Following years of control and regulation, the years since 1980 have seen a massive trend toward the liberalisation of financial markets. This volume provides an analysis of this process and considers likely future developments. It is divided into three parts: the first covers the behaviour of households and firms; the second includes studies on stock, bond and currency markets; and the third part analyses the behaviour and performance of financial intermediaries, particularly banks. The topics examined range from the demand for personal and corporate credit and the allocation of savers' wealth, to innovations in securities and services traded in financial markets, and their regulation.

These essays represent a blend of both theoretical and empirical work, the latter focussing in particular on Europe and the recent integration of financial markets on the Continent. Discussions of the studies are provided by some of the world's leading financial economists.

Financial markets' liberalisation and the role of banks

Financial markets' liberalisation and the role of banks

Edited by
VITTORIO CONTI
and
RONY HAMAUI

CAMBRIDGE
UNIVERSITY PRESS

Published by the Press Syndicate of the University of Cambridge
The Pitt Building, Trumpington Street, Cambridge CB2 1RP
40 West 20th Street, New York, NY 10011-4211, USA
10 Stamford Road, Oakleigh, Melbourne 3166, Australia

First published 1993

Printed in Great Britain at the University Press, Cambridge

A catalogue record for this book is available from the British Library

Library of Congress cataloguing in publication data

Financial markets' liberalization and the role of banks / edited by
Vittorio Conti and Rony Hamaui.
    p.   cm.
Includes index.
ISBN 0 521 41982 4 (hardback)
1. Finance. 2. Banks and banking. 3. Capital market.
4. Finance – European Economic Community countries.
I. Conti, Vittorio. II. Hamaui, Rony.
HG136.F57 1992
332.1 – dc20 92–6551 CIP

ISBN 0 521 41982 4 hardback

HG
136
.F57
1993

Contents

PART II: FINANCIAL MARKETS

PART III: BANKS

Figures

Tables

Preface

SERGIO SIGLIENTI

The papers published in this volume result from a research effort sponsored by the Banca Commerciale Italiana, whose purpose was to evaluate the economic effects of the liberalisation process. We believe that – in this period of transition to a freer economic environment – banks should pay adequate attention to the agents' responses induced by the effort towards European unification and by the ongoing process of financial liberalisation; in particular, it is necessary to anticipate the behaviour of households, non-financial firms, financial intermediaries, and the workings of financial markets, in order to set up appropriate corporate strategies to face the challenge of increasing competitive pressures.

The research work published here logically follows an analogous initiative carried out some years ago. As in that case, the present work was carried out by a team comprising economists working with the BCI Research and Planning Unit and economics professors from various universities. In fact, we have an old tradition of strict relationship between bank and academia, based on the belief that only joint work can produce results whose relevance encompasses banking practice as well as economic theory. Both methodology and results of the papers have therefore been discussed with members of several divisions of BCI, although the research team's independence was also guaranteed.

Initiatives of the kind epitomised by this research – in which the bank is involved not only financially but also in the project layout and completion – are important because they ensure that the cumulated research expertise is properly exploited and put to work. In an ever more competitive and complex environment such as the one we face, the twin efforts of designing strategies and building the know-how necessary to implement them require continuing investment in research to understand the outside world. It is therefore our intention to keep following this path.

Note

Sergio Siglienti is President, Banca Commerciale Italiana.

Acknowledgements

The editors and publishers acknowledge with thanks permission to reproduce the following:

National Institute Economic Review, for Tables 5.3a, 5.3b and 5.4, and for data in Tables 5.5 and 5.6, from S.A.B. Page, 'The choice of invoicing currency in merchandise trade' (1981).

University of Carolina, for Tables 5.5 and 5.6, from S. Black, 'Transaction costs and vehicle currencies' (1989).

North-Holland, for 1973 data in Table 5.7, from S. Black, 'International money and international monetary arrangements' (1985).

IMF, for Table 5.7, from M.P. Dooley, J.S. Lizondo and D.J. Mathieson, 'The Currency Composition of Foreign Exchange Reserves' (1989).

Journal of International Money and Finance, for Tables 5.8–5.10, from 'International capital mobility: net versus gross stocks and flows (1990).

North-Holland, for critical values in Table 10.6, from S.B. Hall and S.G.B. Henry, *Macroeconomic Modelling* (1988).

CEPR, for data in Table 12.5, from D.J. Neven, 'Structural adjustment in European retail banking. Some views from industrial organization' (1989).

EIB Papers, for Tables A.10 and A.18 in Chapter 12, from B. Lygum, E. Peree and A. Steinherr, 'The Spanish financial system' (1989).

Banca d'Italia, *Temi di Discussione*, for Table 1.17 in Chapter 12, from G. Ferri and P. Marullo Reedtz,, 'Mercato interbancario e gestione degli attivi bancari: tendenze recenti e linee di sviluppo' (1989).

Notes on contributors

Orazio P. Attanasio was born in 1959. He graduated in Statistics 1982, and gained his MSc(Econ) from LSE, 1984 and his PhD from LSE, 1988. Current positions are Assistant Professor, Stanford University; Research Fellow, Centre for Economic Policy Research, London.

Angelo Baglioni was born in Milan – where he now lives – in 1960. He studied economics first at Bocconi University, Milan, then at the University of Pennsylvania, Philadelphia, where he received an MA degree. Since 1988 he has been an economist at the Research Department of the Banca Commerciale Italiana. He has been working in the field of monetary economics, with particular interest in the area related to the activity and the regulation of financial intermediaries.

Leo Bonato received his first degree in Economics at the Università di Modena and his MA at Boston University. He is currently an economist at the Economic Research and Planning Department of the Banca Commerciale Italiana. His research interests include macroeconomics and corporate finance.

Umberto Cherubini holds an MA degree in Economics at New York University. Until 1989, he worked in Rome, at the Department of Econometrics and Operational Research of the Banco di Sicilia. Since then, he has been working as Economist at the Economic Research Department of the Banca Commerciale Italiana. He has carried out research in financial markets' economics and applied econometrics.

Massimo Ciampolini is a graduate of Bocconi University, Milan, and holds an MA degree in Economics from the University of Pennsylvania, Philadelphia. He is currently an economist at the Research and Planning Department of the Banca Commerciale Italiana. His main fields of interest are monetary and international economics and applied econometrics.

Alessandro Citanna gained his first degree from Bocconi University, Milan, nd is now doing his PhD at the University of Pennsylvania, Philadelphia. His fields of interest are the theory of finance and econometrics.

Vittorio Conti was born on 25 October 1942 in Lovere (Italy). He graduated in Economics at the Università Cattolica, Milan, and was a PhD Student at Oxford University. In 1971–6 he served as an Economist in the Economic Research Department of the Banca d'Italia, Rome. Since 1981 he has been head of the Economic Research and Planning Department, and since 1976 lecturer in Economic Theory at the Università Cattolica, Milan. He has published articles on inventory investment decisions, productivity in manufacturing industry, input–output models, and international trade. At present he is involved in research concerning the banking industry and strategic planning in banking.

Gregorio De Felice studied at Bocconi University, Milan. After a short period in that university, in 1983 he joined the Economic Research and Planning Department of the Banca Commerciale Italiana, where since 1988 he has been head of the Monetary and Financial Markets division. He is a member of the Editorial Committee of *Monetary Trends*, an economic journal published by the Banca Commerciale Italiana. His research interests are monetary theory and policy, financial markets' analysis and the evolution of the Italian banking system.

Riccardo Faini was born in Lausanne (Switzerland) on 12 April 1951. He graduated from Bocconi University, Milan in 1976 and completed his PhD at the Massachusetts Institute of Technology in 1976. He has taught at the University of Essex, Università di Venezia and the Bologna Center of the Johns Hopkins University. He was also economist at the Research Department of the World Bank. He is now Professor of Industrial Economics at the University of Brescia. He has published widely in the fields of regional development, international trade and development economics.

Paolo Fulghieri was born on 13 July 1956 in Milan. He graduated from Bocconi University, Milan, and received a PhD in economics from the University of Pennsylvania, Philadelphia. He is now an Assistant Professor of Business at the Graduate School of Business of Columbia University. His research interests focus on corporate finance and on the economics of information in its applications to financial economics.

Claudio Giraldi graduated from the University of Florence and obtained an MA from the Johns Hopkins University. He worked as consultant with the Economics and Statistics Department of the OECD in Paris. In 1988 he joined the Economic Research and Planning Department of the

Banca Commerciale Italiana where, since 1990, he has been the head of the International Monetary and Financial Markets division. His main reearch interests are monetary policy, exchange rate determination and dynamics, financial risk management and options and futures theory.

Vittorio Grilli was born in Milan on 19 May 1957. He obtained degrees from Bocconi University, Milan (1981) and the University of Rochester, New York (1985), and his PhD in Economics from the University of Rochester (1986). In 1986, he became a Research Associate of the Rochester Center for Economic Research and in 1989 a Research Fellow, Centre for Economic Policy Research, London. His research interests are in open economy macroeconomics and international finance, and he has published widely in this field.

Rony Hamaui was born on 22 November 1953 in Cairo (Egypt). He graduated at Bocconi University, Milan, and did his masters degree at LSE. He now heads the Economic Research Department of the Banca Commerciale Italiana and is a lecturer at Bocconi University. He formerly lectured at Bergamo University and was a research assistant at IRS (the Institute for Social Research). He has published several articles on exchange rates, international monetary economics and finance.

Mauro Maccarinelli graduated at Bocconi University, Milan, in 1985 and since then has worked for the Banca Commerciale Italiana as an economist in the Research and Planning Department. He is particularly involved in studies on Italian banks and banking structures and evolution of the economies of the main OECD countries.

Giuseppe Marotta studied at the University of Turin (1975) and the London School of Economics (1979) where he obtained his MSc(Econ). In 1981 he joined the Research Department of the Bank of Italy; since 1988 he has been Associate Professor in Economics at the University of Brescia. His main research interests are econometric modelling, firms' real and financial investment decisions and financial intermediation.

Marco Pagano was born in Naples in 1956. After a degree in Law at the University of Naples in 1978, he took a BA in Economics at Cambridge University in 1981, and a PhD in economics at the Massachusetts Institute of Technology in 1985. He was Associate Professor of Economics at the University of Naples until 1991, and now teaches at Bocconi University, Milan. Most of his research has focussed on financial markets. He has investigated the relationship between trading volume, liquidity and volatility in the stock market, as well as the effects of different methods of trading securities. He has also analysed the market for consumer loans, studying both the effects of borrowing constraints on households' consumption decision and the causes of international differences in the volume of consumer lending.

Massimo Prosdocimi graduated at Bocconi University, Milan, in 1981 and since then has worked for the Banca Commerciale Italiana as an economist in the Research and Planning Department where he is responsible for the Planning Office. He is particularly involved in banking and financial studies.

Marco Ratti is an economist with Banca Commerciale Italiana. He holds an MSc(Econ) from LSE and has published in the field of empirical corporate finance.

Ailsa Röell was born in 1955; she obtained her MA (Economics) in 1979 from the Rijksuniversiteit Groningen, Netherlands; her PhD(Econ) in 1983 from the Johns Hopkins University. Since 1984 she has been a lecturer in economics at LSE.

Nicola Rossi (PhD) is professor of Econometrics in the Department of Political Economy of the University of Modena. He has worked as an economist in the Research Department of the Bank of Italy and in the Fiscal Affairs Department of the International Monetary Fund. He has taught at the Universities of Rome and Venice. He is a member of the editorial Board of *Ricerche Economiche*.

Nouriel Roubini was born on 29 March 1958. He took a degree in Economics at Bocconi University, Milan, in 1982 and a PhD in Economics at Harvard University in 1988. He is currently Assistant Professor, Department of Economics, Yale University and was National Fellow in residence at the Hoover Institution, Stanford for the academic year 1991–2. His research interests are in open economy macroeconomics, exchange rate theory, theoretical and empirical studies of political business cycles and partisan models of policy making, and he has published widely in these fields.

Riccardo Rovelli is Professor of Economics at Cagliari University and Bocconi University, Milan. His research is on financial markets' performance and on monetary policy design and institutions.

Guglielmo Weber was born in 1958. He graduated in Economics in 1982 and obtained his MSc(Econ) from LSE in 1983 and his PhD from LSE in 1988. He is currently Lecturer in Economics, University College, London; Research Associate, Institute for Fiscal Studies; and Senior Research Fellow, Innocenzo Gasparini Institute for Economic Research.

Introduction

VITTORIO CONTI and RONY HAMAUI

The changes likely to occur in the competitive environment as a result of the liberalisation process have become a major issue in the current debate about European integration. Two main channels through which competition will produce its effects can now be clearly identified. The former will provide more opportunities for financial intermediaries to expand geographically, as formally allowed under new rules governing mutual recognition and free business location; the latter will be opened by provisions enhancing capital mobility.

Defining the possible impact of the entire process is, however, a difficult task. Some doubts still remain as to whether the markets can evolve towards forms able to provide greater efficiency in production and resource allocation. The main issues at stake concern financial stability, the way in which it will be affected by liberalisation, and the contribution that regulatory reform can make towards the success of the liberalisation programme.

Historical differences among the various countries may affect the timing within which in practice operating conditions can be aligned. As a result, an asymmetric distribution of costs and opportunities may set in, and the degree of convergence could be quite different across markets and agents. Moreover, the complex pattern of regulatory norms and exceedingly protective practices so far prevailing in many European countries will have to change. There is the fear that the laborious matching process currently under way may result in more or less explicit forms of competitive deregulation. Accordingly, policy makers, business men and economists are focussing their attention on the closer links between microeconomic choices and macroeconomic stability.

These issues cannot be solved unless the possible impact of these changes on agents' behaviour and on the working of markets is assessed. The research work presented in this volume is an attempt to contribute towards such an assessment in theoretical, empirical and institutional terms. The basic idea is to carry out a detailed agent- and market-oriented analysis rather than undertake a global analysis of liberalisation.

First we will evaluate households' and firms' financial behaviour. The attention will be particularly concentrated on the allocation of savers' wealth and on the demand for credit from the personal and corporate sectors. This will permit the relative importance of different aspects to be asserted, among which institutional settings seem to play a crucial role in constraining the process of international integration. The focus will then be shifted to financial markets. In this context the analysis will underline the impact of recent changes on the functioning of foreign exchange, bond, and equity markets, so the need for novel regulations will emerge. Finally, we will discuss the problems with which banks are confronted more directly in the liberalisation process and the future role of intermediaries.

1   Private non-banking agents

The empirical analysis of household and firm behaviour has repeatedly shown how the classical assumptions of financial theory based on the complete-markets paradigm are not supported by the evidence. Market imperfections such as liquidity constraints, distortionary taxation, non-marketability of assets, rationing, etc. interfere with financial behaviour in important ways. In one word, agent heterogeneity is a crucial factor in assessing the effect of liberalisation on the economic performance of EC countries and on their financial intermediaries. However, to track the implications of liberalisation, one needs to know exactly what forces are at work, whether they can be affected by government action, and how they differ across the countries.

1.1   Households

Most recent empirical attempts to understand household portfolio allocation have performed poorly, despite dynamic improvements and an enlarged set of assets among which portfolio choice was supposed to take place. Giraldi, Hamaui and Rossi in Chapter 1 make a contribution towards realism by discussing households' wealth allocation choices in a portfolio model in which many institutional factors are explicitly accounted for. Among these, a crucial element is the distinction between marketable and non-marketable (or rather illiquid) assets. This distinction, until now confined to macro levels, shows that the relationships between marketable assets and their yields are very similar in different European countries, whereas substantial differences emerge if the impact of non-marketable assets (social security, pensions, and real estate) is considered. The simulations show that significant differences among households' portfolios in different European countries can survive tax harmonisation. Hence, for European integration to be effective, the need arises to provide broader uniformity across different labour market, social security and pension laws.

This conclusion cannot but raise some doubts as to the possibility of attaining the intended goals in the short run. Accordingly, financial intermediaries may be faced for some time with markets where the demand for largely non-homogeneous financial assets in different countries will prevail. This may offer arbitrage opportunities to those intermediaries who are able to adjust their supply structure in flexible ways to take full advantage of market segmentation. Competition in managing households' liquid financial assets is in fact expected to remain somewhat imperfect for some time under the influence of what we have termed 'non-marketable' assets.

Financial assets provide liquidity services on top of risk–return combinations; hence the need, recognised in the recent literature, to model this feature. Attanasio and Weber's Chapter 2 measures the value of the liquidity service of bank deposits in a time-series model in which consumers are subject to transaction costs and a constraint on net wealth. They explain the yield differential between short-term securities and bank deposits with consumption growth, inflation, real money supply, and the money expenditure ratio; the model is then used to estimate the shadow prices associated with the various capital market imperfections in Italy. The analysis reveals the importance of these imperfections in reducing the degree of liquidity of assets other than money; this suggests that the liquidity services of these assets will increase as a result of the liberalisation process and the spreading of financial innovation.

The relative reduction in the liquidity service provided by money is likely to bring about a reduction in the interest rate spread between bank deposits and securities. This may, in turn, involve reduced margins for banks and the need for a more careful liability management partly to counter the disintermediation process. As regards banks' assets, some indications can be found by an assessment of the effects of a greater availability of consumer credit via reduced constraints on net economic wealth. The evidence is that such constraints existed in Italy, though they were not particularly stringent, especially at times of very high interest rates. As a result, substantial growth opportunities in this interesting business are opened to banks, thus somewhat offsetting the expected reduction in interest margins.

1.2   Firms

The determinants of firms' financial behaviour appears particularly complex because of two main factors. First, the theoretical literature provides useful explanations for single aspects, but no organic approach to a complete understanding of the firms' financial structure. Second, the pattern of this structure has undergone substantial changes in different countries in the last ten years: firms in the United States carried out massive share repurchasing and heavy borrowing, while corporate leverage decreased substantially in Japan, Germany and Italy. No unequivocal models of interpretation can therefore be applied.

This accounts for the eclectic approach chosen by Bonato, Faini and Ratti in Chapter 3, who use the predictions of different available models in the empirical tests. The analysis of balance sheet data shows that the 'relative' tax advantage offered by borrowing over other forms of corporate financing has apparently led Italian firms to favour greater indebtedness. This result seems of particular interest since very few empirical papers have so far been able to detect significant fiscal effects. By contrast, according to the evidence produced in Chapter 3, a favourable performance of stock prices would have led large corporations to turn directly to the equity market for funding. As a result, a greater scope has been indirectly afforded to smaller firms because of the increased competition among banks in the supply of loans.

As in many other countries agency costs appear to play a role in Italy as well. In fact, as predicted by this theory, the econometric results show that firms characterised by a lower operating risk, i.e. with higher tangible assets, lower and more stable rate of growth, etc. have a higher level of indebtedness. This is found to be particularly true for small companies located in the South of Italy, where financial intermediaries have to be more careful about firms' riskiness.

In conclusion, it can be fairly inferred from these findings that, should European integration result in tax harmonisation based on the neutrality principle, the fiscal advantage from borrowing over other forms of corporate funding would disappear in all EC countries, but the effect will be particularly strong in Italy. Moreover should internationalisation result in larger average size and easier access to international equity markets for companies, the larger corporations would have enhanced motives to finance their operations directly through the market. This would cause the banking system to shift its emphasis to the smaller firms and/or play a more active role in the process of industrial restructuring and non-traditional intermediation. This process could, however, take some time in the countries in which the industrial structure is heavily tilted towards small firms, which are typically bank-dependent and often highly geared.

2   Financial markets

Institutions are as important in the analysis of financial markets as in that of household and firm behaviour; however, in the former case both liberalisation and regulatory reform are likely to exert their effects much more quickly. Actually, financial markets have changed at a very fast pace in recent years – due to innovations, reforms, or otherwise – and the very speed that characterises their reaction begs the issue of market stability.

2.1   The foreign exchange market

The internationalisation of financial markets has brought about dramatic changes in market workings even more than in firms' behaviour as the liberalisation process has basically turned financial markets from domestic into international arenas. Trading volumes have accordingly greatly expanded and various new entrants have appeared in the market place. Since most transactions occur through the exchange of assets held by residents in different countries, parallel transactions take place in foreign exchange markets as a result. Furthermore, active management of multi-currency portfolios stimulated the development of adequate instruments to hedge exchange risks.

Special emphasis should be placed on the impact the changes occurring in foreign exchange markets will have on exchange rate variability. Grilli and Roubini tackle this issue in Chapter 4 by a simple model of the relations between the international liberalisation of capital flows, the volume of foreign exchange transactions and the volatility of exchange rates. The authors conclude that, although liberalisation always implies an increase in the number of traders and in all the volumes traded, it has ambiguous effects on exchange rate variability. On one hand, both aggregate and idiosyncratic information shocks amplify exchange rate volatility; on the other, the growing number of traders and increased market depth tend to stabilise prices. As the latter effect may display its full impact only after some time, it can be reasonably expected that an increase in exchange rate volatility will be initially associated with the liberalisation process.

Estimates for a number of countries seem to confirm this view; the lifting of controls on capital mobility is often associated with increased volatility because of the more uncertain environment in which traders have to work in the initial stage. Furthermore, some preliminary empirical evidence seems to indicate that exchange rate volatility declines as the number of transactions increases.

Grilli and Roubini note some interesting implications of these findings for an appraisal of the effects that financial liberalisation, as recently enacted in several European countries, may have on the stability of the European Monetary System (EMS). Although liberalisation may create some problems for the stability of exchange rate parities in the short run, thus requiring more coordination in policy making, a greater stability can be realistically expected in the longer run, and this not only because of larger trading volumes.

Grilli and Roubini also show in Chapter 5 that, in fact, the liberalisation process's fostering of increasingly diversified international portfolios may reduce the well-known exchange rate asymmetry in the EMS. This consists in the fact that European currencies respond asymmetrically to movements of the dollar because of the higher substitutability between dollar-denominated and DM-denominated assets than between dollar-denominated assets and those denominated in the other European currencies. In this case, other things being equal, foreign exchange liberalisation may weaken the EMS. Nevertheless it is reasonable to think that the uneven degree of currency substitutability largely depends on the existence of constraints on capital mobility, which seems to indicate that asymmetries may disappear as these constraints are gradually lifted. This is also shown by empirical evidence showing that the EMS has brought about a reduction in the polarisation of the member countries' currencies as contrasted with other currencies.

Grilli and Roubini's study, however, identifies another 'new type' of asymmetry resulting from the different intensity with which different currencies are used in international transactions. Even in the event of perfect substitutability among all currencies, it is then possible that external shocks will produce different effects in the EC countries if certain currencies are more frequently used in international transactions and are therefore more likely to be held as official reserves.

Even this second type of asymmetry is likely to decline if foreign exchange liberalisation stimulates the use of currencies previously seldom employed because of the constraints on the settlement of foreign trade or borrowing transactions. Financial intermediaries' strategies will become an all-important factor in this respect. For example, in the case of Italy, banks will be faced with the choice of whether to develop the market for Eurolira-denominated deposits and securities, at least in the transition to the full integration of European markets, or to make direct use of the ECU and the other European currencies.

2.2   The stock market

The weakening of the links between trade and forex markets will proceed hand in hand with an increasing link between the latter and different countries' markets for equities, bonds and other financial assets. The gradual liberalisation within the EC will result in keener competition among countries, leading policy makers to reduce taxation on transactions and redesign the workings of their domestic financial markets in order to increase their relative efficiency. This situation is evidenced by a review of the reforms which affected major European bourses during the 1980s. Following London's Big Bang, the Stock Exchanges of Paris, Madrid, Copenhagen and Milan underwent extensive changes in areas of liberalisation of access, new trading methods and deregulated fees.

Pagano and Röell in Chapter 6 provide an appraisal of the effects of the reform of the Paris Bourse which has often led other European countries in introducing innovations. Their overall findings show that the new regulations, particularly the shift to a continuous auction system, reduced price volatility by stimulating the dealers to be more active. The former *agents de change* have been replaced by the new *Sociétés de Bourse*, which can trade on their own accounts as 'dual-capacity dealers' and whose ownership can be controlled by banks and other financial intermediaries.

Trade volumes have expanded considerably, though it is unlikely that this was a result of the newly introduced dealing procedures. The greater liquidity in the Paris market does not appear to be far higher than that offered on the same securities in the London Stock Exchange. Since the most obvious difference between the French and British Stock Market is that the former is based on an auction system while the latter is based on dealership, it is important to understand the relative feature and benefits of each system. Despite the fact that these two systems are the archetypes for all reforms, the theoretical literature has failed fully to analyse their relative advantages.

Pagano and Röell fill this gap in Chapter 7 and argue that dealers provide liquidity to the market. Yet, they are subjected to special obligations and privileges, the most important of which consists in publicly quoting stock prices. In other words, they protect traders against execution risk, i.e. the risk of finding few (or no) other parties to the deal. The question is then whether traders are better off acquiring this protection from the dealers or by directly taking execution risks. Pagano and Röell show that a dealership market is better if the dealers' risk aversion is lower than that of their clients, while an auction-based system will be preferable in the opposite case. Yet, a grey area remains in which the crucial variable is the inherent risk of the securities being traded – the auction market being more appropriate if intrinsic risk is high.

The above findings may provide a standard against which to evaluate conditions under which dealer intermediaries can effectively play their role. This is more likely to happen the larger the dealer's size because individual risks can be more easily managed, the more sound its capital structure, and the greater the guarantees offered by the economic authorities in terms of credit facilities, tax benefits, etc. Also, such high-risk assets as futures should be still traded in auction-based markets.

As mentioned above, the reforms already implemented or currently under way in many European countries allow authorised intermediaries not only to collect and place orders on their clients' behalf but also to trade on their own account. In other words, the so-called 'dual-capacity trading' principle has been introduced. As a stockbroker receives an order from a client, he can be motivated to make a transaction on his own before executing the client's order, thereby using 'front-running' to take advantage of the information implicit in the order he has just taken.

Pagano and Röell in Chapter 8 illustrate the conflicts of interest likely to arise when stockbrokers are allowed to practise front-running. They show that intermediaries profit from front-running and that the related costs are not borne by their clients alone. Public authorities' regulatory action thus appears appropriate as the relationship between brokers and clients cannot eliminate all possible distortions in the pricing process. Yet, it is obviously difficult to prevent dealers from practising front-running between different markets – for example between spot and futures or options markets or between the Paris Bourse and the London Stock Exchange where the same securities are traded.

2.3   The bond market

It has often been noted that futures markets reduce the costs of the underlying illiquid spot assets because trading volumes increase and investors are afforded hedging opportunities at a lower cost. On this basis, Citanna and Rovelli show in Chapter 9 that the introduction of a futures market may even reduce the risk premium on the underlying assets, thus levelling out the interest rate term structure. This result is essentially based on market incompleteness, and so – contrary to common belief – the introduction of futures markets appears to be particularly important in countries with comparatively backward financial structures. The empirical findings on French government bonds seem to confirm these theoretical views, as the risk premium on these securities has virtually disappeared since the MATIF became operational in February 1986.

Since banks have traditionally engaged more heavily in forward markets where transactions take place over the counter, they offer some resistance to the introduction of futures markets, which they view as potential competitors for their intermediation activities in forward contracts. However, banks can benefit from the increased volume of transactions arising from futures markets and the development of related contracts, in which they may play a major intermediation role.

3 Banking intermediaries

To get a better insight into the effects the liberalisation of financial markets may have on banks as financial intermediaries, the recent developments in the structure and behaviour of the banking system should be described in more detail.

3.1 Banks as investors

The proportion of securities in banks' total assets substantially increased in many countries during the 1980s as a result of the gradually shrinking gap between banks and other intermediaries and expanding securities markets. Exceptions have been the United States, Japan and Italy where either the lifting of some constraints – e.g. the ceiling on lending in Italy and the bar on the sale of securities with maturities shorter than one year in Japan – or financial innovation on the liabilities side significantly reduced the amount of securities held by the banking systems.

Chapter 10 by Cherubini, Ciampolini and De Felice tries to identify the determinants of this changed pattern, in particular the reasons why banks invest in securities. A causality and cointegration analysis for four countries seems to confirm the view that securities are a residual variable in banks' balance sheets both in the short and in the long term. They have never determined the performance of either deposits or loans, but have been often influenced by them. Also, deposits and loans seem to be mutually independent variables. This evidence appears to be consistent with the models in which securities are assumed to be a source of secondary liquidity, particularly the Klein–Monti model which also assumes that deposit decisions are fully independent of lending decisions – deposits and loans being regarded as two separate services supplied by banks to customers.

3.2 Liability management

Financial liberalisation and innovation seem to undermine the foregoing model in two respects. First, the possibility of selling loans substantially enhances the liquidity of assets traditionally viewed as entirely illiquid. Second, the spreading of short-term instruments with a wide secondary market leads to a more active liability management.

Just 1.5 per cent of the leading US banks' loans had been sold to other banks or financial intermediaries by mid-1983. This proportion went up to slightly less than 10 per cent in early 1988, and went on growing thereafter. The fast rate of the 'securitisation' process in the United States, where financial markets are larger and more diversified, may rapidly be extended to Europe through market liberalisation and integration. It is then important to see what benefits this process has in store for banks, how it can change the ways in which banks are managed, and what consequences it may have on the system's stability.

Some recent studies have tried to explain the securitisation process as part of an explicitly optimising bank behaviour. Among them, Fulghieri's Chapter 11 assumes that the risk of default introduces a conflict of interest between a bank and its depositors about the optimal monitoring level which, in turn, affects the bank's loan performance. As a result, if the monitoring effort is privately chosen by the bank, this conflict leads to a sub-optimal monitoring level. The bank can achieve a better allocation of its monitoring effect between assets retained and assets sold by selling loans. In particular, it can be shown that the bank will sell the assets with the lowest marginal returns to monitoring, which are usually those involving lower risks and more frequently sold by banks in practice. Unlike other authors, Fulghieri also shows that securitisation enhances the monitoring of retained assets, thus improving the 'quality' of the bank's balance sheet itself for any given amount of loans sold.

Maccarinelli, Marotta and Prosdocimi in Chapter 12 offer instead an international comparison of the liability side of banks' balance sheets. They emphasise customers' increasing concern for returns, resulting in a shift towards fixed-maturity investments or marketable securities.

The shift from formerly widespread retail banking forms of deposits to the use of wholesale instruments often appears the only available choice to stop disintermediation, although the evidence seems to indicate a different possible route. In fact, those forms of deposit that provide a better liquidity service than time deposits or CDs as well as remuneration appear more competitive – e.g. deposits on interest-bearing checking accounts with Italian banks. Although, for this product to be truly competitive, a sufficiently widespread sales network must be available, the entry of foreign competitiors is already driving some systems to introduce it as an innovating instrument to prevent disintermediation in the deposits upmarket. This also provides a useful tool to improve service quality in the expected climate of increasing price competitiveness.

Price competitiveness will shift to third countries after liberalisation because of the funding difficulties that the banks of some countries will have. A meaningful indication of this trend is the increased attention of banks in different national settings for strengthened capital structures. This strengthening seems to be the result partly of the need to comply with regulations governing capital ratios, but also of the need to help funding by establishing a sort of 'coinsurance' by shareholders towards both depositors and subscribers.

Increasing competition and the process of internationalisation of the banking system, supported by the making of the European Single Market, are driving the authorities in major countries to a more general revision of the regulations concerning non-banking intermediaries. Unlike several proposals stimulated by operating needs, very few studies attempt to identify useful indications for proper banking regulations applying the recent theoretical literature on the nature and role of banks.

In the last few years, the origin of banking intermediation has been increasingly accounted for by the information discrepancies between borrowers and lenders, and the economies of scale which can be achieved in screening and monitoring. Major implications of these theories are the banks' special vulnerability to runs and the heavy social costs of liquidation because of the unsaleable nature of their assets. Hence the need for a lender of last resort able to secure stability to the system as well as detailed regulations.

On this basis, Baglioni and Marotta in Chapter 13 focus on deposit insurance – an area whose regulation is still open to change. Their analysis shows that any such insurance agency must have a public nature not only because of a likely systematic risk but also for it to play a supervisory role. Insurance should apply to a broad definition of a bank's role to prevent liquidity risks being shifted to other intermediaries; the premium should be risk-dependent to avoid moral hazard; finally, it should be possible to preserve customer relationships.

Most discussions on deposits insurance are based on the US experience as widespread public interest in European banking systems and the close control European monetary authorities keep on banks make the need of deposit insurance less acute. Only recently, some experiences of insurance on deposits have been recorded in Europe – most of them on voluntary private bases. It is still obvious, though, that as a greater liberalisation sets in this will become a serious issue because risks are bound to increase and deposits can move around among different national banking systems.

4   Some closing remarks

The diversified pictures that emerge from our research efforts provide some insights into the relative significance of the factors likely to impinge upon the process by which financial structures tend to converge and become mutually integrated.

First, it is clear that households' financial choices largely depend on national institutional settings. This fact depends, in turn, on both the varying degrees of efficiency with which domestic financial markets offer liquidity services and on the different nature of non-marketable assets which are affected by labour markets, social-security and other legislative norms.

When the firms' financial attitudes are considered, constraints resulting from different productive structures appear to be less likely to be removed than those arising in connection with different market structures. For example, the size of a firm is a crucial factor in choosing the right debt–equity ratio, while product specialisation and localisation may significantly influence borrowing decisions. The integration process is then likely to be slower and more complex than expected, and so even the intermediaries' competitive condition can be less easily outlined at this transition stage when significant segmentation still prevails.

As far as security markets are concerned, the role they played in determining the new competitive environment has emerged very clearly. Many reforms have shaped the liberalisation process to some extent and impinged upon foreign exchange, stock and bond markets in many countries. This has fostered closer interrelations between different markets, whether domestic or international, and significantly increased their liquidity and trading volumes.

It has been seen that, at least at an early stage, liberalisation may increase the volatility of financial asset prices. As a result, intermediaries will have an opportunity to play roles other than those of pure brokerage. Yet, these new roles require the ability to take risks in order to provide adequate customer service. Finally, the wider scope for substitution among alternative investment and borrowing sources will require banks to engage in the active management both of their liabilities through expanded operations in money markets, and of their assets through loan selling and effectively handling their securities portfolios.

The actors' expanding number and changing role poses the parallel question of how to redefine both the operating mechanisms and the rules of participation to combine improved efficiency with an effective control on the risks rising from increased price volatility and the possibility of transferring risks and information among different markets, thus generating dangerous instability proceses.

In this context, the public authorities' controlling and supervisory roles become more important in order both to secure equitable relations between the intermediaries and the markets and to protect a rich heritage of information, confidence and reputation.

Note

The editors would like to thank Marco Ratti for editorial assistance, Costanza Govino, Simonetta Melotto and Patrizia Zani for research assistance and Giuliana Brenna, Sonia Papandrea and Antonella Patruno for secretarial help.

Part I

Households and firms

1.1 The evolution and allocation of financial wealth

---

1 Marketable and non-marketable assets in households' portfolios: a cross-country comparison

CLAUDIO GIRALDI, RONY HAMAUI and NICOLA ROSSI

1 Introduction[1]

Notwithstanding the differentiated institutional settings prevailing in Europe, the current debate on the ongoing creation of a European internal market largely assumes a substantial degree of homogeneity of agents' behaviour across individual countries. In particular, as far as the European financial liberalisation is concerned, the existing degree of capital mobility provides the basis for the assumption of behavioural similarity underlying the treatment of matters such as fiscal harmonisation. However, a common sense observation would suggest that, along with taxation systems, other institutional arrangements can ultimately affect agents' behaviour, including a certain degree of heterogeneity among European countries which could, in turn, lead to a reconsideration of the fiscal harmonisation process itself.

Following this line of research, the present chapter focusses on the determinants of the structure of households' financial portfolios in order to single out similarities among selected European countries. To this end the chapter discusses and estimates an augmented portfolio model incorporating a number of salient institutional features through the key distinction between marketable and non-marketable assets. The powerful role of non-marketable wealth in determining portfolio allocation has long been recognised in the theoretical as well as in the empirical literature. In principle, the presence of non-marketable (highly if not perfectly non-liquid) assets implies that, even with the assumption of homogeneous expectations, investors do hold different portfolios of marketable assets. It is not surprising, therefore, that empirical applications have been (successfully) confined to the analysis of individual data which capture well the effects due to structural differences. Individual information on households' portfolios is, however, still scattered and certainly not such as to allow the cross-country comparison we want to undertake here. Therefore, in this chapter an attempt will be made to trace the effects of non-marketable assets by using aggregate data.

In doing this, we depart somewhat from the most recent attempts to improve on the empirical performance of portfolio models. Among them is the enlargement of the 'menu' of assets by going beyond the original narrow categories of bonds and equities so as to achieve a finer disaggregation and include tangible assets such as real estate (Stambaugh, 1982). Other authors (Frankel, 1985, most notably) have been looking in the theory for more structure to be imposed on the problem and have noticed that, under rational expectations, the variance–covariance matrix of returns is nothing but the variance–covariance matrix of the error term in the system of inverted asset demands. Finally, time variation of first and second conditional moments has also been investigated (Bollerslev, Engle and Wooldridge, 1988) in the form of generalised autoregressive conditional heteroscedastic processes. Notwithstanding the interest and importance of such efforts, it is difficult to escape the impression that 'despite the theoretical plausibility of significant relative assets supply effects, virtually all empirical research has been unsuccessful in isolating these effects' (Roley, 1982). As this chapter suggests, investigating the role of non-marketable assets could provide a more fruitful avenue of research.

The chapter analyses households' portfolios in three major European countries (Germany, Italy and the United Kingdom) in the period 1970–88, on the basis of an accurate and detailed data set partly drawn from the painstaking work of Davis (1986).[2]

The main findings of the chapter can be summarised as follows. Non-marketable as well as highly illiquid forms of wealth (that is, pension funds, social-security wealth and the housing stock) appear to be very important determinants of the structure of households' portfolios in all countries looked at in the present study. Furthermore, while the relationships among returns on marketable assets appear to be roughly the same across countries, substantial heterogeneity arises as soon as the analysis focusses on the impact of non-marketable wealth on households' portfolios. The latter finding indicates significant differences in the relationships between marketable and non-marketable assets in different countries, and highlights the role played by country-specific institutions in determining the structure of households' portfolios as well as in hampering the full integration of the European market.

The chapter is organised as follows. Section 2 introduces the reader to portfolio composition in the three countries mentioned above. Section 3 presents the theoretical background and discusses the empirical application. Section 4 exploits the estimation results to assess the impact of fiscal harmonisation in Europe. Section 5 concludes the chapter.

2   Portfolio composition

The first step towards a comprehensive analysis of households' portfolios in three major European countries since 1970 lies in a very brief and purely descriptive discussion of portfolio composition. The aim of this preliminary investigation is to detect common trends in different financial markets and highlights the specificity of particular countries. Table 1.1 provides summary information on the evolution of asset shares across countries.[3]

Substantial differences in the composition of households' portfolios emerge from Table 1.1. The share of currency and sight deposits has always been much larger in Italy than in (West) Germany or in the United Kingdom. Large quantities of that asset were held in Italy because checking accounts have always been interest-bearing. Furthermore, until the mid 1970s there were few alternative financial investment opportunities. Finally, constraint on consumer credit induced households to detain substantial amounts of liquid assets for precautionary reasons. As far as deposits with banks and with other financial institutions are concerned, the levels of the shares remain different across countries because of heterogeneous financial structures. For instance, in Germany banks

Table 1.1. *Marketable asset shares, percentages*[a]

	Germany		Italy		United Kingdom	
	1970	1988	1970	1988	1970	1988
Currency and sight deposits	11.41	8.46	27.00	16.93	8.95	7.50
Time and saving deposits with banks	42.11	37.86	19.72	14.28	8.02	4.52
Deposits with other financial institutions	9.87	7.61	11.15	9.05	19.29	21.01
Government bonds	1.42	3.10	4.91	34.56	6.01	3.26
Private bonds	6.83	7.17	13.08	3.61	1.76	0.14
Equities	10.03	6.00	9.35	9.52	28.46	15.68
Foreign assets	0.44	4.68	0.73	1.16	3.46	2.03

[a] Shares of households' total financial wealth.

provide a range of services that in Great Britain, on the other hand, are typically offered by institutions which are classified as 'other financial institutions'. The personal sector in Germany still therefore holds 40 per cent of its financial wealth in time deposits, whereas it owns only 10 per cent of this asset in the United Kingdom.

A further striking feature of Table 1.1 is the boom of households' government bond holdings in Italy: they jumped from 4.9 per cent in 1970 to 34.6 per cent in 1988, mirroring the concurrent decline of corporate bonds in households' portfolios.

Table 1.1 also shows that the sizeable gap in the level of equity holdings (at market value) between Great Britain, on the one hand, and the other two nations has been reducing over the sample period. However at the end of 1988, there still remained a sharp difference between Great Britain and Germany. The low equity absorption in Germany derives, among other things, from a number of supply factors. In Germany stock listing is expensive, and traditionally the debt–equity ratio is far higher than in the United Kingdom. Moreover, a large number of companies are founded as private limited companies (GmbH).

Finally, as far as foreign assets holdings are concerned, they increased in Italy and in the United Kingdom following the financial markets liberalisation which took place in 1979 in the latter country and started in 1985 in the former. With respect to Germany, the 1988 observation should be regarded as the exceptional response to the announcement of a 10 per cent withholding tax on all capital incomes of domestic origin to be implemented as of January 1989. This capital levy was then removed after six months.

3   Asset demand and non-marketable wealth

3.1   Theoretical background

Cross-country analysis of the underlying determinants of households' portfolio choices is largely confined to Davis's paper (1986) which models the behaviour of financial asset and liability accumulation and portfolio selection of the personal and company sector of four major industrialised countries. In that paper, the reference framework is given by a dynamic portfolio model, whereas in our study we investigate, in the context of a traditional optimal portfolio selection rule, a possible source of misspecification given by mandated holdings in specific assets with particular reference to participation in social-security schemes. This topic was investigated, among others, by Mayers (1973), Friedman and Roley (1979) and Hubbard (1985); however, to the best of our knowledge, it was never empirically looked at on aggregate data.[4]

It is well known (Merton, 1969, 1971, 1973) that, under the assumptions of constant relative risk aversion and joint-normally distributed expected asset returns, expected utility maximisation in continuous time subject to a wealth constraint yields a system of asset demand equations in share form depending (linearly) on expected returns according to the variance–covariance structure of asset returns, as follows:

$$s = (1/\rho)AE(r) + B \qquad (1)$$

where s and r denote the $(n \times 1)$ vectors of optimal asset shares (relative to total portfolio size) and real after-tax sales of return on (n) risky assets, the scalar ρ indicates the degree of (constant relative) risk aversion, $E(.)$ denotes the mathematical expectation operator and it is assumed that all assets are marketable and are risky assets. In (1):

$$A = \Omega^{-1} - (i'\Omega^{-1}i)^{-1}\Omega^{-1}ii'\Omega^{-1} \qquad (n \times n) \quad (2)$$

and

$$B = (i'\Omega^{-1}i)^{-1}\Omega^{-1}i \qquad (n \times 1) \quad (3)$$

where Ω denotes the $(n \times n)$ variance–covariance matrix of asset returns and i is a unit $(n \times 1)$ vector.

Over and above the different institutional settings referred to in the previous section, a typical feature of the three economies analysed in this study is, however, the existence of future monetary claims such as social-security payments or the future payments from private retirement programmes that cannot be marketed. Mandatory participation in the social-security system is to be considered as an obvious source of non-marketable assets in households' portfolios but a similar situation can arise if large transaction costs prevent withdrawal from private pension funds or disposal of the housing stock. In such a case, the system of asset demands (1) is still valid if, however, returns on marketable assets are 'adjusted' for the presence of non-marketable assets and the A and B matrices are modified accordingly. Formally, let r^+ represent the $(n \times 1)$ vector of marketable asset real net returns and r^- the $(m \times 1)$ vector of (unobservable) non-marketable asset real net returns. Accordingly let Ω^+ represent the $(n \times n)$ variance–covariance matrix of marketable asset returns and Ω^- the $(n \times m)$ matrix of covariance between marketable and non-marketable asset returns. Finally let s^+ and s^- denote the optimal $(n \times 1)$ vector of marketable asset holdings and the given $(m \times 1)$ vector of non-marketable asset holdings, respectively (both relative to total marketable wealth). In this framework, it then follows that (Mayers, 1973; Hubbard, 1985):

$$\begin{aligned} s^+ &= (1/\rho)a^+[e)r^+) - \rho\Omega^-)s^-)] + b^+ \\ &= (1/\rho)A^+E(r^+) + C^+s^- + B^+ \end{aligned} \qquad (4)$$

with:

$$A^+ = (\Omega^+)^{-1} - [i'(\Omega^+)^{-1}i]^{-1}(\Omega^+)^{-1}ii'(\Omega^+)^{-1} \qquad (n \times n) \quad (5)$$

$$B^+ = [i'(\Omega^+)^{-1}i]^{-1}(\Omega^+)^{-1}i \qquad (n \times 1) \quad (6)$$

and

$$C^+ = -A^+\Omega^- \qquad (n \times m) \quad (7)$$

where i is again a unit vector of appropriate dimension. The asset demand system (4) represents a straightforward extension to the case of more than one non-marketable asset of the restricted asset demand system derived and presented in Hubbard (1985). It highlights the fact that, in the presence of non-marketable wealth, investors tend to tilt their portfolios away from those stocks with which their non-marketable securities are most highly correlated. In other words, the individual investors require different risk premia, attaching relatively higher risk premia to those marketable assets with which their non-marketable returns show the highest covariance.

The main hypothesis we would like to investigate in the present study therefore concerns a substantial homogeneity in investors' responses to changes in relative rates of return coupled with a (too often neglected) heterogeneity induced by country-specific institutional arrangements. While the former homogeneity would imply a substantial degree of integration of European financial markets, the latter heterogeneity would cast some doubt on all attempts to proceed with European integration while keeping national institutions (social-security systems, for example) untouched.

3.2   Estimation

The exercise undertaken in the present study focusses on the following six marketable assets: time and savings deposits with banks; deposits with other financial institutions; government bonds; corporate bonds; corporate equities; and foreign assets.[5] Instead, pension funds, social-security wealth and the housing stock are regarded as non-marketable assets. Needless to say, we recognise that some of the above non-marketable assets are not completely given. For example, private pension wealth could, in fact, be altered by choosing a different job and, even in Italy, the housing stock is not perfectly illiquid. We shall, however, ignore these possible sources of endogeneity.

Another set of problems arises from the measurement of net rates of return. For instance, while we take account of the evolution of with-holding taxes on financial asset returns between 1970 and 1988 it has proved impossible to obtain reliable estimates of marginal tax rates. Problems rising from the treatment of social-security wealth and after-tax rates of return are discussed further in the Appendix.

With respect to the descriptive analysis undertaken in Section 2, the study disregards currency and sight deposits whose demand is assumed mainly to be a demand for liquidity.

For estimation purposes, we notice that all variables and parameters in the theoretical model (4) should actually carry a suffix i, identifying the ith country looked at in this study. The hypothesis of complete geographical heterogeneity is, however, somewhat uninteresting in that it prevents any meaningful comparison of agents' behaviour across countries. Therefore, we initially confine any untested geographical heterogeneity to the constant term, which is therefore assumed to capture shifts in asset shares induced by the different institutional settings described in Section 2. Furthermore, we append an error term to (4) linearly decomposed into two zero mean random components. The first component is assumed to be country-specific and uncorrelated across countries, while the second is an area-wide component which affects all countries equally in the same geographical area.[6]

Notice that since countries are not randomly selected, the area-wide shock cannot be analysed in an 'error component' kind of model. Therefore, disregarding, for the time being, the expected nature of the variables on the right-hand side of equation (4), the appropriate estimator for the above setting is given by what is known, if we can regard each country as a group, as the between-within groups, fixed effects estimator. As Mundlak (1978) shows, this estimator amounts to applying standard techniques to the system of equation (4) expressed in terms of 'transformed' variables, where, for a generic variable x_i, the transformation takes the following form:

$$\tilde{x}_t^i = x_t^i - (1/T)\Sigma_j x_j^i - (1/N)\Sigma_k x_t^k + (1/NT)\Sigma_j\Sigma_k x_j^k$$
$$(j = 1, \ldots, T; k = 1, \ldots, N) \quad (8)$$

where T and N now denote the number of time periods and the number of countries respectively. Notice that the transformation eliminates the constant term (the B^+ vector) and the area-wide error term. In general, the transformation would eliminate all variables not simultaneously indexed on i and t. The analysis of the geographical heterogeneity undertaken later on will therefore focus on the A^+ and C^+ matrices – that is, for a given ρ, on the relationship among marketable assets and between marketable and non-marketable assets.

Furthermore, we let expectations be rationally formed – that is, we let expectation errors be uncorrelated with the information set available at time t. The set of parameters in the system of equations (4) is therefore

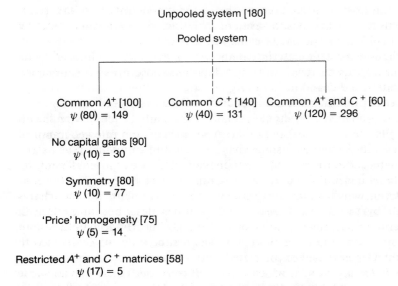

Figure 1.1   **Hypothesis testing in the pooled asset demand system**
Note: The number of free parameters is shown in square brackets, and the number of restrictions in parenthesis.

estimated by three stages' least squares. The instrument list includes lagged values of all rates of return as well as all non-marketable asset shares.[7]

3.3   Empirical results

Figure 1.1, reports on the sequence of tests carried out on the equation system (4). In Figure 1.1, $\psi(q)$ indicates the likelihood ratio test obtained as minus twice the difference between restricted and unrestricted log likelihoods. The statistics is $\chi^2(q)$ distributed under the null.

Letting the maintained hypothesis be the unpooled system, the upper part of Figure 1.1 first tests for behavioural homogeneity defined alternatively as H_0: $A_i^+ = A^+ (\forall i$; common rate of return responses across countries), H_0: $C_i^+ = C^+ (\forall i$; countries non-marketable assets responses across countries) and, finally, as H_0: $A_i^+ = A^+$ and $C_i^+ = C^+ (\forall i$; full pooling). As it turns out, in all cases, the null hypotheses seem to be rejected at conventional significance levels. However, this conclusion changes after adjusting the statistics in order to take into account the results of Meisner (1979), Bera, Byron and Jarque (1981) and Bewley (1983).[8] In this case, the data would admit a substantial degree of homogeneity. However, conventional significance levels are not necessarily appropriate in the present case. The homogeneity hypothesis is in fact a rather loose one and substantially more conservative significance levels could be suggested. In this case, it is easy to notice that the only hypothesis consistent with the data is the one that allows a limited degree of heterogeneity as far as investors' responses to changes in non-marketable assets are concerned. Given (6) and (7), this result immediately implies that the Ω^- matrix significantly differs among countries.

The second step is to test the rate of return definition. In particular, we recall that, under the efficient market hypothesis, the rates of return on equities and foreign assets are given by the sum of a yield plus a zero-mean expectation error. The hypothesis tested is that, in assessing the relative return of different assets, investors do actually disregard the error component which should, in principle, be unforecastable on the basis of the information set available at the time the portfolio allocation decision is taken.[9] This is, clearly, not a test of the efficient market hypothesis but, more simply, a test on the expectation generating process. Again, the null hypothesis is not rejected after small sample adjustment.[10]

The following two hypotheses tested impinge on the theoretical nature of the model and refer to the symmetry of the Ω^+ matrix as well as to the 'price' homogeneity of asset demands. The first hypothesis appears to be soundly rejected while the second appears not to be at variance with the data. However, if again a small sample adjustment of the statistics is carried out,[11] the model tends marginally to pass both tests. The last section of Figure 1.1 finally reports on the possibility of imposing a few zero restrictions in both the substitution matrix A^+ and the matrix C^+.

In brief, if adjustment for the degrees of freedom is performed, we find it legitimate to focus the attention on the most restricted model. The arbitrary nature of small sample adjustment should be openly recognised, and is clearly pointed out by Sargan and Sylwestrowicz (1976). Nevertheless, in the light of small sample problems that undoubtedly exist, degrees of freedom adjustment can be usefully seen as a part of a sensitivity analysis intended to assess the robustness of test results.[12]

On the basis of the test results contained in Figure 1.1, we can turn to Table 1.2 where the parameter estimates for the partially pooled and restricted model (homogeneous and symmetrical) are reported. On the whole, the performance on the model is quite remarkable. In addition to a rather good fit (on the variables transformed as in (9)), there are no clear signs of dynamic misspecification.[13] The immediate reaction to the figures presented in Table 1.2 is that, contrary to most available evidence (Frankel, 1985), the parameters tend to be rather precisely estimated as well as plausible, in particular as far as the substitution matrix A^+ is concerned. This should come as no surprise and in fact does not necessarily contrast with the available evidence. If non-marketable assets are

Table 1.2. *Parameter estimates for the partly pooled and restricted asset demand system[a]*

Dependent variables	Explanatory variables[a]									
	The $[A^+/\rho]$ matrix						The $[C^+]$ matrix (benchmark country: the United Kingdom)			
	Time deposits	Other deposits	Govern. bonds	Private bonds	Equities	Foreign assets	Adults	Elderly people	Pension funds	Housing stock
Time deposits	0.99 (0.18)	-0.33 (0.16)	-0.15 (0.12)	-0.45 (0.11)	-0.27 (0.13)	0.22 (0.07)	-8.75 (0.82)		-0.25 (0.04)	
Other deposits		0.38 (0.23)	0.05 (0.14)	0.28 (0.14)	-0.03 (0.12)	-0.34 (0.09)	7.50 (1.10)	12.51 (2.41)	0.46 (0.05)	0.13 (0.02)
Government bonds			0.57 (0.19)	-0.48 (0.12)	0.13 (0.13)	-0.12 (0.07)	4.59 (1.22)	-6.98 (1.07)	-0.34 (0.06)	0.06 (0.03)
Private bonds				0.81 (0.13)	-0.23 (0.07)	0.07 (0.08)	4.71 (0.54)	-11.05 (2.55)	0.30 (0.03)	
Equities					0.22 (0.19)	0.17 (0.05)	-8.66 (1.32)		-0.14 (0.05)	-0.17 (0.03)

Explanatory variables[a]

Dependent variables	The [C+] matrix (Germany: deviations with respect to benchmark)				The [C+] matrix (Italy: deviations with respect to benchmark)				Single-equation diagnostics	
	Adults	Elderly people	Pension funds	Housing stock	Adults	Elderly people	Pension funds	Housing stock	R^2 adjusted	D.W.
Time deposits	7.25 (1.48)	-15.09 (4.47)		0.09 (0.04)		-8.77 (3.17)	-0.48 (0.05)		0.82	1.41
Other deposits	-6.04 (1.62)	6.98 (3.81)	-0.26 (0.08)	-0.07 (0.04)	-3.14 (1.42)		-0.18 (0.05)	-0.15 (0.03)	0.92	1.53
Government bonds	-8.21 (1.14)			-0.05 (0.03)	-5.14 (1.54)		-0.29 (0.06)	-0.06 (0.04)	0.97	2.07
Private bonds		5.24 (1.95)	0.17 (0.06)	-0.09 (0.02)	3.12 (0.48)		-0.12 (0.03)		0.96	1.42
Equities	6.97 (2.41)	11.86 (6.55)		0.11 (0.06)	6.92 (1.89)	13.39 (3.85)		0.21 (0.04)	0.44	1.50

[a] Asymptotic standard errors are in parenthesis.

an important determinant of asset demands, as they certainly appear to be in Table 1.2, the estimates of the substitution matrix reported in most of the previous literature are biased and inconsistent. Along with the A^+ matrix, Table 1.2 reports also the C^+ matrix which, we recall, differs for each country in that it (presumably) incorporates institutional factors affecting the covariation of marketable and non-marketable assets. Most of the C_i^+ coefficients turn out again to be significantly different from zero in all three countries, therefore underlying the powerful role of non-marketable assets.[14]

A close inspection of Table 1.2 reveals that, in general, the assumption of gross substitutability among all assets, usually regarded as plausible in a large part of the relevant literature, does not appear to be fully consistent with the evidence.[15] With the exception of foreign assets, all assets substitute for bank deposits; deposits with other financial institutions are substitutes of foreign assets; government bonds appear to be close substitutes of corporate bonds and the latter of equities. However, a few assets are complements: for instance, deposits with other financial institutions and corporate bonds on the one hand, and with equities and foreign assets on the other.

Among non-marketable assets, the impact of the age composition of the population is particularly sizeable in all countries. If we take the estimates of Table 1.2 at face value, the current process of population ageing (coupled with a shrinking working age section of the population) would imply a shift to bank deposits in the United Kingdom and from

Table 1.3. *Non-marketable asset shares*

	Germany		Italy		United Kingdom	
	1970	1988	1970	1988	1970	1988
Adults[a]	63.65	69.58	64.63	68.27	62.81	65.57
Elderly people[b]	13.17	15.25	10.77	13.63	12.94	15.37
Pension funds[c]	17.92	25.13	14.05	10.80	24.05	44.51
Housing stock (net)[d]	154.92	116.14	105.88	79.43	39.78	46.76

[a] Share of the population of working age. Proxy for the social-security wealth of this age cohort.
[b] Share of the population of age 65 and over. Proxy for pensioners' social-security wealth.
[c] Share of households' total financial wealth.
[d] The source of the lira value of private residential capital is OECD, *Economic Outlook*. The figure presented in Table 1.3 is the share of households' total financial wealth.

bank deposits to deposits with other financial institutions in Germany, as well as a rather massive shift to government bonds (at the expense of corporate bonds, foreign assets and perhaps equities) in all three countries. Furthermore, it is clear that portfolios dominated by a highly illiquid asset such as the housing stock tend to present a higher share of short-term assets as bank deposits. Finally, the evidence is far more varied for private pension funds which, in fact, correspond to widely different institutional arrangements in the three countries.

In short, non-marketable assets largely contribute to the understanding of asset shares evolution across countries. Their widely different sizes (see Table 1.3), as well as the varied institutional arrangements impinging on the covariation between their implied rate of return and the marketable assets rate of return help explain the huge inter-country differences depicted in Section 2.

4   Portfolio choices and the completion of the European internal market

In evaluating the possible effects of the European financial integration, an important issue is the harmonisation of tax systems within the EC countries.

It is well known that different tax treatments of financial assets may trigger destabilising capital flows. When residual restrictions are lifted, capital will move to countries where the tax treatment of financial assets is more favourable. This is likely to put pressure on the exchange rates but the latter, in a system such as the EMS, are bound to float within given limits and cannot be used to restore equilibrium in capital markets. Countries will have therefore to implement measures to equalise taxation on capital in order to remove the conditions for destabilising capital movements to occur. In this sense, fiscal harmonisation will be a necessary condition for European financial integration, and its effects are examined below.

Prior to describing the kind of simulated harmonisation and its results, it is perhaps useful to say a few words on the way we modelled taxation of financial assets in Germany, Italy and the United Kingdom. In fact, the estimation results previously described have been obtained by using yields net of taxes. In Germany, almost all assets are taxed by income tax. Since we do not know the marginal tax rate of each investor we simply assume that this marginal rate is zero and, therefore that gross returns are equal to net returns. In Italy and the United Kingdom, where assets are taxed by different withholding taxes – those in the case of Italy are final taxes – we used returns net of the above withholding taxes. Equities are treated differently because a system of tax credit on stock dividends exists in all

Table 1.4. *Simulation of tax harmonisation changes in asset shares*

Harmonised variables	Italy						Total change in asset shares	Asset shares after harmonisation	1988 asset shares
	Time deposits	Other deposits	Govern. bonds	Private bonds	Equities	Foreign assets			
Asset shares after tax harmonisation									
Time deposits	2.23	− 0.39	− 0.23	− 0.67	0.00	0.59	1.56	21.34	19.78
Other deposits	− 0.74	0.45	0.08	0.42	0.00	− 0.95	− 0.75	11.79	12.54
Government bonds	− 0.34	0.06	0.88	− 0.71	0.00	− 0.34	− 0.45	47.42	47.87
Private bonds	− 1.01	0.33	− 0.74	1.21	0.00	0.20	− 0.02	4.98	5.00
Equities	− 0.61	− 0.04	0.22	− 0.34	0.00	0.48	− 0.29	12.91	13.20
Foreign assets	0.50	− 0.40	− 0.19	0.10	0.00	0.00	0.01	1.62	1.61

United Kingdom

Harmonised variables	Time deposits	Other deposits	Govern. bonds	Private bonds	Equities	Foreign assets	Total change in asset shares	Asset shares after harmonisation	1988 asset shares
Asset shares after tax harmonisation									
Time deposits	1.31	−0.42	−0.38	−1.23	0.00	0.00	−0.71	8.98	9.69
Other deposits	−0.44	0.49	0.13	0.76	0.00	0.00	0.94	46.00	45.06
Government bonds	−0.20	0.06	1.44	−1.31	0.00	0.00	0.00	6.98	6.98
Private bonds	−0.60	0.36	−1.21	2.21	0.00	0.00	0.76	1.06	0.30
Equities	−0.36	−0.04	0.35	−0.63	0.00	0.00	−0.67	32.95	33.62
Foreign assets	0.29	−0.43	−0.30	0.19	0.00	0.00	−0.26	4.09	4.35

countries. Hence, we use gross yields on equities because we consider dividends as net income.

We simulate a scenario in which tax rates are equalised across assets and thus do not modify relative gross returns. This assumption can be interpreted in several ways. In a sense, this tax system is the same as the one currently in force in Germany, where all assets are taxed by income tax. The same is true in the United States or other developed countries. Another interpretation is that a sizeable reduction of taxes on financial assets (at the limit equal to zero) could also be the ultimate result of institutional competition set off by financial liberalisation in Europe. Finally, this assumption is comparable to the EC proposal of making taxation neutral across financial assets by imposing an even withholding tax on all assets.

Table 1.4 reports the results of the simulation based on 1988 yields and asset shares. As expected, the impact of harmonisation is quite large for Italy, but much less pronounced for the United Kingdom, where the withholding tax evenly affects all assets and is close to the marginal rate of taxation.

In general for Italy the harmonisation seems to favour bank deposits as well as foreign assets and to depress all other assets and in particular government bonds and deposits with other financial institutions. This result seems quite reasonable if we think that bank deposits as well as foreign assets are at present heavily taxed. On the other hand, deposits with other financial institutions, bonds and equities are negatively affected by tax harmonisation, given their pre-simulation tax advantages.

In the United Kingdom, the simulation shows an increase in deposits with other financial institutions at the expense of bank deposits. Furthermore, private bonds tend to increase and replace equities.

In sum, the impact of simulated tax harmonisation on European households' portfolios is quite modest: changes in asset shares brought about by tax convergence towards the German system do not appear to be large either in Italy or in the United Kingdom. This result is not surprising in view of the theoretical background of our model. It has been previously underlined that different non-marketable assets – that is, heterogeneous institutional settings – are expected to result in different asset portfolios across countries: in fact it is the structure of 'adjusted' returns – i.e. yields corrected for the covariances between marketable and non-marketable assets – which drives investors' choices. In this respect, it would have been extremely interesting to compute the vector of adjusted returns. However, in the present case, the approximations involved in deriving a proxy for certain variables (such as the return on equity and social-security wealth) prevent any meaningful computation.

5   Concluding comments

The main conclusion to be drawn from the above results is that the extended portfolio model seems to improve substantially over more traditional alternatives. In fact, the inclusion of non-marketable assets yields precise and reasonable estimates of the impact of relative returns on asset demands and, more generally, provide an adequate description of households' allocation of financial wealth.

However, we would like to stress the drawbacks of the previous approach. First of all, the list of non-marketable assets is far from being exhaustive. It is not difficult to imagine that human wealth could play a crucial role in this respect. In addition the age composition of population (which is supposed to proxy social-security wealth) could actually capture neglected individual heterogeneity and point to aggregation bias.

Finally, it is important to recall that, in some cases, very different financial instruments and intermediaries hide behind an homogeneous terminology. For instance, the definition 'deposits with other financial institutions' is used for both building societies' deposits in the United Kingdom and post office accounts in Italy, even though they are quite heterogeneous instruments due to the different nature of their issuers.

Nevertheless, we believe that the previous results have highlighted a number of important issues in the process of European economic integration. In particular, the empirical evidence suggests that liberalising market entry and adapting fiscal systems are likely to be minor steps towards financial integration if harmonisation does not extend to other institutional arrangements such as social-security systems, pension schemes, labour legislation and the like.

Appendix

Warning

Due to space limitations, it was not possible to include a detailed description of data sources, aggregation of financial assets and the tax treatment of the rate of return used. This information is however available from the authors upon request.

Social-security wealth

In principle, at least, pensioners' gross social-security wealth (denoted by o) could be estimated by multiplying the number of pensioners belonging to the ith age cohort in the tth time period (p_{it}) for the (discounted) expected pension payments (b_{ijt}) accruing to those individuals in any given

(jth) future time period in which they are expected to survive with a given non-zero probability (ϕ_{ijt}). In short,

$$o_t = \Sigma_i p_{it} \Sigma_j (b_{ijt} \phi_{ijt})/(1 + r)^{j-i} \quad (i = \tau, \ldots, T; j = i, \ldots, T) \quad \text{(A.1)}$$

where τ is the age of retirement and T is maximum length of life.

Similarly, for individuals currently belonging to the work force in the ith age cohort (w_{it}), the computation of social-security wealth (denoted by y) implies that expected pension benefits for all workers should be summed up from retirement age up the expected time of death. That is,

$$y_t = \Sigma_i w_{it} \Sigma_j (b_{ijt} \phi_{ijt})/(i + r)^{j-i} \quad (i = \theta, \ldots, \tau; j = \tau, \ldots, T) \quad \text{(A.2)}$$

where θ is initial working age. It easy to check that, in the case of mandatory retirement plans and if the ratio of (discounted) expected pension benefit to marketable wealth is assumed constant (across age cohorts and time periods), pensioners' social-security wealth (o) and workers' social-security wealth (y) could well be proxied by the age composition of population, that is by the share of population of age 65 and over and by the share of the population of working age (14–64).[16]

Net rates of return

A further set of problems refers to the definition and measurement of rates of return. To start with, every effort was made to define net rates of return although it proved impossible to obtain reliable estimates of marginal tax rates. In addition, the gross profit share was used as a measure of the yield on equity. Since equity holding include unlisted stocks, the gross profit share appears to be a more reliable variable than the usual dividend–price ratio. We recognise, however, that the use of such variable as a proxy for the yield of equities makes the standard distinction between yields and capital gains or losses somewhat blurred.

Leaving aside approximations, the rates of return on equity and on foreign assets were defined, as usual, inclusive of capital gains and losses. However, if markets efficiently process all available information, changes in share prices and/or exchange rates from time t to time $t + 1$ should be random variables with mean zero, unpredictable on the basis of information available at time t. The relevant rates of return would therefore be represented by the gross profit share and by the net interest rate respectively.[17] An indirect test of the random walk hypothesis is nevertheless provided (Figure 1.1).

Notes

1 The authors are indebted to Luigi Spaventa and Giuseppe Marotta for their

stimulating comments, to E.P. Davis for rendering his 1986 data set available and to Enrica Croda for updating a part of it. They also wish to thank R. South from the Central Statistical Office, W. Heinelt from the Deutsche Bundesbank and Angela Ancona, Costanza Govino and Agnese Sironi for computer assistance.

2 The exclusion of other European countries (most notably France and Spain) is due to difficulties in finding the relevant data. However, we intend to extend the empirical analysis to the above countries as soon as additional data is collected.

3 A detailed description of data sources and definitions is available from the authors upon request.

4 In fact, previous evidence on the role of non-marketable assets in the allocation of financial wealth is confined to the cross-section studies.

5 In disregarding the pattern of financial liabilities, we implicitly assume that quantity constraints on their long-term component impinge (as in Italy) on households' propensity to save. The availability of short-term financial liabilities should instead be reflected in liquid assets holdings (currency and sight deposits) which are not considered in the present exercise.

6 In the absence of measurement errors, the error term can be shown to be a linear function of expectation errors pertaining to the individual rates of return.

7 In particular, the instrument set includes one-, two- and three-months lagged rates of return, along with the non-marketable asset shares. Since asset shares are as of December, rates of return data used as instruments refer to the month of November or to the last available data. For exchange rates and stock prices, instruments refer to the months of December, November and October. This is a rather important point in that it highlights the fact that we are in fact dealing with a monthly model with missing observations. In this context, the assumption of illiquidity for selected assets should definitely be more palatable.

8 This is true if the small sample adjustment is allowed for as in Pudney (1981, p. 575) with the adjusted likelihood ratio taking the following form,

$$\psi^* = \psi + (I - 1)T\ln[((I - 1)T - p_1)/((I - 1)T - p_0)]$$

where p is the number of parameters and the subscripts 0 and 1 identify the null and alternative hypotheses respectively.

This is also true if the adjustment follows Meisner's (1979) suggestion with:

$$\psi^{**} = \psi[(T - p_1/(I - 1))/T]$$

9 In short, this implies that, for example, the relevant term in, say, the ith equation, is expressed as $a_{i,equities}^+ [E(i_{i,equities}^+) + \gamma_{i,equities} E(g_{equities})]$ where i_i^+ and g_i denote the yield and capital gain components respectively. We test the hypothesis $\gamma_{i,equities} = 0$.

10 In the present case $\Psi^* = 16$ and $\Psi^{**} = 19$. Notice that relevant critical values for theoretically-based hypotheses are computed taking into account the whole sequence of tests so as to ensure an overall significance level of the test approximately equal to, say, 0.05.

11 In this case $\psi^* = 63$ and $\psi^{**} = 53$ for the null given by $H_0: a_{ij}^+ = a_{ji}^+$ and symmetry would be once more rejected. However, things do change if the adjusted statistics are compared with the adjusted critical values computed as in Sargan and Sylwestrowicz (1976, p. 20), that is:

$$k^* = (I - 1)T\ln[1 + qF^*/((I - 1)T - p_1)]$$

and

$$k^{**} = (I - 1)T\ln[1 + qF^{**}/((I - 1)T - p_1)]$$

where F^* and F^{**} are respectively the critical value for the F distribution with $[q, (I - 1)T - p_1]$ and $[q, T - p_1(I - 1)]$ degrees of freedom. If, in particular, the most conservative extension is considered, the symmetry restriction is accepted.

12 It should be underlined that while the literature tends not to test the theoretical restrictions on the A^+ matrix, the theoretical reasons behind them are rather tenuous if we allow for slight changes in the theoretical framework.

13 This is a rather interesting result which should be contrasted with the results on the sources of dynamic misspecification.

14 Notice that both pension funds and the age composition of population play a role. In the light of the remarks of n. 6 above, this result would suggest that the hypothesis underlying the approximation of social-security wealth with the age structure would not be appropriate for private pensions.

15 This is definitely not surprising since the restrictions implied by the usual assumption of gross substitutability are indeed extremely strong.

16 If additional forms of heterogeneity are thought to exist, then demographic variables could well contribute to capture them.

Notice that the age structure of population could also be interpreted as a proxy for human wealth which, in principle, should be the most important form of non-marketable wealth. Finally notice that if the expected private pension benefit–marketable wealth ratio were constant the age structure of the population could also be proxying private pension wealth.

17 In the Italian case, the foreign rate of return takes into account the non-interest-bearing compulsory deposit in force from 1973 to 1987.

References

Bera, A. K., R. P. Byron and C. M. Jarque (1981) 'Further Evidence on Asymptotic Tests for Homogeneity and Symmetry in Large Systems', *Economic Letters*, **8**: 101–5.

Bewley, R. A. (1983) 'Tests of Restrictions in Large Demand Systems', *European Economic Review*, **20**: 257–69.

Bollerslev, T., R. F. Engle and J. M. Wooldridge (1988) 'A Capital Asset Pricing Model with Time-varying Covariance', *Journal of Political Economy*, **96(1)**: 116–31.

Davis, E. P. (1986) 'Portfolio Behaviour of the non-Financial Private Sectors in the Major Economies', **E.P. 17**, Basle: BIS.

Frankel, J. A. (1985) 'Portfolio Crowding-Out Empirically Estimated', *Quarterly Journal of Economics*, **100**: 1041–65.

Friedman, B. M. and V. V. Roley (1979) 'A Note on the Derivation of Linear Homogeneous Asset Demand Functions', **W.P. 345**, Cambridge: NBER.

Hubbard, R. G. (1985) 'Personal Taxation, Pension Wealth and Portfolio Composition', *Review of Economics and Statistics*, **67(1)**: 53–60.

Mayers, D. (1973) 'Non-marketable Assets and the Determination of Capital Asset Prices in the Absence of a Riskless Asset', *Journal of Business*, **46**: 258–67.

Meisner, J. F. (1979) 'The Sad Fate of the Asymptotic Slutsky Symmetry Test for Large Systems', *Economic Letters*, **2**: 223–31.

Merton, R. (1969) 'Lifetime Portfolio Selection Under Uncertainty: The Continuous Time Case', *Review of Economics and Statistics*, **50**: 247–57.

Merton, R. (1971) 'Optimum Consumption and Portfolio Rules in a Continuous Time Model', *Journal of Economic Theory*, **3**: 373–413.

Merton, R. (1973) 'An Intertemporal Capital Asset Pricing Model', *Econometrica*, **41**: 867–87.

Mundlak, Y. (1978) 'On the Pooling of Time Series and Cross Section Data', *Econometrica*, **46**: 69–85.

Pudney, S.E. (1981) 'An Empirical Method of Approximating the Separable Structure of Consumer Preferences', *Review of Economics Studies*, **48**: 561–77.

Roley, V. V. (1982) 'The Effect of Federal Debt-Management Policy on Corporate Bond and Equity Yields', *Quarterly Journal of Economics*, **97**: 645–68.

Sargan, J. D. and J. D. Sylwestrowicz (1976) 'A Comparison of Alternative Methods of Numerical Optimization in Estimating Simultaneous Equation Econometric Models', *LSE Econometrics Programme*, **D.P. 3**.

Stambaugh, R. F. (1982) 'On the Exclusion of Assets from Tests of the Two Parameter Model: A Sensitivity Analysis', *Journal of Financial Economics*, **10**: 237–68.

2 Credit, money and consumption: time-series evidence for Italy

ORAZIO P. ATTANASIO and GUGLIELMO
WEBER

1   Introduction

The main goal of this chapter is to study the implications of intertemporal maximising behaviour for consumption and interest rates in a world where credit markets are imperfect, and to provide some evidence from Italian macroeconomic time series. This is done by generalising the standard Euler equation approach of Hansen and Singleton (1982) to allow for the possibility of net wealth constraints and liquidity services provided by some of the assets available to the representative consumer.

When financial markets are perfect and agents are risk neutral expected rates of return should be equalised. Even if agents are risk averse, assets with similar risk should produce equal expected returns. Thus, if we consider two assets which are affected only by inflation risk we would expect identical returns. An example would be interest-bearing deposits and short-term bonds, as long as the risk of default by both the bank and the company issuing bonds was negligible. Yet, inspection of time-series returns on such assets reveals that bonds stochastically dominate deposits.

The simplest explanation for the (first order) stochastic dominance of short-term bonds over deposits is provided by the existence of transaction costs on the goods market. If goods can be purchased only with money, monetary assets provide liquidity services which are valuable to the consumer. In the extreme case where 'cash in advance' is required, the intertemporal optimisation problem facing individual consumers includes an additional inequality constraint (Lucas, 1982; Svensson, 1985). In more realistic cases where bonds can be used as a means of exchange but a penalty is incurred, the intertemporal budget constraint needs modifying.[1]

In this chapter we model liquidity services of monetary assets by means

36

of a differentiable penalty function associated with low ratios of monetary balances to current expenditure (as in Feenstra, 1986; see also Poterba and Rotemberg, 1987). This allows us to specify an estimable dynamic equation for the excess return of bonds over deposits in terms of consumption growth, real money balances, money balances to expenditure ratios and inflation. We further argue that this equation can be derived in the more general case when an additional net wealth constraint is imposed on the consumer, as long as negative holdings are permitted for individual assets.

The Euler equations derived by solving an intertemporal expected utility maximisation problem provide us with estimates not only of structural parameters but also of the shadow prices associated with various capital markets' imperfections, most notably net wealth constraints and institutional restrictions on trading in foreign assets. This suggests that in future applications to Italian data we could carry out simulation exercises to evaluate the effects of abolishing such restrictions, which involve setting these shadow prices to zero. As a by-product we also obtain estimates of the liquidity function which can be used to discuss the likely effects of financial innovations on money holdings. In this sense, we can interpret ours as a model of money demand.

This chapter is organised as follows. Section 2 presents the theoretical model, Section 3 discusses the data and estimation issues and Section 4 presents empirical results on Italian quarterly time series. We draw some preliminary conclusions and discuss promising developments for future research in Section 5.

2 The model

Let the representative consumer maximise the following intertemporal utility index:

$$E_t\left\{U \equiv \sum_{\tau=t}^{\infty} \beta^{t-\tau}\left[u(c_\tau^1) + v(c_\tau^2)\right]\right\} \tag{1}$$

subject to the following constraints:

$$A_\tau \equiv M_\tau + B_\tau = (1 + r_{\tau-1}^B)B_{\tau-1} \\ + (1 + r_{\tau-1}^M)M_{\tau-1} + y_\tau - X_\tau - p_\tau f(M_\tau, \mathbf{X}_\tau) \tag{2}$$

$$X_\tau \equiv p_\tau^1 c_\tau^1 + p_\tau^2 c_\tau^2 \tag{3}$$

$$p_\tau \equiv s^1 p_\tau^1 + (1 - s^1)p_\tau^2 \tag{4}$$

$$A_\tau \geq \bar{A} \tag{5}$$

where U is the dynasty's utility, β is the time preference parameter, u and v are intraperiod utility of non-durable (c^1) and durable (c^2) goods consumption, with p^1 and p^2 their respective prices.[2] In (2), A is financial wealth, M is (interest-bearing) monetary assets, B is bonds, r^M and r^B are their nominal returns, X is total nominal expenditure (defined in (3)), y is labour income and p is a weighted price index, defined in (4).[3]

The novel aspect of this chapter is the introduction of a lower limit to net wealth (see Zeldes, 1989), namely $\bar{A}$ in (5), *together with* the liquidity services function $f(.)$ in the budget constraint. We assume $f(.)$ to be a twice differentiable function such that:

$$f(.,.) \geq 0, \quad f(M,0) = 0$$

$$f_c(.,.) \geq 0, \quad f_m(.,.) \leq 0$$

$$f_{cc}(.,.) \geq 0, \quad f_{mm}(.,.) \leq 0, \quad f_{mc}(.,.) \leq 0 \tag{6}$$

where subscript m denotes the partial derivative with respect to $m \equiv M/p$, and c the partial derivative with respect to $c \equiv X/p$.

The function $f(.)$ captures the notion that money holdings produce liquidity services: when they are low and a purchase takes place the consumer incurs a monetary cost equal to $pf(.)$.[4] The exact specification of $f(.)$ depends on the assumptions made about the nature of the transaction costs affecting the goods market (Feenstra, 1986).

If we denote by λ_τ the Lagrange multiplier associated with (2), and by μ_τ the Kuhn–Tucker multiplier associated with (5), we can derive the following first order conditions:

$$E_t \left\{ \lambda_{t+1} \frac{1 + r_t^B}{\beta} \right\} = \lambda_t - \mu_t \tag{7}$$

$$E_t \left\{ \lambda_{t+1} \frac{1 + r_t^M}{\beta} \right\} = \lambda_t \left[1 + p_t \frac{\partial f(M_t, X_t)}{\partial M_t} \right] - \mu_t \tag{8}$$

$$\lambda_t p_t^1 + \lambda_t p_t \frac{\partial f(M_t, X_t)}{\partial c_t^1} = \frac{\partial u}{\partial c_t^1} \tag{9}$$

$$\mu_t \geq 0; \quad \mu_t(\bar{A} - A_t) = 0. \tag{10}$$

Subtracting (7) from (8), and using (9), we obtain the following equation for excess returns:

$$E_t \left(\frac{u'(c_{t+1}^1)}{u'(c_t^1)} \frac{r_t^M - r_t^B}{\beta} \frac{p_t^1}{p_{t+1}^1} \frac{1 + \dfrac{\partial f(M_t, X_t)}{\partial c_t} \dfrac{p_t}{p_t^1}}{1 + \dfrac{\partial f(M_{t+1}, X_{t+1})}{\partial c_{t+1}^1} \dfrac{p_{t+1}}{p_{t+1}^1}} \right) = p_t \frac{\partial f(M_t, X_t)}{\partial M_t}. \tag{11}$$

Equation (11) implicitly explains the excess return between monetary and other liquid assets in terms of variances and covariances of consumption growth, inflation on non-durable goods, relative prices, liquidity services and the excess return itself.

It is worth stressing that equation (11) has been derived without setting μ_t to zero, and is thus valid whether the consumer is bound by the net wealth constraint (5) or not. It is an equation that involves observable variables and can be used to estimate by the Generalised Method of Moments (GMM, see below) the deep parameters of $u(.)$ and $f(.)$.

Equation (11) is easily modified to allow for the existence of 'credit goods' (Lucas and Stokey, 1983). If durable goods, for example, can be purchased on credit then X_t becomes nominal expenditure on non-durables only and relative price terms drop out of (11).

Knowledge of the deep parameters allows us to evaluate numerically the Lagrange multipliers λ_t and λ_{t+1}. The Kuhn–Tucker multiplier in each time period can then be computed from (7), but care must be taken in using the projection on the instruments set of the expression within the expectations operator rather than its actual realisation.

3   The data

In our application we use quarterly time series data for Italy, spanning the 13-year period 1976–88.

We take our consumption measure from the new National Account-ancy statistics on consumers' expenditure on non-durable goods and services. We also try a broader definition which includes semidurable commodities (such as clothing).[5] *Per capita* consumption is obtained by dividing total expenditure by total population, while the corresponding implicit deflators are used when computing real consumption and the inflation rate.[6]

In order to estimate equation (11) we need rates of returns on a monetary and a non-monetary financial asset, as well as household holdings of the chosen monetary asset. The monetary financial asset we use is cash plus bank current and deposit accounts (the distinction in terms of liquidity and returns between the two types of account being a minor one in Italy). As for the non-monetary asset, we use three-month Treasury Bills.[7] Treasury Bills (and other similar short-term government bonds) are currently one of the most popular assets in the portfolios of Italian households, and together with bank deposits account for a sub-stantial proportion of Italian households' financial wealth (in 1982, for instance, the sum of bank deposits and government bonds accounted for over 80 per cent of the financial wealth of Italian households). However Treasury Bills hardly existed before 1976: in 1975 the ratio of Treasury Bills to the sum of bank deposits and cash was below 1 per cent.

The impressive growth of Treasury Bills as a popular asset is probably better explained as the establishment of a new financial product than in the framework of a model of liquidity services and interest rate differentials. For this reason, we reluctantly decided to limit ourselves to the analysis of the 1976–88 period.

A theoretical problem is caused by the choice of Treasury Bills as the non-monetary asset: negative holdings of such an asset by individual consumers are not allowed. While our theoretical model allows for a lower limit to total financial wealth, it does not take into account the possibility of restrictions on individual assets (or at least on the individual assets for which we consider the Euler equation). In theory, it is possible that some households will want to borrow at the Treasury Bill rate to get some liquidity services from money holdings. We assume that in equilibrium this does not occur.

The data used in this study are relatively new and deserve some description. Total consumption expenditure grew at an average rate of 3.2 per cent per annum. As in other countries, consumption exhibits very strong seasonality: seasonal variation accounts for about 94 per cent of the variability of quarterly consumption growth. However, unlike in other countries, growth in total expenditure presents negative seasonality in the first and fourth quarter and positive seasonality in the second and third. If we look at the seasonality of the various components it is also very differentiated. Expenditure on durables presents negative seasonality in the third quarter and positive seasonality in the others, with the highest being in the first quarter (seasonality accounts for only 58 per cent of the variability in the growth of expenditure on durables). Semidurables and services present the same pattern as total expenditure.

As stressed in the previous section the use of the liquidity services model is justified by the dominance of one asset over another. The nominal rates of return on Treasury Bills and 'money' are plotted in Figure 2.1. As can be seen, the return on Treasury Bills is always higher: given that both nominal returns are known in advance such a difference cannot be explained by risk considerations (unless we assume that the insolvency risk for the government is higher than for banks). Over the period 1976–87 there was on average a differential of 6.5 percentage points between the return on Treasury Bills and that on money holdings. According to our theory the interest rate differential should be related, via the transaction cost function, to the ratio of expenditure to money. When such a ratio is high (when 'velocity' is high), the liquidity services are particularly high and therefore the interest rate differential should be high (for a related discussion on the role of the transaction demand for money, see Friedman, 1988). A formal study of such a relationship is postponed to the next section, but we believe that a preliminary glance at the data can be useful. Figure 2.2 presents the plot of the interest rate differential

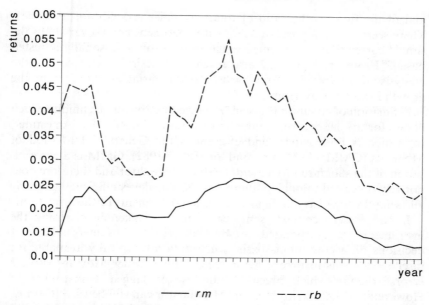

Figure 2.1   Nominal returns

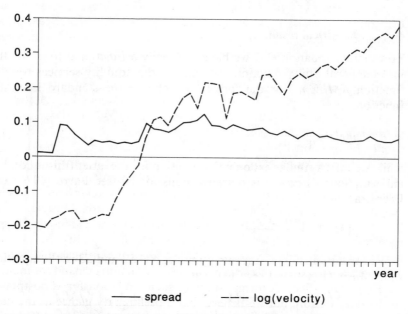

Figure 2.2   The interest rate spread and log of consumption velocity

and of the (log of) the ratio of total consumer expenditure to money. There seems to be a positive relationship between the two variables: the simple correlation coefficient is equal to 0.34 (on a seasonally adjusted basis).[8] However, Figure 2.2 also reveals the desirability of casting the analysis in a dynamic setting, where other variables can explain the growth in velocity over time.

Estimation of equation (11) can be carried out by any technique which allows for the endogenous character of variables timed $t + 1$. An estimator which is both robust and efficient is the Generalised Method of Moments (GMM, see Hansen and Singleton, 1982). GMM is a generalisation of the standard instrumental variable estimator and therefore does not rely on distributional assumptions, and achieves efficiency gains by allowing for time-varying higher conditional moments of the error term.

In the present context, some care must be taken in choosing the instruments set. As pointed out by Hall (1988), consumers take their decisions on a continuous basis, while data are typically available for discrete intervals in time. This induces a First Order Moving Average error structure which precludes the use of lagged 1 instruments.[9] However, an MA(1) corrected GMM estimator can still be used (Cumby, Huizinga and Obstfeld, 1983) and convenient formulae to compute an estimator of its asymptotic variance–covariance matrix are available (Newey and West, 1987).

4   Empirical results

To estimate equation (11) we have to specify a functional form for the intratemporal utility function $u(c_t^1)$ and of the liquidity services penalty function $f(M_t, X_t)$. For the former, we choose the standard isoelastic function:

$$u(c_t^1) \equiv \frac{c_t^{1(1-\gamma)}}{1-\gamma} \tag{12}$$

while we take a similar exponential function for the latter (this is consistent with Barro's generalised transactions model, see Barro, 1976, and Feenstra, 1986):

$$f(M_t, X_t) = \frac{a_0(X_t/M_t)^{a+1}}{a+1} \tag{13}$$

We further introduce seasonal dummies $S1$, $S2$ and $S3$ in the equation as in Miron (1986), and rewrite (9) as:

$$E_t\left\{\left(\frac{c_{t+1}^1}{c_t^1}\right)^{-\gamma} \frac{(r_t^M - r_t^B)}{\beta} \frac{p_t^1}{p_{t+1}^1} \frac{m_{t+1}}{m_t} \frac{m_t + a_0(X_t/M_t)^a}{m_{t+1} + a_0(X_{t+1}/M_{t+1})^a}\right.$$

$$\exp\left(\sum_{i=1}^{3} d_i(S_{i,t+1} - S_{i,t})\right)\right\} = -a_0\beta(X_t/M_t)^{a+1}\frac{1}{m_t} \qquad (11')$$

where $m_t \equiv M_t/p_t$.[10]

Tables 2.1–2.4 report our parameter estimates. The sample we used for estimation is 1976:2–1988:4. Each table is organised as follows: the upper part of the table presents (non-linear) IV estimates, the lower part the more efficient GMM ones. Instruments used include second, third and fourth lags of consumption growth, earnings growth, inflation, the two asset returns and real money holdings, as well as four seasonal dummies. Hence there are 19 overidentifying restrictions which are tested for in the bottom part of the table (the value of the objective function is the appropriate χ^2 test statistic). Each table also presents some summary statistics on the shadow prices of the net wealth constraints (expressed in real terms: $\mu_t p_t$), and a list of their annual averages over the sample period.

In practice we found that β and a_0 are not separately identified, and proceeded by setting $\beta = 1.0075$ (corresponding to a real discount rate of 3 per cent per annum).[11] The identification problem for β is best understood with reference to equation (11'). There β appears only on the right-hand side and is multiplied by a_0: for identification, we require a_0 to be 'pinned down' on the left-hand side. This condition is not met in practice, because the a parameter is estimated to be close to zero, and the ratio $(m_t + a_0)/(m_{t+1} + a_0)$ is insensitive to the value taken by a_0.

Table 2.1 presents results for the model where the narrow definition of consumption is adopted (semidurables are not included in c^1) and all remaining goods are treated as credit goods. Taking the GMM parameter estimates at face value, the elasticity of intertemporal substitution is low $(1/\gamma = 0.31)$. The corresponding parameter (γ) is however poorly determined: its t-value is only 1.75. The liquidity services function is better determined (see the estimate of a_0), but $f(M_t, X_t)$ is effectively linear, thus giving us an insignificant (and incorrectly signed) estimate for the a parameter. The overidentifying restrictions test fails to reject the null of correct specification.

Table 2.2 estimates conform more closely to those typically discussed in the literature, because they are based on the broader consumption measure (which includes semidurables). The elasticity of intertemporal substitution is still rather low $(1/\gamma = 0.363)$, and the existence of the liquidity services function is clearly reflected in a well determined, positive estimate for a_0. Once again, a linear functional form for $f(M_t, X_t)$ cannot be rejected, and the test does not reveal misspecification.

In Tables 2.3 and 2.4 we present results relative to the model where no credit goods exist. Table 2.3 corresponds to the narrower definition of

Table 2.1. *Estimates of (11'): narrow consumption measure, durables and semidurables treated as credit goods*

IV optimization results

Var	Coeff.	Std error	t-stat	P-value
γ	4.393363	6.650542	0.660602	0.512231
d_1	− 0.233610	0.153974	− 1.517200	0.136204
d_2	− 0.226234	0.110861	− 2.040699	0.047166
d_3	0.265715	0.671583	0.395655	0.694227
a_0	0.128756	0.114654	1.122997	0.267389
a	− 0.172064	0.678595	− 0.253559	0.800990

GMM optimisation results
*** Value of objective function: 19.709088 ***

Var	Coeff.	Std error	t-stat	P-value
γ	3.263415	1.862074	1.752570	0.086480
d_1	− 0.192739	0.056808	− 3.392813	0.001443
d_2	− 0.223314	0.060550	− 3.688126	0.000598
d_3	0.148096	0.194904	0.759840	0.451308
a_0	0.119581	0.059463	2.011015	0.050330
a	− 0.238131	0.384997	− 0.618525	0.539344

Notes: 51 observations. Degrees of freedom: 19.

Kuhn–Tucker multipliers (sample period 1976:2–1988:4):

summary statistics

no. of obs.	mean	stand dev.	max	min
51.0000	0.0499	0.7329	2.3068	− 1.9065

annual averages

0.2215	0.3292	0.0926	− 0.2259	− 0.0641	0.1192	− 0.3008
0.2669	− 0.4806	− 0.5004	− 0.7951	0.1891	1.8403	

Table 2.2. *Estimates of (11'): broad consumption measure, durables treated as credit goods*

IV optimization results

Var	Coeff.	Std error	t-stat	P-value
γ	5.415940	9.886072	0.547835	0.586509
d_1	$-$ 0.348121	0.399922	$-$ 0.870473	0.388657
d_2	$-$ 0.345151	0.280014	$-$ 1.232621	0.224112
d_3	0.115644	0.515040	0.224534	0.823357
a_0	0.132748	0.099652	1.332114	0.189524
a	0.031617	0.709035	0.044592	0.964630

GMM optimisation results
*** Value of objective function: 19.592255 ***

Var	Coeff.	Std error	t-stat	P-value
γ	2.754010	2.751390	1.000952	0.322197
d_1	$-$ 0.226217	0.119369	$-$ 1.895114	0.064505
d_2	$-$ 0.282215	0.093231	$-$ 3.027042	0.004068
d_3	$-$ 0.036548	0.148822	$-$ 0.245581	0.807122
a_0	0.140119	0.060449	2.317977	0.025046
a	0.059747	0.405599	0.147305	0.883548

Notes: 51 observations. Degrees of freedom: 19.

Kuhn–Tucker multipliers (sample period 1976:2–1988:4):

summary statistics

no. of obs.	mean	stand dev.	max	min
51.0000	0.0197	0.2807	0.8783	$-$ 0.5124

annual averages

0.1011	0.1041	0.0248	$-$ 0.0766	$-$ 0.0164	0.0503	$-$ 0.0370
0.1112	$-$ 0.2140	$-$ 0.2153	$-$ 0.2810	0.0901	0.6355	

Table 2.3. *Estimates of (11'): narrow consumption measure, no credit goods*

IV optimization results

Var	Coeff.	Std error	t-stat	P-value
γ	3.002923	6.667849	0.450359	0.654611
d_1	− 0.181714	0.150854	− 1.204571	0.234660
d_2	− 0.200195	0.098147	− 2.039735	0.047265
d_3	0.145949	0.668366	0.218367	0.828129
a_0	0.106767	0.061032	1.749362	0.087039
a	− 0.098315	0.589299	− 0.166834	0.868247

GMM optimisation results
*** Value of objective function: 19.797255 ***

Var	Coeff.	Std error	t-stat	P-value
γ	1.688452	1.958946	0.861918	0.393298
d_1	− 1.145201	0.055981	− 1.593736	0.012758
d_2	− 0.202711	0.050601	− 4.006034	0.000220
d_3	0.010478	0.203325	0.051535	0.959127
a_0	0.094739	0.029996	3.158425	0.002824
a	− 0.234595	0.329754	− 0.711425	0.480489

Notes: 51 observations. Degrees of freedom: 19.

Kuhn–Tucker multipliers (sample period 1976:2–1988:4):

summary statistics

no. of obs.	mean	stand dev.	max	min
51.0000	0.0149	0.3001	0.7616	− 0.5600

annual averages

0.0974	0.0615	0.0143	− 0.0856	0.0084	0.0598	0.0642
0.0405	− 0.3098	− 0.0449	− 0.3202	− 0.0035	0.6323	

Table 2.4. *Estimates of (11'): broad consumption measure, no credit goods*

IV optimization results

Var	Coeff.	Std error	t-stat	P-value
γ	4.017460	9.764164	0.411449	0.682694
d_1	− 0.287133	0.394513	− 0.727816	0.470492
d_2	− 0.298083	0.274160	− 1.087262	0.282705
d_3	0.055410	0.509106	0.108838	0.913814
a_0	0.110941	0.066380	1.671296	0.101597
a	− 0.053056	0.631049	− 0.084077	0.933368

GMM optimisation results
*** Value of objective function: 19.962924 ***

Var	Coeff.	Std error	t-stat	P-value
γ	1.533214	2.679579	0.572185	0.570041
d_1	− 0.180294	0.115944	− 1.555017	0.126941
d_2	− 0.243838	0.088963	− 2.740885	0.008749
d_3	− 0.085746	0.146723	− 0.584405	0.561863
a_0	0.112143	0.040583	2.763328	0.008251
a	− 0.066604	0.377360	− 0.176499	0.860693

Notes: 51 observations. Degrees of freedom: 19.

Kuhn–Tucker multipliers (sample period 1976:2–1988:4):

summary statistics

no. of obs.	mean	stand dev.	max	min
51.0000	0.0092	0.1938	0.5727	− 0.3528

annual averages

0.0615	0.0462	0.0102	− 0.0597	− 0.0006	0.0474	0.0265
0.0391	− 0.1824	− 0.0927	− 0.1578	− 0.0079	0.4033	

consumption, and is thus directly comparable to Table 2.1. The elasticity of intertemporal substitution is now larger (0.59), but very poorly determined. The a_0 parameter of the liquidity services function is instead much more precisely estimated. Similar results obtain with the broader definition of consumption (Table 2.4).[12]

Our estimates can be used to determine the importance of various imperfections and institutional restrictions present in the Italian financial markets. If we are confident in the point estimates reported above, equations (7)–(9) can be used to derive the Kuhn–Tucker multipliers associated to the net wealth constraint (5). Furthermore, if we know that investment in a given asset was limited because of institutional restrictions (like capital controls) the estimates of our structural parameter can be used to compute the Kuhn–Tucker multiplier associated to such a restriction. Finally, we can in principle study the effects of a reduction in transaction costs due to financial innovations.

The Kuhn–Tucker multipliers associated to equation (5) were computed first solving equation (7) for λ_t and then solving equation (8) for μ_t. This gives us (ignoring the seasonal dummies for notational simplicity):

$$\lambda_t = \frac{u'(c_t^1)}{p_t^1 + p_t \dfrac{\partial f(M_t, X_t)}{\partial c_t^1}} \tag{14}$$

$$\mu_t = \lambda_t - E_t\left[\lambda_{t+1}\frac{1 + r_t^B}{\beta}\right] \tag{15}$$

In both (14) and (15) estimated parameters replace the unknown coefficients of the utility and liquidity services functions. For this reason, we shall denote calculated λ and μ with hats. Note that $\hat{\mu}$ will also differ from μ because the true conditional expectation of λ_{t+1} is replaced by the projection on the instruments set. This may explain why the estimated shadow price of the net wealth constraint, $\hat{\mu}_t p_t$, goes negative occasionally, while its theoretical counterpart is positive when the constraint is binding and zero otherwise.

If we look at the bottom of Table 2.1, we see that the average value of the real Kuhn–Tucker multiplier is positive (0.05). However, we calculate negative numbers in six of the thirteen years, mostly in the early 1980s. The largest multipliers correspond to 1977, 1983 and 1988. A similar pattern can be detected in Table 2.2: the average multiplier is 0.02, peak years are again 1977, 1983 and 1988. Similar findings emerge from Tables 2.3 and 2.4.

Overall it can be observed that when the *ex post* real interest rate was relatively high, as in the early 1980s, the Kuhn–Tucker multiplier was particularly low. Particularly impressive is the increase of the multiplier in

1988, corresponding to a large decrease of the real interest rate. This observation is consistent with the hypothesis that in the presence of high interest rates there are less incentives (*ceteris paribus*) to borrow against uncertain future labour income. One would therefore expect that restrictions on borrowing would not be binding.

Another factor may help to interpret our results, i.e. credit ceilings imposed by the Bank of Italy. According to Cottarelli *et al.* (1986), overall credit ceilings were binding in 1977 and in the early 1980s. Their analysis does not cover the period after 1984, when credit ceilings were first lifted and then reintroduced for the six months September 1987–March 1988. Whether these restrictions influenced available consumer credit to any appreciable extent is, however, unclear.[13]

5   Conclusions

In this chapter we investigated the importance of capital market imperfections for Italian consumers. We specified an intertemporal maximisation problem where monetary assets yielded liquidity services and consumers were subject to net wealth constraints. This produced a non-standard consumption growth equation which we estimated on Italian aggregate data.

On the basis of our estimates we computed the shadow price of the net wealth constraint over individual quarters of the sample period (1976:2–1988:4) and commented on the likely causes of the varying degree of severity of credit restrictions facing Italian households. These computations could form the basis for a simulation exercise, aimed at assessing the macroeconomic importance of greater availability of consumer credit or of an improved performance of the Italian banking sector which reduced the liquidity services of monetary assets. Such an exercise presupposes the specification of a general equilibrium model which is beyond the scope of this chapter. Alternatively, one can make some simplifying assumptions about the behaviour of some variables and study the effects of changes in the Kuhn–Tucker multipliers on the others. For instance, it is possible to assume that, given EMS membership and the phasing out of capital controls, Italian interest rates cannot dramatically deviate from European levels. Relaxation of various kinds of restrictions and imperfections would then have an effect only on expected consumption growth.

Notes

Helpful discussions with Rob Alessie, Rony Hamaui and Nicola Rossi are gratefully acknowledged. We also wish to thank Simonetta Melotto for providing the data used in this study and COMIT for financial support. G. Weber is grateful to the Center for Economic Policy Research at Stanford for hospitality.

1 In a related study on aggregate asset holdings by Italian households, Bollino and Rossi (1989) find that short-term financial assets like Treasury Bills provide some liquidity services.

2 For notational simplicity we express $v(.)$ as a function of durables' purchases, rather than services from the durables' stocks. This is of no consequence on our derivations, as we do not use the first order conditions with respect to c^2.

3 To keep the analysis simple we do not make s^1 a function of individual expenditure on non-durable goods. Thus p_τ is an economy-wide price index which the consumer takes as given.

4 In general the function $f(.)$ may be expected to be discontinuous. If we take a sufficiently flexible functional form for $f(.)$ we may, however, capture most of the non-linearities and retain the analytical advantages of dynamic programming (MaCurdy, 1983).

5 The consumption series were released during summer 1989, and are known as 'new new' National Accounts.

6 We also use expenditure on all (durable and non-durable) goods to compute the ratio X/M and the price index p in the model without credit goods.

7 We also tried the average return on corporate bonds and found that empirical results were largely unaffected. Corporate bonds would suit our theoretical framework better, as individual consumers are theoretically able to go short on bonds. However, they may be affected by default risk and are rarely found in individual portfolios, possibly because of unfavourable tax treatment or institutional restrictions affecting their supply.

8 In Figure 2.2 both spread (in annual terms) and the logarithm of velocity have been seasonally adjusted by taking the residuals of a regression on four seasonal dummies. For presentational purposes, the sample average has been added back to the spread only.

9 Optimisation errors and durability of goods can also generate on MA(1) error. Note that the expectational character of the error prevents the use of standard filtering techniques (Hayashi and Sims, 1983). While filtering makes the disturbance white noise, it does not ensure orthogonality of the transformed error to the filtered information set.

10 If real money holdings or real expenditure (X/p) are of order of integration 1 then the right-hand side of (11') is going to be non-stationary. For the error term to be stationary, we have to assume that the left-hand side is also I(1). This was borne out in our data set, as augmented Dickey–Fuller tests could not reject an I(1) structure for the product of the excess return and the price ratio.

11 β is the reciprocal of the pure time preference discount factor, expressed in real terms and on a quarterly basis. We would normally expect it to range between 1 and 1.02, even though lower values (0.98, for example) have been reported in the literature. Needless to say, our remaining estimates are insensitive to slight variations in its value.

12 We also tested for a structural break of the liquidity services function by letting a take a different value from 1980:1 onwards. Neither estimate of the parameter was significantly different from zero.

13 A word of caution is in order. Our model is based on the representative agent assumption. This is a standard assumption in the context of complete markets where idiosyncratic risks are fully insurable. Imperfect capital markets imply less than full insurance and make aggregation less straightforward. In order to use aggregate data we not only require an equation which holds for constrained and unconstrained individuals (like equation (11) in the text), but presumably also have to restrict preference variations across consumers. We

do not attempt a formal analysis of aggregation issues in this chapter, but emphasise that econometric work on micro data would lead to more convincing results.

References

Barro, R. J. (1976) 'Integral Constraints and Aggregation in an Inventory Model of Money Demand', *Journal of Finance*, **31**: 77–87.

Bollino, C. A. and N. Rossi (1989) 'The Italian Households' Demand for Monetary Assets and Government Debt', in F. Giavazzi and L. Spaventa (ed.), *High Public Debt: The Italian Experience*, Cambridge: Cambridge University Press.

Cottarelli, C., G. Galli, P. Marullo Reedtz and G. Pittaluga (1986) 'Monetary Policy through Ceilings to Bank Lending', *Economic Policy*, **3**: 673–710.

Cumby, R. E., J. Huizinga and M. Obstfeld (1983) 'Two-Step Two-Stage Least Squares Estimation in Models with Rational Expectations', *Journal of Econometrics*, **21**: 333–55.

Feenstra, R. C. (1986) 'Functional Equivalence Between Liquidity Costs and the Utility of Money', *Journal of Monetary Economics*, **17**: 271–91.

Friedman, M. (1988) 'Money and the Stock Market', *Journal of Political Economy*, **96(2)**: 221–45.

Hall, R. E. (1988) 'Intertemporal Substitution in Consumption', *Journal of Political Economy*, **96**: 339–57.

Hansen, L. P. and K. J. Singleton (1982) 'Generalized Instrumental Variables Estimation of Nonlinear Rational Expectations Models', *Econometrica*, **50(5)**: 1269–88.

Hayashi, F. and C. Sims (1983) 'Nearly Efficient Estimation of Time Series Model with Predetermined, but not Exogenous, Instruments', *Econometrica*, **51(3)**: 783–98.

Lucas, R. E., Jr (1982) 'Interest Rates and Currency Prices in a Two-Country World', *Journal of Monetary Economics*, **10**: 225–59.

Lucas, R. E., Jr and N. L. Stokey (1983) 'Optimal Fiscal and Monetary Policy in an Economy without Capital', *Journal of Monetary Economics*, **12**: 55–93.

MaCurdy, T. (1983) 'A Simple Scheme for Estimating an Intertemporal Model of Labour Supply and Consumption in the Presence of Taxes and Uncertainty', *International Economic Review*, **24(2)**: 265–89.

Miron, J. A. (1986) 'Seasonal Fluctuations and the Life Cycle-Permanent Income Model of Consumption', *Journal of Political Economy*, **94**: 1258–79.

Newey, W. K. and K. D. West (1987) 'A Simple, Positive Semi-Definite, Heteroskedasticity and Autocorrelation Consistent Covariance Matrix', *Econometrica*, **55(3)**: 703–8.

Poterba, J. M. and J. J. Rotemberg (1987) 'Money in the Utility Function: An Empirical Implementation', in W.A. Barnett and K.J. Singleton (eds), *New Approaches to Monetary Economics*, Cambridge: Cambridge University Press: 219–40.

Svensson, L. E. O. (1985) 'Money and Asset Prices in a Cash-in-Advance Economy', *Journal of Political Economy*, **93(5)**: 919–44.

Zeldes, S. (1989) 'Consumption and Liquidity Constraints: An Empirical Investigation', *Journal of Political Economy*, **97(2)**: 305–46.

Discussion

LUIGI SPAVENTA

1   Introduction

Ordinary portfolio models are unable to explain the major differences evidenced by the data in the composition of households' financial assets in different countries. Giraldi, Hamaui and Rossi (hereafter GHR), following the suggestions of some earlier literature, argue that this is due to the neglect of the effects of non-marketable (i.e. illiquid or highly illiquid) assets on the structure of financial wealth. Considering Germany, Italy and the United Kingdom, they test (for the first time on aggregate data) an augmented portfolio model, where such non-marketable assets as pension funds, social-security wealth and the housing stock are made to play an explicit role in explaining assets' demand. They obtain remarkably successful results: the introduction of non-marketable wealth considerably improves the empirical performance of a portfolio model, and the difference in its size and composition in the three countries (which in turn depends on different institutional arrangements) appears to be a major factor of the different structure of marketable wealth. GHR then use their model to simulate the effects of tax harmonisation across the three countries on relative asset demand. Such effects turn out to be surprisingly modest, and this is taken by the authors as further corroboration of their finding: 'in fact it is the structure of 'adjusted' returns – i.e. yields corrected for the covariances between marketable and non-marketable assets – which drives investors' choices'. This leads GHR to conclude that 'liberalising market entry and adapting fiscal systems are likely to be minor steps towards financial integration if harmonisation does not extend to other institutional arrangements such as social-security systems, pension schemes, labour legislation, and the like'.

Though I have no particular competence to discuss the theory, and especially the econometrics of this impressive paper, in what follows I venture to submit two sets of brief comments. The first relates to the explanatory content of the model (irrespective of its econometric specification) and to the policy implication drawn by GHR. The second concerns the definition of illiquid assets and the data used to proxy non-marketable wealth.

Let me say at the outset that my remarks do not intend to be ungenerous to what is a very good study: they can in no way detract either from the ingenuity and the remarkably technical competence displayed by the authors in their search for data and in their estimation procedures, or from the objective relevance of their results.

2   Non-marketable wealth

Non-marketable wealth is not itself a 'primitive object': pension funds and social-security wealth depend, as the authors stress, on institutional arrangements and on the age structure of the population (while the housing stock is itself a variable to be explained). That such factors should somehow affect the relative demand for financial assets is *prima facie* a sound and sensible hypothesis. But why and, especially, how? Without indulging in an exasperating quest for microfoundations, a bit of theory is useful to understand the purpose and the results of empirical analysis. The theoretical foundation of the GHR model is simple and on the whole acceptable: 'in the presence of non-marketable wealth, investors tend to tilt their portfolio away from those stocks with which their non-marketable securities are most highly correlated . . ., attaching relatively higher risk premiums to those non-marketable assets with which . . . non-marketable returns have the highest covariation'. This, however, is hardly enough to explain why the current process of population ageing would imply a shift to bank deposits in the United Kindom, but one from bank deposits to deposits with other financial institutions in Germany, while causing, in all three countries, a rather massive shift to government bonds (which, incidentally, are very different animals in the three cases). Nor does it obviously follow that 'portfolios dominated by a highly illiquid asset such as the housing stock tend to present a higher share of short-term assets as bank deposits'. First, as we know nothing about the covariations between the (unobservable) non-marketable returns and the returns of the six broad categories of financial assets in the three countries, we are unable to check the empirical results against the theory. Second, invoking liquidity may make sense, but it is not necessarily consistent with a theoretical explanation in terms of covariation of returns.

GHR, as we have seen, argue that, to pursue financial integration, liberalisation is not enough and harmonisation should not be confined to the tax treatment but extend to all sorts of institutional arrangements affecting non-marketable wealth. I fail to understand why convergence in the composition of households' financial wealth should in any way be a policy objective: surely, of all the possible reasons for changing social-security systems, pension schemes, etc. that is the least important? Apart from this, are GHR so sure that greater homogeneity of the institutional determinants of non-marketable wealth would by itself harmonise the composition of marketable assets?

First, the authors seem to disregard the relevance of supply factors in affecting the structure of financial wealth in non-fully integrated markets (as those of the three countries were in the period they. consider). Asset composition reflects the degree of intermediation of the financial system: the latter in turn depends not only, and perhaps not so much, on assets demands, as on the role assigned to banks by history, industrial structure and legislation. The differences between 'bank-oriented' and 'market-oriented' systems (say, between Germany and Britain), which has recently attracted the attention of theoretical literature (see Hellwig, 1990), *must* have some bearing on assets' composition. Again, the need to finance huge public sector imbalances may affect composition through the constraints imposed on the supply of competing assets (as witnessed by the Italian case), while on the other hand drastic fiscal corrections, leading to a sharp decline in the public debt–GDP ratio, may leave an unsatisfied appetite for sovereign paper. Financial integration will probably remove this latter cause of divergence, but is unlikely to eliminate the former one.

Second, the GHR model can hardly account for differences in the structure of households' marketable assets within the same country where institutional arrangements affecting non-marketable wealth are necessarily homogeneous. In the case of Italy such differences are remarkable (Banca d'Italia, 1989). As the Italian surveys show, 'portfolio composition changes considerably as the overall size of [the household's] financial wealth rises' (Cannari *et al.*, 1990, p. 35) and is also affected by the regional location of the household and the degree of education of the head of family. I am sure it is possible to rationalise the relevance of such factors (in terms of economies of scale, of transaction and information costs): the only point I wish to make is that they are unrelated to non-marketable wealth and persist even when the heterogeneity of institutional factors affecting the latter is removed.

3   Social-security wealth and pension funds

GHR define non-marketable assets as those which are illiquid and which can be taken as exogenous in the solution of an optimal portfolio model: pension funds, social-security wealth and the housing stock possess in their view these attributes. They use value data for the first and the third variable, while they proxy the pensioners' and workers' social-security wealth by the share in the population of elderly people (over 65) and of people of working age.

Let me first express some doubts concerning the treatment of social-security wealth and the separate consideration of pension funds. Proxying the former in all countries by the age composition of the population is a clever device, but conceals deep differences of the pension systems:

differences in the retirement age, in the number of years of compulsory contributions required to be entitled to a pension above the minimum level, in the ratio of the pension income to the income in the working period, in the existence of ceilings to the pension level. The recourse to non-mandatory pension funds very much depends on how generous social security is: we could hardly understand otherwise why, in spite of relatively high employment termination allowances (the reserves for which are included in the pension funds item), the ratio of pension funds to marketable wealth is so low in Italy with respect to the other two countries (see GHR's Table 2.4). It is therefore likely that the use of the age composition proxy causes a relative underestimation of social-security provisions: overall pension wealth – irrespective of whether it is the result of voluntary or mandatory contributions – would then depend only on the age structure and pension funds may be omitted as a separate explanatory variable.

4   The housing stock

I have slightly more serious problems with the housing stock. First with the data, as the OECD (net) values GHR use for Italy and the United Kingdom bear little (if any) resemblance to the data produced by Fazio (1986), even allowing for the fact that the latter are gross values. The valuation of the housing stock is bound to be a headache in any case, and the use of net values, beside being of doubtful significance, adds to the difficulty. Here as elsewhere one is (ungenerously) led to wonder what trust one can have in the offspring of a marriage between rigidly rigorous models and data for which the margins of error can well run into two digits.

But does the housing stock even qualify as a member of the family of non-marketable (illiquid and exogenously determined) assets? Even if we forget that acquiring a house is part of the decision process concerning the allocation of the household's overall wealth, and that a house, unlike social-security wealth, can be sold, we can hardly neglect that a house is an asset one can borrow against, for investment or for consumption purposes (as the recent UK experience amply shows). Is, then, a house a less liquid asset than, say equity in a company? This admittedly vague query uncovers another source of uneasiness.

5   Households' financial liabilities

Intercountry differences in the composition of gross financial assets are on the whole less striking than differences in the ratios of households' financial *liabilities*, whether to assets or to net wealth or to GDP. Households' liabilities find no place in the chapter. As the authors inform us in a footnote, 'in disregarding the pattern of financial liabilities we implicitly assume that quantity constraints on their long-term component impinge (as in Italy) on households' propensity to save'. I find this a bit weak. The same optimising process must preside over the choice of assets and of liabilities: if so, constrained or unconstrained decisions about the latter interact with the choice of assets and the composition of gross and net wealth.

6   Conclusions

This chapter is an important contribution towards understanding inter-country differences in households' financial decisions. Many problems are as yet unsettled, which may be of greater relevance in the process of financial integration in Europe, and many neglected determinants of the structure of financial wealth deserve more careful consideration. GHR are well equipped to broaden their analysis and to provide the relevant answers.

Note

Luigi Spaventa is Professor, University of Rome, La Sapienza.

References

Banca d'Italia (1989) 'I bilanci delle famiglie italiane nell'anno 1987', *Supplemento al Bollettino Statistico*, 5.
Cannari, L., G. d'Alessio, G. Raimondi and A.I. Rinaldi (1990) 'Le attività finanziarie delle famiglie italiane', Banca d'Italia, *Temi di discussione del Servizio Studi*, 136 (July).
Fazio, A. (1986) 'Debito pubblico, ricchezza e sviluppo dell'economia', Banca d'Italia, *Bollettino Economico*, 6 (February).
Hellwig, M. (1990) 'Banking, Financial Intermediation and Corporate Finance', paper presented at the IMI–CEPR Conference on Financial Intermediation (Rome) (January).

1.2 Financial choices of industrial firms: the Italian case

3 Empirical determinants of corporate debt decisions: some evidence for Italy

LEO BONATO, RICCARDO FAINI and MARCO RATTI

1 Introduction[1]

The state of corporate indebtedness has always attracted considerable attention in both academic and policy circles. More recently the rise in companies' debt has been at the centre of a lively debate in the United States (Volcker, 1986; Kaufman, 1986; Bernanke and Campbell, 1988).

In Italy the evolution of corporate debt has witnessed a dramatic turnabout from the situation in the 1970s, where increasing companies' debt was at the forefront of policy makers' concern, to the more recent trend, characterised by a marked improvement in the main debt indicators. The purpose of this chapter is to provide a detailed account of the determinants of corporate debt choice for Italian firms.

This chapter is organised as follows. In Section 2 we present a brief account of the evolution of corporate financing decisions in Italy. We find that there are significant differences between large companies on the one hand and small and medium-sized firms on the other. We choose therefore to rely on two different samples of balance sheet data, one of small and medium-sized manufacturing firms from the Centrale dei Bilanci (hereafter CdB) data base and the second one of large firms from Ricerche & Studi (hereafter R & S). After a brief survey of the theoretical models of corporate borrowing (Section 3), we present in Section 4 our econometric results. We find a substantial role for cash flow considerations and for fiscal effects. More generally, significant differences in firms' behaviour according to size and location are clearly detected. We also argue that the behaviour of the stock market may have exerted a significant but opposite impact, depending on the firm's size, on the decision to borrow. Section 5 offers some conclusions.

2   The main features of corporate debt in Italy

In the 1980s a large part of the manufacturing sector has seen a remarkable improvement in most performance indicators. Profits have grown rapidly and have been used to finance new investments in fixed assets. At the same time, the availability of funds and the new opportunities offered by financial markets have encouraged firms to acquire large quantities of financial assets, as well as to reduce their financial liabilities, leading thereby to a major decline in the weight of net interest expenses in their profit and loss accounts. Innovations in financial management have played a paramount role in this process. By consolidating many financial operations with a holding company, large corporations have succeeded in achieving significant economies of scale in financial management.

Unfortunately, the improvement in firms' financial health seems to be confined to large companies and has not trickled down to smaller firms, where on the contrary increasing debt ratios and declining profitability combine to paint a much less optimistic picture. Small companies, it appears, after being the stars of the 1970s, have returned to their more ordinary status as the backward segment of the industrial sector.

As a matter of fact, existing evidence suggests that there is cause for concern. In Table 3.1 we distinguish between firms according to their size and find that, whereas the debt–sales and the debt–assets ratios improved for large firms during the 1980s, they significantly deteriorated for small and, to a lesser extent, for medium-sized firms.

The picture does not change much even if we look at financial debt, relying on the more meaningful market value (rather than book value) indicators of indebtedness. Table 3.2 shows some of these indicators for the smaller samples that we selected for empirical work, as described below. Again, it appears that only large firms exhibit an improvement in their debt ratios. Significant differences emerge also with respect to the maturity distribution of outstanding debt (with large firms holding a bigger and tendentially increasing share of long-term debt) and the weight of net interest expenses in earnings.

Finally, if we focus on the distribution of the debt–sales ratio within each size class, we find that most of the deterioration of small and medium-sized firms occurs in the upper tail of the distribution. Indeed for the 90th percentile the debt–sales ratio increases from 69.3 and 57.8 in 1982 to 76.8 and 64.4 in 1987 for small and medium-sized firms respectively.

Table 3.1. *Book-value debt indicators, %, by firm size in manufacturing, Italy, 1982–7*

Year	Debt/Sales (1)			Debt/Assets (2)			Interest expense/ earnings* (3)			Net interest expense†/earnings* (4)		
	small	med.	large	small	med.	large	small	med.	large	small	med.	large
1982	51.00	48.01	56.01	61.97	63.08	64.85	49.73	45.85	46.87	43.56	37.53	28.74
1983	52.69	49.22	56.46	60.50	62.06	64.35	52.20	44.50	43.43	44.99	35.13	23.29
1984	52.95	48.68	55.55	62.61	64.05	65.09	49.35	40.37	36.96	42.17	30.60	17.25
1985	53.15	48.66	53.61	63.38	64.80	63.70	48.73	37.57	31.81	41.65	28.12	13.21
1986	53.94	50.04	55.94	62.77	64.33	61.87	42.08	32.05	24.29	35.51	23.45	6.59
1987	56.88	52.22	55.54	63.54	64.80	61.94	37.86	28.27	21.70	31.42	20.07	4.75

* gross total profits plus interest expenses.
† interest expenses minus interest income.
Source: CdB: total sample of 10,110 private manufacturing companies; small: sub-sample of 5,501 companies with sales between 1 and 10 billion lire in 1987; medium: sub-sample of 3,728 companies with sales between 10 and 50 billion lire in 1987; large: sub-sample of 881 companies with sales of more than 50 billion lire in 1987.

Table 3.2. *Market value debt indicators, %, for selected samples of manufacturing companies, Italy, 1982–7*

Year	Financial debt Fixed assets* (1)	Financial debt Sales (2)	Interest exp. Earnings† (3)	Net exp. Earnings† (4)	L/T fin. debt Tot. fin. debt. (5)
Small (*N* = 2132)					
1982	—	30.53	—	—	36.64
1983	98.89	31.93	48.09	41.23	38.11
1984	98.27	30.87	44.26	37.25	37.61
1985	99.34	30.77	41.70	34.61	37.40
1986	98.34	30.99	35.91	29.34	38.33
1987	99.94	31.61	32.12	25.58	37.39
Medium (*N* = 913)					
1982	—	26.78	—	—	36.62
1983	125.14	27.81	43.15	33.99	35.62
1984	124.95	28.52	40.11	30.33	35.10
1985	118.73	27.78	38.53	28.53	36.10
1986	114.03	28.17	32.94	23.61	38.63
1987	113.56	29.21	29.48	20.30	36.88
Large (*N* = 48)					
1982	75.20	23.55	63.49	39.54	55.55
1983	75.38	23.21	62.54	28.06	58.46
1984	85.92	22.76	48.42	13.87	54.63
1985	73.27	18.45	43.94	13.58	58.35
1986	65.66	16.24	34.84	− 0.78	62.14
1987	74.38	16.80	31.47	− 8.17	59.39

* replacement cost.
† cash flow plus interest expenses.
Source: authors' calculations using the CdB (small and medium-sized firms) and the R & S (large firms) data base. Small and medium-sized firms are grouped in two different fixed samples according to the level of 1982 sales: 1–10 billion lire for small, 10–50 billion lire for medium-sized ones.

In the remainder of this chapter we shall try to understand why borrowing by small and large firms has exhibited such a contrasted behaviour.

3 The determinants of corporate borrowing

Most surveys of the theoretical determinants of corporate debt decisions begin by arguing that today we are short of a general theory of the firm's capital structure. Actually the 'capital structure puzzle' seems as remote from a solution as its better-known analogue, the 'dividend puzzle'.

The main source of the puzzle stems from the fact that the tax system seems to favour borrowing. Yet the typical firm for the purpose of investment relies also on alternative sources of finance, such as retained earnings and new share issues which, relative to the issue of debt, are sometimes heavily penalised by the tax systems. Existing explanations of firms' financing choice, while providing useful insights on the determinants of corporate financial behaviour, still do not add up to a consistent and testable theory.

The impact of this state of affairs is felt on empirical research. Most of the time the empirical researcher is forced simply to list the factors most likely to affect the debt decision and let the data assess their quantitative importance. The theory offers little or no guidance as to the functional form of the relationship and the existence of restrictions which could be usefully exploited in the course of the empirical analysis. This chapter is no exception to the general rule, and we can only apologise by lamenting that the problem is a general one and highlighting the considerable effort produced in assembling a comprehensive and reliable data set.

It is useful to distinguish between two main sets of factors which are said to affect the corporate decision to borrow.

3.1 Tax factors

Let r denote the *required rate of return* by the final investor. If we indicate the *investor's marginal tax rate*, the *corporate tax rate* and the *capital gains tax rate* respectively as τ_p, τ_c and τ_g, then it is possible to show that the *cost of capital*, defined as the pre-corporate tax return which allows the final investor to obtain the required rate r, will be equal to $r/(1 - \tau_p)$ under borrowing, to $r/(1 - \tau_p)(1 - \tau_c)$ under the new equity finance and to $r/(1 - \tau_c)(1 - \tau_g)$ if the investment is financed through retained earnings.

Evidently the firm should never rely on new share issues as a source of investment finance. The relevant cost of capital is always greater than the one prevailing under debt finance. Retained earnings instead can represent, from a fiscal point of view, the privileged source of finance provided that $(1 - \tau_c)(1 - \tau_g) > (1 - \tau_p)$. If we assume that capital gains are effectively untaxed, the comparison boils down to whether τ_c is lower than τ_p. In such a case the advantage of interest deductibility at the corporate level is more than offset by higher tax liability at the personal level. The choice between debt and retained earnings will therefore depend on the personal income tax rate for the firm's marginal investor. In a Miller (1977) equilibrium, higher bracket investors will enter the market until $\tau_p = \tau_c$ and the firm is indifferent between debt and retained earnings. As noticed by DeAngelo and Masulis (1980a, 1980b), however, the corporate tax is also not constant across firms, but varies according to whether the firm is totally or partly *tax-exhausted* because, say, of low earnings and cannot therefore fully exploit the tax advantage of debt. Also there are alternative tax shields (investment tax credit, normal and accelerated depreciation allowances, expenditure on research and development) which make it more likely that a firm will not be able fully to exploit the tax deductibility of debt. Formally we can represent this by asserting that the *effective corporate tax rate* is a declining function of the quantity of outstanding debt, i.e. $\tau_c = \tau_c(D)$, with $\tau_c' < 0$. In other words, an increase in the amount of debt is associated with a reduction in the effective corporate tax rate, in turn lowering the tax advantage of debt.

This tax approach provides several implications for the purpose of empirical analysis. It highlights the fact that both corporate and personal income tax parameters should play a role in affecting corporate borrowing. More crucially, it suggests that the convenience in issuing debt is inversely related to the existence of alternative tax shields (accelerated depreciation, etc.). We shall discuss in the next section how to measure empirically the role of tax factors.

3.2   Capital market imperfections

An alternative approach to explain why firms do not choose an *only debt* capital structure relies on the possibility that a higher level of debt may be associated with increasing costs for the firm. Under these circumstances the firm will choose the debt ratio so that the marginal tax benefits of debt are balanced by the marginal costs.

Several factors are at work here. First, a higher level of debt worsens conflicts between debtholders and shareholders, by providing the latter with an incentive to undertake excessively risky projects, thereby transferring wealth away from bondholders (Jensen and Meckling, 1976). To avoid such an outcome, rational debtholders will interfere, through (say) bond covenants, with the efficient management of the firm. Similarly, in a highly levered firm the conflict between the firm and its specialised suppliers, workers and/or customers will be more severe because of the higher probability that the firm will be wound up irrespective of the costs imposed on (say) its workers (Titman, 1984). As a result, the levered firm will face worse terms of trade with (say) its workers.

A further reason for the firm to limit its leverage is described in Myers (1977), where it is argued that a highly levered firm will have to pass up otherwise profitable investment opportunities. Suppose that the value of the firm's assets is a function of further (discretionary) investment. A highly levered firm will have a lower incentive to undertake such investment insofar as a potentially conspicuous share of the extra profits will be captured by bondholders. The same project would have been undertaken under an *all equity* capital structure (Myers, 1977). Once again this would lead managers to try to contain the firm's level of debt.

The potential conflict between shareholders and the firm's managers works in the opposite direction. Suppose that managers benefit in some way from faster firm growth. They will then have an incentive to invest the surplus cash flow of the firm in low-yield investment projects. By issuing debt (and not retaining the proceeds of the issue) managers credibly commit themselves to pay out future cash flows as interest, and thereby significantly reduce the agency cost of free cash flow (Jensen, 1986).

All the approaches analysed so far presume, with the exception of Miller (1977), that an optimal capital structure exists for the firm, and that the latter will in time tend to converge toward such a structure. The *pecking order* or *financial hierarchy* approach (Myers, 1984; Myers and Majluf, 1984) takes a different view. Suppose that managers possess inside information about the value of the firm. If this inside information is unfavourable, managers will have an incentive to issue new shares. However, by doing so they will signal bad news to potential investors. To avoid such a negative signal managers may pass up an otherwise profitable investment opportunity. Internal finance does not generate such costs. Firms therefore prefer internal finance and will never pass up a profitable project if they can rely on internally generated funds. At an empirical level, the financial hierarchy approach predicts that the firm does not aim at an optimal capital structure and, as a result, that the marginal choice of investment finance will be independent of the firm's actual debt–assets ratio.

4   Empirical analysis

4.1   The data

For the purpose of empirical analysis we rely on two different samples. The first one is drawn from the balance sheet data base of CdB. We focus on private manufacturing firms and eliminate companies with incomplete, missing and/or unreliable data.[2] The resulting sample is heavily biased toward small (2,132) and medium-sized (913) firms. We have reason to believe that large companies in our sample have not been randomly selected and are not sufficiently representative of the corresponding population. For large firms we therefore resort to the R & S data base on major Italian corporations, selecting 48 firms for the period 1975–87.[3]

4.2   The dependent variable

We use as dependent variable in our equations the ratio of long-term financial debt (B) to sales. This choice can be motivated as follows. First of all such a variable is more likely to be affected by tax considerations. The identification of such effects represents an important part of this chapter. Secondly we are interested in the sources of investment finance. Financial debt seems a more appropriate item to focus on in such a context. Last but not least we rely on balance sheet data which are subject to many shortcomings, in particular to *window-dressing* modifications. The problem is likely to be less relevant for long-term debt.

Economic theory indicates that one should rely on market rather than book values of debt. In computing the market value of debt, we amend the procedure developed by Brainard, Shoven and Weiss (1980, hereafter BSW) to allow for some institutional features of debt issues in Italy on the one hand and optimally to exploit the information available in our two samples on the other. The BSW method assumes that debt is reimbursed only at maturity. In our calculations we assume instead, in line with current practices in Italy, a straight line amortisation procedure. The BSW method also requires information and/or assumptions about both maturity and maturity distribution of the firm's long-term debt. For the CdB sample we assume a 10-year maturity and, for lack of better information, a uniform age distribution of outstanding debt in the initial year. For the R & S sample we make use of extensive information about maturity, maturity distribution, anticipated reimbursements (because, say, of call provisions) and coupon rates for the single securities issued by each individual firm. Full details about the procedure used and its effects can be found in Bonato, Govino and Ratti (1990).

For econometric work, debt and all nominal explanatory variables have been deflated with the sectoral output price index.

4.3   The explanatory variables

The various approaches outlined in the previous section provide several indications as to the relevant variables which are most likely to affect the corporate borrowing decision. There are, however, several problems connected with the empirical measurement of these variables and the interpretation of the effect they purport to measure.

4.3.1   Tax factors

Following the definitions outlined in Section 3.1, the tax advantage of debt with respect to *retained earnings* (*TAXRE*) can be measured as $(1 - \tau_{pb})/(1 - \tau_c)(1 - \tau_g)$, where τ_{pb} is the *personal tax rate on interest income*; relative to *new shares* (*TAXNS*), assuming that the proceeds of the project are distributed as dividends, the relevant expression is $(1 - \tau_{pb})(1 - s)/(1 - \tau_{pd})(1 - \tau_c)$ where τ_{pd} and s denote respectively the *personal tax rate on dividends* and the *imputation rate*. As a measure of the effective corporate tax rate we have used the statutory rate for tax-paying firms and a value of zero for non-tax-paying firms.

To proxy the probability that a firm be tax-exhausted we also rely alternatively on its effective tax rate (defined as the average ratio of tax liabilities to pre-tax earnings: *EFFT*) or on the observed frequency of negative earnings (*FRNE*).

Finally, as an indicator of scarcity of non-debt tax shields, we use the ratio of earnings to fiscal depreciation deductions, *E/DEPR*.

4.3.2   The share of fixed assets

Fiscal depreciation of fixed assets (*K*) takes place over a relatively long period. A high share of fixed to total assets may therefore indicate that the firm will be able to rely in the future on fiscal depreciation as a non-debt tax shield. While this effect would lead the firm to rely relatively less on debt, we expect it to be already captured by our indicators of the fiscal status of the firm (see above). Moreover, a high share of fixed assets may also reveal that the scope for discretionary investment is more limited. Finally, fixed assets may be more easily sold on second-hand markets than intangible assets and therefore be more acceptable as collaterals of a debt contract. We expect, then, that a high share of fixed assests, measured at their replacement cost, will be associated with a greater reliance on corporate borrowing.

4.3.3   The variability of earnings

This indicator performs at least two roles. First, risky firms should exhibit a greater variability of earnings. Second, a large earnings variability implies that debt is ineffective as a tax shield. In both cases, we would predict that a greater variability of earnings should be associated with a lower propensity to issue debt. We attempt to distinguish between the two hypotheses and add to the list of explanatory variables the ratio of our measure of earnings variability (*STDE*) to *E/DEPR*. This variable (*STDEE*) should measure the importance of fiscal effects. If earnings are large with respect to existing non-debt tax shields and at the same time are not too variable, then we expect debt to be a favourite source of investment finance and *STDEE* to have a negative sign. As a measure of earnings variability, we use the standard deviation of firm's earnings over time normalised by the level of sales.[4]

4.3.4   The firm's cash flow

Cash flow (*CF*) also plays several roles. It can be taken as an indicator of the availability of internal finance or alternatively of collateral for debt issues. The impact on borrowing is negative in the first case (provided that retained earnings are preferred as a source of investment finance) and positive in the second.

Jensen's theory of free cash flow also predicts that firms with surplus cash flow and low growth prospects should have an incentive to issue more debt. We control for this possibility by introducing the ratio of cash flow to the average growth rate of the firm (*CF/GS*). We expect this effect to be significant only in our sample of large mostly publicly-owned firms, where issues of conflict of interests between management and shareholders are more relevant. We measure cash flow as the sum of post-tax earnings and net additions to the depreciation and other accounts.

4.3.5   The firms's growth rate

There are several reasons to expect this variable (*GS*) negatively to affect the decision to borrow. On the one hand a high average growth rate is likely to be associated with the existence of discretionary growth opportunities. As noticed earlier, this should lead the firm to borrow less. A high growth rate is also likely to occur only if investment expenditures are sufficiently high. The latter in turn allow the firm to increase its flow of fiscal depreciation charges and make debt less palatable as a tax shield.

A different and opposite effect may also be at work, however. Consider the financing hierarchy approach. Because of asymmetric information between managers and potential new shareholders, firms have to pay a *lemon* premium when they issue new shares. Suppose also that retained earnings are insufficient to finance existing investment projects. This is likely to occur when the firm is faced with many investment opportunities and its growth prospects are favourable. Under these circumstances, the financing hierarchy approach would predict that a new (possibly safe) debt issue will represent the marginal source of finance. An increase in growth opportunities will then imply that a larger share of existing investment projects will have to be financed by issuing debt. This variable is measured as the firm's average growth rate of sales.[5]

4.3.6   The stock market index

This variable (SMI) is found to exert a significant effect in many empirical debt studies (MacKie-Mason, 1988; Taggart, 1977). This is a somewhat embarrassing, albeit robust, finding insofar as the inclusion of such a variable is not supported by a strong theoretical background. We need to appeal to the possibility that corporate treasurers possess superior ability in timing new share issues to account for the fact that depressed share prices are often found to be associated with greater reliance on debt. The stock market variable is measured as the yearly average of end-of-month BCI index of industrial share prices on the Milan Stock Exchange.

Other variables which are likely to affect corporate borrowing are found in many existing empirical studies, but have not yet been mentioned. In particular the tax loss carryforward at the firm level and the expenditure in R & D have often been used in empirical debt studies. In our case, while most of this information is in principle available in our balance sheet data, we found that it is not reported by a great majority of firms. We decided therefore with some regret not to include it in our study.

4.4   Econometric methods

Short of a fully-fledged model of debt behaviour, we follow Taggart (1977), Auerbach (1985) and Marsh (1982) in assuming a partial adjustment mechanism where:

$$B_{i,t} - B_{i,t-1} = (1 - \gamma)(B^*_{i,t} - B_{i,t-1}) \tag{1}$$

where $B_{i,t}$ and $B^*_{i,t}$ denote respectively the actual and desired stock of outstanding debt of firm i at time t. Since B^* is not observable, we assume it to be a linear function of its determinants.

In the econometric analysis, we normalise both the dependent and the explanatory variables by the level of sales to reduce heteroscedasticity.[6]

There is a serious econometric issue which needs to be faced when estimating equation (1) on a panel of individual firms' data. It is well known (Nickell, 1981) that in a dynamic panel data the speed of convergence of the coefficient estimates is a function only of T, the number of observations available for each unit. This is likely to be a fairly serious problem for both our panels, in particular for the CdB sample, where only six observations are available for each unit.

We follow Anderson and Hsiao (1982) and Arellano and Bond (1988a) and take first differences of the original equation, removing therefore the firm's fixed effect and thereby the source of the original bias. In doing so, however, the error term, if white noise to begin with, has been transformed into a unit-root moving-average process and will therefore be correlated with the lagged dependent variable. To circumvent this latter problem we use an instrumental variable procedure with $B_{i,t-2}$ as an instrument. To gain in efficiency, we also rely on a Generalised Method of Moments (GMM) estimator, which exploits all the restrictions between the instrument set and the error term (Arellano and Bond, 1988a). To implement this estimator we rely on the DPD package developed by Arellano and Bond (1988b).

4.5   Econometric results: small and medium-sized companies

As mentioned earlier, the CdB sample draws on a large data base of 3,045 firms over the period 1982–7. Several problems arise because of the short time span covered by the sample.

First of all, statutory tax rates during this period are virtually flat. Short of significant variations of the *effective* corporate tax rate across firms, it becomes impossible to identify the impact of tax factors. While empirical evidence (Edwards *et al.*, 1987; Devereux, Ratti and Schiantarelli, 1988) suggests that there are significant differences across firms as far as their tax status is concerned, it appears reasonable to assume that the effective corporate tax rate for any individual firm does not exhibit any significant variation over the period under analysis.[7]

Unfortunately panel data estimation does not allow us to identify the impact of time-invariant variables, even though there may be significant variability across firms. A similar problem arises in connection with other determinants of the firm's decision to borrow. As a matter of fact, it can be reasonably argued that the growth prospects of an individual firm or its riskiness are unlikely to vary over a relatively short period of time.

To circumvent the problems associated with the measurement of the impact of time-invariant variables, we rely on the following procedure (Auerbach, 1985). We first estimate equation (1) as a function of the time-varying determinants of firms' borrowing. We then use the estimated coefficients to compute the individual firm effect, i.e. its intercept. We finally regress the individual firm effect on the time-invariant determinants of corporate borrowing. Alternatively we rely on a logit specification where firms are classified according to whether their individual effect is larger or smaller than the median for the sample. It is then assumed that the probability of belonging to a given group is a logistic function of the time-invariant influences on borrowing.

Our econometric results are presented in Tables 3.3, 3.5 and 3.6. Notice that, following the analysis in Section 1, we have distinguished in our sample between small firms (with 1982 sales less than 10 billion lire) and medium-sized firms (with 1982 sales between 10 and 50 billion lire).

Table 3.3 contains the first stage regression result, with the debt to sales ratio (B/S) as a function of its lagged value, the cash flow to sales ratio (CF/S), the fraction of assets accounted by plant and equipment (K/S) and the stock market index (SMI).

There are several noteworthy results. First of all, while adjustment is found to be slow, the debt to sales ratio appears to converge towards a long-run steady state value contrary to the most extreme prediction of the *financial hierarchy* theory. Second, the ratio of K to sales (with plant and equipment measured at substitution cost rather than book historic cost values) provides a positive contribution to the firms' willingness to borrow. This finding is consistent, as mentioned earlier, with Myers (1977) (if we take K to be negatively related to the quantitative importance of discretionary investment opportunities) and with the role of fixed assets as a collateral in reducing the agency cost of debt.

Cash flow instead does not appear to be a significant determinant of borrowing. Its coefficient is not statistically different from zero for both the small and the medium-sized firms' samples. This may be attributed to the fact that cash flow acts as an indicator of the availability of internal finance and as a collateral, with the two effects tending to offset each other.

The most interesting finding is the existence of a positive impact of the stock market index on borrowing by small but not by medium-sized firms. In the literature, the stock market is generally found to have a negative impact insofar as firms are more likely to issue shares rather than debt when the stock market is overvalued (Taggart, 1977; MacKie-Mason, 1988). Here we find instead a positive effect on borrowing by small firms. We shall see later in the chapter, when we focus on the R & S sample, that there is some evidence that large firms' borrowing is negatively related to the stock market index.

A possible explanation of this diverging behaviour is as follows. Suppose that the credit market is segmented between large, creditworthy firms on the one hand and small, risky firms on the other. Following an increase in the stock market index, the supply of debt (demand for credit) by large firms will decline. If the two markets are segmented but still interrelated, the decline in supply in one market is likely to be compensated in the other. It is therefore not surprising, under these circumstances, to find a positive effect of the stock market on the quantity of borrowing by small firms.

Tables 3.5 and 3.6 contain the results of the second-stage regressions. We are now able to assess the existence of significant tax effects. We regress the estimated individual firm effect on the following variables: the *ex post* effective average tax rate of the firm ($EFFT$, defined as the ratio of tax liabilities to pre-tax earnings), the ratio of gross earnings to fiscal depreciation allowances ($E/DEPR$), the average growth rate of the firm's

Table 3.3. *Panel data estimation results for CdB samples of small and medium-sized companies, 1982–7*

	LHS variable = Long-term financial debt $(B/S)_{i,t}$	
RHS variables	Small firms (N = 2132) (1)	Medium-sized firms (N = 913) (2)
Constant	− 0.005262 (− 2.9297)	− 0.0061 (− 1.566)
$(B/S)_{i,t-1}$	0.5739 (13.118)	0.5385 (5.4049)
$(CF/S)_{i,t}$	− 0.0830 (− 0.1740)	0.7892 (0.8017)
$(K/S)_{i,t}$	0.2755 (3.058)	0.5689 (2.1507)
$SMI_{i,t}$	0.00007 (1.9907)	0.000001 (0.0283)
Diagnostic tests		
Wald [d.f.]	328.7854 [4]	52.2003 [4]
Sargan [d.f.]	5.4516 [6]	2.8012 [6]
AR(1) [n.obs.]	− 7.303 [2132]	− 3.943 [913]
AR(2) [n.obs.]	− 0.843 [2132]	− 0.221 [913]

Robust *t*-statistics in parenthesis.
Four tests are presented: (a) Wald test (asymptotically χ^2) of joint significance of the explanatory variables; (b) Sargan test (asymptotically χ^2) of overidentifying restrictions imposed to the instrument set; tests (asymptotically $N(0,1)$) of (c) first order and (d) second order autocorrelation of residuals. Notice that, after first-differencing, we expect to find some first order but no second order autocorrelation of residuals.

sales (*GS*), the standard deviation of its earnings normalised by the level of its sales (*STDE*), a locational dummy (which takes a value of 1 for firms located in Southern Italy) and the ratio of *STDE* to *E/DEPR* (*STDEE*). As mentioned earlier, we expect *STDEE* to capture purely fiscal effects and exert a negative impact on corporate borrowing.

The locational dummy requires some explanation. It is introduced to capture the effect of the wide array of fiscal and financial incentives granted to firms which locate in Southern Italy and the possibility that the existence of a relatively underdeveloped capital market in that region will affect the firm's capital structure (Galli and Onado, 1990).

As a matter of fact, there are significant differences among firms depending on their location. As Table 3.4 shows, small firms in Southern

Table 3.4. *Mean of some explanatory variables, by location of companies*

	Small			
	Location		Test $H_0: \mu_N = \mu_S$	
Variables	North ($N = 1983$) (1)	South ($N = 149$) (2)	t-test (d.f.) (3)	Wilcoxon test (4)
STDE	0.0218	0.0310	3.19 (159)	2.94
FRNE	0.9627	1.2953	2.30 (162)	1.56
EFFT	0.3396	0.2539	− 8.10* (2130)	− 7.77
E/DEPR	3.4541	2.3904	− 5.07* (2130)	− 6.03
GS	0.1439	0.1098	− 4.43* (2130)	− 4.45
	Medium			
Variables	North ($N = 868$)	South ($N = 45$)	t-test (d.f.)	Wilcoxon test
STDE	0.0172	0.0306	2.31 (45)	2.71
FRNE	0.7903	1.0444	0.96 (47)	0.10
EFFT	0.3507	0.2708	− 3.39 (47)	− 3.88
E/DEPR	3.6189	4.5963	1.09 (45)	− 0.17
GS	0.11184	0.1273	0.62 (47)	0.29

Reported tests for the equality of means: (a) a classical t-test, calculated under the assumption of equal variances (cases marked with an asterisk) unless an F-test allows us to reject $H_0: \sigma_N^2 = \sigma_S^2$; (b) Wilcoxon rank-sum test, whose reported z-value is distributed standard normal.
Source: authors' calculations on CdB data set.

Italy exhibit a statistically significant difference in some of the variables described above: higher variability of earnings (*STDE*), lower effective corporate tax rate (*EFFT*), higher (lower value of the indicator of scarcity) non-debt tax shields (*E/DEPR*), lower growth rate (*GS*). Similar results hold for medium-sized firms relative to earnings variability and tax rate.

Such differences will most probably influence the choice of the capital structure, but many also imply an altogether different relationship between debt behaviour and its determinants. We therefore also investigate whether firms in Southern Italy respond differently to changes in the tax and risk parameters. To this purpose, we allow for a possible interaction between the locational dummy and the other explanatory variables (*EFFTS, E/DEPRS, . . .*).

Our econometric results provide encouraging support to our set-up. Let us consider first the case of small firms (Table 3.5). The locational dummy, together with most of the interaction terms of such dummy with the other explanatory variables, have been found not to contribute in a statistically significant way to the equation, and have been dropped. The noticeable exception is the standard deviation of earnings for Southern Italy (*STDES*). Interestingly enough, the coefficient associated with *STDES* is negative, indicating that risk factors have a more pronounced impact on borrowing in the South. All the other variables have the expected sign and have coefficients significantly different from zero. In particular the effective *ex post* tax rate, the ratio of gross earnings to fiscal depreciation allowances and *STDEE* all contribute significantly to explaining the individual firm effect.

Our results therefore appear to suggest quite clearly that tax factors matter considerably in the firm's decision to borrow. This is a remarkable result if we consider that in the literature, with some noticeable exceptions (Mackie-Mason, 1988), it has been extremely hard to identify the impact of fiscal factors.

When we estimate the logit specification (column (2)), our results change somewhat. In particular, the growth rate of the firm becomes significant, whereas there is no longer any evidence of a significant different in the impact of *STDE* across regions. Possibly this is due to inadequate estimation techniques where no allowance has yet been made for the possible endogeneity of some right-hand-side variables.

Consider in particular the effective corporate tax rate. On the one hand a large value of *EFFT* will prompt firms to increase their level of borrowing. On the other, a sizeable amount of borrowing will be associated with a low value of *EFFT*.

We can account for this simultaneity problem in two ways: first, we can rely on an instrumental variable procedure, using (for instance) the frequency of negative earnings for a firm as an instrument for *EFFT*. Alternatively we can exclude from our sample those firms which pay little or no taxes (less than 10 per cent of their income). Indeed, it is likely that for tax paying firms the direction of causality between *EFFT* and borrowing is better defined. As a matter of fact, the existence of a positive tax liability is an indication that firms have not overborrowed in the past to escape corporate taxation.

The results of these two ways of proceeding are presented in columns (3)–(5) of Table 3.5. They are fairly encouraging. We find that all the results in column (1) of the table are confirmed. Moreover, there is no longer any conflict between the OLS and the logit specification. We conclude therefore that, for small firms, tax factors exert an important influence on corporate financial structure. Risk, as measured by the variability of earnings, is also likely to play a more powerful role for firms located in Southern Italy.

Table 3.5. *Determinants of individual firm effects, CdB sample of small firms*

RHS variables	Type of estimator				
	OLS ($N = 2132$) (1)	Logit ($N = 2132$) (2)	IV ($N = 2132$) (3)	OLS ($N = 1993$) (4)	Logit ($N = 1993$) (5)
Constant	−0.0801	−0.9655	−0.0755	−0.0752	−0.9429
	(−12.897)	(−5.519)	(−11.593)	(−12.554)	(−4.543)
EFFT	0.0465	0.5777	0.0319	0.0443	0.6316
	(3.302)	(1.437)	(1.800)	(3.139)	(1.302)
E/DEPR	0.0050	0.2096	0.0051	0.0048	0.2091
	(7.667)	(8.776)	(8.872)	(7.373)	(8.540)
GS	0.0245	1.5116	0.0284	0.0097	1.5806
	(1.379)	(2.946)	(1.784)	(0.530)	(2.937)
STDE	−0.1027	−5.2906	−0.1289	−0.1448	−7.5809
	(−1.133)	(−2.358)	(−1.918)	(−1.415)	(−2.980)
STDEE	−0.1286	−2.0083	−0.1321	−0.0873	−1.7448
	(−2.258)	(−2.182)	(−4.974)	(−2.292)	(−1.486)
STDES	−0.6617	−4.1424	−0.6716	−1.1389	−13.2704
	(−2.135)	(−0.856)	(−5.450)	(−4.394)	(−1.958)
statistics					
R^2	0.09165	n.a.	0.09104	0.09393	n.a.
Log-lik.	2849.2	−1403.2	2852.0	2773.7	−1311.2
% correct prediction	n.a.	62.99	n.a.	n.a.	62.57

Robust t-statistics in parenthesis.

Matters are somewhat different for medium-sized firms. The results are reported in Table 3.6. Risk factors, as measured by the variability of earnings ($STDE$), keep playing a significant role. Interestingly enough, though, there is no longer any evidence that such a variable has a more pronounced impact on borrowing for firms located in Southern Italy. Indeed the standard deviation of earnings for Southern Italy ($STDES$) is never statistically significant, and has been dropped from the equation. This result can be usefully contrasted with the findings for smaller firms (Table 3.5) where $STDES$ was highly significant. This suggests the existence of a threshold size as far as different regional behaviours toward risk are concerned.

The effect of fiscal factors is more complex. We find again that the ratio of earnings to fiscal depreciation allowances ($E/DEPR$) has a positive

Table 3.6. *Determinants of individual firm effects, CdB sample of medium-sized firms*

RHS variables	Type of estimator				
	OLS ($N = 2132$) (1)	Logit ($N = 2132$) (2)	IV ($N = 2132$) (3)	OLS ($N = 1993$) (4)	Logit ($N = 1993$) (5)
Constant	− 0.1391	0.0721	− 0.1305	− 0.1408	0.0380
	(− 8.673)	(0.250)	(− 9.141)	(− 7.730)	(0.110)
EFFT	− 0.0774	− 2.8549	− 0.1162	− 0.0663	− 2.9795
	(− 2.173)	(− 4.046)	(− 1.863)	(− 1.626)	(− 3.538)
EFFTS	0.0701	3.2810	0.1963	0.1413	3.0757
	(1.370)	(2.294)	(0.342)	(2.029)	(1.939)
E/DEPR	0.0108	0.4257	0.0115	0.0114	0.4937
	(6.603)	(8.604)	(4.753)	(6.602)	(9.002)
E/DEPRS	− 0.0091	− 0.3749	− 0.0123	− 0.0087	− 0.4177
	(− 3.724)	(− 5.006)	(− 0.875)	(− 3.873)	(− 5.130)
GS	0.0683	0.2553	0.0839	0.0633	0.3341
	(1.392)	(0.253)	(1.582)	(1.274)	(0.312)
STDE	− 1.1933	− 33.4898	− 1.1984	− 1.5753	− 47.4771
	(− 3.821)	(− 5.984)	(− 5.197)	(− 5.296)	(− 7.015)
STDEE	0.1728	9.0727	0.1667	0.4225	16.6889
	(0.620)	(2.112)	(1.066)	(1.779)	(2.503)
STDEES	− 2.9407	− 117.786	− 3.3919	− 7.9830	− 67.5449
	(− 1.843)	(− 1.785)	(− 1.828)	(− 1.820)	(− 0.758)
statistics					
R^2	0.16708	n.a.	0.16157	0.19484	n.a.
Log-lik.	855.22	− 548.93	856.73	838.21	− 505.55
% correct prediction	n.a.	71.41	n.a.	n.a.	71.79

Robust *t*-statistics in parenthesis.

impact on borrowing, although the effect virtually disappears for firms located in Southern Italy (the coefficients on *E/DEPRS* and *E/DEPR* have equal size and opposite sign). This is not very surprising if we consider that firms in such a region benefit from widespread tax exemptions. It is more difficult to interpret the coefficients on the effective tax rate (*EFFT* and *EFFTS*) and on the ratio of earning variability to *E/DEPR* (*STDEE* and *STDEES*). Contrary to our *a priori* expectations, the coefficient on *EFFT* is negative. Correcting, as we did for small firms, for the possible endogeneity of *EFFT* does not seem to alleviate the problem. Similarly the coefficient on *STDEE* is positive, albeit not always significant, rather than negative as predicted. For firms located in Southern Italy fiscal effects once again appear to cancel out.

These results seem to confirm the difference in the impact of fiscal factors between northern and southern regions of the country. There are however some puzzling results, in particular the negative coefficient on the effective tax rate for firms located in Northern Italy, which we find difficult to explain.

Finally we find that risk, as measured by the variability of earnings, exerts a significant influence on both small and medium-sized firms. Contrary to what we found for small firms, however, no difference in behaviour dependent on location emerges.

4.6   Econometric results: large companies

The R & S sample draws on balance sheet data for 48 large firms over the period 1975–87. The length of the sample period ensures that there is sufficient variability over time for the main determinants of debt decisions. We therefore emphasise in this section the first-stage regression results.

Some noteworthy differences with respect to the approach used in connection with the CdB sample should be mentioned. As a measure of tax effects, we still rely on the ratio of gross earnings to fiscal depreciation allowances ($E/DEPR$), defined as an indicator of scarcity of non-debt tax shields. Instead of $EFFT$, however, we rely on the theoretically more sound comparison of the tax advantage of debt relative to retained earnings ($TAXRE$) and to new shares ($TAXNS$) defined as in Section 4.3.1.

Other explanatory variables in the regression include the firm's growth rate (GS), the stock market index (SMI), the measures of cash flow (CF) and of plant and equipment (K) normalised by sales and the ratio of cash flow to firm's growth rate (CF/GS), introduced to capture the *free cash flow* effect (Section 4.3.4). We could not perform any analysis by location since no meaningful definition of this attribute could be identified for multi-plant firms.

Equation (1) still represents the basis for estimation. We take again first differences of the equation and use a GMM estimation procedure. The results are presented in Table 3.7. All variables but one have the expected sign, and are highly significant.

Not surprisingly, adjustment appears much faster than in small and medium-sized firms. Once again, the debt–sales ratio seems to converge toward a long-run steady state. Fixed assets confirm their positive substantial contribution to firms' propensity to borrow. Unlike small and medium-sized ones, large firms seem to be markedly affected by cash flow in their decision to borrow. The influence of this variable is actually twofold.

Table 3.7. *Panel data estimation results, R & S sample of large companies, 1975–87*

	LHS variable = Long-term financial debt $(B/S)_{i,t}$									
RHS variables	Constant (1)	$(B/S)_{i,t-1}$ (2)	$(K/S)_{i,t}$ (3)	$(CF/S)_{i,t}$ (4)	$(CF/GS)_{i,t}$ (5)	$GS_{i,t}$ (6)	$SMI_{i,t}$ (7)	$(E/DEPR)_{i,t}$ (8)	$TAXRE_{i,t}$ (9)	$TAXNS_{i,t}$ (10)
	0.0046	0.0417	0.1650	− 0.3846	0.0333	− 0.0051	− 0.0001	0.0174	− 0.2015	0.0337
	(3.2356)	(4.4953)	(14.3643)	(− 3.6725)	(3.8355)	(− 6.4761)	(− 1.6436)	(4.4077)	(− 7.8562)	(9.5406)

Diagnostic tests

Wald [d.f.]		Sargan [d.f.]		AR(1) [n.obs.]		AR(2) [n.obs.]
3122.6 [9]		26.963 [29]		− 2.252 [48]		0.519 [48]

Robust *t*-statistics in parentheses

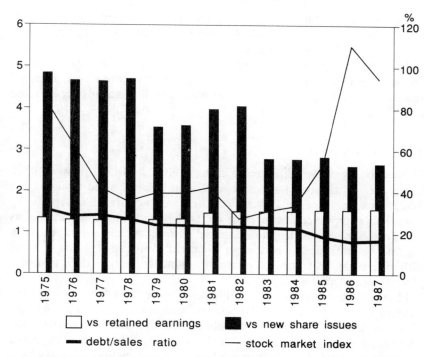

Figure 3.1   Relative tax advantage of debt, R & S sample of large firms, 1975–87
Source: authors' calculations using the R & S sample of 48 large firms; BCI index of industrial share price on the Milan Stock Exchange (yearly average of end-of-month observations).
Note: tax advantage (left scale) is estimated assuming the effective corporation tax rate equal to the statutory rate for tax-paying firms and equal to zero for tax-exhausted firms (see Section 4.3.1).

The *financial hierarchy* approach prediction that firms have a preference for internal finance seems to be verified by the negative coefficient of the cash flow–sales ratio. This effect looks very strong and probably has an important role in the reduction of indebtedness of large firms. On the other hand, a *free cash flow* effect, reflected in the positive coefficient of *CF/GS*, seems to be at work for large firms.

A negative contribution of growth rate has been clearly identified. This is consistent with Myers (1977, 1984), provided that the growth rate of sales is an indicator of discretionary investment opportunities. Some evidence, though not very strong, emerges that the stock market exerts a negative influence on large firms' borrowing decisions, providing some support to the contention that a booming stock market (see Figure 3.1) leads large firms to rely less on debt finance. As far as tax factors are concerned, we obtain an unambiguous result for the tax advantage relative to new share issues, which corroborates the first-sight impression one can get by looking at Figure 3.1.

The only exception to this encouraging picture is the tax effect for retained earnings, which carries an unexpectedly negative sign. This is a somewhat puzzling result, which we hope will find an answer in some future research.

5   Conclusions

There exist significant differences in the evolution of debt between large companies on the one hand and small and medium-sized firms on the other. As a matter of fact, whereas the first group of firms has witnessed a remarkable improvement in most of its debt indicators, no analogous trend can be discerned for the second set of firms, which instead register a marked deterioration in a number of crucial debt ratios. Most of these differences can be traced to economic influences rather than to unexplained size effects.

Financial management is probably responsible for a substantial difference between large and small firms in the costs and velocity of adjustment of the stock of long-term financial debt to its desired level. This difference, often cited as one of the reasons for the diverging behaviour of large and small companies in the 1980s, is confirmed by our results.

A key factor relates to the availability of cash flow. Our results suggest that cash flow exerts a negative effect on corporate borrowing by large companies, but that no significant effect can be identified for small and medium-sized firms.

One possible explanation of this diverging behaviour would emphasise that large, mature firms rely on retained earnings as the marginal source of investment finance. Under these circumstances, any increase in the availability of cash resources would be used by such firms to reduce their stock of debt and/or acquire financial assets. Smaller companies instead use most of their cash availability to finance their investment expenditure. Provided that capital market imperfections are not too severe, they must therefore rely on external sources, mostly debt, as the marginal source of investment finance.

Investment in this situation is constrained by the availability of internal finance. An increase in cash flow will be reflected in higher investment expenditure. There is indeed some evidence (Galeotti, Schiantarelli and Jaramillo, 1990) that cash flow has a positive effect on investment by small firms, but no influence for large firms.

The evolution of the stock market appears to account to some extent for the contrasted behaviour between small and large firms. As the econometric analysis for the R & S sample may indicate, large firms will rely less on debt finance when the stock market is overvalued. Indeed a booming stock market provides large firms with an alternative and apparently less costly source of investment finance. At the same time, as shown by the CdB sample, the evolution of the stock market is instead positively correlated with the quantity of debt issued by small firms. We argued tentatively that this could be attributed to the easing of credit market conditions for small firms following a lower demand of credit by large firms.

The availability of cash flow and the evolution of the stock market are only two among the main determinants of debt behaviour. Our analysis has also uncovered an important role for tax factors and some significant behavioural differences dependent on the firm's location.

Consider tax influences first. They appear to be important, but hard to measure. As a matter of fact, we would need a measure of both the effective corporate tax rate for each individual firm and of the personal tax rate for the marginal investor in the firm. None of this information is available and some of the puzzling results we have obtained (for instance, in relation to the effect of the tax cost for retained earnings) may perhaps be traced to these measurement problems. Still, our results suggest that tax factors are undoubtedly an important determinant of borrowing decisions. We would venture the judgement that the introduction of a personal capital gains tax in 1991 has provided new incentives to the use of debt finance.

With respect to regional differences, we found that risk factors were important for small firms, but more so if the company was located in Southern Italy. For medium-sized firms risk, as measured by the variability of earnings, is important but no significant difference can be identified as a function of the firm's geographical location. Possibly the banking sector in Southern Italy is less equipped to lend to small firms, or alternatively small firms in that region are intrinsically more risky.

The limits of this chapter should again be emphasised. We did not rely on any formal theory as a strict guide for the specification of our estimating equation, but simply listed what various and not always compatible theories indicate as the main determinants of corporate borrowing. Still, we believe that our results may provide some useful indications for future research on the debt behaviour of Italian firms, a fairly underresearched subject so far.

Notes

1 The authors are grateful to Costanza Govino and Luca Rigotti for invaluable help with managing respectively the Centrale dei Bilanci (CdB) and the Ricerche & Studi (R & S) data sets; Marzio Galeotti, Fabrizio Guelpa, Rony

Hamaui and Pippo Ranci for useful comments; Giuliana Brenna, Maristella Guerrina and Antonella Patruno for help with the editing. The usual disclaimer applies.

2 The selection procedure has been based on the following criteria:

(a) annual account closing date on December 31
(b) no involvement in mergers and acquisitions operations
(c) squared statements of sources and uses
(d) capital stock consistent with the depreciation account
(e) nominal yearly growth rate of sales between −50 per cent and +100 per cent
(f) sales above 1 bn lire
(g) labour cost, employees, interest paid, ordinary depreciation allowance, liquid assets, net capital stock (book value and replacement cost), long-term financial debt (book value and market value) greater than zero

over the whole period 1982–7.

3 We applied the same criteria as above, with the difference that we did not require a firm to satisfy all the criteria for the whole time period to be selected. Hence the panel, unlike that of CdB, is not balanced.

4 In the literature the standard deviation of first differences is commonly used instead. This measure is the forecast error for earnings predictions by investors if earnings, as the accounting literature has often found for other countries, follow a random walk. Since there is no such solid evidence for Italy, we tested this hypothesis for our samples of small and medium-sized firms running an autoregressive model on first differences. The instrumental variable estimates (see Section 4.4) of this model allow us to reject this hypothesis for both samples:

small f.: $\Delta(earnings)_{i,t} = \underset{(s.e. = 0.0852)}{0.1367} \Delta(earnings)_{i,t-1}$

Wald test = 2.57 (1 d.f.)
Sargan test = 14.18 (6 d.f.)
AR(1) test = − 3.27 (2132 n.obs.)
AR(2) test = − 1.87 (2132 n.obs.)

medium f.: $\Delta(earnings)_{i,t} = \underset{(s.e. = 0.1203)}{0.3746} \Delta(earnings)_{i,t-1}$

Wald test = 9.70 (1 d.f.)
Sargan test = 5.28 (6 d.f.)
AR(1) test = − 1.67 (913 n.obs.)
AR(2) test = − 0.68 (913 n.obs.)

5 Six-year average growth rate for CdB samples, four-term moving average of yearly growth rate of sales for R & S sample.

6 This is a standard procedure in the literature (Bernanke and Campbell, 1988; Auerbach, 1985). It is not, however, immune from criticism. As a matter of fact, if sales – or more generally the variable which is used to normalise the equation – happens to be endogenous, ordinary least squares estimation of equation (1) will lead to biased and inconsistent estimates. To account for this possibility, the equation is estimated by instrumental variable methods and the exogeneity of the instrument set is carefully tested for. Notice that we have experimented with alternative normalisation rules only to find that this did not significantly affect our results.

7 Recall that, because of first-differencing of the data and instrumenting, our sample period effectively begins in 1984.

References

Anderson, T. W. and C. Hsiao (1982) 'Formulation and Estimation of Dynamic Models Using Panel Data', *Journal of Econometrics*, **18**: 47–82.

Arellano, M. and S. Bond (1988a) 'Some Tests of Specification for Panel Data: Montecarlo Evidence and an Application to Employment Equations', Institute for Fiscal Studies, *Working Paper*, **4**.

Arellano, M. and S. Bond (1988b) 'Dynamic Panel Data Estimation Using DPD – A Guide for Users', Institute for Fiscal Studies, *Working Paper*, **15**.

Auerbach, A. J. (1985) 'Real Determinants of Corporate Leverage', in B. M. Friedman (ed.), *Corporate Capital Structures in the United States*, National Bureau of Economic Research, Chicago: University of Chicago Press.

Bernanke, B. S. and J. Y. Campbell (1988) 'Is There a Corporate Debt Crisis?', *Brookings Paper on Economic Activity*, **1**: 83–125.

Bonato, L., C. Govino and M. Ratti (1990) 'A Methodology for Calculating the Market-Value of Corporate Debt in Italy' (mimeo).

Brainard, W. C., J. B. Shoven and L. Weiss (1980) 'The Financial Valuation of the Return to Capital', *Brookings Paper on Economic Activity*, **2**: 453–502.

DeAngelo, H. and R. W. Masulis (1980a) 'Optimal Capital Structure Under Corporate and Personal Taxation', *Journal of Financial Economics*, **8**: 3–29.

DeAngelo, H. and R. W. Masulis (1980b) 'Leverage and Dividend Irrelevancy Under Corporate and Personal Taxation', *Journal of Finance*, **35(2)**: 453–64.

Devereux, M., M. Ratti and F. Schiantarelli (1988) 'Modelling the Corporate Tax System in Italy', Consiglio Nazionale delle Ricerche, *Working Paper*.

Edwards, J. S. S., C. P. Mayer, P. Pashardes and J.M. Poterba (1987) 'The Effects of Taxation on Corporate Dividend Policy in the U.K.', Institute of Fiscal Studies, *Working Paper*, **96**.

Galeotti, M., F. Schiantarelli and F. Jaramillo (1990) 'Investment Decisions and the Role of Debt, Liquid Assets, and Cash-flow: Evidence from Italian Panel Data' (mimeo).

Galli, G. and M. Onado (1990) 'Dualismo territoriale e sistema finanziario', in Banca d'Italia, *Il sistema finanziario del Mezzogiorno*, Special Issue of *Contributi alla ricerca economica*.

Jensen, M. C. (1988) 'Agency Costs of Free Cash Flow, Corporate Finance, and Takeovers', *American Economic Review*, **76(2)**: 323–9.

Jensen, M. C. and W. Meckling (1976) 'Theory of the Firm: Managerial Behaviour, Agency Costs and Ownership Structure', *Journal of Financial Economics*, **3**: 305–60.

Kaufman, H. (1986) 'Debt: The Threat to Economic and Financial Stability', in Federal Reserve Bank of Kansas City, *Debt, Financial Stability and Public Policy*: 15–26.

MacKie-Mason, J. K. (1988) 'Do Taxes Affect Corporate Financing Decisions?', National Bureau of Economic Research, *Working Paper*, **2632**.

Marsh, P. (1982) 'The Choice Between Equity and Debt: An Empirical Study', *Journal of Finance*, **37(1)**: 121–44.

Miller, M. H. (1977) 'Debt and Taxes', *Journal of Finance*, **32(2)**: 261–75.

Myers, S. C. (1977) 'Determinants of Corporate Borrowing', *Journal of Financial Economics*, **5**: 146–74.

Myers, S. C. (1984) 'The Capital Structure Puzzle', *Journal of Finance*, **39(3)**: 575–92.

Myers, S. C. and N. S. Majluf (1984) 'Corporate Financing and Investment Decisions when Firms Have Information that Investors Do Not Have', *Journal of Financial Economics*, **13**: 187–221.

Nickell, S. J. (1981) 'Biases in Dynamic Models with Fixed Effects', *Econometrica*, **49**: 1399–1416.

Taggart, R. A. (1977) 'A Model of Corporate Financing Decisions', *Journal of Finance*, **32(5)**: 1467–84.

Titman, S. (1984) 'The Effect of Capital Structure on a Firm's Liquidation Decision', *Journal of Financial Economics*, **13**: 137–51.

Volcker, P.A. (1986) 'The Rapid Growth of Debt in the United States', *Federal Reserve Bank of Kansas City Review*, **71**: 3–12.

Discussion

PIPPO RANCI

The chapter by Bonato, Faini and Ratti (hereafter BFR) examines the debt decision by Italian firms during the 1980s. The chapter was part of a project investigating debt, investment and dividend decisions on the same data base, so I shall say something on the project as well as remark on the study. The BFR chapter presents both an accurate description of what has happened and an attempt to interpret the facts by applying theoretical models presented and discussed in the recent literature of other countries. I shall not deal with the discussion of the models; I shall rather focus on the problems arising when they are applied to the Italian context of the period.

The task of describing what has really happened should not be under-estimated. It has entailed an extremely patient work of cleaning and reclassification of the data, which has been carried on for the first time within the present project. Praise is well deserved, and it should go together with hope that the job will be continued so as to provide longer series of comparable data, to the benefit of further research. In fact, by applying rigorous methods to the available data, the chapter shows how unsatisfactory our level of information is in the area of business decisions. The provision of such a large sample of firm accounts as the Centrale dei Bilanci data base, while greatly increasing our knowledge on the wide variety of conditions and behaviour across size classes, industries and regions, has made it quite clear to us that it would be a mistake to rely on aggregate data for the purpose of exploring business decisions. Since detailed information is available only for a short time period, we are now bound to be much more cautious in drawing conclusions on behaviour patterns than we were before. It is not the first time that an increase in knowledge produces a decrease in certainty.

When reading the chapter a few general characteristics of the 1980s should be kept in mind, since they bear on the phenomena under scrutiny. A wide reorganisation of industrial firms took place, producing a remarkable increase in the profitability of the large and medium-sized firms. Dividends have followed this positive change. Debt has been drastically reduced, again with the exception of small firms; profitability increase and debt reduction have been remarkable, but causal relations go both ways and are difficult to isolate. One reason for such difficulty is inflation. It was above 20 per cent at the beginning of the decade and has declined regularly, leaving a heritage of heavily distorted values in the firms' accounts. Among other consequences, it has become difficult to separate income from industrial activity and income from financial operations in the profit and loss account, whereas a correct assessment of the two is essential in order to isolate relations going from debt reduction to profits or the other way round. A high level of investment, even in the face of recession and high interest rates, has puzzled macroeconomic model builders, defying well-established theories.

A new actor, the investment fund, entered the Italian financial stage by virtue of new legislation introduced in 1983; no doubt the institutional discontinuity played a role in the stock exchange boom of 1984–6, with consequences for the relative costs of debt and equity and for their relative weight in corporate liabilities, which cannot be explained by any conventional model assuming institutional continuity.

On the econometric methods applied I have no competence to comment in detail, but I wish to express my uneasiness with the way the authors have got over the scarcity of observations. I must make it clear that I have no better way to suggest, so the issue is only how reliable the conclusions are one can draw from using sophisticated econometrics on scarce data. The best answer will come from future research on the longer series that will become available year after year.

The authors use two sets of data: the large CdB sample over a short time span and the thin R & S sample over a long period. The results of tests of the same hypotheses on both samples are discussed jointly. Since CdB included all manufacturing business, the R & S sample of large firms could be considered as a sub-set of CdB, the extreme one in the distribution by size. Yet comparisons of R & S with a sub-set of CdB ordered by size show disturbing characters. Profitability is growing with firm size in CdB but is lower in R & S. Capital intensity is decreasing with firm size in CdB but is higher in R & S. Either the firms discussed are non-linearly distributed with respect to size, or R & S is heavily influenced by a few large and somewhat peculiar firms, or the accounting procedures are not homogeneous. The hypothesis of a U-shaped distribution of profitability and capital intensity is too simple to be accepted lightheartedly; after all, the characters of R & S firms should reflect the average characters of the CdB sub-set of the large firms. The authors rely heavily on panel analysis in order to overcome the data problem. The number of observations is thus always large enough, but the amount of information they carry is quite different whether one looks for variability in time or variability among firms. A CdB panel is only six years long; when using first differences and lagged variables the useful time span is reduced to four, three or even two observations. Clearly no variability over time can be inferred from such data, whatever amount of econometric skill is applied. It may be suggested that the different time length of R & S and CdB, rather than the difference in average firm size, has something to do with the different results obtained when testing the same hypothesis: clearly the effect of time-varying variables can be detected only in R & S. It is also not surprising that the coefficient of the lagged dependent variable is very high in an equation allowing for an adjustment process; my own conclusion would not be that adjustment is particularly slow in that particular set of firms, but rather that the term picks up too large a share of the variance because of the lack of observations. When the regressors accounting for the 'desired' level of the dependent variable are not varying at all (over time) within the available data set, I would conclude that no adjustment process can be caught. The fact that such variables may vary among firms does not help us with our problem.

The lag structure is perforce very simple, usually only a one-year lag, in such circumstances, but again one can suspect that useful results could be obtained by testing a more complex lag structure if there were enough observations. It cannot be done now, but interpretation of the present results must take account of the likely distortion induced by imposing too simple a lag structure.

More specifically, BFR provide an accurate description of corporate debt in Italy, with interesting insights on the differences among firms of different size and location. The international comparison is stimulating, but the basic statistics of the various countries are probably not quite comparable. The really interesting question is whether there is a pattern of convergence towards some average level of indebtedness, and I would be inclined to answer that there is one in Europe and Japan. The debt–assets ratio falls in Italy, and it would show a greater fall if assets were corrected for inflation. It also falls in the economies where it was higher and increases where it was lower. The debt–sales ratio does not fall in Italy, but the debt–value added ratio (not shown here) does fall. Conventional wisdom on the reduction in debt runs approximately as follows: it has been made possible by better profitability and desirable by the sharp increase in interest rates that occurred at the beginning of the decade and was maintained thereafter.

What is the relationship between such beliefs and the theories tested by BFR? The basic recognition that both desirability and possibility must be considered is in agreement with the search by BFR for imperfections and constraints in the financial markets. A role of interest rates in setting the optimal level of debt is not recognised by BFR. This exclusion seems to imply that the costs of the different sources of capital move together, which takes us again into the unlikely realm of perfect capital markets. If the authors had considered interest rates, though, they could not have taken into account the abrupt change that took place at the end of the 1970s, since the available data on firm accounts start in 1982; but it is likely that the adjustment process induced by that change has lasted a number of years. According to well-established theories, BFR stress tax factors; but tax laws and rates have not changed during the short period for which data are available. Perhaps a cross-country analysis could help. The authors notice that effective corporate tax rates do vary among firms, and rely on a two-stage regression procedure in order to separate the time-varying from the time-invariant determinants of the firms' borrowing; they find that tax variables are indeed recognisable among the latter. The procedure is ingenious, and yet I do not feel quite sure whether it allows recognition of a causal relation going from tax rates to indebtedness rather than one going from indebtedness to effective tax rates.

Note

Pippo Ranci is Professor, Catholic University of Milan.

Part II

Financial markets

Financial markets

4 Financial liberalisation and exchange rate volatility

VITTORIO GRILLI and NOURIEL ROUBINI

1 Introduction

The structure and openness of the international financial markets has significantly changed since 1970. Financial deregulation has led to the internalisation of the financial services industry while the progressive liberalisation of international capital movements has allowed, and has been followed by, large-scale cross-country portfolio diversification. These developments have stimulated the growth of the world foreign exchange markets. In a related study (Arcelli *et al.*, 1990), we described the liberalisation process that occurred in the foreign exchange markets after 1980. The analysis revealed that the size of these markets has increased enormously during this period. One main factor has been the separation between trade-motivated transactions and total transactions in foreign exchange. Most of the turnover in the foreign exchange markets that we analysed was generated by financial operations, and a large part of them were of a speculative nature.

In this chapter, we study whether the growth of the market and the dramatic changes in the type of transactions and traders have had a major impact on exchange rate volatility. In particular, we analyse the relationship between financial innovation, capital liberalisation, transaction volume and exchange rate volatility. First we present, in Section 2, a model of the foreign exchange market which produces a simple relationship between volume of transactions and exchange rate variability. One of the implications of the model is that there exist changes in the structure of financial markets which generate a simultaneous increase in the volume of transactions and of the distribution of exchange rates. Next, in Section 3, we turn to the data. We search for possible switches in the stochastic process generating exchange rates, and ask whether these switches could be related to liberalisation measures. The conclusion that we reach is that, for most currencies, changes in the process generating the exchange rate have occurred, and they happened close to the time in which major capital market innovations took place.

2   The model

In this section we adapt previous work on stock market volatility and volume of transactions to the analysis of the foreign exchange market. The main reference is Tauchen and Pitts (1983). Consider a foreign exchange market where currency A is traded for currency B. Suppose that there are J traders operating in this market. For simplicity we assume that the desired net position in currency A of trader j at time t is a linear function of the form:

$$Q_{tj} = a[e_{tj}^* - e_t] \tag{1}$$

where e_t is the spot exchange rate (defined as units of B currency for one unit of A currency) and e_{tj}^* is the reservation exchange rate for trader j, a function of his or her expectations. Contrary to the representative agent approach to exchange rate markets, we want explicitly to account for differences in the market participants. We introduce heterogeneity in the model by assuming that the information held and processed is different across agents and that, therefore, expectations (e_{tj}^*) vary among traders. If $e_{tj}^* > e_t$, currency A is priced below trader j's reservation level, and thus he or she will want to have a positive net position in currency A. Conversely, if $e_{tj}^* < e_t$, currency A is more appreciated than trader j's reservation level, and he or she will want to have a net positive position in currency B.

In equilibrium:

$$\sum_{j=1}^{J} Q_{tj} = 0 \tag{2}$$

must hold, that is, the exchange market clears. Together (1) and (2) imply:

$$\frac{1}{J} \sum_{j=1}^{J} e_{tj}^* = e_t \tag{3}$$

i.e. the average of the reservation exchange rate clears the market. From (3) it is immediately clear that:

$$\mathrm{var}(e_t) = \frac{1}{J^2} \mathrm{var}\left(\sum_{j=1}^{J} e_{tj}^* \right) \tag{4}$$

that is, the variance of the exchange rate depends on the distribution of the reservation exchange rate of the traders on the market. We assume that informational shocks hit the economy every period, both at the aggregate level and at the individual level. In the present context, these shocks will be related to the changes in the regulatory structure of the markets. Formally, therefore, the individuals' reservation prices are distributed:

$$e_{tj}^* = \phi_t + \psi_{tj} \tag{5}$$

where:

$$E(\phi_t) = \phi \qquad \mathrm{var}(\phi_t) = \sigma_\phi^2 \tag{6}$$

and

$$E(\psi_{tj}) = \psi \qquad \mathrm{var}(\psi_{tj}) = \sigma_\psi^2$$

Accordingly, ϕ_t is an economy-wide shock, while ψ_{tj} an idiosyncratic component. If we assume that the shocks are mutually independent, both across traders and over time, then:

$$e_t = \frac{1}{J} \sum_{j=1}^{J} e_{tj}^* = \phi_t + \frac{1}{J} \sum_{j=1}^{J} \psi_{tj} \tag{7}$$

From (7) it follows that

$$\mathrm{var}(e_t) \equiv \sigma_e^2 = \sigma_\phi^2 + \frac{\sigma_\psi^2}{J} \tag{8}$$

Thus, other things being equal, an increase in the number of traders (J) tends to reduce the volatility of the exchange rate. On the other hand, a larger variance of both the aggregate and idiosyncratic informational shocks corresponds to a larger exchange rate variance.

Consider now the determination of turnover. The volume of transactions on the markets at period t is given by the change in position of the traders between period $t-1$ and t. Using (5) and (7), we can rewrite (1) as:

$$Q_{tj} = a\left(\psi_{tj} - \frac{1}{J} \sum_{j=1}^{J} \psi_{tj}\right) \tag{9}$$

The volume of transaction at t is therefore given by:

$$V_t = \frac{a}{2} \sum_{j=1}^{J} \left|\left(\psi_{tj} - \frac{1}{J} \sum_{j=1}^{J} \psi_{tj}\right) - \left(\psi_{t-1j} - \frac{1}{J} \sum_{j=1}^{J} \psi_{t-1j}\right)\right| \tag{10}$$

Assuming that ψ_{tj} are i.i.d. $\sim N(0, \sigma_\psi^2)$ it can be shown that:

$$E(V) = a\sigma_\psi \sqrt{\frac{J(J-1)}{\pi}} \tag{11}$$

The expected value of the trading volume is therefore an increasing function of the number of traders in the market. A larger variance of the idiosyncratic shock will also induce an increase in average volume.

What does this model tell us about the effect of liberalisation of capital markets? This approach highlights the importance of distinguishing between short–medium-run effects and long-run effects. In this framework it is natural to interpret the short-run effects of a liberalisation as an increase in the variance of both the aggregate and of the idiosyncratic shocks. The regime change brought about by the elimination of capital controls implies that a larger set of variables will now be relevant for the determination of exchange rates. This will be reflected in a higher degree of uncertainty, and thus will be associated with larger σ_ϕ and σ_ψ. This will produce a positive correlation between exchange rate variance and the average volume of transactions. As it can be noted from (8) and (11), in fact, the variance of the exchange rate is an increasing function of both σ_ϕ and σ_ψ, and expected volume is a positive function of σ_ψ. This result depends on the assumption that, in the short run, the number of traders does not change (at least, not too much). The main effect of the liberalisation, in this case, is to increase the volume of transactions because of the increase in the uncertainty produced by the regime switch. This, in turn, could require large swings in the exchange rate, i.e. an increase in variance.

Over time, the liberalisation also tends to increase the number of potential traders and thus expand the size of the market. If this is the case, the correlation between exchange rate variability and volume may reverse sign in the long run. In fact, as can be seen from (8) and (11), the volume is a positive function of the number of traders (J), while the variance of the exchange rate is a negative function of J. As J increases, the markets become 'thicker' and this reduces the need for large variation in the exchange rate in order to equilibrate the market. In the long run, therefore, the financial liberalisation would tend to increase transaction volume and reduce the exchange rate fluctuations. In the medium run, the long-run effect and the short-run effect on the exchange rate volatility will tend to offset each other.

As we noted in Section 1, liberalisation processes have always generated considerable increases in the volume of transactions in the foreign exchange market. In this section we will investigate whether, in fact, the various liberalisations have generated an increase in the volatility of exchange rates, and if it is already possible to detect the reversal due to the thickening of the market. A first piece of evidence is provided in Table 4.1. Using daily data, we constructed the monthly coefficient of variation (i.e. sample standard deviation normalised by the sample mean) for eight countries: Australia, Canada, France, Germany, Italy, Japan, the United

Table 4.1. *Coefficient of variation, average of monthly data*

	Australia against:						
	Canada	France	Germany	Italy	Japan	UK	US
Jan. 71–Dec. 74	0.540	0.900	1.007	0.831	0.660	0.738	0.449
Jan. 75–Dec. 79	0.631	0.752	0.801	0.760	0.786	0.812	0.498
Jan. 80–Dec. 84	0.699	1.068	1.051	1.083	1.001	0.970	0.693
Jan. 85–May 89	1.262	1.586	1.663	1.652	1.605	1.612	1.314

	Japan against:						
	Australia	Canada	France	Germany	Italy	UK	US
Jan. 71–Dec. 74	0.660	0.641	0.796	0.886	0.728	0.702	0.599
Jan. 75–Dec. 79	0.786	1.019	0.912	0.940	1.043	1.034	0.854
Jan. 80–Dec. 84	1.001	1.061	1.128	1.070	1.155	1.159	1.171
Jan. 85–May 89	1.605	1.284	0.829	0.839	0.939	1.072	1.273

	UK against:						
	Australia	Canada	France	Germany	Italy	Japan	US
Jan. 71–Dec. 74	0.738	0.549	1.697	0.777	0.601	0.702	0.554
Jan. 75–Dec. 79	0.812	0.988	0.805	0.864	0.887	1.034	0.881
Jan. 80–Dec. 84	0.970	0.942	0.976	0.937	1.043	1.159	1.114
Jan. 85–May 89	1.612	1.353	0.814	0.839	1.017	1.072	1.423

	France against:						
	Australia	Canada	Germany	Japan	Italy	UK	US
Jan. 71–Dec. 74	0.900	0.797	0.669	0.796	0.705	0.697	0.767
Jan. 75–Dec. 79	0.752	0.901	0.523	0.912	0.737	0.805	0.759
Jan. 80–Dec. 84	1.068	1.120	0.350	1.128	0.602	0.976	1.259
Jan. 85–May 89	1.586	1.337	0.180	0.829	0.542	0.814	1.325

	Germany against:						
	Australia	Canada	France	Japan	Italy	UK	US
Jan. 71–Dec. 74	1.007	0.864	0.669	0.886	0.822	0.777	0.872
Jan. 75–Dec. 79	0.801	0.946	0.523	0.940	0.844	0.864	0.835
Jan. 80–Dec. 84	1.051	1.061	0.350	1.070	0.583	0.937	1.198
Jan. 85–May 89	1.663	1.427	0.180	0.839	0.538	0.839	1.415

Table 4.1. (*Cont.*)

	Italy against:						
	Australia	Canada	France	Germany	Japan	UK	US
Jan. 71–Dec. 74	0.831	0.625	0.705	0.822	0.728	0.601	0.586
Jan. 75–Dec. 79	0.760	0.893	0.737	0.844	1.043	0.887	0.722
Jan. 80–Dec. 84	1.083	1.097	0.602	0.583	1.155	1.043	1.193
Jan. 85–May 89	1.652	1.354	0.542	0.538	0.939	1.017	1.343

	US against:						
	Australia	Canada	France	Germany	Italy	Japan	UK
Jan. 71–Dec. 74	0.449	0.212	0.767	0.872	0.586	0.599	0.554
Jan. 75–Dec. 79	0.498	0.397	0.759	0.835	0.722	0.854	0.881
Jan. 80–Dec. 84	0.693	0.427	1.259	1.198	1.193	1.171	1.114
Jan. 85–May 89	1.314	0.483	1.325	1.415	1.343	1.273	1.423

	Belgium	Denmark	Ireland	Netherlands
Jan. 71–Dec. 74	0.784	0.809	0.569	0.854
Jan. 75–Dec. 79	0.820	0.808	0.814	0.821
Jan. 80–Dec. 84	1.229	1.175	1.194	1.161
Jan. 85–May 89	1.380	1.367	1.335	1.402

Kingdom and the United States. In Table 4.1 we report five-year averages of these coefficients of variation. It is interesting to notice that in all cases we observe an increase in this measure of volatility coinciding with the liberalisation periods. In some cases, e.g. for Japan, we also notice a reduction in the volatility towards the end of the sample.

The evidence presented in Table 4.1 suggests that a liberalisation of capital movements might lead, at least in the short–medium run, to an increase in exchange rate volatility. Our next step is therefore to try to test more formally the hypothesis of a relation between capital liberalisation and exchange rate volatility.

3   A test for the change in regime

If capital liberalisation leads to a change in the volatility of the exchange rate it must be the case that, coinciding with the liberalisation of capital controls, there is a change in the stochastic process of the variance of the exchange rate. We therefore implement a test to determine the timing of the change in the stochastic process for the variance of the exchange rate and to test whether this timing is coincident with liberalisation episodes. The procedure has the objective of determining the most likely data for the change in regime, conditional on the assumption that the change occurred all in one period (this is also the approach followed by Mankiw et al., 1987).

Suppose that the process for the coefficient of variation (cv_t) of the exchange rate follows the following:

$$\log cv_t = s_1 + \epsilon_t \qquad t = 1, \ldots, T_s$$

$$\log cv_t = s_2 + \epsilon_t \qquad t = T_s + 1, \ldots, T$$

where T_s is the switch date, i.e. the first period of the new regime. The objective is to use a maximum likelihood procedure to estimate T_s.

If we assume normal errors, the log likelihood function for the model is:

$$\log L = - T \log(\sigma) + \sum_{t=1}^{T_s} \log N \left(\frac{cv_t - s_1}{s_1} \right) + \sum_{t=T_s+1}^{T} \log N \left(\frac{cv_t - s_2}{s_1} \right)$$

where s_1 and s_2 are the means of the coefficient of variation in the old and new regimes, σ^2 is the variance of the error ϵ_t and $N(.)$ is the density function of a standardised normal distribution. As in Mankiw et al. (1987), the maximum density likelihood value for T_s is found by computing the maximum likelihood estimates of the three parameters of the model (s_1, s_2 and σ^2) for all possible T_ss and then taking the value of T_s with the maximum likelihood.

One of the disadvantages of the test we are using is that it gives an exact dating of the change in regime while in reality the process of liberalisation of capital controls is usually never a one-shot event. The process of liberalisation occurs over time, and it is more sensible to talk about a liberalisation period rather than an exact liberalisation date. In order to take into consideration this issue and to give a degree of confidence to the point estimates of the date of the regime change, we therefore compute the posterior odds ratio for alternative dates of regime switch. This ratio allows us to find a region of dates over which it is likely that the change in regime has occurred, i.e. it gives a confidence measures of how likely it is that the liberalisation actually occurred in the period around the estimated regime switch date. This posterior odds ratio is computed as:

$$\text{POR} = \exp(\log L_t - \log L_{T_s})$$

i.e. the posterior odds ratio is the ratio of the likelihood values for different switch dates.

Finally, in order to test for the presence of a structural break in the mean of the coefficient of variation at the estimated break date, we test the hypothesis of a change in the value of this mean. The hypothesis to be tested is:

$$H_0: s_1 = s_2$$

versus:

$$H_1: s_1 \neq s_2$$

The test is a simple log likelihood ratio test:

$$2(\log NR - \log R) \rightarrow \chi_1^2$$

where NR refers to the non-restricted model and R to the restricted model.

The results of the above tests are presented for seven countries (Australia, France, Germany, Italy, Japan, the United Kingdom and the United States) in Tables 4.2–4.8. The reasons why there might be a structural change in the volatility of exchange rates are numerous but here we advance the hypothesis that the main reasons for a structural break should be significant changes in regimes, such as the abolition of capital controls or, for the EMS countries, the movement to a system of fixed exchange rates. In particular, the model presented above suggests that the liberalisation of capital movements might lead to a change in the volatility of exchange rates and to an increase in the volume of transactions in the foreign exchange market. The second effect, the one on the volume of transactions, is theoretically unambiguous since an increase in the number of traders in the exchange market should lead to an increase in the volume of transactions. The evidence presented in Arcelli *et al.* (1990) regarding the increase in the volume of transactions in a number of foreign exchange rate markets following the liberalisation of capital controls is consistent with this hypothesis.

The effects of capital liberalisation on the volatility of exchange rates is ambiguous. On one side, the liberalisation can be seen as leading to a generalised increase in uncertainty, both economy-wide and trader-specific uncertainty. On the other side, the increase in the number of traders in the exchange rate market should lead to an increase in the thickness of the market and to a reduction of exchange rate volatility. Following a liberalisation of capital movements, exchange rate volatility might therefore increase or fall, depending on whether the first effect dominates the second or vice versa. One might argue that, while the liberalisation leads to an immediate increase in uncertainty, the number of traders will increase only slowly over time, in which case the volatility will first increase and then decline when the market becomes very thick.

Of the seven countries for which the test was conducted, three witnessed a significant liberalisation of capital movements in the period con-

Table 4.2. *United States*

	Switching point	CV1	CV2	CV	Likelihood ratio test
Belgium	80:2	0.72	1.15	0.94	25.18
Denmark	80:2	0.73	1.13	0.93	24.42
France	79:8	0.64	1.12	0.89	29.89
Germany	80:2	0.77	1.16	0.97	21.99
Ireland	77:11	0.49	1.03	0.84	46.56
Italy*	82:9	0.73	1.16	1.06	193.27
Netherlands	80:2	0.75	1.14	0.95	21.66
Australia*	81:7	0.31	0.90	0.63	75.81
Canada	76:10	0.22	0.38	0.33	26.37
Japan	77:9	0.42	1.05	0.80	61.68
UK	77:11	0.49	1.05	0.86	49.68

* For Italy and Australia two variances were considered. The likelihood ratio test is H_0 two means and two variances against H_1 one mean and two variances.

sidered (Australia, Japan and the United Kingdom) while in two others (France and Italy) a partial liberalisation occurred in the later part of the period (the late 1980s). Two caveats should be kept in mind: first, since different countries liberalise in different periods, the change in the volatility of bilateral exchange rates might reflect the effects of either liberalisation so that more than one structural break is possible. Second, the (three) EMS countries should be considered separately because the inter-EMS volatility has been importantly affected by the creation of the EMS and because two of the EMS countries (France and Italy) started their liberalisation only very recently.

Consider first the three countries (Australia, Japan and the United Kingdom) with major liberalisations. We can use the bilateral volatility with the dollar as a first test of the hypothesis that structural breaks are due to capital liberalisation. The estimated dating of the change in regime suggests that the structural break occurred in August 1981 for the Australian dollar, September 1977 for the yen and November 1977 for the British pound (see Table 4.2). These dates are very close to the actual dating of the liberalisation in these three countries (1978 for the United Kingdom, 1978–9 for Japan and 1982 for Australia). One could argue that the structural break might not be due to a change in regime in these countries (i.e. the liberalisation of capital controls) but rather to a break in the volatility of the US dollar, but this hypothesis does not seem to be supported by the data. In fact, the dates for the structural break differ for the three countries. Also, if one considers the bilateral rates of the dollar with the other three currencies (German mark, French franc and Italian lira), the break in volatility occurs at quite different dates (1980, 1979 and 1982 respectively) suggesting that country-specific effects rather than changes in the volatility of the dollar are behind the break in volatility of the liberalising countries.

It should also be observed that the posterior odds ratio for the volatility of these currencies with the dollar suggests that the regime change occurred with a high likelihood around the estimated dates; this strengthens the hypothesis that the capital liberalisation in these countries is the source of the estimated structural break in volatility.

3.1   Australia

In the case of Australia, the hypothesis of a break in volatility due to the liberalisation is confirmed by the estimated break dates of the bilateral rates of the Australian dollar with the British pound (October 1982) and Canadian dollar (June 1982) (see Table 4.3): these match well the liberalisation period (1981–2). The different estimated break date of the Australian dollar with Japan (February 1978) should probably be imputed to the effects of the Japanese liberalisation (1978). The study of the posterior odds ratios for the Australian dollar suggests that the regime change occurred with high likelihood around the estimated dates, reinforcing the argument that the capital liberalisation was the source of the estimated structural break in volatility.

The main puzzling result is the estimated break of volatility with the German mark (January 1985), that is some time after the liberalisation of the Australian dollar. For our concern, the effects of the liberalisation on the volatility of the exchange rate, the data for the Australian dollar show a systematic increase in this volatility after the estimated break date. Also,

Table 4.3. *Australia*

	Switching point	CV1	CV2	CV	Likelihood ratio test
France	80:9	0.66	1.17	0.90	33.95
Germany	85:1	0.81	1.47	0.94	29.92
Italy	80:2	0.59	1.21	0.89	51.21
Canada	82:6	0.44	0.96	0.61	58.72
Japan	78:2	0.49	1.05	0.83	48.32
UK	82:10	0.64	1.25	0.84	39.89
US*	81:7	0.31	0.90	0.63	75.81

* For the US two variances were considered. The likelihood ratio test is $H0$ two means and two variances against $H1$ one mean and two variances.

the likelihood ratio test confirms that this increase in volatility is statistically very significant (the critical value of the ratio for rejecting the null hypothesis is equal to 3). These results suggest that the increase in uncertainty following the liberalisation has dominated the effects of an increased number of traders in affecting the volatility of the Australian dollar.

3.2   Japan

The results for Japan (Table 4.4) also confirm the hypothesis that the structural break in volatility was due to the liberalisation of the yen in 1977–9 period. The estimated break date with the US dollar (September 1977) coincides with the estimated break date with the British pound and Canadian dollar. The estimated break date with the other countries also falls in the liberalisation period (February 1978 with the Australian dollar and the Italian lira and August 1979 with the German mark and the French franc). The study of the posterior odds ratio suggests that the structural break of the yen occurred with high likelihood in the period around the estimated data (see Figure 4.1). The likelihood ratio for the yen rate relative to the franc, mark, lira and pound suggests a wider interval in the period 1978–80 in which the structural break might have occurred (see, for example, Figure 4.2).

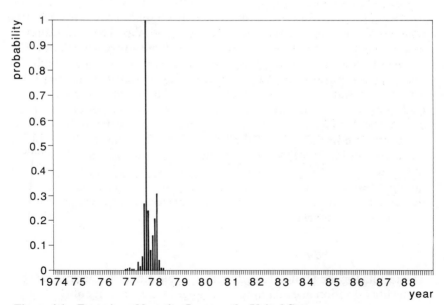

Figure 4.1   Posterior odds ratio, Japan vs the United States

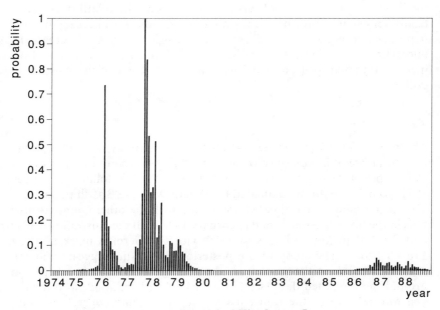

Figure 4.2   Posterior odds ratio, the United Kingdom vs Japan

It can also be observed that the changes in the volatility of the yen following the liberalisation seem to be consistently in the direction of a greater volatility in the post-liberalisation period; the likelihood ratio test shows that the increase in volatility is statistically very significant. The results of Table 4.4 also suggest that the increase in volatility might be only temporary and due to the dominant role of uncertainty in the period after the liberalisation with a reduction in volatility when the number of traders increase. In fact, when we split the sample in two periods, as in the case of the yen/German mark rate, we find that a first break in 1979 led to an increase in volatility of the bilateral rate but that a second break (occurring in late 1981) led to a reduction of the volatility. One could then interpret the initial increase in volatility as being due to the initial dominant effect of an increase in uncertainty after the liberalisation, while the reduction after 1981 could be due to the effects of an increaed number of traders in the market.

3.3   The United Kingdom

The results for the United Kingdom (see Table 4.5) also confirm the role of the liberalisation in explaining the change in the volatility of the British pound. The estimated break date is November 1977 with the US dollar

Table 4.4. *Japan*

	Switching point	CV1	CV2	CV	Likelihood ratio test
France1**	79:8	0.80	1.36	0.92	17.57
France2**	88:10	0.88	0.39	0.84	13.89
Germany1**	79:8	0.84	1.38	0.96	15.47
Germany2**	81:11	1.08	0.74	0.86	17.48
Italy	78:2	0.75	0.97	0.89	9.17
Australia	78:2	0.49	1.05	0.83	48.32
Canada	77:9	0.52	1.04	0.85	39.42
UK	77:9	0.69	1.00	0.90	16.06
US	77:9	0.42	1.05	0.80	61.88

** The sample period is 73:1–89:5, with the exceptions of France and Germany (2 samples 73:1–81:12 and 77:1–89:5).

Table 4.5. *United Kingdom*

	Switching point	CV1	CV2	CV	Likelihood ratio test
France1**	80:9	0.65	0.92	0.72	6.07
France2**	87:6	0.80	0.44	0.72	17.72
Germany1**	74:5	0.97	0.71	0.74	2.77
Germany2**	87:4	0.79	0.44	0.71	16.60
Italy	79:5	0.62	0.91	0.78	15.62
Australia	82:10	0.64	1.25	0.84	39.89
Canada	77:9	0.60	1.00	0.87	30.19
Japan	77:9	0.69	1.00	0.90	16.06
US	77:11	0.49	1.05	0.86	46.68

** The sample period is 73:1–89:5, with the exceptions of France and Germany (2 samples 73:1–81:12 and 77:1–89:5).

and August 1977 with the Canadian dollar and the Japanese yen. The posterior odds ratio (see Figures 4.2–4.4) puts a high likelihood on the hypothesis that the structural break occurred close to the estimated dates. This would confirm the role of the 1979 liberalisation as the cause of the structural break. It should, however, be observed that the estimated dates of structural break anticipate by several quarters the actual liberalisation date. Two explanations of this result are possible. First, while capital controls were completely eliminated only in October 1979, significant liberalisation had already started in 1977: for example, capital controls on non-residents were eliminated in 1977 and foreign exchange restrictions on financial intermediaries were reduced in the same period.

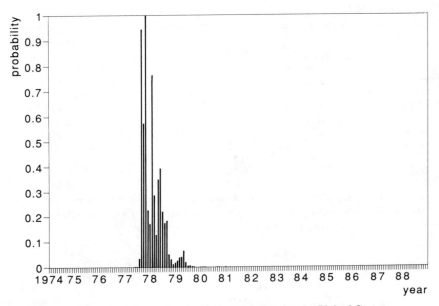

Figure 4.3   Posterior odds ratio, the United Kingdom vs the United States

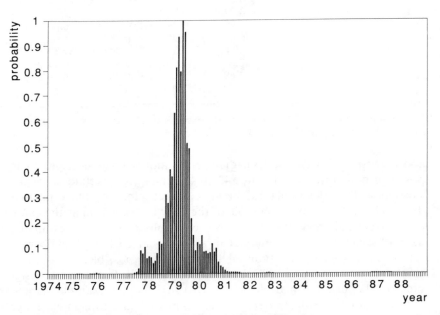

Figure 4.4   Posterior odds ratio, Italy vs the United Kingdom

This also suggests that the volatility of the exchange rate might have increased in the 1977–9 period on the expectation that capital controls would eventually be completely eliminated. Second, the change in monetary control procedures in 1976–7 – i.e. the introduction of explicit monetary targets – might have led to increased interest rate and exchange rate volatility.

The late 1982 break of the bilateral rate with the Australian dollar (Table 4.5) can be imputed with high likelihood to the Australian liberalisation in that period. The estimated break date with the German mark is quite off target (May 1975 for the first sub-period); however, the likelihood test shows that this break is not statistically significant. The unreliability of the 1975 estimated date for the break in the pound/mark rate is also confirmed by the picture of the posterior odds ratio, that shows a quite flat distribution throughout all the 1974–83 sub-period. In the pound/mark and pound/franc case, we estimated the model for two different sub-periods (1973–83 and 1978–89), the second corresponding to the post-liberalisation period. The reason for this approach is the following: we expected that the liberalisation of the pound in 1978 would lead to an increase in the volatility of the pound bilateral rates and all the volatility measures in the post-liberalisation period statistically confirm that hypothesis. However, the British pound, while not being a formal member of the EMS, started an informal policy of pegging to the EMS currencies during the late 1980s. This informal EMS membership is confirmed by the estimate for the second sub-period showing a structural break (in the direction of significantly reduced volatility) in April 1987 (with the German mark) and June 1987 (with the French franc).

3.4   Italy

The cases of Italy (and France) are harder to analyse because these two countries have not yet completely liberalised their capital movements in the period under investigation. One could argue that, for these two countries, the main structural break was represented by the creation of the EMS, but this is only partially correct. First, if the EMS had any immediate effect, it would have affected the volatility of the lira and the franc relative to other EMS currencies (such as the mark) but not their volatility relative to other currencies. Second, the start of the EMS did not mark an immediate change in the economic policies of divergent countries such as Italy and France. In the case of Italy, a more stable policy and exchange rate environment had already started before the EMS, following a number of major exchange rate crises, the last of which occurred in early 1976. Third, the early EMS experience was characterised by frequent exchange realignments (seven by 1983) and only in 1983 can one detect a drastic change in policy stance both in France (see Sachs and Wyplosz, 1986, on this) and in Italy (the wage indexation reform).

If we then consider the results for Italy (Table 4.6) we observe that the estimates of the structural break of the volatility of the lira relative to the mark and the franc are dated at October 1976 and January 1977 respectively. The posterior odds ratio figures suggest that the probability estimate of the date of the regime switch is highly concentrated around the estimated date. This could be interpreted as suggesting that the January–March 1976 exchange crisis of the lira marked a dramatic shift in policy. In fact, an exchange rate collapse of the lira of that magnitude has not occurred since then (see Penati and Pennachi, 1989, for a study of that episode). Moreover, Table 4.6 shows that the volatility of the lira has fallen in a statistically significant way since the above structural breaks.

One can also observe that the estimated dates of a regime change of the lira relative to the currencies of Japan, the United Kingdom and Australia

Table 4.6. *Italy*

	Switching point	CV1	CV2	CV	Likelihood ratio test
France	76:10	0.87	0.49	0.56	37.10
Germany	77:1	0.87	0.51	0.58	31.91
Australia	80:2	0.59	1.21	0.89	51.21
Canada	80:1	0.68	1.13	0.91	35.88
Japan	78:2	0.75	0.97	0.89	9.17
UK	79:5	0.62	0.91	0.78	15.62
US*	82:9	0.73	1.16	1.06	193.27

* For the US two variances were considered. The likelihood ratio test is $H0$ two means and two variances against $H1$ one mean and two variances.

coincide with the liberalisation periods for these countries. Moreover, the posterior odds ratio for the estimated dates of regime switch confirms that the regime change did probably occur close to the estimated dates. One should also observe that the volatility of the lira with respect to the above currencies significantly increases after these changes in regime.

3.5   France

The case of France is similar to the Italian one, since capital controls have been lifted only recently. The structural break with the German mark occurred only in September 1982, more than three years after the creation of the EMS (see Table 4.7). This estimated date is quite consistent

Table 4.7. *France*

	Switching point	CV1	CV2	CV	Likelihood ratio test
Italy	76:10	0.87	0.49	0.56	37.10
Germany1*	82:9	0.42	0.13	0.26	86.65
Australia	80:9	0.66	1.17	0.90	33.95
Canada	80:9	0.80	1.11	0.95	15.14
Japan1**	79:8	0.80	1.36	0.92	17.57
Japan2**	88:10	0.88	0.39	0.84	13.89
UK1**	80:9	0.65	0.92	0.72	6.07
UK2**	87:6	0.80	0.44	0.72	17.72
US	79:8	0.64	1.12	0.89	29.89

** The sample period is 73:1–89:5, with the exceptions of United Kingdom (2 samples 73:1–83:12 and 78:1–89:5) and Japan (2 samples 73:1–81:12 and 77:1–89:5).

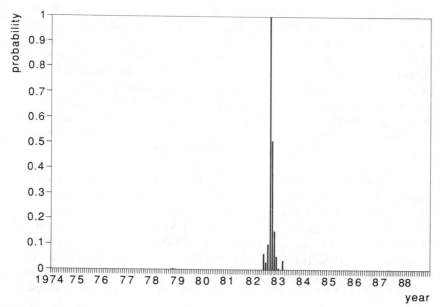

Figure 4.5   Posterior odds ratio, France vs Germany

with the radical shift in French economic policy in 1982 after the failed attempt of Mitterrand to go it alone and follow an expansionary monetary and fiscal policy in the 1981–2 period. As discussed by Sachs and Wyplosz (1987), the policy debate in France in 1982 centred on the two alternatives of abandoning the EMS and pursuing a divergent policy stance or remaining in the EMS and accepting the policy constraints of a fixed rate regime. The estimates for France show a significant reduction in the franc/mark volatility after 1982 and the posterior odds ratio dates this structural break around September 1982 with a very high degree of confidence (see Figure 4.5). As discussed above, the estimated structural break date with the Italian lira (October 1976) can be imputed with a certain degree of confidence to a structural change in Italy. Similarly, the estimates of the regime change relative to other currencies (such as the Japanese yen, Australian dollar and British pound) appear to be in the period of liberalisation of these currencies (the analysis of the posterior odds ratio confirms this interpretation). In all these cases, the volatility of the franc relative to these currencies increases after their liberalisation. However, as discussed above, if we split the estimation sample into two parts for the franc/yen and the franc/pound rates we observe a second structural break (in June 1987 for the franc/pound rate and in October 1988 for the franc/yen rate). In both cases the volatility falls significantly after the second break. In the case of the franc/pound rate, this is likely to be the result of the effective pegging of the pound to the EMS currencies since 1987 (engineered by the former British Chancellor Lawson) and the reduction in volatility implied by an increase in market thickness after a liberalisation (we have discussed in Arcelli et al., 1990, the huge increase in transaction volumes in the London market in the 1980s). In the case of the franc/yen rate, increases in the numbers of participants in the exchange market and thickening of the transaction volumes could be the source of the second structural break; however, the posterior odds ratio suggests that this second break might have occurred with high probability in the two years before the estimated date of October 1988.

In conclusion, the above empirical analysis suggests that episodes of capital liberalisation are associated with significant structural breaks in the volatility of the exchange rate. In the first stage, liberalisation appears systematically to lead to an increase in volatility as the degree of uncertainty faced by the agents increases. In the longer run, the evidence suggests that the increase in volatility might be dampened or reduced as the number of participants in the exchange rate market increases, the transaction volumes become larger and the thickness of asset markets is increased.

4   Conclusions

The growth in the volume of transactions in the foreign exchange rate markets has risen dramatically since 1980, to an extent that cannot be explained just by the increase in the volume of trade in goods and services.

In fact, most of the turnover in the foreign exchange markets is generated by financial operations and a large part of these are of a speculative nature. Moreover, this increase in the volume of transactions has occurred coincidentally with an increase in the degree of volatility of exchange rates. Exchange rate markets have become more unstable, leading to concern about the 'excess volatility' of exchange rates under unrestricted capital mobility.

In this chapter, we attempted to test the hypothesis of a relation between international capital *liberalisation*, increase in the *volume* of transactions and greater exchange rate *volatility* in foreign exchange rate markets. While the effects of capital liberalisation on the volume of transactions in the exchange rate market are theoretically unambiguous (liberalisation leads to increased volumes), the effects of liberalisation on the volatility of the exchange rate are more ambiguous. On one side, liberalisation will lead to increased economy-wide and investor-specific uncertainy, and will therefore increase the volatility of exchange rates. On the other, an increase in the number of participants in the exchange rate market should reduce such volatility. In the short run, the uncertainty effect might be dominant while in the medium–long run an increase in the number of traders should thicken otherwise 'thin' markets and tend to reduce the volatility of exchange rates.

We therefore estimate whether changes in the distribution of exchange rate volatility have occurred, and the exact timing of these switches. We find that, for most currencies, changes in the process of exchange rate volatility have occurred, and that they have taken place close to the time in which major capital liberalisation episodes have occurred. These results suggest that liberalisation of capital movements is associated with significant breaks in the volatility of exchange rates. Initially, the liberalisation of international capital appears to lead to a systematic increase in the volatility of exchange rates as the degree of uncertainty faced by agents increases. However, there is also some preliminary evidence that, in the longer run, the increase in the number of traders, the growth in transaction volumes and the increased thickness of exchange rate markets have tended to reduce the volatility of exchange rates.

The implications of this process of liberalisation of capital movements for the stability of exchange rate in the EMS region are twofold. In the short run, liberalisation might increase the potential effects of disturbance on the inter-EMS exchange rates. An even greater degree of exchange rate intervention and coordination will therefore be required to ensure the stability of exchange rates in the EMS bands. In the longer run, however, the reduction in 'thinness' in exchange rate markets deriving from the increase in the number of market participants should tend to reduce potential exchange rate volatility. Finally, as shown in related work of ours (Grilli and Roubini, 1990) liberalisation of capital movements should lead to a greater degree of diversification of international asset portfolios. This final effect should also contribute to a reduction of exchange rate asymmetries in the EMS deriving from shocks external to the system.

Note

We thank Rudiger Dornbusch and Rony Hamaui for helpful comments and Paolo Pesenti for excellent research assistance.

References

Arcelli, M., G. de Kock, V. Grilli, M. Pasinelli and N. Roubini (1990) 'Foreign Exchange Rate Markets: A Primer', Yale University (March) (mimeo).

Grilli, V. and N. Roubini (1990) 'Capital Mobility, Vehicle Currencies and Exchange Rate Asymmetries in the EMS', Yale University (March) (mimeo).

Mankiw, N.G., J.A. Miron and D.N. Weil (1987) 'The Adjustment of Expectations to a Change in Regime', *American Economic Review*, **77**: 358–74.

Penati, A. and G. Pennachi (1989) 'Optimal Portfolio Choice and the Collapse of a Fixed Exchange Rate Regime', *Journal of International Economics*, **27 (1/2)** (August: 1–24).

Sachs, J. and C. Wyplosz (1986) 'The Economic Consequences of President Mitterrand', *Economic Policy*, **2**: 261–313.

Tauchen, G.E. and M. Pitts (1983) 'The Price Variability–Volume Relationship on the Speculative Markets', *Econometrica*, **51**: 485–505.

5 Capital mobility, vehicle currencies and exchange rate asymmetries in the EMS

VITTORIO GRILLI and NOURIEL ROUBINI

1 Introduction

Given the EC decision to liberalise capital movements by 1990, it is important to analyse the effects of this removal of capital controls on the inter-EMS exchange rates. This issue is important because, according to a popular point of view,[1] disturbances external to the EMS (such as movements of the dollar driven by US monetary and fiscal policies) have led in the past to inter-EMS exchange rate tensions. This point of view is supported by the empirical observation that, in periods of strength (weakness) of the dollar, the Deutsche mark appears to be weak (strong) relative to the other EMS currencies.[2]

One possible explanation of this empirical fact is based on the assumption that assets denominated in different currencies are imperfect substitutes in the portfolios of international investors. In particular, it is argued that the degree of asset substitutability between dollar and Deutsche mark-denominated assets is greater than the one between the dollar and other European currencies-denominated assets (such as the French franc or the Italian lira).[3] In the presence of this type of imperfect asset substitutability, portfolio shifts (driven by changes in expectations and/or changes in fundamentals) will have asymmetric effects on the exchange rates between the Deutsche mark and the EMS currencies.[4] For example, shocks that lead to an increase (decrease) in the demand for dollar assets will reduce (increase) the demand for the Deutsche mark more than the demand for French francs or Italian lire. Then, in correspondence with the dollar appreciation (depreciation) relative to the other currencies, we will also observe a depreciation (appreciation) of the Deutsche mark relative to the other EMS currencies: i.e. we will observe asymmetric effects of the disturbances on the EMS exchange rates.

If the source of this inter-EMS asymmetry is imperfect asset substitutability, then capital controls might be justified as an instrument aimed at reducing inter-EMS exchange rate tensions deriving from disturbances external to the EMS. In particular, some authors[5] have argued that the EMS has been a viable regime of semi-fixed exchange rates because widespread capital controls in countries like France and Italy have limited the potentially disruptive effects on the inter-EMS exchange rates of movements of the dollar due to changes in monetary and/or fiscal policy in the United States. If this view is correct, the liberalisation of capital controls in the EMS area might exacerbate the inter-EMS tensions caused by external shocks. In this sense, if we take the objective of maintaining stable exchange rate in the EMS area as an exogenously given goal,[6] capital controls might be justified as a second best instrument aimed at this objective while a liberalisation of capital movements might not be welfare improving.[7]

An alternative view also identifies imperfect asset substitutability as the main source of asymmetric effects in the EMS. However, according to this approach, imperfect substitutability is not an exogenous datum but is rather caused by the very existence of capital controls. In other words, it is capital controls that reduce the substitutability of different currencies and assets in the investors' portfolios. The view that capital controls lead to a lower asset substitutability has been theoretically argued in a number of different ways.[8] In one formulation,[9] the risk of future capital controls increases the variance of the rate of return of an asset and makes the asset less substitutable. In another view, 'even if the probability of tighter capital controls in the future is zero, assets are less substitutable because of market thinness, endogenously generated by capital controls' (Giavazzi and Giovannini, 1989, p. 233). From a normative point of view, if capital controls are the cause of the low substitutability of a certain asset, the removal of capital controls will increase the substitutability and therefore reduce exchange rate asymmetries.

In Grilli and Roubini (1989), we investigated the role of different potential sources of asymmetries. Our argument was based on the observation that the foreign exchange market structure is fundamentally asymmetric, because of the different role that currencies have as means of payment. We model there the intuitive, but never formalised, idea that the reserve and vehicle currency role of certain currencies might affect their equilibrium exchange rates. Certain currencies (such as the US dollar, the Japanese yen and the Deutsche mark) are used both as reserve assets and as currencies with which international transactions of goods and services are conducted, while other currencies have a much more limited or non-existent role as reserve assets and/or international transaction currencies. We show that these differences have important implications for the determination of exchange rates. In this chapter we use the results derived there to demonstrate that this type of framework can be fruitfully applied to explain the existence of asymmetries in the EMS. In particular, we will address the question of whether inter-EMS exchange rate asymmetries might be due to the fact that the Deutsche mark is an international transaction currency, while the other EMS currencies are not.

In our analysis, we focus on two interrelated issues. First, we study the interaction between vehicle currency role and the source of the shocks, in order to identify which types of disturbance lead to inter-EMS asymmetries and which types of disturbance do not. In particular, it is important to analyse whether monetary disturbances can be a source of asymmetries or whether these inter-EMS exchange rate tensions are due only to external real disturbances.

Second, we study the interaction between the vehicle currency role and the degree of international portfolio diversification. Given that the elimination of capital controls will increase the ability of investors to diversify their equity and bond portfolios, it is important to analyse whether this will have an impact on exchange rate asymmetries.

The theoretical framework used in Grilli and Roubini (1989) allows us to analyse separately the role of the three above factors (alternative disturbances, portfolio diversification effects and reserve currency effects) in driving exchange rate asymmetries. It uses a three-country cash-in-advance model similar to those introduced in the international literature by Helpman (1981), Helpman and Razin (1979, 1982, 1984) and Lucas (1982). One can think of two of the countries as being Germany and Italy (the EMS bloc) while the third represents the non-EMS bloc (the US for simplicity). In Section 2 we first investigate empirically the existence and the extent of exchange rate asymmetries. In Sections 3 through 6 we summarise and reinterpret the theoretical results obtained in Grilli and Roubini (1989). Section 3 presents the general model for the case of imperfect capital mobility (no equity diversification, so that claims on domestic output are held only by domestic residents) and where both the US and the German currencies have a potential reserve currency role. Section 4 considers the effects on exchange rates of monetary and real shocks for the special case in which the US dollar is the only reserve currency (here marks and lire are not used for international transactions of goods and services); while Section 5 discusses the effects of the same shocks for the case where more realistically both the dollar and the mark are reserve currencies.

Section 6 starts the analysis of the effects of capital liberalisation by expanding the model to allow for different degrees of international equity diversification. Next, we consider asset diversification in the two-vehicle currency model case. Section 7 presents the empirical evidence on the asymmetries in the vehicle currency and reserve currency roles of different currencies and presents data on the degree of international diversification of asset portfolios. Section 8 presents some concluding remarks.

2   Assessing the empirical importance of asymmetries

Before presenting a formal analysis of the potential causes of inter-EMS asymmetries it is interesting to review the evidence on these asymmetries to assess the empirical importance of the phenomenon. In Table 5.1 and 5.2 we replicate and extend results obtained by Giavazzi and Giovannini on this polarisation by running regressions of the percentage change in daily bilateral mark exchange rates on percentage changes of an effective dollar index. The main differences with Giavazzi and Giovannini is that we consider two extra currencies (the Irish punt and the Australian dollar) and we use two-year longer time series continuing until May 1989. The results in Table 5.1 confirm those already found by Giavazzi and Giovannini:

(1)   There is strong evidence that a weakening of the effective US dollar exchange rate is associated with an appreciation of the Deutsche mark with respect to all the other currencies. In particular all the EMS currencies weaken with respect to the mark when the dollar is weak.

(2)   This phenomenon also strongly holds for the two extra currencies in our sample, the Irish punt and the Australian dollar.

(3)   After 1979, the polarisation with the mark is smaller for all currencies, but the reduction in polarisation is more pronounced for the currencies in the EMS than for the currencies outside the EMS.

(4)   The hypothesis that the polarisation for the EMS is larger in periods of dollar depreciation is partially correct in the 1970s (the 1977–8 period) but not the 1980s.

In Table 5.2 we try to test the hypothesis that EMS realignments have often been triggered by sudden downward movements of the dollar, as suggested by Giavazzi and Giovannini. In Table 5.2 we regress the bilateral mark exchange rates on the effective dollar for the two months prior to each of the ten EMS realignments. As Table 5.2 shows, our results do not support the hypothesis. There is a lack of polarisation in concomitance with EMS crises and realignments. This evidence does not necessarily imply that dollar movements have not been a cause of inter-EMS tensions. It is quite likely that, given the commitment to maintain the exchange rates in the EMS bands, variables other than the exchange rate (for example, foreign exchange reserves) would reflect the pressures on the EMS parities deriving from movements of the dollar.

Two aspects of these results are particularly important. First, the polarisation effect is significantly reduced for the EMS countries after the formation of the EMS; this result is consistent with the hypothesis that the EMS has been effective in reducing inter-EMS exchange rate movements.

Table 5.1. *The effective dollar and bilateral Deutsche mark exchange rates*

	Pound sterling	French franc	Belgian franc	Italian lira	Irish punt	Danish kroner	Dutch guilder	Japanese yen	Australian dollar	Canadian dollar
(1971:1:6–1973:5:31)	−0.44	−0.35	−0.46	−0.41	−0.45	−0.44	−0.39	−0.43	−0.18	−0.65
(1973:6:1–1979:3:9)	−0.63	−0.12	−0.19	−0.56	−0.63	−0.27	−0.12	−0.50	−1.04	−1.45
(1979:3:12–1989:5:17)	−0.20	−0.05	−0.07	−0.10	−0.07	0.00*	−0.04	−0.17	−0.81	−1.05
(1977:5:13–1978:10:31)	−0.31	−0.13	−0.12	−0.69	−0.31	−0.33	−0.10	0.02*	−0.86	−1.30
(1978:11:1–1981:8:5)	−0.38	−0.11	−0.11	−0.28	−0.23	−0.13	−0.04	−0.19	−0.93	−1.14
(1981:8:6–1985:3:18)	−0.21	0.01*	−0.08	−0.05*	−0.02*	−0.07	−0.06	−0.19	−0.66	−0.98
(1985:3:19–1987:12:31)	−0.18	−0.06	−0.07	−0.08*	−0.08	−0.10	−0.02	−0.23	−0.97	−1.12
(1988:1:2–1989:5:17)	−0.03*	−0.05	−0.01*	−0.09*	−0.05	0.68*	−0.01	0.03*	−0.55	−0.98

* Not significant at the 5 per confidence level.

Table 5.2. *The mark–dollar asymmetry and EMS realignments*

Pound sterling	French franc	Belgian franc	Italian lira	Irish punt	Danish kroner	Dutch guilder	Japanese yen	Australian dollar	Canadian dollar
(1979:7:24–1979:9:24)									
0.33*	− 0.16*	0.09*	− 0.67	0.36*	0.00*	0.01*	0.07*	− 0.77	− 1.19
(1979:9:30–1979:11:30)									
− 0.29*	− 0.10*	− 0.09*	− 0.09*	− 0.06*	− 0.43*	− 0.08*	− 0.15*	− 0.81	− 1.04
(1981:1:22–1981:3:22)									
− 0.51	0.14	− 0.09*	− 0.31	− 0.07*	− 0.21	− 0.05*	− 0.85	− 1.28	− 1.35
(1981:8:5–1981:10:5)									
− 0.16*	− 0.13*	− 0.11*	− 0.25*	− 0.19*	− 0.23	− 0.02*	− 0.29	− 0.99	− 1.11
(1981:12:22–1982:2:22)									
− 0.19*	− 0.18*	− 0.56*	− 0.22*	0.01*	− 0.22*	− 0.12	0.14*	− 0.99	− 0.80
(1982:4:14–1982:6:14)									
− 0.25*	0.79	0.09*	0.13*	0.12*	0.13*	− 0.13	0.05*	− 0.62	− 0.69
(1983:1:21–1983:3:21)									
− 0.30	0.34*	0.13*	0.07*	0.04*	− 0.09*	− 0.08	0.08*	0.31*	− 0.95

Table 5.2. (*cont.*)

	Pound sterling	French franc	Belgian franc	Italian lira	Irish punt	Danish kroner	Dutch guilder	Japanese yen	Australian dollar	Canadian dollar
(1985:5:21–1985:7:21)	− 0.19*	− 0.04*	− 0.02*	− 0.14*	− 0.05*	− 0.15	− 0.03*	− 0.70	− 0.61	− 1.13
(1986:2:7–1986:4:7)	− 0.50	0.02*	− 0.06*	− 0.01*	− 0.02*	− 0.01*	− 0.03*	− 0.29	− 1.19	− 1.35
(1986:11:19–1987:1:19)	− 0.69	0.05*	0.02*	0.30*	− 0.18	− 0.05*	0.00*	− 0.30*	− 1.75	− 1.25

* Not significant at the 5 per cent confidence level.

Second, while the reduction in the dollar–mark polarisation after 1979 is much stronger for the EMS currencies, one observes a substantial reduction in the polarisation also for the non-EMS currencies (Japanese yen, British pound, Canadian dollar and Australian dollar). This fact suggests that the constraints posed by a fixed exchange rate like the EMS might not be the exclusive explanation of the general reduction in the degree of polarisation after 1979. In particular, given the process of liberalisation of capital controls in Britain, Japan and Australia in the 1978–80 period, an alternative explanation of this phenomenon might be that the elimination of capital controls in these countries has increased the degree of substitutability among different assets and currencies and has therefore led to a reduction in the dollar–mark polarisation. In other words, given the liberalisation of capital controls in these countries, portfolio movements out of the dollar may not lead to an excess demand for marks but rather to symmetric increases in the demand for marks, pounds, yen and Australian dollars.

If this interpretation is correct, part of the reduction in degree of polarisation in the EMS region (in particular, the apparent lack of polarisation in the period of dollar weakness after 1985) could also be due to the progressive liberalisation of capital controls in that region (the ongoing removal of capital controls in France and Italy) rather than being only the effect of the EMS constraints. In this sense, the general reduction in polarisation in the 1980s, inside and outside the EMS, might be mostly due to the generalised process of capital liberalisation observed in the OECD area since 1980.

3   The model

In this and in the next three sections we use the model developed in Grilli and Roubini (1989) to show that the presence of vehicle currencies can be the source of the type of exchange rate asymmetries that we have documented in the previous section. The model is a cash-in-advance model similar to those introduced in the international literature by Helpman and Razin (1979, 1982, 1984), Helpman (1981), Stockman (1980), Lucas (1982) and Persson (1984).[10] It differs from traditional cash-in-advance models in a number of ways:

(1) It is a three-country model instead of the standard two-country model used in the literature.[11] Given that the focus of the analysis is the study of asymmetries deriving from disturbances external to the EMS countries, a three-country model is the minimum set necessary for our analysis.

(2) It develops a richer cash-in-advance technology that allows for a reserve and transaction role for different sub-sets of the three currencies.[12]

(3) It allows explicitly for different degrees of equity diversification across countries and analyses the implications of different degrees of capital mobility and asset diversification.[13]

The three countries in the model may be regarded as a non-EMS bloc represented by the US (country *1*) and an EMS group represented by Germany (country *2*) and Italy (country *3*).

We will describe now the structure of the model starting from the determination of the nominal side. We first define the notation of the variables as it will be used throughout the study.

Definitions
c_j^i = consumption by country *j* of the good produced in country *i*.
p_j^i = nominal price of the good produced in country *i* as expressed in the currency of country *j*.
M_j^i = amount of currency of country *i* held by residents of country *j*.
p_{ij} = relative price of good *j* in terms of good *i*.
e^{ij} = nominal exchange rate between currency *j* and currency *i* (units of currency *i* per unit of currency *j*).
G_j = public consumption of the home final good by the government of country *j*.

The goods of the three countries are imperfectly substitutable in consumption so that purchasing power parity will not hold in this model.[14] However, goods arbitrage implies that the price of each good should be equal when expressed in different currencies (i.e. the law of one price will hold). It then follows that:[15]

$$e^{ij}p_j = p_i p_{ij} \quad (i = 1, 2, 3; \quad j = 1, 2, 3) \tag{1}$$

The general cash-in-advance technology of the model is defined as follows:

(i) For domestic goods all purchases are made with the domestic currency.
(ii) For consumption of foreign goods by each of the three countries: a fraction (*k*) of the transactions are made using US dollars; a fraction (*1 − k*) of the transactions are made using Deutsche marks.

This specification of the cash-in-advance technology captures the observed fact that dollars and marks are used as currencies of denomination and transaction in the international exchange of goods and services, while the currencies of smaller EMS countries (like Italy) are not international transaction currencies.[16]

Given these definitions, the cash-in-advance constraint for country *1* (the US) will be given by the demand for dollars by US residents (M_1^1), and the demand for marks by US residents (M_1^2). The first is equal to:[17]

$$p_1 c_1^1 + ke^{12}p_2 c_1^2 + ke^{13}p_3 c_1^3 + p_1 G_1 = M_1^1 \tag{2}$$

while M_1^2 is similarly given by:

$$(1 - k)p_2 c_1^2 + (1 - k)p_2 p_{23} c_1^3 = M_1^2 \tag{3}$$

Similar cash-in-advance constraints for country 2 (Germany) and country 3 (Italy) can be derived. We can also observe that the total demand for dollars must be equal to the exogenous supply of dollars (M^1) or:

$$M_1^1 + M_2^1 + M_3^1 = M^1 \tag{4}$$

In order to solve the model in explicit form we will assume that in each country there is a representative agent whose utility depends on his or her consumption of each of the three goods produced in the three countries. It is assumed that the utility function describing the preferences of the representative agent is identical for all three countries and given by a general CES specification:[18]

$$U_i = [c_i^{1^a} + c_i^{2^a} + c_i^{3^a}]^{\frac{1}{a}} \qquad i = 1, 2, 3 \quad a \leq 1 \tag{5}$$

It is a standard feature of these cash-in-advance models that a separation exists between the real and monetary decisions of the agents.[19] We can then express the budget constraint for the representative agent of the three countries as:

$$c_i^1 + p_{12} c_i^2 + p_{13} c_i^3 = W_i \qquad i = 1, 2, 3 \tag{6}$$

where W_i represents the real private disposable income of the agent in country i (expressed in terms of good 1) and is equal to his or her real consumption (in terms of good 1) of the three goods.

In the market for good i the total demand for the good must be equal to its exogenous supply Y_i, or

$$c_1^i + G_i + c_2^i + c_3^i \equiv Y_i \tag{7}$$

After tedious substitutions we obtain that e_{12} (the US dollar/Deutsche mark exchange rate) and e_{32} (the Italian lira/Deutsche mark exchange rate) are equal to

$$e_{12} = \frac{M_1}{M_2} \frac{[A]\tilde{Y}_2^{a-1} G_2 + \{\tilde{Y}_1^a[(1-k)(\tilde{W}_2 + \tilde{W}_3)] + \tilde{Y}_2^a[\tilde{W}_2 + (1-k)(\tilde{W}_1 + \tilde{W}_3)] + \tilde{Y}_3(1-k)(\tilde{W}_1 + \tilde{W}_2)\}}{[A]\tilde{Y}_1^{a-1} G_1 + \{\tilde{Y}_1^a[\tilde{W}_1 + k(\tilde{W}_2 + \tilde{W}_3)] + \tilde{Y}_2[k(\tilde{W}_1 + \tilde{W}_3)] + \tilde{Y}_3^a k(\tilde{W}_1 + \tilde{W}_2)\}} \tag{8}$$

$$e_{32} = \frac{M_3}{M_2} \frac{[A]\tilde{Y}_2^{a-1} G_2 + \{\tilde{Y}_1^a[(1-k)(\tilde{W}_2 + \tilde{W}_3)] + \tilde{Y}_2^a[\tilde{W}_2 + (1-k)(\tilde{W}_1 + \tilde{W}_3)] + \tilde{Y}_3(1-k)(\tilde{W}_1 + \tilde{W}_2)\}}{[A]\tilde{Y}_3^{a-1} G_3 + \tilde{Y}_3^a \tilde{W}_3} \tag{9}$$

where:

$$\tilde{W}_i = a_i \tilde{Y}_1^a + \beta_i \tilde{Y}_2^a + \gamma_i \tilde{Y}_3^a \qquad i = 1, 2, 3 \tag{10}$$

$$\tilde{Y}_i = Y_i - G_i \qquad i = 1, 2, 3 \tag{11}$$

$$A = \tilde{Y}_1^a + \tilde{Y}_2^a + \tilde{Y}_3^a \tag{12}$$

and

as a_i = share of country *1* output owned by residents of country i
β_i = share of country *2* output owned by residents of country i
γ_i = share of country *3* output owned by residents of country i

4   The model solution for the case of no pooling and one reserve currency

Given our interest in the effects of capital controls on exchange rates, let us study the implications of the model in the case of limited capital mobility and one reserve currency. Given that capital controls limit the amount of equity pooling across countries, we will start from the extreme assumption of no pooling. In this case, the ownership claims on the output of each country are held only by the residents of the country.

In order to abstract, for the moment, from cases of exchange rate asymmetries due to the different reserve currency role of the Deutsche mark and the Italian lira, we consider first the case in which only one currency, the dollar, is used in international transactions; in this case the parameter k is equal to *1*. Here, marks and lire have a symmetric role in that both of them are not used in international transactions.[20] We will consider the effects of a number of disturbances (monetary and real shocks) on the equilibrium exchange rates.

In order to facilitate the understanding of the results below, we first summarise some basic results on the effects of disturbances on exchange rates in a simplified two-country version of our model. Then, we show how these standard results are modified in our more complex framework. In the simple two-country setting with no pooling and a seller's currency transaction technology, the nominal exchange rate would depend on the relative money supplies of the two countries while the terms of trade (p_{12}) would not be affected by nominal variables such as money supplies. As is well known, the effect on the nominal exchange rate of a real shock such as a permanent increase in the output of the first country is ambiguous: on the one side, the exchange rate will tend to appreciate because the increase in output in country *1* leads to an increase in demand for money in country *1*; on the other side, the exchange rate will tend to depreciate since the increase in output will cause a worsening of the terms of trade of

Example 5.1. *No pooling*

	One vehicle currency DM/$	DM/£	Two vehicle currencies DM/$	DM/£
Y_{US}	$-$ (if $a < a^*$)	$+$ (if $\tilde{g}_3 > \tilde{g}_2$)	$-$ (if $a < a^*$)	$-$
G_{US}	$+$ (if $a < 1/2$)	$-$ (if $\tilde{g}_3 > \tilde{g}_2$)	$+$ (if $a < 1/2$)	$+$
M_{US}	0	0	0	0

country 1 (an increase in p_{12}). The net effect on the exchange rate will depend on the elasticity of substitution between the two goods and on the share of government spending relative to output. In particular, it is easy to show that a necessary and sufficient condition for a dollar appreciation relative to the mark is that the parameter a in the utility function is greater than the share of public spending in output (g).

Unlike the case of an output shock, the effect of a fiscal shock on the exchange rate is unambiguous: real money demands are unaffected while the terms of trade effect is positive (p_{12} falls). It then follows that the nominal exchange rate will appreciate with certainty as long as $a < 1$ (i.e. the goods are not perfect substitutes). Also, the appreciation of the exchange rate is greater the lower is the elasticity of substitution. In fact, the lower a is, the more inelastic the demand for good 1 and the greater the terms of trade improvement necessary to clear the market for good 1 following a permanent increase in the public consumption of the good.

The results of the three-country version of the model are summarised in Example 5.1, which reports the sign of the partial derivatives of the exchange rates with respect to US output, US government spending and US money supply.

4.1   The effects of supply shocks

We are now ready to consider the effects of real disturbances in our three-country framework. We will first consider the effects of a permanent increase in Y_1, the US output. The condition for a dollar appreciation relative to the mark following an output shock in the United States differs from the similar condition for the two-country case. The condition $a > g$ is now only sufficient, and not necessary and sufficient as before; this implies that the dollar will appreciate even if $a < g$. In particular, the critical value of a (a^*) below which the dollar depreciates will be positive but lower than g ($0 < a^* < g$). The reason for this result is simple: in both cases the terms of trade effects deriving from the output shock are identical and will tend to cause a depreciation. However, in our three-country one-reserve currency case, the increase in the real money demand for dollars (that leads to a dollar appreciation) will come not just from the direct effect of the increase in Y_1 on the demand for US goods. In addition to these effects, the demand for dollars will rise because the increase in US income will lead to an increase in US demand for foreign goods (that are paid for in dollars given the one-currency assumption). The fall in the relative price of good 1 will also reduce the German demand for German goods, and the ensuing reduction in the demand for marks will also contribute to the dollar appreciation. This extra increase in the demand for dollars explains why the condition $a > g$ is only sufficient.

What is the effect of the same shock on the lira/mark exchange rate (e_{32})? It can be shown that the lira will appreciate relative to the mark if $\tilde{g}_3 > \tilde{g}_2$, where $\tilde{g}_i = (G_i/(Y_i - G_i))$. This result may be intuitively explained in the following way. The US output shock leads to a reduction in the relative price of US goods and therefore causes a fall in the consumption of German goods by German residents and Italian goods by Italian residents. Then, if G_3 is large relative to G_2, the fall in c_3^3 will reduce the demand for lire less than the fall in c_2^2 reduces the demand for marks. It then follows that the lira will appreciate relative to the mark.

In a one-reserve currency world, therefore, an output shock in the US will cause an exchange rate asymmetry. Whether or not the asymmetry will be of the type characteristic of the EMS (a weak mark relative to the lira when the dollar is strong relative to the mark), depends on the degree of substitutability of goods. If we accept that the condition for a lira/mark appreciation is likely to hold in practice because the Italian output (public spending) is lower (greater) than the German one, for the EMS asymmetry to be present we need a high degree of substitutability between US and foreign goods.

4.2 The case of demand shocks

We next consider the effects of a US demand shock in the form of a permanent increase in the public consumption of US goods by the US government. Consider first the effects of this shock on the dollar/mark exchange rate. It can be shown that a sufficient condition for a dollar/mark appreciation is $a < 1/2$. This is only a sufficient condition for obtaining a dollar appreciation following a US fiscal expansion. However, it differs from the simple result in the two-country model above because in that former case the dollar always appreciated while now the dollar will depreciate if the parameter a is greater than a critical value a^* where $1/2 < a^* < 1$. How to explain this dollar depreciation following a US fiscal expansion? The terms of trade effect is identical in both cases, and should lead to a dollar appreciation. Here, however, there is also a money demand effect that goes in the opposite direction. In particular, the fiscal shock leads to an increase in the relative price of US goods. This, in turn, reduces the demand for US goods and increases the demand for foreign goods; these effects tend to lead to a depreciation of the dollar.

Consider now the effects of the US fiscal shock on the lira/mark exchange rate. It can be shown that the effect of a fiscal shock on e_{32} is precisely the opposite of the effect of a supply shock. The result is intuitively clear: the lira/mark exchange rate depends only on the net US income $(Y_I - G_I)$ so that the effect of a US fiscal shock on e_{32} is going to be opposite to the effect of a US supply shock. Given the previous observation that Italian output is lower and public spending greater than the German case, the lira will depreciate relative to the mark following a US fiscal shock. Again, it can be concluded that a US fiscal expansion might lead to EMS exchange rate asymmetries, but these asymmetries may or may not correspond to those characterising the EMS.

4.3   The case of monetary shocks

A final important observation is required before moving to the analysis of the model with two reserve currencies. This section has shown that real disturbances (both supply and demand) external to the EMS (such as US shocks) will affect e_{32}, the lira/mark rate. However, contrary to the case of real disturbances, monetary disturbances that are external to the EMS do not affect the lira/mark rate in this model. In particular, it can be shown that US monetary shocks have no effect on the lira/mark rate; US monetary shocks therefore cannot cause exchange rate asymmetries in the EMS. This result has been obtained here for the particular case of one reserve currency and imperfect capital mobility (no asset pooling). However, the result is more general and can be replicated under alternative assumptions about the degree of capital controls and the reserve currency role of different currencies.

5   The no-pooling two-reserve currency case

We next consider the effects on the exchange rate of various disturbances in the case in which two currencies, the dollar and the mark, are used in international transactions. The results are summarised in Example 5.1.

5.1   The effects of supply shocks

The effects of a US supply shock on the dollar/mark rate are similar to those obtained in the one-reserve currency case. Now, however, the effects of Y_I on e_{12} are even more ambiguous than in the case of one reserve currency. The sign of the derivative is ambiguous because, as in the case of one currency, the terms of trade effect and the money demand effects go in opposite directions. The terms of trade effect here is unambiguous and identical to the one obtained in the one-currency case. The money demand effect is more complex. First, the increase in Y_I leads to a direct increase in the demand for dollars and will tend to appreciate the dollar. Second, the reduction in the relative price of US goods will lead to a reduction in the demand for foreign goods and an increase in the demand for US goods. Third, the increase in US income leads to an increased US demand for all goods, both domestic and foreign. Now, however, international transactions are paid both in dollars and marks: then, the smaller k, the share of US dollars in international transactions, is the smaller the demand for dollars and the stronger the tendency towards a dollar depreciation. Therefore, in the two-reserve currency model, a dollar depreciation is more likely.

In the two-reserve currency case, a depreciation of the lira relative to the mark also becomes more likely. The intuitive reason for this effect is simple: the fall in the relative price of US goods leads to a net increase in the demand for US goods by all countries. Given that the mark is an international currency while the lira is not, the net demand for the mark will tend to increase and lead to a lira depreciation.

It can then be concluded that as long as a is not too large, an increase in US output will lead to a dollar depreciation relative to the mark and a mark appreciation relative to the lira. Therefore compared to the case where the mark was not a reserve currency ($k = 1$), the weak dollar-cum-strong mark asymmetry will be more likely in the case where the mark has a role as an international reserve currency.

5.2   The effects of demand shocks

A sufficient condition for a dollar/mark appreciation following a US fiscal shock is identical to the one obtained in the one-currency case ($a < 1/2$). However, a lira appreciation relative to the mark is now more likely than in the one-currency case. In fact, recalling that the lira/mark rate depends only on net US output ($Y_I - G_I$), the effect of a US fiscal shock on e_{32} will be precisely opposite to the one of a US output shock discussed above. In particular, a lira appreciation relative to the mark is going to be likely for the same reasons as a US output shock was likely to lead to a depreciation of the lira. It then follows that, as long as $a < 1/2$, a US fiscal expansion will lead to a dollar/Deutsche mark polarisation: a strong dollar relative to the mark and a weak mark relative to the lira.

In conclusion, the introduction of the Deutsche mark as a reserve

Example 5.2. *Pooling*

	One vehicle currency		Two vehicle currencies	
	DM/$	DM/£	DM/$	DM/£
Y_{US}	−	− (if $a_2 > a_3$)	−	− (if $a > 0$)
		0 (if $a_2 = a_3$)		
G_{US}	+	+ (if $a_2 > a_3$)	+	+ (if $a > 0$)
		0 (if $a_2 = a_3$)		
M_{US}	0	0	0	0

currency in addition to the dollar increases the likelihood of exchange rate asymmetries typical of the EMS. In the case of one reserve currency, these asymmetries were possible but the effects of US shocks on the lira/mark exchange rate were quite ambiguous. The introduction of the mark as a reserve currency importantly reduces those ambiguities about the lira/mark exchange rate by introducing channels through which the demand for marks is significantly increased (or reduced). It can then be argued that the observed role of the mark as a reserve currency strengthens the possibility of exchange rate asymmetries in the EMS.

6   The effects of capital liberalisation

The discussion has been limited so far to the analysis of the effects of disturbances in the case of imperfect capital mobility. In particular, we have considered only the extreme case of no pooling of equity assets where the output of each country is owned only by the residents of the country. Will capital liberalisation exacerbate these asymmetries, or reduce them? Will a perfect pooling of equity assets eliminate these asymmetries? The answers to these questions are important in order to understand the potential effects of capital liberalisation on the inter-EMS exchange rates. The results of our analysis are summarised in Example 5.2.

6.1   The one-reserve currency case

6.1.1   The case of supply shocks
The effects of a supply shock on the dollar/mark exchange rate are hard to derive unequivocally in the general case in which the shares of equity ownership claims assume any feasible value. We have already seen in Section 4 that, even in the particular case of no pooling, the effects of a US output shock on e_{12} are ambiguous because of the opposing terms of trade and money demand effects. Here the terms of trade effect is identical

to the case of no pooling, and would lead to a dollar depreciation, but the money demand effect (that goes in the other direction) is even more complex. In fact, given that each country holds ownership claims on US output, a permanent supply shock will affect wealth not only in the US (as in the case of no pooling) but also in Germany and Italy.

However, we can obtain stronger results if we consider the particular case of perfect pooling, where the share of ownership claims on output is equally distributed across countries. The case of perfect pooling is important because it represents the extreme case of complete asset diversification across countries in the presence of complete capital mobility (the perfect pooling case is the one considered by Lucas, 1982). In the case of perfect pooling it can be shown that if the degree of substitutability among goods is small (i.e. a is below a critical value a^*), the usual money demand effect that leads to a reduction in the demand for dollars and a dollar depreciation is stronger than the terms of trade effect that leads to a dollar appreciation, so that e_{12} will increase.

The effect of the US output shock on the lira/mark rate can be derived for the more general case of partial pooling of equity claims. In particular, it can be shown that the lira will depreciate relative to the mark if the share of US assets in German portfolios (a_2) is greater than the share of US assets in Italian portfolios (a_3). This condition also implies that if the German and Italian assets are similarly pooled with respect to claims to US output, ($a_2 = a_3$) a US supply disturbance will not affect e_{32}, i.e. it will not lead to inter-EMS exchange rate asymmetries. This result suggests that as long as capital controls in smaller EMS countries prevent the agents in these countries from diversifying their portfolios towards US assets in the same way as German agents can do, exchange rate asymmetries will occur as a consequence of US output shocks. It also suggests that as the liberalisation of capital movements in the EMS will allow a more uniform and similar asset diversification in the EMS bloc, exchange rate asymmetries deriving from US output shocks will be dampened and eventually eliminated in the case of perfect asset pooling. In this sense, the model suggests that the process of liberalisation of capital controls will reduce rather than exacerbate inter-EMS asymmetries.

6.1.2   The case of demand shocks

Quite comparably to the case of a US output shock, the effects of US fiscal shocks on the dollar/mark exchange rate are ambiguous. The dollar may appreciate or depreciate depending on the value of a and the distribution of equity claims among the three countries. In the particular case of perfect pooling, some more specific results can be obtained: in particular, we get that the dollar will appreciate relative to the mark if $a \leq 1$. This condition implies that, with the exclusion of the case of perfect substitutability ($a = 1$) when e_{12} does not change, the dollar will always appreciate following a US fiscal expansion. In this case of perfect pooling, the previous ambiguities about the effects of US fiscal expansions on the dollar exchange rate are therefore eliminated.

The effects of the US output shock on the lira/mark rate can easily be derived for the general case of partial pooling of equity claims by observing that e_{32} depends on the US net output ($Y_1 - G_1$). The effect of G_1 on e_{32} will therefore be the opposite of the effect of Y_1. It then follows that, if liberalisation of capital movements allows German and Italian portfolios to be similarly diversified towards dollar assets ($a_2 = a_3$), US fiscal disturbances will not affect the lira/mark exchange rate and therefore will not be a source of exchange rate asymmetries. Conversely, capital controls that prevent such a diversification will increase the degree of inter-EMS exchange rate asymmetries.

The main result of this section is that capital controls limiting the degree of international diversification of asset portfolios are a cause of exchange rate asymmetries in the EMS. Supply and demand disturbances external to the EMS affect the lira/mark rate as long as the share of US assets held by Germans is different from the share held by Italians. This analysis then suggests that these asymmetries will be significantly reduced (or eliminated) if the liberalisation of capital movements in the EMS leads to a more balanced international diversification of the portfolios of the EMS countries. These results, however, have been obtained for the case where the dollar is the only reserve currency. We will next consider whether perfect pooling eliminates inter-EMS asymmetries in the case where the mark also has a reserve currency role.

6.2   Exchange rate asymmetries where the mark is a reserve currency

On the basis of our previous discussion, we already know that the lack of asset diversification plays an important role in generating these asymmetries. In order to isolate the specific role of reserve currencies in causing asymmetries, we will consider only cases of perfect asset pooling. As we know from the previous section, in the case of one reserve currency the assumption of perfect pooling is enough to eliminate movements in the inter-EMS exchange rates caused by US disturbances. Does this result hold in the case where the mark is an additional reserve currency?

Where perfect pooling is holding, the introduction of the mark as an additional reserve currency does not change the qualitative results regarding the effects of real disturbances from the US on e_{12}.

Consider now the effect of a change in the US net output $\tilde{Y}_1$ on e_{32} (since e_{32} depends only on this net output, the exercise can be alternatively thought of as a permanent increase in Y_1 or a permanent reduction in G_1).

It can be shown that, for $a > 0$, an increase in $\tilde{Y}_I$ will lead to a depreciation of the lira relative to the mark if $k < 1$. This result implies that perfect pooling will not eliminate inter-EMS exchange rate asymmetries if the Deutsche mark has a reserve currency role that the Italian lira does not have. Only in the special case where the dollar is the only reserve currency ($k = 1$), the derivative will be 0 and US shocks will not affect the lira/mark rate. The reasons for this persistence of inter-EMS asymmetries with perfect pooling are clear. Changes in US net output affect relative prices and the import demand for the three goods. When the mark is a reserve currency, the changes in import demand affect the demand for marks because the mark is used in international transactions. Conversely, the lira is not a reserve currency so that the demand for lire is not affected by these changes in import demands. It then follows that US shocks will affect differently the demand for marks and lire and the lira/mark exchange rate will change even if there is perfect pooling of equity claims.

This result has important implications for the EMS because of the particular and unique role of the Deutsche mark as an international reserve currency (among the EMS currencies, only the French franc has a similar, if limited, reserve currency role). It suggests that, while the current process of liberalisation of capital movements in the EMS might contribute to the reduction of exchange rate asymmetries deriving from disturbances external to the EMS, these asymmetries will persist even after this liberalisation has been accomplished. The particular, and so far unique, role of the Deutsche mark as an international currency among the EMS currencies is likely to remain a cause of inter-EMS tensions that have their source in disturbances external to the EMS area. It also suggests that only the future growth of the ECU as a full international reserve currency might prevent the dollar-driven inter-EMS exchange rate asymmetries that have recurrently buffetted the EMS since its inception in 1979.

7   Empirical evidence on vehicle and reserve currencies and the international diversification of asset portfolios

7.1   Vehicle currencies in international trade

The above theoretical analysis in the chapter suggests that asymmetric effects on the inter-EMS exchange rates may occur even in the presence of perfect pooling of assets whenever the EMS currencies have different vehicle currency roles in international trade. In particular, if the Deutsche mark has a vehicle role in international trade transactions that other EMS currencies do not have, shocks that should otherwise have a neutral effect on the inter-EMS exchange rates will actually affect these inter-EMS parities.

The issue of the currency used in the invoicing of exports has been formally analysed in a number of papers.[21] Rao and Magee (1980) prove an 'irrelevance proposition' according to which the currency of denomination in exports and imports should be irrelevant. In fact, the equilibrium price of the good should incorporate the different foreign exchange risks faced by exporters and importers because of the choice of the currency of invoice. However, this result is true only if both parties have the same degree of risk aversion. McKinnon (1979), instead, argues that exporters will prefer invoicing in their own currency because importers can raise the domestic price of the imported good if an unexpected devaluation occurs while exporters cannot change *ex post* the costs of their production inputs. This idea was rigorously formalised by Bilson (1983). Also, as argued by Cornell (1980) the result of Rao and Magee is valid only when exchange rate variations are due to relative price changes. In a more recent contribution, Bissaro and Hamaui (1989, p. 2) criticise the approach of Baron (1976) and Giovannini (1985) because these contributions 'fail to specify in a proper way the mechanism of bargaining between the exporter and the importer'. They then present an explicit intertemporal model of the price and invoicing choice where the exchange rate risk has an important role for both the exporter and the importer. Bissaro and Hamaui (1989) find that, while the 'irrelevance proposition' is true in the long run, in the short run exporters and importers will face asymmetrical contract risks. The choice of the currency of invoicing will therefore depend on the expected exchange rate, its volatility and the degree of risk aversion of exporters and importers.

In more general terms, we need to understand why we observe the existence of vehicle currencies in the first place. Krugman (1980) and Chrystal (1984) build models that explain the existence of vehicle currencies on the basis of transaction costs and increasing returns to scale in the transaction technology. Under the assumption that transaction costs are inversely proportional to volume in each bilateral currency market, a vehicle currency will emerge whenever indirect exchange costs through the vehicle are less than direct exchange costs between two non-vehicle currencies. Black (1989) extends the model of Chrystal by constructing an explicit model of transaction costs based on volatility and volume and models the interaction between falling transactions costs and increasing vehicle currency use.

What is the empirical evidence about the vehicle currency role of different national currencies? The available evidence suggests a significant vehicle currency role for four currencies, the US dollar, the German mark, the Swiss franc and the British pound. Consider, for example, the

Table 5.3a. *Currencies used in world trade*

Share of each country's exports in:

Country	Dollars	DM	Sterling	French francs	Own
Austria	10.4	24.2	2	1.2	51.9
Belgium	12.5	17.9	2.6	13	42.2
Denmark	16	12	8	1.3	51
Finland	27.2	9.4	9.9	2.8	2.4
France	11.6	10.2	3.2	62.4	62.4
Germany	7.2	82.3	1.5	2.8	82.3
Ireland	21.9	1.5	40	0	23.5
Italy	31.1	21.5	2.7	6.4	31.3
Netherlands	16.5	21.7	4.2	5.4	43.5
Norway	28	9	22	1	
Sweden	14.1	4.8	4.6	0.7	67.4
Switzerland	7.1	7.8		1.2	82.8
United Kingdom	17	3	76	2	76
Other OECD Eur.	38	6	6	4	
Canada	85	0.2	1	0.1	
United States	98	1	1		98
Japan	61.5	1.9	0.9	0.3	32.7
Australia	70	1	1	1	
Centrally planned	67	13	5	2	
Oil exporters	100	0	0	0	
Other LDCs	85	0	15	0	
Non-OECD develop.	85	2	7	3	
World	54.8	14.4	7.5	6.1	

Source: Page (1981) Table 1.

figures in Tables 5.3a and 5.3b. The US dollar share as the currency of invoicing in exports and imports is very significant for a number of countries and regions. On the exports side, the dollar's share as the invoicing currency is over 2/3 in Canada, the United States, Japan, Australia, centrally planned economies, oil exporters, other developing countries and non-OECD developed countries. Among the other OECD countries, the dollar share is large for Italy, Finland, Norway and the other smaller European OECD countries. On the import side, the US dollar share is high not only among oil exporters, centrally planned economies and LDCs but also among most OECD countries. In fact, as many primary commodities imported by the OECD bloc (oil for example) are priced in dollars in international commodity markets, the dollar

Table 5.3b. *Currencies used in world trade*

Share of each country's imports in:

Country	Dollars	DM	Sterling	French francs	Own
Austria	17	39.4	2.3	1.8	25.1
Belgium	23.4	18.3	4.9	10.5	28.4
Denmark	27	17	5	1.9	27
Finland	56.1	9.7	6.2	1	2.7
France	28.7	14.1	3.8	35.8	35.8
Germany	33.1	42.8	3.1	3.3	42.8
Ireland	10.5	3.8	53.4	1.4	26.9
Italy	50.6	20.2	5.1	6.8	9.1
Netherlands	29.4	22.9	4.7	4.4	27.9
Norway	30	12	12	3	
Sweden	20	19.7	10.3	2.1	25.7
Switzerland	27	24	5	6	38
United Kingdom	29	9	38	5	38
Other OECD Eur.	50	11	11	5	
Canada	95	1	2	1	
United States	85	4.1	1.5	1	85
Japan	93	2	2	1	2
Australia	52	14	9	4	
Centrally planned	58	13	4	6	
Oil exporters	50	10	8	7	4
Other LDCs	72	7	4	6	
Non-OECD develop.	52	14	9	4	
World	54.3	13.9	6.9	6.4	

Source: Page (1981) Table 1.

share on the import side will tend to be high for all the industrialised countries.

The importance of the dollar as a vehicle currency is summarised in Table 5.4: while the US share in total world exports is only 11.7 per cent, the share of the dollar as an invoicing currency in export trade is equal to 54.8 per cent. Also, 32 percentage points of this 54.8 per cent share is accounted by 'third country' use.[22] As evident from Table 5.4 only the German mark, the British pound and the Swiss franc have a similar vehicle currency role. For Germany the mark share in exports is equal to 14.4 per cent while Germany's share in world exports is only 11.1 per cent. The corresponding shares for Britain are 7.5 per cent versus 5.9 per cent, while they are 2.1 per cent versus 1.7 per cent for the Swiss franc. All the

Table 5.4. *International use of currencies*

Country	Country share in world exports	Currency share in exports
Dollar	11.7	54.8
Deutsche mark	11.1	14.4
Sterling	5.9	7.5
French franc	6.3	6.4
Netherlands guilder	4.1	3
Belgian franc	3.6	2.6
Yen	6.6	2.3
Swiss franc	1.7	2.1
Italian lira	4.7	1.9
Swedish krona	1.8	1.7
Schilling	1	0.8
Danish krone	0.9	0.8
Irish punt	0.5	0.3
Finnish markka	0.7	0

Source: Page (1981) Table 2.

other countries have currency shares in exports that are lower than their country share in world exports.[23] In particular, among the major exporting countries, Japan and Italy have a currency share in exports that is significantly lower than their share in world exports.[24] It should also be observed that the role of the British pound as a reserve currency is mostly due to the fact that some primary commodities are priced in pounds (15 per cent of developing countries' exports are priced in pounds). The German mark, instead, owes its role of reserve currency to the fact that it is significantly used in the export invoicing of many European countries. This evidence is therefore consistent with the hypothesis in the chapter that the US dollar and the German mark have a vehicle currency role that the other EMS currencies do not have. Asymmetries in the inter-EMS parities deriving from these vehicle currency asymmetries are therefore quite possible.

It should be observed that the above data regarding the invoicing currencies in exports and imports refer to the late 1970s (mostly the 1978–80 period). Data on the invoicing currency of exports and imports for more recent years are available only for a selected group of countries (the United States, Germany, the United Kingdom, France, Japan, Italy, OPEC) and are presented in Tables 5.5 and 5.6 for imports. The data suggest that the currency denomination of exports and imports is quite stable between 1980 and 1987: the only main changes are the increase in own-currency share in the invoicing of imports for Japan, France and Italy and the reduction in the dollar share in OPEC's imports.

Table 5.5. *Share of currencies in exports*

1980	Dollar	Dmark	Yen	Pound	Franc	Lira
Share of currency	0.572	0.168	0.336	0.085	0.080	0.027
Share of world exports	0.117	0.102	0.069	0.058	0.061	0.04
Share of group exports	0.193	0.168	0.114	0.096	0.101	0.067
1987	**Dollar**	**Dmark**	**Yen**	**Pound**	**Franc**	**Lira**
Share of currency	0.451	0.225	0.0629	0.09	0.089	0.046
Share of world exports	0.108	0.125	0.098	0.055	0.063	0.049
Share of group exports	0.195	0.226	0.177	0.1	0.11	0.089

Source: Elaboration of data from Page (1981), Black (1989) and IMF–IFS.

The dollar share in exports has declined from 57.2 per cent in 1980 to 45.0 per cent in 1987 mostly because of the collapse of oil exports that are almost completely priced in dollars. Conversely the share of the German mark and the yen has increased, the first from 16.7 per cent to 22.4 per cent and the second from 3.3 per cent to 6.2 per cent. On the imports side, the picture is similar: the US dollar, German mark, British pound and French franc appear as vehicle currencies in imports while the yen and the Italian lira do not. The decline in the dollar share between 1980 and 1987 and the corresponding increase in the mark and yen shares is also a feature of the imports figures.

Finally, one can observe that the move from a world with a single vehicle currency (the US dollar) to one with many vehicle currencies (dollar, mark and, perhaps, yen) suggest that the asymmetries in inter-

Table 5.6. *Share of currencies in imports*

1980	Dollar	Dmark	Yen	Pound	Franc	Lira
Share of currency	0.563	0.138	0.009	0.071	0.074	0.023
Share of world imports	0.133	0.097	0.073	0.059	0.069	0.051
Share of group imports	0.24	0.176	0.132	0.108	0.126	0.093
1987	**Dollar**	**Dmark**	**Yen**	**Pound**	**Franc**	**Lira**
Share of currency	0.486	0.185	0.033	0.073	0.092	0.042
Share of world imports	0.175	0.094	0.062	0.063	0.065	0.052
Share of group imports	0.317	0.171	0.113	0.115	0.118	0.09

Source: Elaboration of data from Page (1981), Black (1989) and IMF–IFS.

EMS exchange rates deriving from the vehicle currency role of the German mark may be now more important than they were in the 1970s.

7.2   Official foreign exchange reserves

The central role of the US dollar, German mark and British pound as reserve and vehicle currencies is also highlighted by the data on the currency composition of official foreign exchange reserves.

The main trends in the currency composition of foreign exchange reserves are presented in Table 5.7. The share of reserves denominated in US dollars is the largest, but has declined from 78.4 per cent in 1973 to 66.2 per cent in 1986. Conversely, the share held in German marks has

Table 5.7. *Share of national currencies in official holdings of foreign exchange*

	1973	1976	1980	1981	1986
All countries					
US dollar	78.4	78.8	68.8	71.5	66.2
Pound sterling	6.5	2.2	2.9	2.2	2.8
Deutsche mark	5.5	8.2	15	13	15
French franc	0.9	2	1.7	1.5	1.2
Yen	n.a.	2.5	4.4	4	7.6
Unspecified	8.7	6.2	7.4	7.5	7.2
Industrial countries					
US dollar		87	77.6	78.8	68.8
Pound sterling		1.8	0.8	0.7	1.6
Deutsche mark		4.4	14.4	13	17.8
French franc		0.5	0.5	0.5	0.6
Yen		1.9	3.5	3.8	8.1
Unspecified		4.3	3.2	3.2	3.1
Developing countries					
US dollar		71.9	59.8	64.1	62.3
Pound sterling		2.4	5	3.6	4.6
Deutsche mark		11.5	15.5	12.9	10.7
French franc		3.3	2.9	2.5	2.2
Yen		3	5.3	4.9	6.8
Unspecified		7.9	11.5	12	13.5

Source: Dooley, Lizondo and Mathieson (1989); Black (1985) for 1973 figures.

increased from 5.5 per cent to 15 per cent. The yen share has increased from 2.5 per cent in 1976 to 7.6 per cent in 1986, but it still remains substantially below the German share. The data also show a significant decrease of the pound sterling share, from 6.5 per cent to 2.8 per cent. These general trends (a reduction in the US dollar share, an increase in the mark and yen share) are even more striking when one looks at the figure for the industrialised countries only. Here, the US dollar share falls from 87 per cent in 1976 to 68.8 per cent in 1986 while there is a significant increase in the shares held in marks (from 4.4 per cent to 17.8 per cent) and in yen (from 1.9 per cent to 8.1 per cent).

The differential in the shares of the German mark and the Japanese yen can be explained by the Japanese authorities' attempts in the 1970s to resist the internationalisation of the yen as a reserve asset and the later liberalisation of capital movements in Japan (1979–80) compared with Germany (early 1970s). Table 5.7 shows that, while the German mark share rose steadily in the period considered, the yen share increased significantly only in the 1980s after the elimination of capital controls in Japan.

A number of models have been proposed to explain the currency composition of foreign exchange reserves.[25] Some authors have used (and tested) a standard 'mean–variance approach' that suggests a comparison between the expected returns and the risks associated with holding particular reserve assets (see for example Clark, 1970; Kelly, 1970; Ben-Bassat, 1980; Macedo, 1980, 1982; and Horii, 1986).[26] Alternatively, the 'transaction approach' suggests that the currency composition of foreign reserves will depend on the transaction activities (and their costs) of the monetary authorities in the foreign exchange markets. In particular, Heller and Knight (1978) and Dooley, Lizondo and Mathieson (1989) find evidence that transaction variables are more important than the risk and return variables in explaining the currency composition of official reserves:[27] 'countries increased the proportion of their foreign exchange reserves held as a given reserve currency if they pegged their exchange rate to that currency or if the reserve center was an important trading partner'.[28] This evidence suggests that the 'transaction' variables that determine the vehicle currency role of certain monies are the same that affect the currency composition of foreign exchange reserves. This explains the close correlation between *vehicle* currency shares in trade and *reserve* currency shares in the portfolios of central banks.

7.3   *Evidence on international asset diversification (pooling)*

The model presented above suggests that inter-EMS asymmetries might be also due to the absence (or limited size) of international diversification

Table 5.8. *Foreign assets and liabilities: all assets, as a ratio of domestic assets' cumulative flows, per cent*

	1970–9			1980–6		
	Share of OECD financial wealth	Foreign liabil./ Domest. assets	Foreign assets/ Domest. assets	Share of OECD financial wealth	Foreign liabil./ Domest. assets	Foreign assets/ Domest. assets
US	32.6	4.7	5.3	35.2	5.6	2.8
Japan	18.8	2.4	3.5	19.2	7.2	11.3
Germany	7.4	10.1	12.6	5.9	14.1	17.9
France	6.8	11.9	11.6	6.6	10.5	8.8
UK	7.5	30.6	30.3	8.1	28.3	31.9
Italy	6.9	5.1	5.7	5.8	7.2	5.7
Canada	4.2	9.8	5.1	3.6	14.2	9.8
Netherlands	2.4	15.3	18.6	1.6	11.8	21.9
Belgium	1.8	20.2	20.3	2.4	39.9	34.9
Sweden	1.7	8.6	5.3	1.6	9.7	5.9
Spain	2.4	8.9	6.5	2.2	6	4.5
Finland	0.5	11.8	6.7	0.7	14.5	11
Average (unweighted)		11.6	11		14.1	13.9

Source: Golub (1990).

of asset portfolios. When the degree of international pooling of assets is not complete, economic disturbances exogenous to the EMS area will affect inter-EMS exchange rates because of the differential effects of these disturbances on the wealth of the various European countries.

Figures on the degree of international diversification of asset portfolios are still limited. One attempt to estimate the stock of gross foreign assets and liabilities of OECD countries is that of Golub (1990). The figures constructed by Golub (1990) reject the hypothesis of international asset diversification. Countries tend to hold mostly domestic assets and liabilities and the share of foreign assets (and liabilities) is very small. Some summary results are presented in Table 5.8. The data show an increase in the degree of international asset diversification as the share of foreign assets increased from 11.6 per cent to 14.1 per cent between the 1970s and the 1980–6 period and the share of foreign assets increased from 11 per cent to 13.9 per cent between these two periods. Also, 75 per cent of the 12 OECD countries in the sample show an increase in asset diversification between the two periods. However, these shares are still very far from those required for a perfect pooling of assets across countries; even the

Table 5.9. *Foreign assets and liabilities: bonds, as a ratio of domestic assets' cumulative flows, per cent*

	1970–9			1980–5		
	Share of OECD bond issues	Foreign liabil./ Domest. assets	Foreign assets/ Domest. assets	Share of OECD bond issues	Foreign liabil./ Domest. assets	Foreign assets/ Domest. assets
US	43.5	1.3	4	46.4		1.2
Japan	18.5	4.2	n.a.	18.3		n.a.
Germany	6.5	5.5	2.9	5.9		17.8
France	3.4	13	6.4	4.6		0.2
UK	3.8	9.3	1.8	4.3		67.2
Italy	7.5	0.5	1.2	4.9		0.5
Canada	5	28.7	– 0.1	3.7		7
Netherlands	0.7	34.7	6.7	1.2		24.3
Belgium	0.5	1.5	11.5	0.5		18.5
Sweden	2.4	12.2	0	2.1		1.2
Spain	0.8	0.2	0	0.7		5.5
Finland	0.2	50.2	12.7	0.3		3.7
Average (unweighted)		13.4	4.3		17.1	13.4

Source: Golub (1990).

countries with the largest degree of international asset diversification (Germany, the United Kingdom, the Netherlands and Belgium) have shares of foreign assets (liabilities) that are below one-third of domestic assets.

As observed by Golub, looking at aggregates of all assets might be misleading because these include banking flows that are difficult to classify between domestic and foreign. Disaggregated data for bonds and equities, presented in Tables 5.9 and 5.10, suggest a somewhat different picture. The data for bonds are consistent with those for total assets: they show an increase in portfolio diversification over time and a significant share of foreign bond liabilities (or assets) for Germany, the United Kingdom, the Netherlands, Belgium and Finland.

The data for equities suggest a much greater degree of international asset diversification. The degree of diversification is very high for the Netherlands, Germany and the United Kingdom (these last two especially with regard to foreign assets) and growing for Japan, Belgium and Spain.

The above evidence on the small degree of international portfolio diversification is puzzling because economic theory suggest that portfolio

Table 5.10. *Foreign assets and liabilities: equities, as a ratio of domestic assets' cumulative flows, per cent*

	1970–9			1980–5		
	Share of OECD equity issues	Foreign liabil./ Domest. assets	Foreign assets/ Domest. assets	Share of OECD equity issues	Foreign liabil./ Domest. assets	Foreign assets/ Domest. assets
US	22.2	24.3	2.8	18.8	24	7.8
Japan	10.4	− 2.2	n.a.	5.9	11.5	n.a.
Germany	6.7	40.3	60.4	4.8	63.7	79.6
France	15.1	25.5	25.5	22	12.3	10.7
UK	6.7	36.8	70.8	12.1	31.3	105.8
Italy	10.1	9.6	8	10.1	3.3	18.6
Canada	5.2	0	n.a.	8.3	4.9	n.a.
Netherlands	3.5	72.3	163.9	2	92.8	156.4
Belgium	2.1	1.6	12.3	1.8	14.4	17
Sweden	2.1	0.8	21.3	2.4	6.5	19.1
Spain	6.3	17.6	6.6	3.1	40.4	10.4
Finland	2.4	2.7	5.5	1.7	2.9	12.3
Average (unweighted)		19.1	37.7		25.7	43.8

Source: Golub (1990).

diversification leads to an international pooling of national consumption risks.[29] How, then, to explain the modest amount of international pooling of assets? Capital controls that limit the degree of international asset diversification can be only part of the answer. In fact, international diversification appears to be small also in countries like the United States, Japan, the United Kingdom and Germany that have eliminated capital controls. Other factors must account for the apparent investors' preference for home assets and liabilities.

Cole and Obstfeld (1989) suggest that 'the direct welfare gains from cross border portfolio diversification . . . are likely to be quite small'. If the gains from diversification are small, then even minor restrictions to asset trade might eliminate them completely. The reason why welfare gains from diversification might be small is that 'fluctuations in international terms of trade may play an important role in automatically pooling national economic risks, since they contribute to a negative correlation between a country's relative output growth rate and its terms of trade' (Cole and Obstfeld, 1989, p. 4).

The same authors suggest that the prevalence of industry-specific shocks compared with country-specific shocks reduces the potential gains from international asset diversification. However, as they point out, the evidence in Stockman (1988) implies that a nation-specific shock may be important suggesting potential welfare benefits from international pooling of assets.

It can be concluded that capital controls and industry-specific shocks are not sufficient to explain the small degree of international diversification of asset portfolios that is observed in the data. Further theoretical and empirical work is required to explain the above stylised facts.

8   Conclusions

This chapter presented a theoretical model explaining inter-EMS exchange rate asymmetries driven by disturbances external to the EMS. The main results of the study are that demand and supply shocks external to the EMS can affect the inter-EMS exchange rates if the degree of international diversification of asset portfolios is limited and if some currencies in the EMS have a vehicle and reserve currency role that other currencies do not have. The empirical evidence in the chapter confirms the existence of asymmetries or dollar–mark polarisation, inside and outside the EMS. Moreover, the chapter presents evidence that the degree of international pooling of assets and liabilities is still limited in the OECD area. Finally, it is shown that the US dollar, the German mark, and, in a minor measure, the British pound, have a vehicle and reserve currency role that other EMS currencies do not have.

The implications of these results are twofold. First, the liberalisation of capital controls in the EMS, by allowing a greater degree of international pooling of asset and liability positions, should reduce rather than increase inter-EMS tensions. From this point of view the liberalisation should facilitate the objective of maintaining exchange rate stability in the EMS area. It should, however, be observed that the model presented in the paper does not consider excess volatility of exchange rates driven by non-fundamental factors. If one believes that greater capital mobility will lead to such speculative volatility of exchange rates, second best arguments in favour of limited capital controls can be presented.

Second, while increased liberalisation of capital movements may reduce inter-EMS tensions, a fundamental asymmetry in the system persists. This asymmetry is the increasing vehicle and reserve currency role of the German mark. This is an independent and increasing source of potential inter-EMS tensions since the level of the exchange rate is affected by the relative role of different currencies in international trade transactions. In a minor measure, only the French franc has such a vehicle role among the EMS currencies. The particular, and so far almost unique, role of the

Deutsche mark as an international currency among the EMS currencies is likely to remain a cause of inter-EMS tensions that have their source in disturbances external to the EMS area. It also suggests that only the future growth of the ECU as a full international reserve and vehicle currency may prevent the dollar-driven inter-EMS exchange rate asymmetries that have recurrently buffeted the EMS since its inception in 1979.

Notes

We thank Rudiger Dornbusch and Rony Hamaui for helpful comments.
1 See for example Giavazzi and Giovannini (1986, 1989), Frankel (1986b) and Marston (1985).
2 Giavazzi and Giovannini (1989) define this as the 'dollar–Deutsche mark polarization view'. These authors analyse in detail the empirical evidence on this issue.
3 See Frankel (1986a) for a test of this hypothesis.
4 See Marston (1985) for a model where imperfect asset substitutability drives a result of this type.
5 See Giavazzi and Pagano (1986), and Giavazzi and Giovannini (1989).
6 We will not discuss here the optimality of fixed exchange rates in an area like the EMS.
7 Capital controls might also be justified if exchange rates are not driven only by fundamentals. If bubbles or non-fundamental changes in expectations lead to 'excess volatility' of exchange rates and if this excess volatility has effects on real variables, capital controls or other restriction to short-term 'speculative' capital transactions might be welfare improving. See Tobin (1976) and Dornbusch (1986) on this issue.
8 See Giavazzi and Giovannini (1989) for a good discussion.
9 See Claassen and Wyplosz (1982).
10 For a survey of this literature see Kimbrough (1987).
11 See Helpman (1981), Helpman and Razin (1979, 1982, 1984), Lucas (1982), Persson (1984).
12 In the traditional formulations of Helpman and Razin (1982), Stockman (1980) and Lucas (1982) it is assumed that purchases of goods are performed only with the seller's currency. Helpman and Razin (1984) consider the other extreme where purchases of goods take place only with the buyer's currency. Finally, Helpman and Razin (1985) introduce cash-in-advance constraints in commodity as well as in asset markets.
13 In the traditional formulations of the cash-in-advance model the assumption is either the one of perfect pooling of equity assets as in Lucas (1982), or the other extreme of no pooling, as in Helpman (1981), and Helpman and Razin (1982, 1984). Here we formulate the general case where the degree of pooling may vary among these extremes and consider the extreme cases as special cases of the analysis.
14 Helpman (1981), and Helpman and Razin (1984, 1985) assume perfect substitution of domestic and foreign goods in consumption so that PPP holds. Helpman and Razin (1982) introduce a non-traded good in the analysis while Lucas (1984) considers a two-good model where the two goods are imperfectly substitutable in consumption.

15 Time subscripts are missing through the chapter since we consider only the steady-state solutions and comparative statics exercises. The equilibria we will solve below can then be thought of as the steady-state solutions of more general dynamic cash-in-advance models as those solved by Helpman (1981), and Helpman and Razin (1982, 1984).

16 This general specification is flexible enough to allow for the case where the US dollar is the only international reserve currency (when $k = 1$) or the other extreme where only the mark is used in international transactions ($k = 0$).

17 In this type of cash-in-advance models, it can be shown that under quite general conditions the nominal interest rate is positive so that the cash-in-advance constraint is always binding with equality. Agents facing positive nominal interest rates do not hold idle cash balances, and the velocity of money is unity. For modifications of this basic set-up see Lucas (1984) and Svensson (1985a, 1985b).

18 For $a = 0$, the elasticity of substitution ϵ between any pair of goods is equal to 1, and we collapse to the Cobb–Douglas case. Also, $\epsilon > $ or < 1 as $a > $ or < 0. For $a = 1$, we obtain the linear utility case where the elasticity of substitution is infinite.

19 See Helpman (1981) for example.

20 The case considered here might be taken as representing the situation during the Bretton Woods period when the US dollar was the dominating world currency.

21 This brief survey relies on Bissaro and Hamaui (1988) who present a broader survey of this literature.

22 See Page (1981) p. 61.

23 In the case of France the two shares are practically identical.

24 We will discuss the Japanese and Italian cases in more detail below.

25 See Black (1985) and Dooley, Lizondo and Mathieson (1989) for a more systematic survey of these models.

26 See Dooley (1986) for a critical discussion of the difficulties with the mean–variance approach to the portfolio choice of central banks among different reserve assets.

27 Authors like Ben-Bassat (1980) and Macedo (1980) who have calculated 'optimal portfolios' of reserve assets on the basis of a mean–variance approach have found that OECD countries hold dollar shares in their portfolios that are much larger than the optimal ones. This is indirect evidence that transaction factors might be more important than risk and expected return in explaining reserve shares.

28 See Dooley, Lizondo and Mathieson (1989) p. 389.

29 See Lucas (1984).

References

Baron, D. P. (1976) 'Fluctuating Exchange Rates and the Pricing of Exports', *Economic Inquiry*, **13(3)**: 25–38.

Ben-Bassat, A. (1980) 'The Optimal Composition of Foreign Exchange Reserves', *Journal of International Economics*, **10** (May): 285–95.

Bilson, J. F. O. (1983) 'The Choice of an Invoice Currency in International Transactions', in J. S. Bhandari and B.H. Putnam (eds), *Economic Interdependence and Flexible Exchange Rates*, Cambridge, Mass.: MIT Press: 384–401.

Bissaro, G. and R. Hamaui (1988) 'The Choice of Invoice Currency in An Inter-temporal Model of Price Setting', *Giornale degli Economisti e Annali di Economia*, **3–4**: 139–61.

Black, S. (1985) 'International Money and International Monetary Arrangements', in R. W. Jones and P. B. Kenen (eds), *Handbook of International Economics*, vol. 2: 1153–93, Amsterdam: North-Holland.

Black, S. (1989) 'Transaction Costs and Vehicle Currencies' Chapel Hill: University of Carolina (September) (mimeo).

Chrystal, K. A. (1964) 'On the Theory of International Money', in J. Black and G. S. Dorrance (eds), *Problems of International Finance*, New York: St Martin's Press.

Claassen, E. M. and C. Wyplosz (1982) 'Capital Controls: Some Principles and the French Experience', *Annales de l'INSEE*, **47/48**.

Clark, P. B. (1970) 'Optimum International Reserves and the Speed of Adjustment', *Journal of Political Economy*, **75**: 356–76.

Cole, H.-L. and M. Obstfeld (1989) 'Commodity Trade and International Risk-sharing: How Much do Financial Markets Matter?', *NBER Working Paper*, **3027**.

Cornell, B. (1980) 'The Denomination of Foreign Trade Contracts Once Again', *Journal of Finance and Quantitative Analysis*, **15** (November): 933–45.

Dooley, M. (1986) 'An Analysis of the Management of the Currency Composition of Reserve Assets and External Liabilities of Developing Countries', in R. Z Aliber (ed.), *The Reconstruction of International Monetary Arrangements*, New York: Macmillan.

Dooley, M. P., J. S. Lizondo and D.J. Mathieson (1989) 'The Currency Composition of Foreign Exchange Reserves', *IMF Staff Papers*, **36(2)** (June): 385–434.

Dornbusch, R. (1986) 'Flexible Exchange Rates and Excess Capital Mobility', *Brookings Papers on Economic Activity*, **1**, 209–26.

Frankel, J. (1986a) 'The Implications of Mean–Variance Optimization for Four Questions in International Finance', *Journal of International Money and Finance*, **5**.

Frankel, J. (1986b) 'Comments on Williamson, Giavazzi and Giovannini', in A. Giovannini and R. Dornbusch (eds), *Europe and the Dollar*, Torino: Istituto Bancario San Paolo di Torino.

Giavazzi, F. and A. Giovannini (1986) 'The EMS and the Dollar', *Economic Policy*, **2**.

Giavazzi, F. and A. Giovannini (1989) *Limiting Exchange Rate Flexibility: The European Monetary System*, Cambridge, Mass.: MIT Press.

Giavazzi, F. and M. Pagano (1985) 'Capital Controls and the European Monetary System', in *Capital Controls and Foreign Exchange Legislation*, occasional paper, Euromobiliare, Milan.

Giovannini, A. (1985) 'Exchange Rates and Traded Goods Prices', Columbia University (unpublished).

Golub, S. (1990) 'International Capital Mobility: Net versus Gross Stock and Flows', *Journal of International Money and Finance* **4**.

Greenwood, J. and K. P. Kimbrough (1987) 'An Investigation in the Theory of Foreign Exchange Controls', *Canadian Journal of Economics*, **XX(2)**: 271–88.

Grilli, V. and N. Roubini (1989) 'Vehicle Currencies and Exchange Rates', Yale University (May) (mimeo).

Heller, H. R. and M. Knight (1978) 'Reserve-Currency Preferences of Central Banks', *Princeton Essays in International Finance*, **131**, Princeton University.

Helpman, E. (1981) 'An Exploration in the Theory of Exchange-Rate Regimes', *Journal of Political Economy*, **89(51)**: 865–90.

Helpman, E. and A. Razin (1979) 'Towards a Consistent Comparison of Alternative Exchange Rate Systems', *Canadian Journal of Economics*, **XII(3)**: 394–409.

Helpman, E. and A. Razin (1982) 'Dynamics of a Floating Exchange Rate Regime', *Journal of Political Economy*, **90(4)**: 728–54.

Helpman, E. and A. Razin (1984) 'The Role of Saving and Investment in Exchange Rate Determination under Alternative Monetary Mechanisms', *Journal of Monetary Economics*, **13**: 307–25.

Helpman, E. and A. Razin (1985) 'Floating Exchange Rates with Liquidity Constraints in Financial Markets', *Journal of International Economics*, **19**: 99–117.

Horii, A. (1986) 'The Evolution of Reserve Currency Diversification', *BIS Economic Papers*, **18**, Basel.

Kelly, M. G. (1970) 'The Demand for International Reserves', *American Economic Review*, **60**, 655–67.

Kimbrough, K. P. (1987) 'International Linkages, Exchange Rate Regimes, and the International Transmission Process: Perspectives from Optimizing Models', in L. H. Officer (ed.), *International Economics*, Dordrecht: Kluver Academic Publishers.

Krugman, P. (1980) 'Vehicle Currencies and the Structure of International Exchange', *Journal of Money, Credit and Banking*, **12(3)** (August): 513–26.

Lucas, R. E., Jr (1982) 'Interest Rates and Currency Prices in a Two-Country World', *Journal of Monetary Economics*, **10**: 335–59.

Lucas, R. E., Jr (1984) 'Money in a Theory of Finance', *Carnegie–Rochester Conference Series on Public Policy*, **21**.

Macedo, J. B. (1980) 'Portfolio Diversification across Countries', International Finance Section, working paper, Princeton University (November).

Macedo, J. B. (1982) 'Portfolio Diversification Across Currencies', in R. N. Cooper *et al.* (eds), *The International Monetary System under Flexible Exchange Rates: Essays in Honor of Robert Triffin*, Cambridge, Mass.: Ballinger.

Marston, R. C. (1985) 'Financial Disturbances and the Effects of an Exchange Rate Union', in J. P. Bhandari (ed.), *Exchange Rate Management under Uncertainty*, Cambridge, Mass.: MIT Press.

McKinnon, R. C. (1979) *Money in International Exchange*, Oxford: Oxford University Press.

Page, S. A. B. (1981) 'The Choice of Invoicing Currency in Merchandise Trade', *National Institute Economic Review*, **85**: 60–72.

Persson, T. (1984) 'Real Transfers in Fixed Exchange Rate Systems and the International Adjustment Mechanism', *Journal of Monetary Economics*, **13**: 349–69.

Rao, R. K. S. and S. P. Magee (1980) 'The Currency Denomination of International Trade Contracts', in R. M. Levich and C. Wihlbourg (eds), *Exchange Rate Risk and Exposure*, Lexington, Mass.: D.C. Heath: 61–79.

Stockman, A. (1980) 'A Theory of Exchange Rate Determination', *Journal of Political Economy*, **88** (August): 673–98.

Stockman, A. C. and A. Hernandez (1988) 'Exchange Controls, Capital Controls and International Financial Markets', *American Economic Review*, **78(3)**: 362–74.

Svensson, L. E. O. (1985a) 'Money and Asset Prices in a Cash-in-Advance Economy', *Journal of Political Economy*, **93(5)**: 919–44.
Svensson, L. E. O. (1985b) 'Currency Prices, Terms of Trade, and Interest Rates. A General Equilibrium Asset-Pricing Cash-in-Advance Approach', *Journal of International Economics*, **18**: 17–41.
Tobin, J. (1986) 'A Proposal for International Monetary Reform', *Eastern Economic Journal*.

Discussion

RUDIGER DORNBUSCH

The chapters dealing with foreign exchange markets by Grilli and Roubini offer a comprehensive and valuable accomplishment and, at the same time, an agenda for further research. In my comments I will try only to highlight a few issues, rather than comprehensively taking issue with the many points of interest that invite comment. Specifically, I will briefly take up three issues: the efficiency of forex markets, the asymmetry question and volatility, including the neglected role of bid–ask spreads as indicators of market turbulence of exchange markets.

1   The efficiency of forex markets

The overview of foreign exchange markets in the world does well in supplying us with detailed institutional information regarding the participants and the coverage of their activities. One might ask a further question: how well do foreign exchange markets work in different locations? Foreign exchange markets operate as wholesale and as retail markets. The former must certainly operate on a highly competitive basis, with little room for discrepancies in spreads across locations, at least at those times where more than one market is open.

It would be of interest to know whether there is some hierarchy of markets: for example, Tokyo, London and New York as the world wholesale markets and Paris, Frankfurt and Melbourne (to name a few) as retail markets. And if such a structure exists, what are the margins at the wholesale and retail level? And at what transactions' levels do actors shift from retail to wholesale? And are margins the same in the wholesale market when major centres are jointly open and when only one is open for business?

All this information is difficult to come by, but ultimately we really do not know how well a market functions, i.e. how competitive is the intermediation process, unless we can make comparison among markets across space and also comparison between foreign exchange markets and other financial markets such as those for financial assets such as stocks, bonds and commodities.

A further question worth asking is how capacity, in the sense of the overhead capital in the form of human resources and physical assets of the foreign exchange market, relates to exchange rate regime. Traders are kept alive by margins and by volatility. What would happen if Europe went to zero margin, par clearing as is practised within national boundaries? Clearly there would be a vast excess capacity in foreign exchange markets. It is worth bearing this possibility in mind as countries like Italy individually open up to increase foreign exchange trading in the context of capital flow liberalisation while Europe at large is heading for more fixed exchange rates.

2   The asymmetry issue

The Giavazzi and Giovannini finding, reinforced by the evidence of Grilli and Roubini, is altogether striking. Figure D5.1 highlights this finding once more, using this time percentage changes of the monthly average of

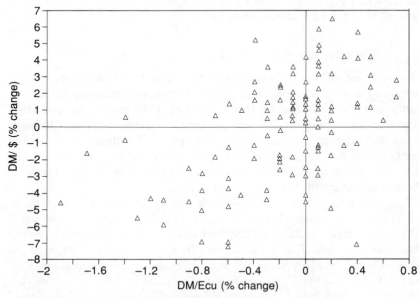

Figure D5.1   The Giavazzi–Giovannini phenomenon

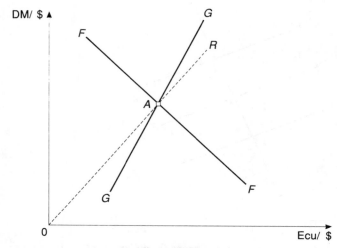

Figure D5.2   Three-currency equilibrium

the DM/$ and the DM/ECU exchange rates in the 1980–90 period. The finding is that when the DM strengthens relative to the dollar it also strengthens relative to other currencies – those in the EMS, but also third currencies.

A simple theoretical formulation, drawing on Mundell (1968) can help understand what might be at work here. The key assumption is that in a three-currency world – the DM, the $ and the (non-DM) ECU – all currencies are gross substitutes. The ECU here is a hypothetical composite of all currencies rather than the real thing. In Figure D5.2 we show along FF the equilibrium in the market for ECUs. Equilibrium obtains at point A which determines the three exchange rates DM/$, ECU/$ and, as the slope of the ray OR, the DM/ECU rate.

$$F(\text{DM}/\$, \text{ECU}/\$, \ldots) = 0 \tag{1}$$

$$G(\text{DM}/\$, \text{ECU}/\$, \ldots) = 0 \tag{2}$$

Suppose now, as shown in Figure D5.3, that there are shifts in the excess demand for dollars, leaving unaffected the excess demand for ECUs. Accordingly we get equilibrium exchange rates given by points like A, B, C. Note that when the demand for dollars is high, the equilibrium reached at point B implies a strong dollar and a weak DM in terms of both dollars *and* ECUs. Conversely, when the dollar is weak (point C), the DM is strong in terms of dollars *and* ECUs. This is precisely the Giavazzi–Giovannini finding. The observed pattern of exchange rates in

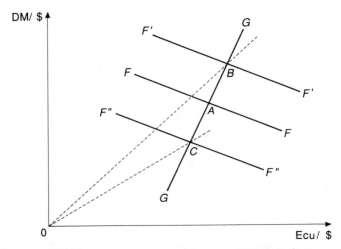

Figure D5.3   Effect of a shift in the excess demand for dollars

Figure D5.1 thus corresponds to a Mundellian gross substitute situation when the shifts of excess demand curves are predominantly between the dollar and the DM, leaving the excess demand for ECUs unaffected.

The finding is striking, but the explanation for this phenomenon remains open. It is clear from the high correlation of nominal and real exchange rate changes that it will be hard to disentangle whether this finding represents observations about changes in equilibrium real exchange rates in response to disturbances that stem from asset or from goods markets. A first step, it would seem, is to look at relationships of changes in exchange rates and asset yields, specifically short- and long-term interest rates. Note, too, from the correlations shown in the Appendix that across sample periods the correlations are not very stable. As the last row for each period shows, there are predominantly negative correlations between the DM/$ and the bilateral DM rates. But the correlations are all over the place, suggesting that there is no single factor that neatly aggregates the world into a three-country model.

3   Volatility

The discussion of exchange market volatility offers an especially challenging issue. The authors highlight the link between market volatility and divergences of speculative opinion on the part of traders. For convenience their basic model is restated here in equations (3) and (4), omitting for simplicity the time subscript. There are J traders each of whom holds an idiosyncratic expectation about the future exchange rate, e_j. Foreign exchange demand is given by:

$$Q_j = a(e_j - e) \tag{3}$$

Market equilibrium requires that the excess demand be 0, $\Sigma Q_j = 0$, which yields the equilibrium spot rate as a function of speculative opinion:

$$e = \Sigma e_j / J \tag{4}$$

This equation is used to establish that the variance of the exchange rate is related positively to the variance of opinion, v^2, and negatively to the number of traders:

$$\sigma^2 = v^2 / J \tag{5}$$

This finding in turn is used to argue that with the opening to capital mobility we should expect at first an increase in volatility as a larger variety of opinion comes to influence the market. Then, as traders enter over time, volatility is brought down. I will now offer a few comments on these findings.

The most important point to recognise is the role of the central bank.[1] The central bank will have intervened prior to liberalisation, and it may continue to do so afterwards. But there is no reason to expect that there is not a change in the intervention rule. Central bank intervention can be modelled by an intervention rule of leaning against the wind:

$$I = -\lambda(e - e^*) \tag{6}$$

where e^* is the mean exchange rate expected by the market. Next we note that market clearing now includes the central bank intervention: $\Sigma Q_j + I = 0$:

$$\Sigma_j a(e_j - e^* - e) - \lambda(e - e^*) = 0 \tag{7}$$

$$e = e^* + \theta \Sigma(e_j - e^*); \quad \theta = a/(\lambda + aJ) \tag{4a}$$

The equilibrium exchange rate in (4a) can now be compared to the result in (4). Central bank intervention dampens fluctuations, more so the larger the coefficient λ. Of course, the presence of intervention affects also the volume of transactions that are undertaken. Consider various possible consequences of liberalisation.

- Liberalisation implies that a larger number of potential market participants can translate their opinion into an effect on the actual exchange rate.
- Liberalisation may increase the variance of opinion.
- Liberalisation may change the intervention rule.
- Liberalisation may increase the number of traders who can profitably operate in the market.

Table D5.1. *Daily bid–ask spreads in the London market*

	1974–7	1978–80	1981–9
$/DM			
Mean	0.055	0.048	0.048
St. dev.	0.030	0.040	0.019
$/Pound			
Mean	0.039	0.044	0.065
St. dev.	0.045	0.044	0.030

Source: DRI.

Some of these factors can lead in the direction of increased variance, but they need not. First, liberalisation is unlikely to occur except when there is a quite firm expectation that the exchange rate can be maintained through intervention or interest rate policy. Second, in this model there is no distinction between the number of participants and the number of traders in the sense of market makers. Third, the central bank would certainly react to increased variability by a more aggressive intervention stance. Finally, there is a link between volatility and the number of traders that can be sustained. The model offers an excellent starting point for a discussion, but it must go much further to exploit more of the opportunities that this interesting structure offers.

The authors argue that foreign exchange market volatility increases as countries liberalise capital flows. I am not sure that the evidence is as stark as they suggest. Table D5.1 shows bid–ask spreads in the London market for various sub-periods. If 1978–80 is considered as the period of opening for sterling then we should expect an increase in spreads and presumably (because of increased volatility of news) also an increase in the variability of the premium. These facts are not present in Table D5.1.

Likewise, Table D5.2, which shows the volatility of daily exchange rates, does not support the view that opening must imply increased volatility.

In summary, the research brings up exceptionally interesting issues

Table D5.2. *Variability of daily spot rates*

	1974–7	1978–80	1981–9
$/DM	5.66	6.02	18.6
$/Pound	13.6	4.86	14.9

Table DA5.1. *Correlations between exchange rates shown in rows, monthly data, 1970:1–1979:12*

	Dated monthly (1970:1–1979:12)						
	(1)	(2)	(3)	(4)	(5)	(6)	(7)
(1) Danish kroner/DM	1.000						
(2) Italian lira/DM	0.960	1.000					
(3) Canadian $/DM	0.973	0.946	1.000				
(4) Japanese yen/DM	0.570	0.642	0.573	1.000			
(5) French franc/DM	0.972	0.971	0.940	0.580	1.000		
(6) Sterling/DM	0.929	0.987	0.918	0.657	0.943	1.000	
(7) DM/US$	−0.960	−0.947	−0.983	−0.643	−0.932	−0.936	1.000

Table DA5.2. *Correlations between exchange rates shown in rows, monthly data, 1980:1–1989:12*

	Dated monthly (1980:1–1989:12)						
	(1)	(2)	(3)	(4)	(5)	(6)	(7)
(1) Danish kroner/DM	1.000						
(2) Italian lira/DM	0.973	1.000					
(3) Canadian $/DM	0.265	0.368	1.000				
(4) Japanese yen/DM	−0.867	−0.909	−0.174	1.000			
(5) French franc/DM	0.993	0.979	0.266	−0.885	1.000		
(6) Sterling/DM	0.864	0.891	0.620	−0.718	0.871	1.000	
(7) DM/US$	−0.111	−0.197	−0.951	0.018	−0.104	−0.463	1.000

Table DA5.3. *Correlations between exchange rates shown in rows, monthly data, 1980:1–1984:12*

	Dated monthly (1980:1–1984:12)						
	(1)	(2)	(3)	(4)	(5)	(6)	(7)
(1) Danish kroner/DM	1.000						
(2) Italian lira/DM	0.982	1.000					
(3) Canadian $/DM	-0.834	-0.894	1.000				
(4) Japanese yen/DM	-0.716	-0.807	0.917	1.000			
(5) French franc/DM	0.991	0.985	0.850	-0.750	1.000		
(6) Sterling/DM	0.756	0.715	-0.439	-0.330	0.761	1.000	
(7) DM/US$	0.857	0.911	-0.992	-0.918	0.871	-0.481	1.000

Table DA5.4. *Correlations between exchange rates shown in rows, monthly data, 1985:1–1990:12*

	Dated monthly (1985:1–1990:12)						
	(1)	(2)	(3)	(4)	(5)	(6)	(7)
(1) Danish kroner/DM	1.000						
(2) Italian lira/DM	0.919	1.000					
(3) Canadian $/DM	0.775	0.848	1.000				
(4) Japanese yen/DM	-0.483	-0.419	-0.195	1.000			
(5) French franc/DM	0.960	0.920	0.805	-0.472	1.000		
(6) Sterling/DM	0.797	0.732	0.864	-0.078	0.824	1.000	
(7) DM/US$	-0.911	-0.953	-0.952	0.332	-0.932	-0.867	1.000

linking exchange markets and exchange rate regimes. The authors have opened up a fertile area of research; their strong conclusions are provocative and they will without doubt lead to a large volume of fruitful research in this area which until their work had been largely unexplored.

Appendix

Tables DA5.1–DA5.4 show the correlations between the logs of bilateral nominal exchange rates (levels in monthly averages) and the DM/dollar exchange rate. For example, -0.947 is the correlation between the lira/DM exchange rate and the DM/$ exchange rate in 1970–9.

Notes

Rudiger Dornbusch is Ford International Professor, MIT.
1 There is also room to look at transactions costs. Specifically the demand equations might reflect the fact that traders will transact only if the expected gain on a transaction exceeds the transactions costs. With fixed costs, that opens a minimum difference of opinion or a minimum transactions size before it is profitable to enter.

Reference

Mundell, R.A. (1968) *International Economics*, New York: Macmillan.

2.2 The equity market

6 Shifting gears: an economic evaluation of the reform of the Paris Bourse

MARCO PAGANO and AILSA RÖELL

> Paris [is] the financial surprise of the late 1980s . . . capital markets
> that learnt to run before they walked have stumbled amazingly little.
> (*The Economist*, 16 December 1989)

1 Introduction

Until 1985, the Bourse de Paris was still working according to the blueprint
laid down at the beginning of the nineteenth century, the same blueprint
that had been adopted by several other exchanges on the European Continent: each stock was traded in a single auction per day (apart from
bilateral trading later in the day), exchange members were public officials
(*agents de change*) appointed by the Ministry of Finance and could not trade
on their own account, all transactions had to be channelled through the
floor of the Exchange, and commissions were statutorily determined.

Today, none of the hallmarks of the nineteenth century blueprint has
remained unchanged: in the late 1980s, the Bourse has gone through the
most drastic process of institutional change in its history. The single batch
auction per day has been replaced by a continuous auction, taking place
via a computer system. The *agents de change* have been replaced by
corporate intermediaries (*sociétés de bourse*) that can be owned by banks
or security firms and can operate transactions on their own account.
Within limits, these new intermediaries can trade large blocks of shares
off the floor at prices that differ from the price reigning on the floor.
Finally, commissions have been liberalised.

The main motivation for the overhaul of the old system and the breakneck pace of the reforms has been the danger of losing business to the London market. In the late 1980s, the competition from London became a serious threat to the Bourse, owing to the creation of SEAQ International (the City's screen-based market specialising in international equities) and the liberalisation of commissions and exchange membership in the London market (known as 'Big Bang').

The French reforms have been aimed at increasing the competitiveness of the Paris exchange and regaining the ground lost to London. The assessment of their results has thus an immediate relevance for policy, considering that these reforms are also being currently emulated in Madrid and Milan, whose stock exchanges have traditionally been organised along lines similar to the Paris Bourse.

Even aside from its immediate relevance, the experience of the Bourse in the late 1980s is of great interest for research on the comparative efficiency of stock trading mechanisms. On one hand, the switch of the Bourse from discrete to continuous trading provides evidence on the effect that trading frequency has on prices and volumes. On the other, since several French stocks are now traded simultaneously in London and Paris, one can directly compare the performance of a market makers' system and that of an auction market.

This chapter is a first attempt to analyse the evidence that the Paris Bourse experiment has started to produce. The time elapsed since the beginning of the experiment is short, so our results should be taken at best as a provisional assessment. To place the evidence in perspective, in Section 2 we survey the main institutional changes that have occurred in Paris since 1986. In the subsequent sections, we concentrate on two distinct points. First, we try to assess the effects that the transition from discrete to continuous trading has had on price volatility and trading volume. Second, we evaluate the liquidity offered by the Paris continuous auction market, using minute-by-minute data from the Bourse and providing comparative evidence on the liquidity supplied by London dealers for the French stocks traded on SEAQ International.

2   The reform of the Bourse: motivation and key points

As explained above, the innovations that occurred in 1985–6 in the British stock market have been the main reason for the reform of the Paris Bourse and for the sense of urgency with which it has been carried out. In 1985, the London's International Stock Exchange (ISE) created SEAQ International, a screen-based quotation system specialising in non-British stocks where market makers competed by quoting bid and ask prices. In October 1986, the London exchange proper went through the so-called

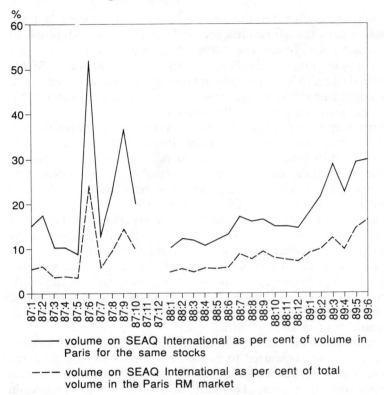

—— volume on SEAQ International as per cent of volume in
Paris for the same stocks

– – – volume on SEAQ International as per cent of total
volume in the Paris RM market

Figure 6.1   Cross-listed French stocks: trading volume in London (SEAQ International), as percentage of trading volume in Paris
Note: SEAQ International volume data are divided by 2 (see n. 2).

'Big Bang': dealership was opened to competition by banks and other financial institutions, commissions were liberalised, and the use of screen-based price quotation was extended to all stocks listed on the ISE (see Tonks and Webb, 1989). Moreover, the stamp duty was halved. As a result, the competitiveness of the London exchange increased considerably: on large deals, transactions costs fell by about one-third.[1]

The threat posed by London's increased competitiveness was compounded by two concomitant factors: the gradual liberalisation of capital flows in the EC and the increasing mobility of institutional investors across national borders. Figure 6.1 reveals the extent to which SEAQ International has been able to attract trade in French equities in the late 1980s. The bottom line shows how London trading in French stocks compares to total trading in domestic shares in the *marché à règlement mensuel* (RM), the segment of the Bourse where the most active stocks are traded. The top line displays instead London trading in French stocks as a proportion of trade in the *same* stocks in the Paris RM market, which is a more accurate indicator of the gravitational pull of SEAQ International.[2]

Figure 6.1 shows that the Paris Bourse lost a large share of trade to London in 1987 and, after recovering somewhat in 1988, started losing ground again. In the first 10 months of 1987, for the 23 French 'blue chip' stocks then traded on SEAQ International, turnover in London was on average 20.6 per cent of the Paris turnover for the same stocks (and 8.7 per cent of the total turnover on the Bourse). The 1987 experience can be partly explained by SEAQ's 'grey market' on the shares of the French public corporations undergoing privatisation: the privatisation of Paribas partly accounts for the surge in trading in January and February, whereas those of CGE, Société Générale and Suez can explain the spikes in the second half of 1987. However, no such explanation can be given for the more recent episode of 1989, when London trading in French stocks climbed back to levels comparable with those of 1987: on average, in the first half of 1989 turnover on SEAQ International was 25.1 per cent of the turnover for the same stocks in Paris, and the number of French stocks traded on SEAQ rose to 29. This indicates that competition by London dealers still poses a real threat for the Paris Bourse.

The response of French policy makers to this threat has turned on four key innovations, that have been introduced sequentially. These innovations have eliminated or deeply modified the four main rules on which the organisation of the Bourse had in the past relied. The first to go has been the rule that there should be a single auction per day on each stock; then, in rapid succession, the rules that trading should be operated by public officials and that their fees should be statutorily fixed have been scrapped; and finally also the principle that trade should be concentrated on the floor of the exchange has been partly amended. In what follows we outline how these rules have been changed.

2.1   Switch to continuous trading

The first step of the reform has been the introduction of a computerised facility for continuous trading (CAC: *Cotation Assistée en Continu*) closely patterned after that of the Toronto stock market (CATS: Computer Assisted Trading System). Before this innovation, more than 90 per cent of trading volume in Paris was concentrated in the opening batch auction *à la criée*; later, trade would normally occur via bilateral deals in the crowds until closing time (see Whitcomb, 1985) or, if there was high trading interest, via additional batch auctions during the day. With the introduction of CAC, bilateral trading during the day has been replaced with a centralised continuous auction, even though the opening batch auction has been retained.

In the CAC system orders can be routed to the market from the terminals of the brokers. If they reach the market before the opening, they are transacted in the batch auction at 10:00 a.m.; currently transactions executed in this auction account for about 10 per cent of trading volume. Orders sent later in the day (up until the 5:00 p.m. close) are instantly and automatically crossed with orders outstanding on the book, if possible, or otherwise are placed in the order book to await execution. Price and volume information is disseminated at two different levels: a network for the general public, named CHRONOVAL, reports prices and quantities of the best outstanding buy and sell limit orders, plus recent price and volume information; a network for market professionals, named TOPVAL, also displays real-time information about the order book.

Starting in July 1986, stocks have been gradually transferred to CAC's trading system. The first ones have been the more active stocks listed on the Bourse (those of the *côté officielle*), except for 13 highly active stocks forming the basis for option contracts that were traded *à la criée* with continuous auctions. By the end of 1989 these stocks, as well as those of the smaller companies (those of the *second marché*), had also been listed on the new system.

2.2   Introduction of dual-capacity dealers

Since January 1988 the monopoly of stock trading has been assigned to a set of new corporate intermediaries, the *sociétés de bourse*, who can act as counterparties to transactions, operating as dual-capacity dealers. This has ended the French tradition of single-capacity intermediaries, the *agents de change*, and has opened stock exchange membership to banks and securities firms.

To appease the *agents de change*, this part of the reform has been phased in gradually. The transition has been softened by granting the status of société de bourse to all the existing *agents de change* and forbidding the creation of new such intermediaries until the end of 1991, so that the *agents* have a chance gradually to transform their businesses by opening up their capital to banks and other intermediaries. This has happened at a rather brisk pace: as of the end of 1989 about two-thirds of the existing *sociétés de bourse* had already opened their capital to banks and securities firms, often foreign ones.

2.3   Liberalisation of commission charges

Traditionally, in Paris the fees of exchange members (*droit de courtage*) were statutorily fixed according to a regressive rate schedule.[3] In July 1989 all existing regulations of commission charges were scrapped, leaving their determination to competitive forces.

2.4   Permission to carry out block trading off the floor

Of the traditional features of the Paris market, one has resisted longer than the others: the principle that all the orders must be concentrated in the stock exchange. In the past, transactions could not be operated off the exchange: brokers were not permitted to conduct upstairs dealing for blocks, as often happens in other markets.

However, this feature of the Bourse has also been increasingly criticised, and was finally modified in 1989. The motivation, once more, was competition with the wholesale market of SEAQ International in London: institutional investors often seem to prefer to trade French stocks in London because they value the possibility of getting immediate firm quotes, even for sizeable orders. Some French firms have thus started to imitate London market makers, quoting prices outside the Bourse. In 1989 this practice, thus far illegal, was allowed by new regulations introduced by the Conseil des Bourse de Valeurs: now a selected group of sociétés de bourse can buy and sell blocks of shares on own account outside the Bourse at prices different from those prevailing on the market. To coordinate these trades (called opérations de contrepartie) with the auction market of the Bourse, market makers must report them within 5 minutes to the floor. Moreover, if the off-exchange transaction has occurred at a price outside the fourchette, i.e. the spread between the best buy and sell order outstanding on the market, the market maker must place an order at that price on the floor, so as to exhaust all the orders in the interval between that price and the fourchette. In other words, he has to align the price on the floor with that of the off-exchange transaction. In this fashion, market makers have been allowed to live side-by-side with the continuous auction on the Bourse.[4]

3   The switch to continuous trading: effects on volatility and trading volume

From the above description, it is apparent that some of the institutional changes implemented in Paris are still too recent to be evaluated empirically: at best, the evidence can shed light on the two first innovations introduced in the Bourse – the switch to continuous trading and the introduction of dual-capacity dealing. In fact we shall focus particularly on the switch to continuous trading: the reason is that we can isolate its effects from other influences better than for other institutional changes, exploiting the wide variation of switch-over dates across companies (from late 1986 to early 1988 in our sample). The introduction of dual-capacity trading has instead taken place at the same time for all companies (in January 1988), and its effect is harder to disentangle from contemporaneous market-wide phenomena (especially considering the turbulence of late 1987). Thus, on the effects of dual-capacity trading, we cannot go much beyond conjectures.

In principle, switching from a discrete to a continuous auction can affect both the behaviour of prices and the volume of trade effected in the market. This section briefly outlines how price volatility and trading volume might be expected to react to more frequent trading, and then confronts the evidence from the Paris experience.

3.1   Effects on volatility

3.1.1   The hypotheses
When a market switches from a single batch auction per day to a continuous auction, one expects the order flow to spread itself more thinly during the day. Does this imply that prices at any given moment will be more volatile? Not necessarily. It all depends on how different groups of traders change the timing of their transactions, and thus the composition of the pool of market participants, at each moment in time.

Suppose, for simplicity, that there are only two classes of traders: 'speculators', who buy low and sell high by conveying price-elastic schedules to the market via limit orders; and 'liquidity' or 'noise traders', who convey price-inelastic demands to the market via market orders. Speculators exert a stabilising influence on market prices, in that they absorb the demand shocks caused by the order flow from noise traders. Their ability to stabilise prices depends on their risk tolerance as well as on their number: other things being equal, the higher their number, the more effectively can they share risk and thus stabilise market prices. The reverse is true for liquidity traders: the higher their number, the larger the noise in the aggregate order flow, and thus the higher the price volatility. The effect of the intradaily reallocation of trade on price volatility thus depends on the change in the relative numbers of speculators and noise traders who participate in the market at each moment.

This point is illustrated by a very simple model in the Appendix. In particular, the model shows that if more frequent clearings produce an equiproportionate reduction in both groups of traders participating in each auction, price volatility will increase. Intuitively, this is because the reduction of the noise injected in prices by liquidity traders is more than offset by the reduction in the number of speculators and thus in their price-smoothing action.

This obviously need not be the case if the increase in trading frequency induces the number of speculators to fall proportionately less than that of the liquidity traders participating in each auction: one would expect this to occur if speculators face lower costs to maintain a presence on the market. As an extreme example, more frequent trade will definitely reduce price volatility if it lowers the number of liquidity traders participating in each auction, but leaves the number of speculators unchanged.

The critical factor is thus how costly it is for speculators to maintain a market presence over a longer time interval. In the French case, speculators may actually have faced a *decrease* in the cost of maintaining a market presence, if one considers that the switch to continuous trading has been accompanied by much greater visibility of the market price and of the order book: the CAC screens continuously update all market participants on prices, volumes and on trading interest on both sides of the market, whereas in the old system prices off the batch auction were struck via bilateral matching. The new trading system may thus have cut considerably the cost of monitoring the market and operating transactions outside of the opening auction.

In addition, one has to consider that the *quality* of the speculators present in the market changed after the introduction of the CAC system: for many stocks (though not for all of them) the transition to continuous trading roughly coincided with the introduction of well-capitalised dual-capacity intermediaries (*the sociétés de bourse*), endowed with greater resources and greater incentives to maintain a continued market presence.

3.1.2   The evidence

Most of the existing empirical studies on the relative performance of batch and continuous trading have focussed on the return volatility associated with these two mechanisms. Since in many exchanges trade starts with a batch auction and proceeds with continuous dealing until the close, these studies have generally compared the volatility of open-to-open returns to that of close-to-close returns. This type of comparison can obviously be performed also for the Paris Bourse. But, as we shall see, the Paris Bourse offers more direct evidence on the comparison between batch and continuous trading: for each stock, one can compare return volatility before and after the transition to the continuous auction system.

Using daily price data from January 1985 to July 1989 for 16 companies listed on the Bourse, we have computed open-to-open and close-to-close returns for each company and their quarterly variances.[5] We have computed the close-to-close returns also for the period before the introduction of CAC, because at that time one could also trade after the opening auction, by striking bilateral deals: for that period, our closing prices are bilateral matching prices.

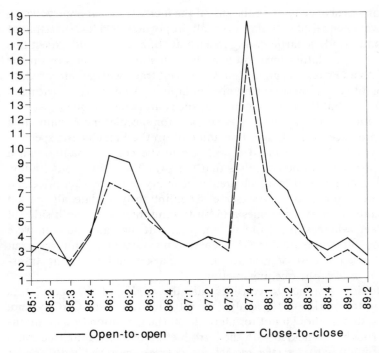

Figure 6.2   Volatility of open-to-open and close-to-close returns, variance of percentage daily returns, average for 16 stocks

Taking the average variance of the 16 companies in each quarter as a measure of volatility, we have compared the open-to-open with the close-to-close volatility. As shown by Figure 6.2, the returns of the opening auction are in general more volatile than those of the closing continuous market (14 out of 18 cases): on average, their variance is 16 per cent higher. This result is in line with the studies by Amihud and Mendelson (1987, 1989) on the New York and Tokyo stock exchanges and that by Amihud, Mendelson and Murgia (1990) on the Milan exchange – and, as in those studies, the greater price volatility of the batch auction may be attributed to greater uncertainty at the opening rather than to the difference between the two trading mechanisms.[6]

In any event, this evidence does not tell us how volatility has been affected by the introduction of the continuous auction in place of the earlier traditional bilateral trading system. To investigate this, we have regressed the return volatilities for the companies in our sample (measured by the quarterly standard deviations of daily returns) on 'continuous trading dummies', set equal to 0 before the transition to the

Table 6.1. *The transition to continuous trading: effect on return volatility*[a]

Dependent variable	Volatility of open-to-open returns	Volatility of close-to-close returns
Intercept	0.614	0.762
	(4.76)	(6.30)
CAC dummy	− 0.108	− 0.168
	(− 1.53)	(− 2.55)
CRIEE dummy	0.440	0.056
	(3.31)	(0.46)
Market volatility	1.323	1.133
	(22.90)	(21.25)
$\bar{R}^2$	0.728	0.702
No. of observations	250	249

[a] *T*-statistics in parenthesis. Data are quarterly, 1985:1–1989:2; volatility is measured as the quarterly standard deviation of daily stock returns. The *CAC* dummy is set equal to 1 from the quarter in which the relevant stock starts trading on the *CAC* system; the *CRIEE* dummy is set equal to 1 from the quarter in which the stock starts trading continuously *à la criée*. For the quarters within which a stock started trading continuously, the two dummies were set equal to 1 or 0 according to whether it traded continuously for the greater part of the quarter. Both regressions include also individual company dummies (not reported for brevity).
Source: Société des Bourses Françaises.

continuous auction system and to 1 afterwards.[7] In our sample, however, only 11 companies switched over to the CAC system: for the remaining 4 companies (Michelin, Saint Gobain, Paribas and Midi), continuous trading has been implemented by a continuous open outcry system (*à la criée*) rather than via the computerised CAC system. We have therefore built two distinct dummies: a '*CAC* dummy' for the 11 companies that switched to CAC in the sample period; and a '*CRIEE* dummy' for the remaining 4. In addition, we have included among the regressors a constant, a company dummy to control for individual company effects and the volatility of the market to control for changes in aggregate risk.

The estimates are reported in Table 6.1 (omitting company dummies for brevity). For the stocks that have switched to the CAC system, volatility has decreased: for open-to-open returns, volatility has declined slightly (by 5 per cent relative to its average value), but the coefficient of the *CAC* dummy is not significant; for close-to-close returns, the decrease in volatility is larger (8.3 per cent of its average value) and significant at the 2.5 per cent level. The results are strikingly different for the stocks that have switched to the continuous auction *à la criée*: the volatility of open-to-open returns has risen considerably (as shown by the large coefficient on the *CRIEE* dummy), whereas that of close-to-close returns has not changed significantly.

How do we interpret these findings? For the stocks that have switched to the CAC system, replacing sporadic bilateral trading with the computerised continuous auction has stabilised closing prices, and has not destabilised prices in the opening batch. In terms of the model proposed above, the lower price volatility at the close suggests that the stabilising action of speculators during the day is now more effective, given the order flow coming from noise traders. And the fact that the volatility of the opening price has not risen indicates that the reallocation of trade away from the opening auction has reduced the noise due to liquidity traders by more than the stabilising action of speculators. In this interpretation, the CAC system has faced speculators with lower costs or greater incentives to maintain a market presence than the previous system of sporadic bilateral trades.

It is harder to explain the results for the stocks that have switched to the continuous auction *à la criée*: here the reallocation of trade away from the opening auction has made its price more volatile, and has not decreased the volatility at the close. This may indicate that the switch to screen-based trading matters more than the switch from bilateral to centralised trading: the critical factor would be the visibility of the CAC screens, rather than the continuous auction *per se*. However, the evidence on this point should be taken very cautiously, since it is based only on 4 stocks. Moreover, all 4 stocks switched to continuous trading shortly before or at the same time as the creation of the corresponding option market, and one of them (Paribas) soon after the company had undergone privatisation. These events may well have raised the volatility of their opening and closing prices.

3.2   *Effects on volume*

When a single auction per day is replaced by a continuous auction, the market offers greater immediacy (i.e. possibility of trading at short notice): one would expect that this would induce a larger volume of trade, other things being equal. In fact, continuous trading was introduced in Paris largely on the assumption that the lack of immediacy of the Paris market was causing trading in French stocks to migrate to London.

Using volume data for 15 of the companies in our sample,[8] we have compared trading volume before and after each stock started trading continuously. As shown in Table 6.2, the switch to continuous trading is associated with a significant increase in trading volume for most of the

Table 6.2. *The transition to continuous trading: test statistics for changes in the volume[a]*

Company	Date of the transition to continuous trading (1)	T-test on the level of own-volume measured at market values (2)	T-test on the level of own-volume measured by the number of shares traded (3)	T-test on the ratio of own-volume to the volume of the market (4)
Schneider	22/08/86	8.05	9.17	3.18
Alsthom	24/10/86	6.65	6.52	− 4.76
Auxiliaire	23/01/87	4.79	6.07	− 1.41
Total	20/02/87	− 0.91	1.74	− 11.67
Eaux	23/04/87	2.80	2.92	− 0.51
Midi	23/06/87	10.17	7.02	3.33
Carrefour	23/06/87	4.64	2.50	− 10.25
Paribas	23/06/87	0.09	− 2.11	− 2.06
Club Méd.	23/12/87	4.53	2.65	− 5.70
Bancaire	23/12/87	4.40	− 3.96	− 8.60
BSN	22/01/88	8.02	3.92	− 5.29
Saint Gobain	22/01/88	− 5.30	− 2.56	− 2.76
Michelin	22/01/88	18.81	6.59	− 16.41
Bouygues	22/01/88	7.30	7.91	2.01
Havas	22/02/88	− 3.24	− 0.18	− 0.12

[a] The test is implemented on daily data for turnover on the *marché a règlement mensuel*. A value of the test statistic above + 1.96 (below − 1.96) indicates that the transition to continuous trading has been associated with a significant increase (decrease) in turnover (at the 5 per cent level of significance).
Source: Société des Bourses Françaises.

stocks in our sample if turnover is measured in levels – whether at market prices (column (2)) or in number of shares traded (column (3)). However, this seems due mostly to the increase in the total volume of trade in the Paris Bourse rather than to the effect of the switch to continuous trading: when the test is effected on the ratio between each company turnover and total market turnover, it turns out that for 10 out of the 15 companies considered the increase in trading volume has been *significantly lower* than for the market as a whole (column (4)). The dates in column (1) of Table 6.2 show that the hypothesis is accepted at least as frequently for the 'late movers' as for the 'early movers'.

A reasonable objection to the simple test in Table 6.2 is that it does not control for the effect of the changes in individual stock prices on trading volume (it is well known that volume is positively related to price variability: see Tauchen and Pitts, 1983, and the studies quoted there). As a check on this point, we have regressed the daily volume for each stock on a constant, a 'continuous trading dummy', the lagged values of own-volume, the current and lagged values of total market volume and of percentage price changes. Specification tests have suggested the need to enter all the volume variables in logarithmic form, as well as the need to introduce lags of the dependent and independent variables to eliminate serial correlation from the residuals. In the specification used for the results reported in Table 6.3, we have used three lags of own-volume, of market volume and of price changes among the regressors (except for Total, Eaux, Midi and BSN, where we have used five lags). The Box–Pierce Q-statistics (column (4)) and the Durbin h-statistics (not reported) signal that there is no significant residual autocorrelation in the regressions.

In Table 6.3 we show the coefficient on the continuous trading dummy in the regression for each stock (column (1)) and the implied percentage change in volume associated with listing on CAC, holding the effect of all the other variables constant (column (2)). The results broadly confirm those obtained by comparing the ratios of own-volume to market volume in Table 6.2: for 7 companies the transition to continuous trading is associated with a statistically significant decrease in volume (and in some cases a sizeable one); for the rest instead there is no significant effect in either direction.

This negative association between longer trading hours and lower volume is rather puzzling, especially considering that in Paris the opening batch auction is still an option for any trader who prefers that trading mechanism. It is possible that the explanation for this puzzle lies in purely technical or statistical reasons: the new system may have required some learning effort by traders, and in its early stages may have occasionally failed when faced with heavy volume; or some systematic statistical discrepancy may have arisen from new methods in the collection of volume statistics associated with the switch to the new trading systems.

Another possible explanation is that, contrary to the French authorities' intentions, the existence of a continuous market in Paris has ended up reinforcing the comparative advantage of London market makers, and thus the business drain from Paris. The new system may have helped SEAQ market makers by providing a continuously updated source of price information and also a market of 'last resort' where they can unwind their positions at any time. Though seemingly paradoxical, this argument may contain some truth: in the next section we shall see that SEAQ market makers make a tighter market in French stocks when the Bourse is operating, so that the quality of the market in London feeds off price information from Paris.

Table 6.3. *The transition to continuous trading: regressions for trading volume*[a]

Company	Continuous market dummy (1)	Volume change associated with switch to continuous trading[b] (2)	$\bar{R}^2$ (3)	Box–Pierce statistic significance level (4)	No. of observations (5)
Schneider	0.023 (0.34)	2.33%	0.679	14.3%	1,121
Alsthom	− 0.200** (3.45)	− 18.13%	0.571	39.9%	1,116
Auxiliaire	− 0.080 (− 0.98)	− 7.69%	0.588	24.6%	636
Total	− 0.207** (− 3.80)	− 18.70%	0.518	46.9%	1,124
Eaux	0.011 (0.26)	1.11%	0.716	25.3%	1,124
Midi	0.031 (0.76)	3.15%	0.666	58.6%	1,091
Carrefour	− 0.177** (− 4.05)	− 16.22%	0.446	35.9%	1,126
Paribas	0.000 (0.35)	0.00%	0.986	23.4%	509
Club Méd.	− 0.066* (− 1.77)	− 6.39%	0.496	23.9%	1,116
Bancaire	− 0.296** (− 5.62)	− 25.62%	0.579	31.6%	1,121
BSN	− 0.068** (− 1.98)	− 6.57%	0.602	69.3%	1,110
Saint Gobain	− 0.028 (− 0.83)	− 2.76%	0.519	51.4%	595
Michelin	− 0.162** (− 5.03)	− 14.95%	0.809	62.3%	1,089
Bouygues	0.002 (0.06)	0.20%	0.376	35.4%	505
Havas	− 0.037 (− 0.60)	− 3.63%	0.640	43.0%	1,116

[a] *T*-statistics in parenthesis; * and ** indicate that the variable is different from 0 at the 5 per cent and 1 per cent significance level respectively. Daily data.
[b] Since all variables except the dummy enter the estimated equation as logarithms, the percentage change in volume associated with the switch to continuous trading is equal to $\exp(\beta) - 1$, where β is the coefficient in column (1).
Source: Société des Bourses Françaises.

4   **The liquidity of the Bourse after the reforms: a comparison with London's dealership market**

Since the reform of the Paris Bourse was largely promoted by the challenge from the British market makers operating on SEAQ International, it is interesting to compare the liquidity offered by the two exchanges using data for French cross-listed stocks. The comparison must be limited to the current situation because of data availability. Even so, the evidence is quite novel: in the existing empirical literature, no study performs a direct comparison between a pure auction market – such as the Paris Bourse – and a pure dealership market – such as SEAQ International. Most authors focus in fact on the experience of the United States and Canada, where no stock exchange is organised as a pure auction market.

In comparing two trading mechanisms as different as dealership and auction, the crucial problem is to find a measure of liquidity that is conceptually equivalent in the two contexts. In a dealership market, the bid–ask spread provides an immediate measure of liquidity. If different dealers quote different bid and ask prices, one can focus on the gap between the best bid and ask quotes, the so-called 'market touch'. What about an auction market? In fact, an implicit bid–ask spread exists there also: even in an auction market, when selling even a modest amount of stock one generally gets a lower price than one pays to buy it. The reason is that, at each instant, the demand curve for stocks is not perfectly elastic: to satisfy an incoming order, speculators require a premium from buyers and impose a penalty on sellers, for the same reasons that induce dealers to demand a bid–ask spread – they need to be compensated for taking risky long or short positions, for the danger of trading with insiders, and for the costs sustained in maintaining a presence on the market. Thus, as we shall see below, measuring the liquidity of the Bourse has meant finding a way to quantify this implicit 'market spread'.

To control for other factors, we compare the liquidity that the two markets supply for the same stocks and over the same time period, by comparing contemporaneous data for French shares traded both on the Paris Bourse and on SEAQ International in London. There are 28 such stocks, but in Paris only 16 of them are traded on the computerised support of the CAC system (the others are traded with the continuous open outcry system), and only for these stocks is there an automatic record of the best outstanding limit orders (and thus of the *fourchette*, i.e. the gap between the two best outstanding limit prices), transaction prices and quantities. The Paris Bourse has provided minute-by-minute data for these stocks from 19 June to 13 July 1989, and SEAQ International has supplied a record of bid and ask prices in London for the same stocks from 3 July to 13 July 1989, at various times of each day.

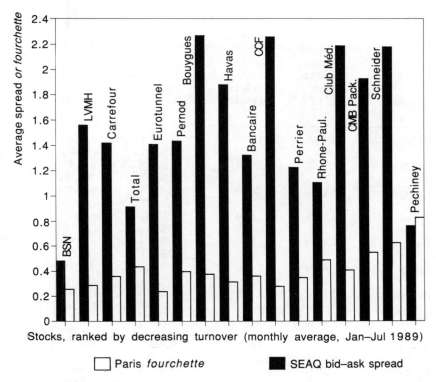

Figure 6.3 shows _Stocks, ranked by decreasing turnover (monthly average, Jan–Jul 1989)_

☐ Paris *fourchette*   ■ SEAQ bid–ask spread

Figure 6.3   Spreads in London and *fourchettes* **in Paris, by stock, average percentage values, 3–13 July 1989**

These data allow a perfect match by time of day. Using all the matched observations, the SEAQ average touch for these stocks is 1.52 per cent, whereas the Paris *fourchette* is 0.41 per cent. The *fourchette* measures the round-trip cost for small trades, so it provides a measure of liquidity for traders placing *small orders*. Clearly, for these orders the Bourse is more liquid than SEAQ International. Figure 6.3 shows how the figures for the *fourchette* and the SEAQ touch compare across the 16 stocks, ranked by decreasing average turnover (left to right). Both the SEAQ touch and the *fourchette* tend to rise as turnover declines, although the SEAQ touch rises by slightly more: the difference between them is 0.87 per cent for the largest 6 companies and 1.25 per cent for the smaller 10.

We can also compare the liquidity offered by London and Paris to traders who place relatively *large orders*. To do so, we have gone through the following steps. First, we have obtained from SEAQ International data on the size for which the bid and ask prices quoted by London dealers are firm, for each of these 16 French stocks (Table 6.4, column

Table 6.4. *Market liquidity in Paris and London, measured on cross-listed French stocks[a]*

Company	Average 'market touch' on SEAQ (1)	Size for which SEAQ quotes are firm (no. of shares) (2)	Average *fourchette* on the Paris Bourse[b] (3)	Average market spread on the Paris Bourse[c] (4)
BSN	0.48%	2,500	0.139% (16.89)	0.282% (13.47)
LVMH	1.56%	500	0.307% (10.05)	0.314% (5.32)
Carrefour	1.42%	500	0.391% (7.40)	0.484% (9.80)
Total	0.92%	2,000	0.501% (18.54)	0.540% (20.73)
Eurotunnel	1.41%	10,000	0.243% (27.85)	0.411% (14.60)
Pernod–Ricard	1.44%	1,000	0.345% (16.90)	0.421% (16.16)
Bouygues	2.27%	2,000	0.514% (13.54)	0.807% (13.16)
Havas	1.88%	2,000	0.358% (6.14)	0.441% (4.76)
Bancaire	1.33%	1,000	0.464% (20.89)	0.497% (18.83)
CCF	2.26%	5,000	0.367% (44.46)	0.594% (11.98)
Source Perrier	1.23%	1,000	0.326% (13.87)	0.439% (13.87)
Rhone-Poulenc	1.11%	2,500	0.546% (7.25)	0.706% (8.16)
Club Méd.	2.19%	2,000	0.481% (8.31)	0.570% (6.10)
CMB Packaging	1.93%	2,000	0.523% (10.48)	0.705% (10.50)
Schneider	2.18%	2,000	0.564% (8.05)	0.852% (6.70)
Pechiney	0.76%	2,500	0.709% (17.14)	0.939% (16.17)

[a] *SEAQ data:* observations at selected times between 3 July and 13 July, from 9:00 a.m. to 4:00 p.m. (UK time). *Paris Bourse data:* all the transactions between 19 June and 13 July 1989, except those at the batch auction of 10:00 a.m. (French time), those inside the *fourchette* and those where the same trader appears as both the buyer and the seller (the latter two groups largely coincide). The number in brackets are *t*-statistics.
[b] Being computed on the entire sample, this average *fourchette* is not the same as that displayed in Figure 6.3, where it was computed using only observations that are time-matched with those from SEAQ International.

(2)): on average, SEAQ quotes are firm up to FF 1,368,021 in the sample period. These numbers tell us the order size for which the bid–ask spread can be expected to be constant in London. Our next step has been to analyse by how much prices move in Paris when one attempts to carry out transactions of the same magnitude: this movement gives us a natural way to measure the 'market spread' for large transactions in Paris, and to compare it with the (constant) spread quoted in London.

To understand how our measure of the market spread is constructed, consider what happens when a new buy order is placed on the market. If the order has a limit price above the current ask (or is a market order), it will immediately execute against the best outstanding sell order, i.e. against the upper bound of the *fourchette*. However, if the buy order is abnormally large, it will exceed the sell order at the upper bound of the *fourchette*, and part of it will execute against sell orders that carry a higher limit price: the buyer will 'slide' along the instantaneous supply curve of the market, and the prices at which he transacts with each seller will trace out this curve. The price at which the entire order will actually execute is the average of these observed transaction prices. The same argument can be repeated for a large sell order. The difference between the average price at which large buy and sell orders execute on the market is what we call 'market spread', and will obviously vary according to the size of the order.

Since the available data relate to actual transactions rather than to orders, to estimate market spreads we had to reconstruct the underlying orders. To do so, we have assumed that if we observe a series of contemporaneous or consecutive sales (of purchases) by the same broker,[9] these correspond to a single customer order that is being fractionally executed against the order book. Our aggregation procedure stops as soon as the series of consecutive sales (or purchases) is interrupted by a transaction operated by another broker or if the original broker switches sides on the market (for example, turns from a seller into a buyer).[10] Once we reconstruct an order with this procedure, we compute the price at which it has been executed as the weighted average of the corresponding transaction prices. In the process, we also delete from the data all observations referring to the 10:00 a.m. batch auction (where by definition there is no

Table 6.4 (*cont.*)
[c] The Paris spread is computed as twice the percentage deviation of the price at which an order is transacted from the middle of the *fourchette* observed at the same time. Here the average spread is computed *for orders of size ranging from half to twice the size reported in column (2)* (the size for which SEAQ quotes are firm). *Data sources:* SEAQ International and Société des Bourses Françaises, respectively.

fourchette and no spread) and all the transactions performed inside the *fourchette*. A large portion of the most sizeable transactions are in fact arranged outside the market and then executed at a price within the outstanding *fourchette* via a special procedure that allows the two orders to reach the market as a joint buy–sell order.

The results are reported in Table 6.4. For each company we report the average market spread in Paris for orders of size comparable to that for which SEAQ dealers quote firm prices (column (4)). The SEAQ *market touch* and the average *fourchette* are also reported (in columns (1) and (3) respectively) for ease of comparison. It turns out that large transactions have virtually no appreciable price pressure effect in Paris. Even when it is computed for orders of the same size for which the SEAQ quotes are firm, the Paris spread is not much larger than the *fourchette*, and stays substantially lower than the SEAQ bid–ask spread (except for Pechiney). Thus, our data say that the Paris Bourse also offers greater liquidity than the London market for French stocks to traders who place relatively large orders. This conclusion deserves a note of caution: we have no information on market liquidity for extremely large orders, because in our data from the Bourse we observe virtually no such order, and SEAQ bid and ask prices are not available for orders exceeding the size for which quotes are firm.

Does this imply that an investor who wants to place a large order should prefer to trade on the Paris Bourse rather than on SEAQ International? The answer on this point must consider not only the difference between the London spread and the Paris spread in Table 6.4, but also the relative magnitude of transaction costs – taxes and commissions – on the two marketplaces. When this element is taken into account, things become less clear cut. Most estimates of transaction costs on equity trading in Paris and London say that for large transactions they are lower in London, although by a very slight margin (see *Quality of Markets Quarterly*, January–March 1989, p. 29) – so that, on balance, Paris retains an overall competitive advantage. However, on SEAQ International dealers often quote their prices *net* of commissions ('about half of all non-UK equity deals are transacted without a commission', *Quality of Markets Quarterly*, p. 29). For the deals settled without commission, transaction costs on SEAQ are zero (in the UK there is no stamp duty on foreign equity deals): in this case London's advantage on this account becomes significant, and slightly outweighs the spread differential in favour of the Paris Bourse. The choice between the two markets thus depends quite sensitively on whether or not SEAQ dealers require a commission on the transaction.

In addition, it should be recalled that transaction costs and market liquidity are only two of the factors that investors value in choosing a marketplace, although they are the only measurable ones. Immediacy is also important for them: especially for large institutional investors, getting quotes over the phone from a London dealer and striking deals in a matter of seconds may be preferable to securing a slightly tighter spread on the Paris Bourse at the cost of waiting for a counterparty. In fact, there is indirect evidence that large traders who transact in Paris tend to give up immediacy: we find that on average the *fourchette* is lower when large traders place their orders than it is in the entire sample. This suggests that, before placing an order, large traders wait for the market to be sufficiently liquid: if so, the results in Table 6.4 overestimate the liquidity really offered by the Bourse.

Finally, our data confirm that there is intense competition between the two markets. The Bourse and SEAQ International are very well arbitraged: on 380 observations, all perfectly matched by time of day, we have not identified a single unexploited opportunity for arbitrage. The competition is visible also in the intradaily movement of the London spread: Figure 6.4 displays the intradaily movements of the market touch in London and of the *fourchette* in Paris, for cross-listed French shares: each observation is the average value of the spread for the 16 stocks listed in Figure 6.3, in the 2 trading weeks from 3 July to 13 July 1989. Before 9:00 a.m. (London time), only the SEAQ International market in London is open, and its spread for French stocks is on average above 3 per cent. At 9:00 a.m. the Paris Bourse opens: the London spread drops to 1.5 per cent and stays there until the Paris market closes at 4:00 p.m. (UK time). During these 7 hours, the *fourchette* stays constantly between 0.4 and 0.5 per cent. Finally, as soon as the Bourse stops trading, the London spread shoots back up almost to 3 per cent.

Thus in the early morning and in the evening, the SEAQ spread on French stocks is about 100 per cent higher than in the interval from 9:00 a.m. to 4:00 p.m.. This increase in the spread exceeds by far that recorded for British stocks on the London market. Using evidence reported by Lee (1989), one can estimate by how much the market touch for British stocks rises outside the 'mandatory quote period' (from 9:00 a.m. to 5:00 p.m.) on the International Stock Exchange in London: in the evening and early morning the average touch is 14.3 per cent higher for Alpha stocks, 9.9 per cent higher for Beta stocks and 8.2 per cent higher for Gamma stocks. These estimates are based on a sample of 195 stocks, evenly divided among the three groups.[11]

Given their size and timing, the intradaily swings of the market touch for French stocks on SEAQ International are clearly linked to the trading activity on the same stocks in Paris. There are in fact two possible interpretations, each of which probably holds part of the truth. The first is that when the Paris Bourse is open, it exerts a competitive discipline on

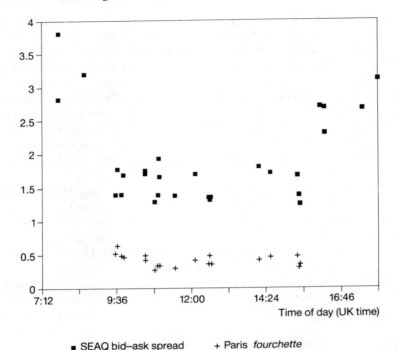

■ SEAQ bid–ask spread   + Paris *fourchette*

Figure 6.4   Spreads in London and *fourchettes* in Paris, by time of day, average percentage values, 3–13 July 1989

the dealers that operate in the French sector of SEAQ. This 'discipline' hypothesis is consistent with most of the available evidence on the effects of intermarket competition in the United States (Branch and Freed, 1977; Hamilton, 1979; Neal, 1987; SEC 1986a, 1986b).

An alternative explanation for the intradaily movements of the SEAQ spread could build on asymmetric information. When the Paris Bourse is closed, London dealers cannot count on the French prices as a guide for setting their quotes and feel more exposed to traders using privileged information, possibly operating from the Continent: widening their bid–ask spread would then be a strategy to protect themselves from such traders. In either case, it is clear that trading activity in Paris from 9:00 a.m. to 4:00 p.m. (London time) benefits also the users of the London market, by making it more liquid than it would otherwise be.

5   Summary of the results

(1) The introduction of the continuous computer-supported auction system in the Paris Bourse has been associated with a significant decrease of the volatility of close-to-close returns, and a smaller and less significant decrease of the volatility of open-to-open returns. No such decline in volatility is found for stocks for which the continuous auction has been implemented via the open outcry system, rather than via screen-based trading (actually the volatility of their open-to-open returns has risen).

The switch to continuous trading has also been associated with lower trading volume, holding other factors constant. Both the results on the volatility and those on trading volume have to be taken with some caution, in view of the small size of the data set used in the tests.

(2) The Paris Bourse currently offers greater liquidity than London dealers, based on the sample of French stocks that are listed on CAC and traded also on SEAQ International. However, this may partly reflect the fact that traders on SEAQ International are often not required to pay any commission expenses, so that the bid–ask spread embodies all the costs they have to pay. For the deals effected with no commission, SEAQ International is actually slightly more competitive than the Paris Bourse.

(3) On cross-listed stocks, there is intense competition between Paris and London, as witnessed by the lack of arbitrage opportunities. Another possible symptom of competition between the two exchanges is the sharp fall in the SEAQ spread on French stocks during the trading hours of the Paris Bourse. This may indicate either that the Bourse exerts competitive pressure on SEAQ market makers or that the latter can make a tighter market in French stocks when they can exploit on-line price information from the Bourse. Obviously these two interpretations are not mutually exclusive.

Appendix

In this Appendix we propose a very simple model to capture the idea that an increase in the frequency of trade can affect price volatility via its effect on the number of traders participating in each auction. In the model people trade only to achieve efficient risk-sharing in the presence of heterogeneous endowments or beliefs (there is no information-based trade), and everyone behaves as a price taker.

There are two classes of traders, N risk averse speculators and M liquidity (or 'noise') traders. The only difference between the two types of traders is that speculators submit price-elastic demands to the market (they buy low and sell high), whereas liquidity traders' net demands are inelastic. The demand for the stock by the ith speculator (k_i^d) is assumed to be linear, and to contain an additive iid random component e_i, with mean 0 and variance σ_e^2:

$$k_i^d = a - bp + e_i \qquad i = 1, 2, \ldots, N \tag{1}$$

This linear demand curve can be derived from a portfolio choice problem under the assumption of mean–variance utility, or negative exponential utility and normal variates. The i.i.d. individual disturbance can instead reflect cross-sectional differences in endowments or beliefs about the fundamental value of the asset.

The supply of the asset K^s is given by a constant K plus the aggregate net supply by the M liquidity traders:

$$K^s = K + \Sigma_j u_j \qquad j = 1, 2, \ldots, M \tag{2}$$

where u_j is the supply of the asset by the jth liquidity trader (an i.i.d. random variable with mean zero and variance σ_u^2). The equilibrium price (obtained by setting $\Sigma_i k_i^d = K^s$) is

$$p = 1/b[a - K/N + (\Sigma_i e_i - \Sigma_j u_j)/N] \tag{3}$$

It is immediate that the variance of the price is decreasing in N, the number of the speculators, and increasing in M, the number of liquidity traders:

$$\text{var}(p) = (1/b)^2(\sigma_e^2 + M\sigma_u^2/N)/N \tag{4}$$

As the frequency of auctions increases, the number of participants per auction – M, N or both – will tend to decrease. The implied effect on price volatility is given by equation (4). If the liquidity traders and the speculators participating in each auction decrease in the same proportion – so that their ratio remains constant – price volatility increases. The same happens if the ratio of liquidity traders to speculators increases above the initial value. If instead the ratio M/N decreases, things can go either way. If the ratio M/N remains above a critical level, volatility will increase, otherwise it will decrease: the latter case will always occur if the number of speculators N remains constant.

Notes

We are grateful to Robert Shiller, as well as to Isabelle Bajeux, Ragnar Lindgren and other participants to a CEPR–ESF Workshop at the University of Lausanne, for their helpful comments. We would also like to thank, for contributing to this chapter with data, information and advice: Denis Richard of the French Treasury, Gilles Oudiz of Banque Stern, Patrick Artus of the Caisse des Dépôt et Consignations, Charles Wyplosz, Hans–Eric Roller and Gabriel Hawawini of INSEAD,

Robert Raymond of the Banque de France, Pierre Fleuriot and Olivier Combe of COB, Bruno Gizard, Jean-Pierre Baron, Patrick de Marteville, M. Bonnet and Odile Tissier of the Société des Bourses Françaises, Christian de Boissieau of Université de Paris I, in France; Doris Sew Hoy of the Quality of Markets Unit, Paul Henderson and Chris Walker of SEAQ International and Ruben Lee of Nuffield College in the United Kingdom; Pier Luigi Parcu of the research department of CONSOB, in Italy. We are also indebted to Costanza Govino of the research department of Banca Commerciale Italiana for her precious help in reorganising the data, and Carlos Ortiz for able research assistance. Marina Margheron is also to be thanked for inputting data. Of course, we are solely responsible for any errors or inaccuracies. Financial support from Banca Commerciale Italiana is gratefully acknowledged.

1 The total cost of a round-trip transaction of £500,000, before and after 'Big Bang', changed as follows:

	Before 'Big Bang' (%)	After 'Big Bang' (%)
Stamp duty	1.00	0.50
Commission	0.31	0.25
Average touch	1.56	1.24
Total	2.87	1.99

The figures for commissions are drawn from Table 4.2 of the *Quality of Markets, Second Report* (March 1987); the figures for the average touch are touches at maximum size for Alpha, Beta and Gamma stocks (Table 2.5), weighted by turnover (Table 2.2), *Quality of Markets Quarterly* (Summer 1987).

2 The data for the first 10 months of 1987 are drawn from the table in Conseil National du Crédit (1988), Annexe XV, whereas figures for 1988 and 1989 have been computed from data supplied directly from the Société des Bourses Françaises and SEAQ International. Since SEAQ International counts both purchases and sales, we divided the London volume data by two. Even so, the data for volume in London and Paris are not fully comparable, since inter-dealer business is included in the former but not in the latter. The gap in the lines in Figure 6.1 reflects the fact that no data are available for November and December 1987.

3 The fees ranged from a maximum rate of 0.65 per cent for transactions below FF 900,000 to a minimum of 0.215 per cent for those above FF 2.2 milion (to which one must add 18.6 per cent VAT on the fee itself).

4 This dual system resembles closely that of the New York Stock Exchange, where an 'upstairs market' specialising in block trading and maintained by investment banks coexists with the centralised market managed by the specialist on the floor of the Exchange. When the upstairs traders strike a deal, they report the trade to the specialist on the floor, and must take any limit orders on the specialist's book that can be executed at the reported price. A similar mechanism operates also in the Amsterdam Bourse: although this retains its old trading system (run by the *hoekman*, a single-capacity trader similar to the now extinct London *jobber*), since 1987 it has supplemented it with the Amsterdam Inter-professional Market (AIM) – a bloc trading system designed for the needs of institutional

investors. AIM allows institutional investors, banks and brokers to trade directly for large deals, but obliges them to report trades promptly to the floor, so as to keep prices in the two markets in line with each other.

5 The companies are Schneider, Alsthom, Auxiliaire Entrep., Total, Eaux (Gle des), Midi (Cie du), Carrefour, Paribas, Club Méditerranée, Bancaire (Cie), BSN, Saint Gobain, Michelin, Havas, Bouygues and Pernod.

6 These authors also find that volatility is higher in the batch auction than in the continuous market, and suggest that this result is accounted for by the greater uncertainty reflected in the prices of the opening auction, rather than by the trading method used: since the opening transaction generally follows a long period of no trade, traders are more uncertain about equilibrium prices.

7 There is a distinct dummy for each company. The companies in the sample are those listed in n. 5, except for Pernod, that switched to continuous trading in a period for which the data were missing.

8 Again, we dropped Pernod because of unavailability of data.

9 In our data set, we have the codes (though not the names) of the brokers who are on the two sides of each transaction, but obviously not those of the customers who placed the order with them.

10 The idea behind this procedure is to reconstruct market orders given by impatient customers who are unwilling to place a limit order and wait until it is executed. In fact, our aggregation procedure stops not only if the series of consecutive sales is interrupted by someone else's transaction, but also if there is an intervening sale by the same broker at an advantageous limit price (we assume implicitly that the corresponding limit order to sell has been placed by another customer acting via the same broker).

11 Lee (1989) calculates the average ratio of the market touch to the minimum dealer spread in each stock, both within and outside the 'mandatory quote period' (Figure IV; 30 p. 91b). The estimates reported in the text are based on his figures, on the assumption that the minimum dealer spread was constant over time. This assumption is reasonable, since Lee reports that individual market makers tend to keep their absolute bid–ask spread constant over time (pp. 84–5): only 13 of the 195 stocks of his sample saw dealers varying their spreads.

References

Amihud, Y. and H. Mendelson (1987) 'Trading Mechanisms and Stock Returns: An Empirical Investigation', *Journal of Finance*, **42**: 533–53.

Amihud, Y. and H. Mendelson (1989) 'Call Auction and Continuous Auction: Effects on Market Volatility and Liquidity', Graduate School of Business Administration, New York University (mimeo).

Amihud, Y., H. Mendelson and M. Murgia (1990) 'Stock Market Microstructure and Return Volatility: Evidence from Italy'; *Journal of Banking and Finance*, **14**: 423–40.

Branch, B. and W. Freed (1977) 'Bid–Asked Spreads on the AMEX and on the Big Board', *Journal of Finance*, **32**: 159–63.

Conseil National du Crédit (1988) 'La fiscalité de l'épargne dans le cadre du marché intérieur Européen', Rapport du Groupe de Travail.

Hamilton, J.L. (1976) 'Competition, Scale Economies, and Transaction Cost in the Stock Market', *Journal of Financial and Quantitative Analysis*, **11**: 779–802.

Hamilton, J.L. (1979) 'Marketplace Fragmentation, Competition, and the Efficiency of the Stock Exchange', *Journal of Finance*, **33**: 171–87.

Lee, Ruben (1989) *Market-making on the UK Stock Exchange*, Ph.D dissertation, Nuffield College, Oxford.

Neal, R. (1987) 'Potential Competition and Actual Competition in Equity Options', *Journal of Finance*, **42**: 511–31.

Securities and Exchange Commission (SEC) (1986a), Office of the Chief Economist, 'Potential Competition and Actual Competition in the Options Markets'.

Securities and Exchange Commission (SEC) (1986b), Office of the Chief Economist, 'The Effect of Multiple Trading on the Market for OTC Options'.

Tauchen, G.E. and M. Pitts (1983) 'The Price Variability–Volume Relationship on the Speculative Markets', *Econometrica*, **51**, 485–505.

Tonks, I. and D. Webb (1989) 'The Reorganization of the London Stock Market: the Causes and Consequences of "Big Bang"', London School of Economics, Financial Market Group, special paper, **20**.

Whitcomb, D.K. (1985) 'An International Comparison of Stock Exchange Trading Structures', in Y. Amihud, T.S.Y. Ho and R.A. Schwartz (eds), *Market Making and the Changing Structure of the Securities Industry*, Lexington, Mass.: Lexington Books: 237–55.

7 Front-running and stock market liquidity

MARCO PAGANO and AILSA RÖELL

1 Introduction

When a stockbroker receives an order from a client, he may have an incentive to trade on his own account to take advantage of the information contained in the order. When he does so before executing the client's order, he is 'front-running' the order, a practice which has become the object of increasing debate and attention by stock exchange regulators.[1] The main reason for this increasing interest is that the introduction of dual-capacity trading in many stock exchanges has eliminated the traditional barriers between the brokerage and dealership function: the same intermediaries are allowed to collect orders from clients and trade on their own account as dealers. In London the 'Big Bang' in 1986 eliminated the distinct roles of 'jobbers' and 'brokers'. In Paris and Madrid, the reforms of 1988 and 1989 respectively allowed stock exchange members also to deal on their own account. In other countries, such as Italy and Germany, the major banks have traditionally dealt in dual capacity on a massive scale, acting as the main conduit for public orders and as the most important players in the stock market, either via representatives (in Germany) or via exchange members (in Italy). In these two countries, the opportunity to front-run clients' orders has thus always been open to banks.[2]

By front-running a broker–dealer can exploit privileged information about the order flow that is about to come onto the market. This information is valuable because the order flow can affect or predict future stock prices, either because it on average reflects news about fundamentals or because it affects the risk premium required by stockholders. Thus the dealer who front-runs by placing his own orders before those of his clients effectively behaves as an agent with inside information, and the effects on the quality of the market are not dissimilar from those of insider trading, as shown in Sections 2 and 3.

178

It should be noted that front-running is not the only way in which dual-capacity traders can take advantage of their special position in the market. Another profitable opportunity arises if they are free to report a time of execution for their clients' orders that differs from the actual execution time. There is then an obvious incentive to report a time and corresponding price that is less favourable than the true execution price. A related method of cheating clients is by placing a number of orders and retaining the best ones oneself, while leaving the clients with the worst deals. Obviously the profits that can be obtained by such misreporting of execution times are larger, the longer the time span over which the dealer has discretion to execute his clients' orders. Finally, a rather different source of profit for dual-capacity dealers arises when they are able to identify the customers who place orders with them and judge their motives for wishing to trade. Long-standing relationships with customers or knowledge of their financial position can help broker–dealers to sort out potential insiders from uninformed liquidity-motivated traders, and offer better terms to the latter. This aspect of dual-capacity trading has been analysed by Röell (1990).

In this chapter we will assume that dual-capacity dealers cannot judge the trading motives of their customers or juggle the time of execution of orders. Their only advantage lies in observing the aggregate orders placed with them in advance of the (preset) time of execution of the orders. This enables them to trade on their own account before filling the customer's order, and thus obtain a price that is different from the one at which customer orders are eventually filled. We show how opportunities for profit can arise in this setting.

We consider a series of two-period models that share a common basic set-up. Customers place their orders via a dual-capacity trader, with orders placed at time 0 for execution at time 1. The dealers can 'front-run' on their clients, i.e. trade themselves at time 0 after observing the orders that have accumulated on their order book.

It is commonly argued that this practice drives up prices against the customers. To analyse this issue, we consider two fundamentally distinct settings. In Section 2, we propose a model where markets are made by competitive risk neutral speculators. The only reason that orders move the price is the prevalence of trading by insiders. In Section 3, there is no insider trading. Instead, the order flow exerts price pressure because competitive market makers are risk averse in the aggregate.

The conclusions reached are rather similar: in both settings, the effects of front-running are experienced by traders in the market at large and not just by the front-runners' customers. In fact, their customers are not necessarily worse off in the equilibrium where the market as a whole is aware that front-running is endemic as compared to a world without front-running. In all but the first case presented, however, any particular customer would benefit if his agent refrained from front-running. Front-runners' profits do generally exceed their clients' losses as a result of front-running, so that one would not expect private contracting to eliminate front-running. Instead, front-runners could implicitly compensate their clients for damage as a result of front-running by lowering the commission rate suitably.

2   Models with insider trading

We consider a series of two-period models. All orders to be executed in the second period (period 1) are channelled through one of a set of dual-capacity dealers, who receive all orders before trade at time 0, and can trade themselves at both time 0 and time 1 after observing their order book. Orders originate from either uninformed liquidity-motivated 'noise' traders or agents with superior information or 'insiders', of whom we assume there is only one in each period.[3] It is assumed that both these groups trade via dual-capacity intermediaries: in our model both will suffer equally (if at all) from front-running by their broker–dealer. Note that they may require a cut in the brokerage commission fee if they are to make use of the services of a front-running dealer.

We assume for simplicity that there is only one monopolistic dual-capacity dealer, who collects the entire order flow. One would expect the outcome of such a model to be rather similar to one with competitive broker–dealers, as long as each one of them has exclusive knowledge of his clients' orders.[4]

The market is cleared by a set of competitive, jointly risk neutral uninformed speculators or market makers. They are aware of the equilibrium strategies of the strategic players: the insiders and the broker–dealers. Hence the market price is set equal to the best estimate of the value of the security, given total market demand from the three types of traders described above.

The three models that we propose in this section are of increasing complexity. In the first, insider trading takes place only in period 1: broker–dealers who front-run in period 0 on their clients' orders are certain to be trading with uninformed 'noise' traders. In the second model, there is an insider trading in both periods but the two insiders have different independent pieces of information, so they do not compete directly against each other. The third model investigates what happens when the two insiders have the same piece of information, so that front-running broker–dealers indirectly exert competitive pressure on the period 0 insider by front-running on the order of (amongst others) the period 1 insider.

Model 1

We start with a very special illustrative case in which front-running has no effect on the broker–dealer's clients. The model assumes that there are no insiders trading in period 0, only noise traders and front-runners. In period 1, orders from both insiders and noise traders are executed. Finally, after trade in period 1, the security's true liquidation value, $V + v$, is publicly revealed, where V is the best initial public estimate of the value of the security, while in periods 0 and 1 only the insider knows v.

The model is the following:

$$y_0 = z_0 + u_0 \tag{2.1}$$

$$y_1 = z_1 + x_1 + u_1 \tag{2.2}$$

where

y_i = total net market demand in period i ($i = 0, 1$).

u_i = noise trading demand in period i, distributed $N(0, \sigma_i^2)$ independently across periods.

z_i = broker–dealers' demand in period i. z_i may depend on $(x_{i+1} + u_{i+1})$, the next period's customer orders observed at time i by the broker-dealers, as well as on the current and past order flow.

x_i = informed traders' demand in period i. This may depend on v, the insider's best informed estimate of the discrepancy between the security's true value and the best public initial estimate V. To all other traders (non-insiders), v is distributed $N(0, \Sigma)$.

In the following proposition we characterise the equilibrium of the model.

Proposition 1

In a two-period model with front-running without any informed trading in the first period, there is a linear equilibrium of the form:

$$P_0 = V + \lambda_0 y_0 \tag{2.3}$$

$$P_1 = V + \lambda_{10} y_0 + \lambda_{11} y_1 \tag{2.4}$$

$$x_1 = \beta_1 v \tag{2.5}$$

$$z_0 = \delta u_0 + \gamma(u_1 + x_1) \tag{2.6}$$

$$z_1 = 0 \tag{2.7}$$

where

$$\lambda_0 = \sqrt{\frac{1}{2} \frac{\Sigma}{\sigma_0^2}} \tag{2.8}$$

$$\lambda_{10} = 0 \tag{2.9}$$

$$\lambda_{11} = \tfrac{1}{2}\sqrt{\frac{\Sigma}{\sigma_1^2}} \tag{2.10}$$

$$\beta_1 = \sqrt{\frac{\sigma_1^2}{\Sigma}} \tag{2.11}$$

$$\gamma = \tfrac{1}{2}\sqrt{\tfrac{1}{2}\frac{\sigma_0^2}{\sigma_1^2}} \tag{2.12}$$

$$\delta = -\tfrac{1}{2} \tag{2.13}$$

Proof. See Appendix.

In equilibrium, the parameter λ_i is an inverse measure of market liquidity at time i: it measures the price pressure per unit of order flow passed on to the market by the broker–dealer. The coefficient β_i denotes the intensity of trading by insiders in response to their information about the security's value. The parameters δ and γ instead show how the front-runner's trading responds to the orders that are to be executed in this period (u_0) and the next ($u_1 + x_1$).[5] The negative sign on the equilibrium value of δ reflects the fact that the broker–dealer absorbs part of the current order flow imbalance. The positive sign on γ shows instead that the broker–dealer exploits his knowledge of next period's orders by trading in the same direction in the current period. γ is an indicator of the intensity of front-running: the proportion of the period 1 order bought in advance by the broker–dealer on his own account.

In this special case, front-running does not harm the dual-capacity firms' brokerage customers: period 0 market demand does not affect the period 1 price. The reason is that any relevant information contained in period 0 demand is spurious once a sharper signal, period 1 demand, is observed (period 0 demand is simply a multiple of period 1 demand plus noise). The front-runners make a profit at the expense of the market at large: the noise traders whose orders are executed in period 0, who find the market less liquid than otherwise. The price moves against them by:

$$\frac{dP_0}{du_0} = \frac{dP_0}{dy_0} \cdot \frac{dy_0}{du_0} = \lambda_0(1 + \delta) = \tfrac{1}{2}\sqrt{\tfrac{1}{2}\frac{\Sigma}{\sigma_0^2}} \tag{2.14}$$

In the absence of front-running, λ_0 would be zero, so that period 0 trades would exert no pressure on the market price.

In the specific model there seems to be an externality attached to front-running. Period 1 customers do not care whether their broker–dealer front-runs or not (though, of course, they would prefer at least a part of their order to be executed in the current rather than in the subsequent period). However, the quality of the market in period 0 would improve if front-running were prohibited. This suggests one reason why explicit rules and laws proscribing front-running are required: customers may not have a strong enough reason to shun front-runners.

Model 2

We now consider a similar model in which there are two different sets of insiders. One knows v_0 (and trades x_0 in period 0), the other knows v_1 (and trades x_1 in period 1). The best estimate of the security's value is $V + v_0 + v_1$, where V is publicly known and v_0 and v_1 are independently distributed with variances Σ_0 and Σ_1, respectively; neither v_0 nor v_1 is publicly revealed until after the end of period 1. Other notation follows that of model 1.

Proposition 2

In the model with front running and distinct informed insiders in the two periods, there is a linear equilibrium provided that σ_0 is large enough relative to σ_1. It takes the form:

$$P_0 = V + \lambda_0 y_0 \tag{2.15}$$

$$P_1 = V + \lambda_{10} y_0 + \lambda_{11} y_1 \tag{2.16}$$

$$x_0 = \beta_0 v_0 \tag{2.17}$$

$$x_1 = \beta_1 v_1 \tag{2.18}$$

$$z_0 = \delta(u_0 + x_0) + \gamma(u_1 + x_1) \tag{2.19}$$

$$z_1 = 0 \tag{2.20}$$

where

$$\lambda_0 = \frac{1 + \tfrac{1}{2}\Sigma_1/\Sigma_0}{1 + \tfrac{1}{4}\Sigma_1/\Sigma_0} \, \frac{1}{2} \sqrt{\frac{\Sigma_0 + \tfrac{1}{2}\Sigma_1}{\sigma_0^2}} \tag{2.21}$$

$$\lambda_{10} = \frac{1}{2} \frac{1 + \tfrac{1}{2}\Sigma_1/\Sigma_0}{(1 + \tfrac{1}{4}\Sigma_1/\Sigma_0)^2} \sqrt{\frac{\Sigma_0 + \tfrac{1}{2}\Sigma_1}{\sigma_0^2}} \tag{2.22}$$

$$\lambda_{11} = \frac{1}{4} \frac{1 + \tfrac{1}{2}\Sigma_1/\Sigma_0}{1 + \tfrac{1}{4}\Sigma_1/\Sigma_0} \sqrt{\frac{\Sigma_1}{\sigma_1^2}} \tag{2.23}$$

$$\beta_0 = \sqrt{\frac{\sigma_0^2}{\Sigma_0 + \tfrac{1}{2}\Sigma_1}} \tag{2.24}$$

$$\beta_1 = \sqrt{\frac{\sigma_1^2}{\Sigma_1}} \tag{2.25}$$

$$\delta = -\frac{\frac{1}{4}\Sigma_1/\Sigma_0}{1 + \frac{1}{2}\Sigma_1/\Sigma_0} \tag{2.26}$$

$$\gamma = \frac{1}{2}\frac{1 + \frac{1}{4}\Sigma_1/\Sigma_0}{1 + \frac{1}{2}\Sigma_1/\Sigma_0}\sqrt{\frac{\Sigma_1}{\sigma_1^2}\frac{\sigma_0^2}{\Sigma_0 + \frac{1}{2}\Sigma_1}} \tag{2.27}$$

and we assume that:

$$\sqrt{\frac{\sigma_1^2}{\sigma_0^2}} \le 2(1 + \frac{1}{4}\Sigma_1/\Sigma_0)^2 \sqrt{\frac{\Sigma_1}{\Sigma_0}}\sqrt{\frac{1}{1 + \frac{1}{2}\Sigma_1/\Sigma_0}} \tag{2.28}$$

Proof. See Appendix.

As in the previous case, the liquidity of the market in the first period worsens as a result of front-running: dP_0/du_0 increases beyond its value of $\frac{1}{2}\sqrt{(\Sigma_0/\sigma_0^2)}$ in the absence of front-running:[6]

$$\frac{dP_0}{du_0} = \lambda_0(1 + \delta) = \frac{1}{2}\sqrt{\frac{\Sigma_0 + \frac{1}{2}\Sigma_1}{\sigma_0^2}} \tag{2.29}$$

so period 0 traders bear the cost of front-running.

How do the dual-capacity firms' customers fare? As before, in equilibrium they are not affected:

$$\frac{dP_1}{du_1} = \lambda_{10}\frac{dy_0}{dy_1} + \lambda_{11}\frac{dy_1}{dy_1}$$

$$= \lambda_{10}\gamma + \lambda_{11}$$

$$= \frac{1}{2}\sqrt{\frac{\Sigma_1}{\sigma_1^2}} \tag{2.30}$$

Why is the liquidity of the market for period 1 traders unaffected? The reason is that in the given equilibrium, net market demand $y_1 = u_1 + x_1$ is known to the competitive price-setting speculators just as it would be without front-running; and this is for them the only relevant piece of information available to make inferences about v_1, the private information that is used by the insiders who trade in period 1.

Although in equilibrium the welfare of customers whose orders are executed in period 1 is not reduced by front-running, individually they would fare better if it were possible to force their broker–dealer not to front-run (so that $dy_0/dx_1 = 0$, the hence $dP_1/dx_1 = \lambda_{11}$). Indeed, if a customer could do so he would be better off in equilibrium than he would be in the equilibrium without any front-running.

So, in contrast to Model 1, there is here a private incentive for the clients to seek out 'honest' broker–dealers who do not front-run or, alternatively, to require a compensating reduction in brokerage fees from broker–dealers who do front-run. The condition under which the broker–dealer's profits from front-running exceed his client's losses is:

$$\sqrt{\frac{\sigma_0^2}{\sigma_1^2}} \geq 2 \frac{(1 + \frac{1}{4}\Sigma_1/\Sigma_0)^2}{(1 + \frac{1}{2}\Sigma_1/\Sigma_0)^{3/2}} \sqrt{\frac{\Sigma_0}{\Sigma_1}} \tag{2.31}$$

as shown in the Appendix. This condition is satisfied if σ_0^2/σ_1^2 is large enough relative to Σ_0/Σ_1, because a relatively large amount of noise trading in period 0 (σ_0^2) raises the broker–dealer's profits by allowing him to trade more aggressively on his knowledge of the future order flow. The large profits he obtained at the expense of period 0 traders in this case induce him to prefer front-running to 'honesty', even if he knows that he will have to compensate period 1 clients via a cut in brokerage fees.

Model 3

The last model to be considered here is one where two different insiders with the *same* information ($v \sim N(0, \Sigma)$) are present, one in each trading period. Here, interestingly enough, front-running provides competition for the period 0 insider, thus reducing transaction costs for ordinary traders in period 0. However, period 1 traders are rendered worse off in equilibrium.

Proposition 3

With two distinct insiders, one in each period, using the same information, and provided σ_1^2 is small enough relative to σ_0^2, there is a linear equilibrium of the form:

$$P_0 = V + \lambda_0 y_0 \tag{2.32}$$

$$P_1 = V + \lambda_{10} y_0 + \lambda_{11} y_1 \tag{2.33}$$

$$x_0 = \beta_0 v \tag{2.34}$$

$$x_1 = \beta_1 v \tag{2.35}$$

$$z_0 = \delta(u_0 + x_0) + \gamma(u_1 + x_1) \tag{2.36}$$

$$z_1 = 0 \tag{2.37}$$

where

$$\lambda_0 = \frac{\sqrt{(2\sqrt{13} - 4)}}{3} \sqrt{\frac{\Sigma}{\sigma_0^2}} \tag{2.38}$$

$$\lambda_{10} = \frac{4}{5 + \sqrt{13}} \sqrt{\frac{\sqrt{13} - 2}{2}} \sqrt{\frac{\Sigma}{\sigma_0^2}} \tag{2.39}$$

$$\lambda_{11} = \frac{2}{5 + \sqrt{13}} \sqrt{\frac{\Sigma}{\sigma_1^2}} \tag{2.40}$$

$$\beta_0 = \sqrt{\frac{\sqrt{13} - 2}{2}} \sqrt{\frac{\sigma_0^2}{\Sigma}} \tag{2.41}$$

$$\beta_1 = \sqrt{\frac{\sigma_1^2}{\Sigma}} \tag{2.42}$$

$$\gamma = \frac{1}{3} \sqrt{\frac{\sqrt{13} - 2}{2}} \sqrt{\frac{\sigma_0^2}{\sigma_1^2}} \tag{2.43}$$

$$\delta = \frac{\sqrt{13} - 5}{6} \tag{2.44}$$

Proof. See Appendix.

Note that here period 0 liquidity actually improves:

$$\frac{dP_0}{du_0} = \lambda_0(1 + \delta) = \sqrt{\frac{(5\sqrt{13} - 1)}{9}} \sqrt{\frac{\Sigma}{\sigma_0^2}} < \frac{1}{2} \sqrt{\frac{\Sigma}{\sigma_0^2}} \tag{2.45}$$

However, the period 1 price for any given order deteriorates somewhat. To see this, note that in the same model without front-running ($\gamma \equiv 0$), the solution is:[7]

$$\lambda_0 = \frac{1}{2} \sqrt{\frac{\Sigma}{\sigma_0^2}} \tag{2.46}$$

$$\lambda_{10} = \frac{1}{3} \sqrt{\frac{\Sigma}{\sigma_0^2}} \tag{2.47}$$

$$\lambda_{11} = \frac{1}{3} \sqrt{\frac{\Sigma}{\sigma_1^2}} \tag{2.48}$$

$$\beta_0 = \sqrt{\frac{\sigma_0^2}{\Sigma}} \qquad (2.49)$$

$$\beta_1 = \sqrt{\frac{\sigma_1^2}{\Sigma}} \qquad (2.50)$$

With front-running, a client trading in the second period will see the market price move in response to his order as follows:

$$\frac{dP_1}{du_1} = \lambda_{10}\gamma + \lambda_{11} = \frac{2}{3}\frac{1 + \sqrt{13}}{5 + \sqrt{13}}\sqrt{\frac{\Sigma}{\sigma_1^2}} \qquad (2.51)$$

Without front-running,

$$\frac{dP_1}{du_1} = \lambda_{11} = \frac{1}{3}\sqrt{\frac{\Sigma}{\sigma_1^2}}$$

So period 1 liquidity deteriorates somewhat as a result of front running.

This deterioration in period 1 liquidity may seem puzzling at first sight. The explanation is that period 0 trading reveals less information about v than it would otherwise, because period 0 insiders curtail their trading relative to the scenario without front running (they trade

$$\sqrt{\frac{\sqrt{13} - 2}{2}}\sqrt{\frac{\sigma_0^2}{\Sigma}}$$

rather than

$$\sqrt{\frac{\sigma_0^2}{\Sigma}}$$

times v). Meanwhile, period 1 insiders trade as much as they would without front-running. Hence y_0 and y_1 together reveal less insider information than they would otherwise, obliging period 1 speculators to protect themselves against trading by insiders by making the market less liquid in period 1.

The net effect on total transaction costs for uninformed traders in both periods taken together depends on the relative sizes of σ_0^2 and σ_1^2. If period 0 noise trading is large enough, there is a net fall in transaction costs.

In evaluating the welfare consequences of front-running in the context of all these models, it should be noted that period 0 traders in our models are agents who, if the models were iterated over time, would have placed their orders in period -1. Even if they are not directly damaged by the activities of their own dealers, they are affected by front-running on the next period's orders. Thus in a market with endemic ongoing front-running the net effect on noise traders would be some average of the effects obtained for period 0 and period 1 traders separately. The steady-state parameters of an interated version of our models would be well worth investigating in this context.

3   A model with risk averse speculators

We consider now a model in which there is no insider trading. Instead, the order flow exerts price pressure because speculators are risk averse and require a risk premium to induce them to absorb noise traders' orders.

Again, we assume that there is noise trading in both periods, but for simplicity with a common variance σ^2. It is assumed that the random order flow at time 0, u_0, is absorbed by offsetting noise demand at time 1. In addition, a new order shock, u_1, independent of u_0, hits the market at time 1.

It is assumed that the broker–dealer trades on own account only in period 0, i.e. he liquidates his holding at time 1: $z_1 \equiv - z_0$ by assumption. Stockholding by broker–dealers in period 1 would not change the nature of the equilibrium, as they would just behave as market makers in that period, sharing risk with the other speculators.

The market makers are also assumed to have a one-period holding horizon in each period. They can best be visualised as short-term specula-tors, providing liquidity and risk-sharing in the market by placing limit orders or price-elastic demand functions. In each period N such market makers take part in trading; those trading in period 0 sell their shares y_{0i} inelasticity in period 1, and those trading in period 1 obtain the liquida-tion value $V + v$ for each of their y_{1i} shares.

Consider first the last period, 1. In that period there are only noise traders and constant absolute risk averse market makers $i = 1, \ldots, N$ who maximise:

$$E[- e^{-bW_{1i}}] \tag{3.1}$$

where $W_{1i} = (V + v - P_1)y_{1i} + W_i$

where y_{1i} is i's demand for equities, and W_i and W_{1i} are initial and final wealth respectively. It is assumed that wealth can also be held in the form of a zero-yield safe asset ('cash').

Under the assumption that $v \sim N(0, \Sigma)$ we get:

$$y_{1i} = (V - P_1)/b\Sigma \tag{3.2}$$

and imposing the market-clearing condition $(y_{11} + \ldots + y_{1N}) + u_1 = 0$, we obtain the period 1 price:

$$P_1 = V + \beta\Sigma u_1 \tag{3.3}$$

where $\beta \equiv b/N$

Now turn to the market equilibrium in period 0. The front-running broker–dealer chooses z_0 so as to maximise his expected utility:

$$E[-e^{-B(P_1 - P_0)z_0}|u_1] \tag{3.4}$$

where B is his coefficient of risk aversion.

However, since he knows u_1 (and hence P_1) he faces no risk and simply maximises his wealth,

$$(P_1 - P_0)z_0 = \{\beta \Sigma u_1 - \lambda(z_0 + u_0)\}z_0 \tag{3.5}$$

where we have made use of (3.3) and we have assumed that the dealer's conjecture about the period 0 price is:

$$P_0 = V + \lambda(z_0 + u_0) \tag{3.6}$$

From (3.5) we find that the optimal broker–dealer's trade is:

$$z_0 = \frac{\beta \Sigma}{2\lambda}u_1 - \tfrac{1}{2}u_0 \tag{3.7}$$

The N risk averse market makers who trade at time 0 instead maximise:

$$E[-e^{-bW_{0i}}|u_0 + z_0] \tag{3.8}$$

where $W_{0i} = (P_1 - P_0)y_{0i} + \underline{W_i}$

and notation is as in (3.1), with all variables simply lagged once.

The maximand in (3.8) can be rewritten as:

$$E[(P_1 - P_0)y_{0i}|u_0 + z_0] - \frac{b}{2}\text{var}(P_1 y_{0i}|u_0 + z_0) \tag{3.9}$$

which yields the demand by market maker i at time 0:

$$y_{0i} = \frac{E[P_1|z_0 + u_0] - P_0}{b\,\text{var}(P_1|z_0 + u_0)} \tag{3.10}$$

Period 0 market clearing requires $y_{01} + \ldots + y_{0N} + u_0 + z_0 = 0$, i.e.:

$$\frac{E[P_1|z_0 + u_0] - P_0}{\beta\,\text{var}(P_1|z_0 + u_0)} + u_0 + z_0 = 0 \tag{3.11}$$

where again $\beta \equiv b/N$. As shown in the Appendix, using this market-clearing condition we obtain the value of the parameter λ consistent with the initial conjecture (3.6):

$$\lambda = \frac{\beta^3 \Sigma^2 \sigma^2}{2}\left(1 + \sqrt{1 + \frac{4}{\beta^4 \Sigma^2 \sigma^4}}\right) \tag{3.12}$$

Substituting equations (3.7) and (3.12) in the expression for the period 0 price, (3.6), one can evaluate the sensitivity of that price to the orders placed by period 0 noise traders:

$$\frac{dP_0}{du_0} = \frac{\beta^3 \Sigma^2 \sigma^2}{4} \left(1 + \sqrt{1 + \frac{4}{\beta^4 \Sigma^2 \sigma^4}} \right) \tag{3.13}$$

This expression can be compared with what would happen if the broker–dealer were forbidden to use the information to trade on his own account – and thus to front-run. If it is assumed that the broker–dealer simply acts as one of the other competitive risk averse market makers, the price sensitivity is found to be:

$$\frac{dP_0}{du_0} = \beta^3 \Sigma^2 \sigma^2 \frac{B}{\beta + B} \tag{3.14}$$

$$= \beta^3 \Sigma^2 \sigma^2 \frac{N}{N + 1} \qquad \text{if } B = b \tag{3.15}$$

where B and b are the broker–dealer's and the market makers' respective coefficients of absolute risk aversion. It is readily seen that the sensitivity of the market price to the order flow of noise traders is not necessarily lower when front-running is banned (equation 3.14) than when it is allowed (equation 3.13).[8] This result runs counter to one's prior intuition that period 0 market liquidity should worsen when the broker–dealer is allowed to exploit his informational advantage by front-running. However, it should be noted that in the context of this model the front-running dealer also has another effect: he has a more precise estimate of the next period's price than the rest of the market because of his advance knowledge of next period's order flow, and can therefore afford to speculate more aggressively than others to smooth out temporary imbalances in the order flow u_0. In fact, in the model he knows P_1 with certainty so that he can act as a risk neutral speculator, and the only reason he does not stabilise the market completely (so that $dP_0/du_0 = 0$) is that he behaves strategically, recognising that his actions affect the market price. In conclusion, in a model with risk aversion, front-running has two opposing effects on market liquidity: a negative one, because the front-runner has the status of a kind of insider, against whom market makers need to protect themselves; and a positive one, because that very same information reduces the risks the front-runner faces and thus enhances his willingness to stabilise prices.

We conclude that if the second effect exceeds the first, noise traders will actually benefit from front-running because the market becomes more liquid. However, the competing market makers will always be harmed by the presence of such a privileged competitor. If it is assumed, for simplicity, that the broker–dealer is as risk averse as other market makers ($B = b$), it is readily shown that the *ex ante* expected utility of the other market makers is lower in the presence of front-running. As shown in the Appendix, the ratio of the two values of expected utility is in fact given by:

$$\frac{\log(E[U|\text{front-running}])}{\log(E[U|\text{no front-running}])} = \left(\frac{N+1}{2N}\right)^2 \tag{3.16}$$

4   Conclusions

One of the advantages enjoyed by broker–dealers on speculative markets is their advance knowledge of the order flow of their clients, and the possibility of exploiting such information by trading on their own account before executing clients' orders. One would expect this practice, known as 'front-running', to be damaging to their clients and to the market in general. In this chapter we try to analyse this contention in the context of a series of models, in which the assumptions of asymmetric information and risk aversion play different roles. In Section 2 we present a sequence of models where it is assumed that, even in the absence of front-running dealers, the market features insider trading, and all market participants are risk neutral. In Section 3, instead, we rule out insider trading but allow both the market makers and the front-running dealer to be risk averse.

One conclusion that is common to all these models is that front-running is generally profitable for broker–dealers, but that the corresponding costs are not borne by their clients alone. Indeed, in all the models except one (the third model in Section 2), the customers are unaffected in equilibrium and profits are obtained at the expense of other market participants – namely, of agents who are trading at a time when front-running is known to be prevalent. This suggests that private incentives may be insufficient to prevent front-running by broker–dealers, and that public intervention may be in order. Private agreements between clients and broker–dealers to eliminate front-running generally will not work: front-runners can outbid 'honest' broker–dealers by offering lower brokerage fees so as to offset the implicit transaction cost arising from the price pressure effect of front-running.

Where the various models do disagree somewhat is on the issue of who suffers from front-running. In the first and second models of Section 2 the front-runner's profits are obtained entirely at the expense of those who trade directly with him – that is, not at the expense of his own customers. In the third model in Section 2, however, the front-runner's profits are gained at the expense of insider traders, and market liquidity actually improves from the viewpoint of the initial noise traders. The reason is that in that model advance knowledge of the order flow reveals to the broker–dealer some of the current insiders' information, so that he ends up competing with insiders and improving market quality for other market participants.

Finally, in the model with risk aversion of Section 3, the effect of front-running on market liquidity as perceived by ordinary traders is ambiguous, while the market makers that compete with the front-runner are sure to be damaged by his presence. The reason why front-running may benefit liquidity traders is that in this model front-running has two opposing effects on market liquidity. On the one hand, the front-runner's information about next period's order flow effectively turns him into an insider, with the usual adverse consequences for market liquidity; on the other hand, this information, by enabling a more accurate forecast of next period's price, increases the front-runner's risk taking capacity and induces him to absorb larger imbalances in the current order flow. If the second effect dominates, front-running may actually improve market liquidity.

Appendix

Proof of Proposition 2

(Proposition 1 is a special case with $v_0 \equiv 0$, $\Sigma_0 = 0$, $v_1 = v$ and $\Sigma_1 = \Sigma$).

The proof proceeds in two stages. In order to economise on notation we first assume that z_1, second-period trading by the broker–dealer, is zero. We show that under this restriction, given that other players employ the linear strategies of Proposition 2, each player optimally responds with a linear strategy of the form given. Secondly, we check for conditions on the parameters such that it is indeed optimal for the broker–dealer not to trade in the second period.

Considering the maximisation problems of the different players:

Insider 0

$$\max_{\{x_0\}} E[(V + v_0 + v_1 - P_0)x_0 \,|\, v_0] \tag{A.1}$$

i.e.

$$\max_{\{x_0\}} (v_0 - \lambda_0(1 + \delta)x_0)x_0 \tag{A.2}$$

since the price P_0 expected by the insider, who does not know the extent of noise trading u_0 or indeed v_1, but realises that the broker–dealer will see his order and supply a proportion δ of it on his own account, is given by:

$$E[P_0] = V + \lambda_0 E[y_0]$$
$$= V + \lambda_0(1 + \delta)x_0 \tag{A.3}$$

The first order condition for maximising (A.2) yields:

$$x_0 = \frac{1}{2\lambda_0(1 + \delta)} v_0 \tag{A.4}^*$$

Insider 1

$$\max_{\{x_1\}} E[(V + v_0 + v_1 - P_1)x_1 | v_1] \tag{A.5}$$

i.e.

$$\max_{\{x_1\}} (v_1 - \lambda_{10}\gamma x_1 - \lambda_{11}x_1)x_1 \tag{A.6}$$

since the agent knows that front runners will trade γ times his order x_1 in period 0. Hence

$$x_1 = \frac{1}{2(\lambda_{10}\gamma + \lambda_{11})} v_1 \tag{A.7}*$$

Broker–dealer

$$\max_{\{z_0\}} E[(V + v_0 + v_1 - P_0)z_0 | u_0 + x_0, u_1 + x_1] \tag{A.8}$$

i.e.

$$\max_{\{z_0\}} (E[(v_1 | u_1 + x_1] + E[v_0 | u_0 + x_0] - \lambda_0(u_0 + x_0) - \lambda_0 z_0)z_0 \tag{A.9}$$

But

$$E[v_1 | u_1 + x_1] = \frac{\beta_1 \Sigma_1}{\beta_1^2 \Sigma_1 + \sigma_1^2} (u_1 + x_1) \tag{A.10}$$

And

$$E[v_0 | u_0 + x_0] = \frac{\beta_0 \Sigma_0}{\beta_0^2 \Sigma_0 + \sigma_0^2} (u_0 + x_0) \tag{A.11}$$

Hence

$$z_0 = \frac{1}{2\lambda_0} \left[\frac{\beta_1 \Sigma_1}{\beta_1^2 \Sigma_1 + \sigma_1^2} (u_1 + x_1) + \left(\frac{\beta_0 \Sigma_0}{\beta_0^2 \Sigma_0 + \sigma_0^2} - \lambda_0 \right) (u_0 + x_0) \right] \tag{A.12}*$$

Market efficiency

Competitive speculators set prices equal to the best estimate of the security's value in both periods:

$$P_i = E[V + v_0 + v_1 | y_i, y_{i-1}] \quad \text{for } i = 0, 1 \tag{A.13}$$

Period 0:

$$P_0 - V = E[v_0 + v_1 | y_0 = (1 + \delta)(u_0 + \beta_0 v_0) + \gamma(u_1 + \beta_1 v_1)] \tag{A.14}$$

$$= \frac{(1 + \delta)\beta_0 \Sigma_0 + \beta_1 \gamma \Sigma_1}{(1 + \delta)^2 \beta_0^2 \Sigma_0 + (\gamma \beta_1)^2 \Sigma_1 + (1 + \delta)^2 \sigma_0^2 + \gamma^2 \sigma_1^2} y_0 \tag{A.15}$$

Period 1:

$$P_1 - V = E[v_0 + v_1 | y_0 = (1 + \delta)(u_0 + \beta_0 v_0) + \gamma(u_1 + \beta_1 v_1),$$
$$y_1 = u_1 + \beta_1 v_1] \tag{A.16}$$

$$= \frac{\beta_0 \Sigma_0}{\beta_0^2 \Sigma_0 + \sigma_0^2} \left(\frac{y_0 + \gamma y_1}{1 + \delta} \right) + \frac{\beta_1 \Sigma_1}{\beta_1^2 \Sigma_1 + \sigma_1^2} y_1 \tag{A.17}*$$

Equating coefficients in the five starred equations with those in equations (2.15)–(2.19):

$$\beta_0 = \frac{1}{2\lambda_0(1 + \delta)} \qquad \text{from (A.4) and (2.17)} \tag{A.18}$$

$$\beta_1 = \frac{1}{2(\lambda_{10}\gamma + \lambda_{11})} \qquad \text{from (A.7) and (2.18) etc.} \tag{A.19}$$

$$\gamma = \frac{1}{2\lambda_0} \frac{\beta_1 \Sigma_1}{\beta_1^2 \Sigma_1 + \sigma_1^2} \tag{A.20}$$

$$\delta = \frac{1}{2\lambda_0} \frac{\beta_0 \Sigma_0}{\beta_0 \Sigma_0 + \sigma_0^2} - \frac{1}{2} \tag{A.21}$$

$$\lambda_0 = \frac{\beta_0(1 + \delta)\Sigma_0 + \beta_1 \gamma \Sigma_1}{\beta_0^2 \Sigma_0 + (\gamma \beta_1)^2 \Sigma_1 + \sigma_0^2(1 + \delta) + \gamma^2 \sigma_1^2} \tag{A.22}$$

$$\lambda_{10} = \frac{\beta_0 \Sigma_0}{\beta_0^2 \Sigma_0 + \sigma_0^2} \frac{1}{1 + \delta} \tag{A.23}$$

$$\lambda_{11} = \frac{\beta_1 \Sigma_1}{\beta_1^2 \Sigma_1 + \sigma_1^2} - \gamma \lambda_{10} \tag{A.24}$$

The parameter values given in the statement of the proposition satisfy these equations.

It remains to be checked that given the proposed equilibrium there is no incentive for the broker–dealer to trade in period 1. Consider his choice of z_1 at that stage, given a value of z_0 determined in period 0.

$$\max_{\{z_1\}} E[(V + v_0 + v_1 - P_1)z_1 | x_0 + u_0, x_1 + u_1] \tag{A.25}$$

where

$$P_1 = V + \lambda_{10}(u_0 + x_0 + z_0) + \lambda_{11}(u_1 + x_1 + z_1) \tag{A.26}$$

and

$$E[V + v_0 + v_1 | x_0 + u_0, x_1 + u_1]$$
$$= V(1 + \delta)\lambda_{10}(x_0 + u_0) + (\lambda_{11} + \lambda_{10}\gamma)(x_1 + u_1) \tag{A.27}$$

Hence the problem reduces to:

$$\max_{\{z_1\}} \{\lambda_{10}(\delta(u_0 + x_0) - z_0) + \lambda_{10}\gamma(u_1 + x_1) - \lambda_{11}z_1\}z_1 \tag{A.28}$$

F.O.C.

$$z_1^* = \frac{1}{2} \frac{\lambda_{10}(\delta(u_0 + x_0) + \gamma(u_1 + x_1) - z_0)}{\lambda_{11}} \tag{A.29}$$

which confirms that $z_1 = 0$ whenever z_0 is as in the proposed equilibrium, given by equation (2.19).

Expected profits from Period 1 trading by the broker–dealer, given z_0 and choosing a corresponding optimal z_1, are given by:

$$\frac{1}{4\lambda_{11}} [\lambda_{10}(\delta(u_0 + x_0) + \gamma(u_1 + x_1) - z_0)]^2 \tag{A.30}$$

Going back to the first-period choice of z_0 to check that total profits in both periods are concave in z_0, we have the second derivative given by:

$$-2\lambda_0 + \frac{\lambda_{10}^2}{2\lambda_{11}} \tag{A.31}$$

≤ 0 under condition (2.28) of Proposition 2.

We conjecture that when that condition fails, the equilibrium involves sufficient randomisation by the broker–dealer in Period 0 (in effect adding noise variance to σ_0^2) so that condition (A.31) just holds with equality, and the broker–dealer is indifferent as to his choice of z_0. Thus he in effect misleads the market in Period 0 to take advantage of this in Period 1.

Proof of condition (2.31)

Inserting the broker–dealer's choice of z_0 (equation (A.12)) into his expected profits (equation (A.9)), his expected profit after observing the order flow in both periods is given by:

$$\frac{1}{4\lambda_0} \left[\frac{\beta_1 \Sigma_1}{\beta_1^2 \Sigma_1 + \sigma_1^2} (u_1 + x_1) + \left(\frac{\beta_0 \Sigma_0}{\beta_0^2 \Sigma_0 + \sigma_0^2} - \lambda_0 \right) (u_0 + x_0) \right]^2 \tag{A.32}$$

Hence on average, before knowing $(u_0 + x_0)$, his profit from knowledge of $(u_1 + x_1)$ is:

$$\frac{1}{4\lambda_0} \left(\frac{\beta_1 \Sigma_1}{\beta_1 \Sigma_1 + \sigma_1^2} \right)^2 (u_1 + x_1)^2 \tag{A.33}$$

The loss to the client from the broker–dealer's front-running is the adverse effect on the price, $\lambda_{10}\gamma(u_1 + x_1)$, times the size of the order, i.e.:

$$\lambda_{10}\gamma(u_1 + x_1)^2 \tag{A.34}$$

(A.33) exceeds (A.34) provided that:

$$\sqrt{\frac{\sigma_0^2}{\sigma_1^2}} \geq 2 \frac{(1 + \frac{1}{4}\Sigma_1/\Sigma_0)^2}{(1 + \frac{1}{2}\Sigma_1/\Sigma_0)^{3/2}} \sqrt{\frac{\Sigma_0}{\Sigma_1}} \tag{A.35}$$

Proof of Proposition 3

Here the two distinct insiders operating in periods 0 and 1 have the same information, namely the realised value of v.

Insider 0

$$\max_{\{x_0\}} E[(V + v - P_0)x_0|v] \tag{A.36}$$

i.e.

$$\max_{\{x_0\}} (v - \lambda_0((1 + \delta)x_0 + \gamma\beta_1 v))x_0 \tag{A.37}$$

Hence, taking the first order condition and equating the coefficient of v with equation (2.35),

$$\beta_0 = \frac{1 - \lambda_0\gamma\beta_1}{2\lambda_0(1 + \delta)} \tag{A.38}*$$

Insider 1

$$\max_{\{x_1\}} E[(V + v - P_1)x_1|v] \tag{A.39}$$

i.e.

$$\max_{\{x_1\}} (v - \lambda_{10}(\beta_0(1 + \delta)v + \gamma x_1) - \lambda_{11}x_1)x_1 \tag{A.40}$$

Hence, equating the coefficient of v in the first order condition with that in equation (2.35),

$$\beta_1 = \frac{1 - \lambda_{10}(1 + \delta)\beta_0}{2(\lambda_{11} + \gamma\lambda_{10})} \tag{A.41}*$$

Broker–dealer

$$\max_{\{z_0\}} E[(V + v - P_0)z_0|u_0 + x_0, u_1 + x_1] \tag{A.42}$$

i.e.

$$\max_{\{z_0\}} E[(v - \lambda_0(u_0 + x_0 + z_0))z_0|u_0 + x_0, u_1 + x_1] \tag{A.43}$$

where

$$E[v|u_0 + x_0, u_1 + x_1] = \frac{\beta_0\sigma_1^2\Sigma(u_0 + x_0) + \beta_1\sigma_0^2\Sigma(u_1 + x_1)}{\sigma_0^2\sigma_1^2 + \beta_0^2\sigma_1^2\Sigma + \beta_1^2\sigma_0^2\Sigma} \tag{A.44}$$

Hence, taking the first order condition and equating the two coefficients with equation (2.36),

$$\delta = \frac{1}{2\lambda_0} \frac{\beta_0\sigma_1^2\Sigma}{\sigma_0^2\sigma_1^2 + \beta_0^2\sigma_1^2\Sigma + \beta_1^2\sigma_0^2\Sigma} - \frac{1}{2} \tag{A.45}*$$

$$\gamma = \frac{1}{2\lambda_0} \frac{\beta_1 \sigma_0^2 \Sigma}{\sigma_0^2 \sigma_1^2 + \beta_0^2 \sigma_1^2 \Sigma + \beta_1^2 \sigma_0^2 \Sigma} \tag{A.46}*$$

Market efficiency

Period 0:

$$P_0 - V = E[v \mid y_0 = (1 + \delta)(u_0 + \beta_0 v) + \gamma(u_1 + \beta_1 v)]$$

$$= \frac{((1 + \delta)\beta_0 + \gamma\beta_1)\Sigma}{((1 + \delta)\beta_0 + \gamma\beta_1)^2 \Sigma + (1 + \delta)^2 \sigma_0^2 + \gamma^2 \sigma_1^2} y_0 \tag{A.47}$$

Hence, equating coefficients of (A.47) and (2.32):

$$\lambda_0 = \frac{((1 + \delta)\beta_0 + \gamma\beta_1)\Sigma}{((1 + \delta)\beta_0 + \gamma\beta_1)^2 \Sigma + (1 + \delta)^2 \sigma_0^2 + \gamma^2 \sigma_1^2} \tag{A.48}$$

Period 1:

$$P_1 - V = E[v \mid y_0 = (1 + \delta)(u_0 + \beta_0 v) + \gamma(u_1 + \beta_1 v), \, y_1 = u_1 + \beta_1 v]$$

$$= \frac{\beta_0 \sigma_1^2 \Sigma}{\sigma_0^2 \sigma_1^2 + \beta_0^2 \sigma_1^2 \Sigma + \beta_1^2 \sigma_0^2 \Sigma} \frac{(y_0 - \gamma y_1)}{1 + \delta}$$

$$+ \frac{\beta_1 \sigma_0^2 \Sigma}{\sigma_0^2 \sigma_1^2 + \beta_0^2 \sigma_1^2 \Sigma + \beta_1^2 \sigma_0^2 \Sigma} y_1 \tag{A.49}$$

Hence, equating coefficients with (2.33):

$$\lambda_{10} = \frac{\beta_0 \sigma_1^2 \Sigma}{\sigma_0^2 \sigma_1^2 + \beta_0^2 \sigma_1^2 \Sigma + \beta_1^2 \sigma_0^2 \Sigma} \frac{1}{1 + \delta} \tag{A.50}*$$

$$\lambda_{11} = \frac{\beta_1 \sigma_0^2 \Sigma}{\sigma_0^2 \sigma_1^2 + \beta_0^2 \sigma_1^2 \Sigma + \beta_1^2 \sigma_0^2 \Sigma} - \gamma\lambda_{10} \tag{A.51}*$$

The seven starred equations determine the parameters β_0, β_1, γ, δ, λ_0, λ_{10} and λ_{11}.

Again, condition (A.31) given at the end of the proof of Proposition 2 must hold for concavity of expected broker–dealer profits in z_0. In this case, that reduces to:

$$\sqrt{\frac{\sigma_1^2}{\sigma_0^2}} \leq \frac{5 + \sqrt{13}}{3} \sqrt{\frac{2}{\sqrt{13} - 2}} = 3.20 \tag{A.52}$$

Derivation of equation (3.12)

Notice that the conditional expectation of the period 1 price is:

$$E[P_1 \mid z_0 + u_0] = V + 2\lambda \frac{\beta^2 \Sigma^2}{\lambda^2 + \beta^2 \Sigma^2} (z_0 + u_0) \tag{A.53}$$

and the conditional variance:

$$\text{var}(P_1 | z_0 + u_0) = \frac{\lambda^2 \beta^2 \Sigma^2 \sigma^2}{\lambda^2 + \beta^2 \Sigma^2} \tag{A.54}$$

Substituting (A.53) and (A.54) into equation (3.11) and equating the coefficient of $(z_0 + u_0)$ with λ, one obtains a second order equation in λ:

$$\lambda^2 - \beta^3 \Sigma^2 \sigma^2 \lambda - \beta^2 \Sigma^2 = 0 \tag{A.55}$$

The unique positive root of this equation is reported in expression (3.12).

Derivation of equation (3.16)

Using equations (3.9), (3.10), (3.11) and (A.54) the expected utility of market makers in the presence of front-running can be computed:

$$\log(E[U | \text{no front-running}]) = \frac{1}{8N} \beta^2 \Sigma^2 \sigma^4 \tag{A.56}$$

and its analogue when front-running is inhibited:

$$\log(E[U | \text{no front-running}]) = \frac{N}{2(N+1)^2} \beta^2 \Sigma^2 \sigma^4 \tag{A.57}$$

Taking the ratio of (A.56) to (A.57), we obtain expression (3.16) in the text.

Notes

We thank Anat Admati, Hayne Leland and Robert Shiller for their comments on earlier drafts.
1 In the United States, front-running within the major exchanges is strictly proscribed. But there is considerable scope for front-running across exchanges by, for example, trading on the Chicago options exchange in advance of a NYSE order. Market authorities are currently setting up a framework for detecting and eliminating such activity. A similar problem may arise in the future in Europe if one exchange were to forbid front-running without coordinating with others. The ban would be rendered ineffective by the increasing integration of European exchanges, especially via cross-listing.
2 See Pagano and Röell (1990, 1992).
3 A many-insider model would have the same qualitative features, as is clear from the work of Kyle (1989).
4 This is the case in the related model of Röell (1990).
5 Alternatively, one may assume that the broker–dealer does not observe the current order flow, u_0, but conditions his demand on his special information $(u_1 + x_1)$ and the current market price:

$$z_0 = \frac{\delta}{(1 + \delta)\lambda_0}(P_0 - V) + \frac{\gamma}{1 + \delta}(u_1 + x_1)$$

6 See Kyle (1985) for the computation of equilibrium parameters for this case.

7 Calculated by setting $\gamma \equiv 0$ in the starred equations for the remaining parameters in the proof of Proposition 3 in the Appendix.

8 This result is qualitatively unchanged if we assume that the broker–dealer does not act as a price taker even when not allowed to front-run, in which case we obtain:

$$\frac{dP_0}{du_0} = \beta^3 \Sigma^2 \sigma^2 \frac{\beta + B}{2\beta + B}$$

Similarly, if we assume he retires from market making altogether we obtain:

$$\frac{dP_0}{du_0} = \beta^3 \Sigma^2 \sigma^2$$

References

Kyle, A.S. (1985) 'Continuous Auctions and Insider Trading', *Econometrica*, **53**: 1315–35.

Kyle, A.S. (1989) 'Informed Speculation with Imperfect Competition', *Review of Economic Studies*, **56**: 317–55.

Pagano, M. and A.A. Röell (1990) 'Trading Systems in European Stock Exchanges: Current Performance and Policy Options', *Economic Policy*, **10**: 63–115.

Pagano, M. and A.A. Röell (1992) 'Shifting Gears: an Economic Evaluation of the Reform of the Paris Bourse', Chapter 6 in this volume.

Röell, A.A. (1990) 'Dual Capacity Trading and the Quality of the Market', *Journal of Financial Intermediation*, **1**: 105–24.

8 Auction markets, dealership markets and execution risk

MARCO PAGANO and AILSA RÖELL

1   Introduction

An economist's immediate picture of a speculative market is that of a Walrasian auction: all market participants submit their orders to buy and to sell, and an anonymous auctioneer finds the price that balances supply and demand. However, in practice many speculative markets are run by market making dealers, who quote bid and ask prices and stand ready to satisfy incoming orders at the stated quotes. Practitioners often describe the difference between the two market regimes by referring to auction markets as 'order-driven' and to dealership markets as 'quote-driven' markets.

Does the difference between these two market systems have substantive economic implications? For instance, are the differences between the two systems so great as to result in a different set of transactions, asset prices, and welfare consequences for market participants? The existing literature on these issues is quite thin, possibly because the auction and the dealership systems differ along many dimensions, and in rather subtle ways.

A reflection of this can be seen in the lack of clear agreement on what really distinguishes the two systems from an economic standpoint. In some models, the distinctive feature of dealership markets is that bid and ask prices are constrained to be constant, independent of aggregate trading volume (Pythiachariyakul, 1986; Mendelson, 1987). But in practice dealers do quote prices that depend on the size of transactions: the bid–ask spread is known to widen for orders of large size. A second characteristic generally associated with dealership markets is that they allow continuous trading, while traditionally auction markets have been characterised by clearing at discrete intervals. However, the frequency of trading cannot be the central difference, because continuous auction markets are not uncommon and are actually becoming increasingly wide-

200

spread: until 1986 Tokyo and Toronto were the only two important exchanges that operated via a continuous auction, but in the late 1980s a number of exchanges in Europe adopted this trading system.[1] Others focus on the fact that dealers have monopoly power; but in Europe, the only dealership system is the competitive UK one, while even on American exchanges with monopoly specialists (NYSE and AMEX) there is effective competition from floor or upstairs traders.

Probably the best way to focus on the meaningful differences between auction and dealership markets is to start from the recognition of what is similar in the two trading systems. It is important to realise that the professional traders that speculate in auction markets play a role quite similar to the market makers of a dealership market: they provide liquidity to other traders. In an auction, speculators supply liquidity by placing limit orders to buy and to sell, against which incoming orders can be executed; in a dealership system, market makers perform the same function by posting bid and ask quotes.

However, despite this functional similarity, dealers are a special breed of speculators because of the many implicit and explicit obligations and privileges conferred upon them. Some of the institutional constraints on dealers' behaviour are rather nebulous, as the exchange authorities form some opinion of what constitutes 'good behaviour' for a dealer, and set indirect rewards and punishments (for example, NYSE specialists who were considered to set a tight market and provide high liquidity in the October 1987 crash were rewarded by having attractive newly-listed securities allocated to their care). This can lead dealers to adopt strategies that are not profit-maximising in the short run, for example by quoting narrow spreads in an extremely unstable market. A more obvious example of the constraints on dealers' behaviour is their obligation to quote firm prices publicly: this is a handicap insofar as it forces them to reveal much of their trading strategy to all other market participants; the offsetting advantage is that other traders cannot compete with them by exposing limit orders directly to the rest of the market.

The fact that dealers have to quote firm prices has an important implication for other traders: in contrast with what happens in auction markets, each trader is insured against execution risk, i.e. the risk of finding few or no counterparties to trade. In an auction market, a trader who places a market order faces an execution risk because his order may execute at an unfavourable price if no offsetting order reaches the market at the same time. On the other hand, if the trader tries to insure against this kind of outcome by placing a limit order, he runs the risk that his order may simply not be executed: execution risk takes the form of uncertainty on the actual execution of the order, rather than that of uncertainty on the price at which it will execute. In a dealership market, by contrast, either form of execution risk is absent: the dealer quotes a bid and an ask price, and at those prices he stands ready to trade against incoming orders.

The dealer can thus be seen as a provider of insurance against execution risk. The crucial point is then whether provision of such insurance is socially efficient: in other words, when is it that customers are better off buying insurance from dealers rather than bearing the risk themselves? In this chapter we present a simple model to address this normative issue. The model is based on the idea that in an auction market a liquidity trader faces a lottery: if lucky, he will cross his orders with an offsetting order by another liquidity trader; if not, he will trade with a professional speculator at a less favourable price to compensate the speculator for the extra risk involved in going short or long on the asset. In a dealership market, the liquidity trader would not face this lottery, since he would go through a dealer for all his trades; the dealer, on the other hand, 'charges' a bid–ask spread to his customers as a compensation for risk.[2] We then analyse whether the expected utility from the lottery implied by the auction is higher or lower than that obtained when 'paying' the bid–ask spread to a dealer.

2   The model

To compare the efficiency of the auction and dealership mechanisms, we propose an illustrative model of the market for a risky security under the two regimes. The security is traded at time 0 and it pays a liquidation value x at time 1. Transactions are carried out by two classes of traders, customers (or liquidity traders) and professional traders.

The *customers* have constant absolute risk aversion (CARA) utility functions $U(x) = - Ae^{-\beta x}$ and place market orders of 1 unit, i.e. have inelastic demand functions. The execution of their orders cannot be fractioned: each order must be filled in a single transaction with another agent. For analytical simplicity, we assume that there are only two potential customers that may wish to trade at time 0: one a potential seller, one a potential buyer. Each of them places an order, independently, with probability q. The *professional traders* have CARA utility $V(x) = - Be^{-bx}$; they act as competitive *speculators* in the auction, placing limit orders at prices l_a (ask) and l_b (bid), and as competitive *dealers* in the dealership market, quoting firm prices p_a (ask) and p_b (bid) for trades of 1 unit of the asset.[3]

2.1   The auction market

In the auction market, competitive speculators contribute to market liquidity by placing limit orders at the ask price l_a and at the bid price l_b. These prices in equilibrium just compensate them for the risk borne by adding 1 unit of the asset to their inventories (or going short by 1 unit). Customers bear execution risk in the form of price uncertainty: if a customer is lucky, he will cross his order directly with an offsetting order at the market mid-price, $(l_a + l_b)/2$; if instead no counterpart order arrives, he will trade with the speculators at the less favourable prices l_a and l_b, that reflect the risk premium required by the speculators.

Competition ensures that the limit prices l_a and l_b are set by the speculators at a level just sufficient to induce them to buy and sell 1 unit of the security, i.e. the certainty-equivalent

$$E[V(-x)] = V(-l_a), \tag{1}$$

$$E[V(x)] = V(l_b). \tag{2}$$

The gap between the two limit prices $L = l_a - l_b$ is increasing in the fundamental riskiness of the security and in the risk aversion of the speculators. For example, if the liquidation value of the security x is a normal random variable with mean μ and variance σ^2, $l_a = \mu + b\sigma^2/2$, $l_b = \mu - b\sigma^2/2$, and the gap between the two prices is $L = b\sigma^2$.

When a buyer and a seller arrive simultaneously, their orders are crossed instead at the mid-price $(l_a + l_b)/2$; when x is normally distributed, this price equals the expected liquidation value μ. One may object that in a continuous auction (the natural benchmark in a comparison with a dealers' market) the chance of two offsetting market orders hitting the market *at the same instant* is practically zero: a market order will almost certainly execute against the best outstanding limit order. But a liquidity-motivated trader can follow this strategy: *first*, place a limit order inside the current market quotes, i.e. between the best outstanding limit buy and sell order, hoping that it might be crossed promptly by an offsetting order; *then*, if this order does not execute, turn it into a market order and transact at the relevant market quote. Our model captures precisely the situation that arises if a trader follows this strategy: the customer will transact inside the pre-existing market quotes l_a and l_b if he is lucky, and will instead trade at these quotes if he is not.

To summarise, there are four possible outcomes in the market:

Probability	Buyer	Seller	Price
q^2	Customer	Customer	$(l_a + l_b)/2$
$(1-q)q$	Customer	Speculator	l_a
$(1-q)q$	Speculator	Customer	l_b
$(1-q)^2$	None	None	—

2.2   The dealership market

In the dealership market, liquidity is provided by dealers who competitively quote an ask price p_a and a bid price p_b. The bid–ask spread $P = p_a - p_b$ is just sufficient to keep the dealers content with being in business. Dealers are assumed to have the same degree of risk aversion as the speculators of the auction market. The key difference with the auction is that in this case even offsetting customer orders are intermediated by the dealer, who charges the bid–ask spread (the 'jobber's turn'); the other side of the coin is that the customer is protected against execution risk.

We assume that when both a buy and a sell order hit the market, the *same* dealer carries out both transactions, and thus earns the bid–ask spread $p_a - p_b$.[4] Competition ensures that the expected utility that a dealer derives from operating equals the expected utility of doing nothing:

$$q^2 V(p_a - p_b) + (1 - q)q EV(x - p_b)$$
$$+ (1 - q)q EV(p_a - x) + (1 - q)^2 V(0) = V(0) \qquad (3)$$

or, replacing expected utilities with their certainty equivalents,

$$qV(p_a - p_b) + (1 - q)[V(l_b - p_b) + V(p_a - l_a)] = (2 - q) V(0) \quad (3')$$

Although there is some latitude in determining equilibrium values of p_a and p_b within the range $[l_a, l_b]$ from this single equation, we shall presume that they are symmetrically determined (i.e. $p_b - l_b = l_a - p_a$), given the symmetric structure of our problem. Using the notation $P \equiv p_a - p_b$ and $L \equiv l_a - l_b$, we then have

$$qV(P) + 2(1 - q)V[(P - L)/2] = (2 - q)V(0) \qquad (4)$$

or, recalling that $V(x) = - Be^{-bx}$,

$$qe^{-bP} + 2(1 - q)e^{-b(P - L)/2} = 2 - q \qquad (4')$$

This equation determines the spread P that makes dealers just indifferent between operating and not operating, relative to the limit order spread L.

3   Choice of market mechanism and customers' welfare

For a typical seller (buyers are analogous) to be indifferent between the two market mechanisms, the following condition must hold:

$$U(p_b) = (1 - q)U(l_b) + q U[(l_a + l_b)/2], \qquad (5)$$

where the expression on the left-hand side is the utility from selling to a dealer, and that on the right-hand side is the expected utility from selling on the auction market. Using the CARA specification of $U(\cdot)$ and deducting $(l_a + l_b)/2$ from wealth in all states, (5) can be rewritten as

$$U(-P/2) = (1-q)U(-L/2) + qU(0) \qquad (5')$$

or, recalling that $U(x) = -Ae^{-\beta x}$,

$$e^{\beta P/2} = (1-q)e^{\beta L/2} + q. \qquad (5'')$$

The dealers' indifference condition $(4')$ and the customers' indifference condition $(5'')$ define two loci in P, L space, that we shall call the D locus (for dealers) and the C locus (for customers), respectively. When the D locus lies *above* the C locus, the minimum spread P required by dealers to operate is higher than that which customers are ready to pay to be as well off as in an auction, so that the dealership market is dominated by the auction. Conversely, when the D locus lies *below* the C locus, the dealership system dominates the other.

Both loci are upward-sloping, as can be seen by total differentiation of equations $(4')$ and $(5'')$: the slope of the D locus is

$$\left.\frac{dP}{dL}\right|_D = \frac{1-q}{qe^{-b(P+L)/2} + 1 - q}, \qquad (6)$$

and that of the C locus is

$$\left.\frac{dP}{dL}\right|_C = 1 - qe^{-\beta P/2}; \qquad (7)$$

both are positive, equal to $(1-q)$ at the origin and to 1 at the asymptote. In the Appendix we show that also the two second derivatives are positive, so that the two curves are strictly convex.

Since at the origin the two loci have the same slope, in a neighbourhood of zero the D locus will lie above the C locus if and only if its second derivative is larger at the origin. As shown in the Appendix, this condition is equivalent to

$$b > \beta/(2-q). \qquad (8)$$

If condition (8) is met, one can prove that the D locus will stay above the C locus *everywhere*, not only in a neighbourhood of the origin:

Proposition 1

If $b \geq \beta/(2-q)$, then the D locus lies above the C locus for any value of L (except at $L = 0$, where they coincide), i.e. dealership is dominated by the auction.

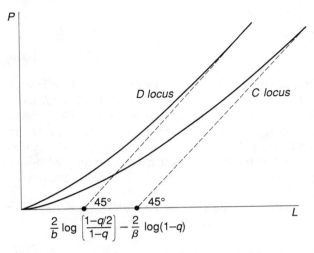

$$\frac{2}{b} \log \left[\frac{1-q/2}{1-q} \right] - \frac{2}{\beta} \log(1-q)$$

Figure 8.1   The indifference loci of dealers (*D*) and of customers (*C*): the case in which dealership is dominated by the auction

Proof. See Appendix.

This case is portrayed in Figure 8.1. Clearly, if dealers are more risk averse than their customers ($b > \beta$), or equally risk averse ($b = \beta$), condition (8) holds and Proposition 1 applies.

Conversely, when the dealers' risk aversion coefficient is less than half that of the customers, dealership turns out to be a superior trading mechanism:

Proposition 2

If $b < \beta/2$, the *D* locus lies above the *C* locus for any value of *L* (except at $L = 0$, where they coincide), i.e. dealership dominates the auction.

Proof. See Appendix.

It must be noticed that $b < \beta/2$ is a sufficient, not a necessary, condition: the region of parameter values over which dealership actually dominates the auction may be larger than this. In fact, for certain values of *L*, the spread between the auction limit prices, we can show that the dealership system dominates also under the less stringent condition $b < \lambda\beta$, where

$$\lambda \equiv \log \left(\frac{1 - q/2}{1 - q} \right) \left[\log \left(\frac{1}{1 - q} \right) \right]^{-1} > \tfrac{1}{2}.$$

More precisely, in the interval between $\beta/2$ and $\lambda\beta$, we can prove that dealership dominates when L is in a neighbourhood of 0 and when $L \to \infty$ (see Proposition 4 in the Appendix), although we conjecture that this may hold also for intermediate values of L.

Finally, there is an interval of values of b and β where the two loci cross. In this intermediate region of parameter values the comparison between the two trading systems is ambiguous:

Proposition 3

If $\lambda\beta < b < \beta/(2 - q)$, where

$$\lambda \equiv \log\left(\frac{1 - q/2}{1 - q}\right)\left[\log\left(\frac{1}{1 - q}\right)\right]^{-1},$$

then the D locus lies below the C locus near the origin, and above it at the asymptote (for $L \to \infty$).

Proof. See Appendix.

In this region, then, the dealership mechanism dominates for small values of L and the auction dominates for large values of L. Recalling that L is an increasing function of the fundamental risk of the security (when x is a normal variate $L = b\sigma^2$), this means that the dealership system is more efficient when fundamental risk is low, while the auction is to be preferred for high-risk securities. Although this result may be rather specific to our simple model, it is consistent with the fact that some high-risk securities, like futures, are traded in auction markets, whereas low-risk ones are often traded by dealers. It also parallels the point made by Grossman and Miller (1987), who argue that assets with high intrinsic risk require a centralised market structure managed by a specialist or an auctioneer, whereas a broker–dealer market is more likely to emerge when risk is comparatively low (they quote the market for real estate as an example of the latter).

To summarise, in our model it is efficient for dealers to perform their insurance role only if they are sufficiently less risk-averse than their customers. The dealership market is superior if dealers are risk-neutral and customers are risk averse, while it is dominated by the auction market if dealers have the same degree of risk aversion as their customers, or a higher one.

These results are illustrated in Figure 8.2, which plots on a line b, the degree of risk aversion of the dealers, and shows that, depending on the value of b relative to β, the degree of risk aversion of their customers, we

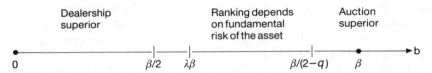

Figure 8.2   Efficiency ranking of the two market structures, b = risk aversion of the dealers, β = risk aversion of the customers, $\lambda < |\, 1/(2-q)\,| < 1$

may be in one of three regions: in the left-most region, b is smaller than $\lambda\beta$ (where $\lambda < 1$) and the dealership system dominates;[5] in the intermediate region, where b is larger but still below β, the result is ambiguous and depends on the riskiness of the security; in the third region, b is larger than $\beta/(2-q)$ and the auction market dominates. In view of the fact that $\beta/(2-q)$ is smaller than β, this means that even if dealers are less risk averse than their customers, they may be unable to offer them a valuable insurance.

4   Conclusion

The main point of the model is that if dealers are to offer an efficient insurance arrangement against execution risk, a necessary condition (though not a sufficient one) is that they must be less risk averse then their customers, or at least act *as if* they were less risk averse. Even if each dealer is individually just as risk averse as everyone else, dealers as a group will act as if they were less risk averse if incoming orders can be fractioned across many dealers, so that the risk borne by each individual dealer will be correspondingly reduced. The same can happen if dealers have access to particularly favourable lines of credit to finance their positions or enjoy special tax or regulatory advantages on their operations. Clearly, the reason why dealers are superior suppliers of insurance against execution risk is not irrelevant from a normative viewpoint: if, for instance, their performance is dependent on tax or regulatory privileges, the social welfare cost of these privileges must be evaluated alongside the immediate benefit for their customers.

Appendix

Second derivatives of the C and D loci

The second derivative of the D locus is:

$$\left.\frac{d^2 P}{dL^2}\right|_D = \frac{(1-q)q\,\dfrac{b}{2}\left(1+\left.\dfrac{dP}{dL}\right|_D\right)e^{-b(P+L)/2}}{(qe^{-b(P+L)/2}+1-q)^2} > 0 \tag{A.1}$$

that at $P = L = 0$ becomes:

$$\frac{d^2 P}{dL^2}\bigg|_D = \frac{b}{2}(1 - q)q(2 - q) \tag{A.2}$$

and that of the C locus is:

$$\frac{d^2 P}{dL^2}\bigg|_C = (1 - q)\frac{\beta}{2}e^{\beta(L - P)/2}\left(1 - \frac{dP}{dL}\bigg|_C\right) \tag{A.3}$$

that at $P = L = 0$ becomes:

$$\frac{d^2 P}{dL^2}\bigg|_C = \frac{\beta}{2}(1 - q)q \tag{A.4}$$

Using (A.2) and (A.4), one can immediately obtain condition (8) in the text. To show that the second derivative in (A.3) is also positive, use equations (5″) and (7) to rewrite it as:

$$\frac{d^2 P}{dL^2}\bigg|_C = \frac{\beta}{2}(1 - qe^{-\beta P/2})qe^{-\beta P/2} > 0 \tag{A.4'}$$

Proof of Proposition 1

Consider the borderline case $b = \beta/(2 - q)$, in which the two second derivatives are equal at the origin. In this case, the first derivative of the D locus is

$$\frac{dP}{dL}\bigg|_D = \frac{1 - q}{qe^{-\frac{\beta}{2}\frac{(P + L)}{2 - q}} + 1 - q} \tag{A.5}$$

On the other hand, using (5″), the first derivative of the C locus in (7) becomes

$$\frac{dP}{dL}\bigg|_C = \frac{1 - q}{qe^{-\frac{\beta}{2}L} + 1 - q} \tag{A.6}$$

Clearly, if the expression in (A.5) is larger than that in (A.6), the D locus lies above the other, and, this being true in the borderline case, it will *a fortiori* hold if $b > \beta/(2 - q)$. Now notice that, for (A.5) to exceed (A.6), one must have $(P + L)/(2 - q) > L$, i.e. $P > L(1 - q)$. But this is true of the D locus, because its slope is $(1 - q)$ at the origin and higher elsewhere (due to the positive second derivative).

Proof of Proposition 2

Consider the borderline case $b = \beta/2$. The first derivative of the D locus becomes

$$\left.\frac{dP}{dL}\right|_D = \frac{1 - q}{qe^{-\frac{\beta}{4}(P + L)} + 1 - q} \tag{A.7}$$

If this expression is smaller than the derivative of the C locus in (A.6), then the D locus lies below the other in the borderline case, and therefore *a fortiori* also when $b < \beta/2$. But notice that P is always smaller than L along both loci. Hence $e^{-\beta(P+L)/4} > e^{-\beta L/2}$, implying that the expression in (A.7) is always smaller than that in (A.6).

Proof of Proposition 3

First, notice that $b < \beta/(2 - q)$ means that condition (8) is violated, implying that the D locus lies below the C locus near the origin. Second, since the asymptote of $(L - P)$ is:

$$\lim_{L \to \infty} (L - P) = \frac{2}{b} \log\left(\frac{1 - q/2}{1 - q}\right), \quad \text{for the } D \text{ locus} \tag{A.8}$$

$$\lim_{L \to \infty} (L - P) = -\frac{2}{\beta} \log(1 - q), \quad \text{for the } C \text{ locus} \tag{A.9}$$

the necessary and sufficient condition for the D locus to lie below the other at the asymptote is:

$$b < \log\left(\frac{1 - q/2}{1 - q}\right)\left[\log\left(\frac{1}{1 - q}\right)\right]^{-1} \beta = \lambda\beta \tag{A.10}$$

Finally, we have to show that the interval $[\lambda\beta, \beta/(2 - q)]$ is non-empty, i.e. that $\lambda < 1/(2 - q)$. With a few algebraic steps, this inequality can be rewritten as:

$$\log(1 - q/2) + (1 - q) \log\left(1 + \frac{q/2}{1 - q}\right) < 0 \tag{A.11}$$

If one takes the linear approximation $\log(y) \cong y - 1$ to the right-hand side of (A.11), one finds that it equals 0. But, considering that $\log(y)$ is in fact smaller than $(y - 1)$ by concavity of the logarithm, the inequality in (A.11) is verified.

Proposition 4

Suppose that $\beta/2 < b < \lambda\beta$. Then the D locus lies below the C locus near the origin and at the asymptote (for $L \to \infty$).

Proof

First of all, we have to show that the interval $[\beta/2, \lambda\beta]$ is non-empty, i.e. that $\lambda > 1/2$. With a few algebraic steps, it is easy to see that this condition is equivalent to:

$$\log(1 - q/2) > (1/2)\log(1 - q), \tag{A.12}$$

which is obviously verified for $q > 0$. Assume then that b is in this interval $[\beta/2, \lambda\beta]$. From the proof of Proposition 3, we know that $\lambda\beta < \beta/(2 - q)$; combining that with the fact that we are assuming $b < \lambda\beta$, this implies that $b < \beta/(2 - q)$, i.e. the D locus lies below the C locus at the origin. Similarly, from that proof, we know that if $b < \lambda\beta$, the D locus lies below the other also for $L \to \infty$.

Notes

We are grateful to Rafael Repullo for providing many insightful comments and suggestions. Any remaining errors are our sole responsibility.
1 Paris, Madrid, Brussels and Copenhagen have already adopted a continuous auction system, where the routeing of orders and the clearing of the order book are effected via computer; the Milan stock exchange is in the process of switching to the same system. A continuous auction works as follows: if possible, new orders are crossed immediately with the best outstanding orders on the limit order book; if they carry a limit price that prevents their immediate execution, the new orders are added to the order book to await later execution according to price priority. See Pagano and Röell (1990, 1992a) for an overview and evaluation of these new developments in European stock markets.
2 Ho and Stoll (1980, 1981) produce a model where the bid–ask spread arises from the riskiness of dealers' inventories. But, in practice as well as in the relevant literature, the size of bid–ask spread is explained also by informational asymmetries: the bid–ask spread compensates the dealer not only for carrying risky inventories but also for the danger of trading with insiders, who profit from their superior information at the dealer's expense. Obviously the asymmetric information problem exists also in auction markets: to the extent that they are in danger of trading with insiders, the auction's speculators will widen the gap between the limit prices at which they place buy and sell orders. In fact, the comparison between auction and dealership proposed in this chapter has been reworked in an asymmetric information model, where both the bid–ask spread of the dealers and the gap between the limit prices of the auction's speculators result from the presence of insider traders (Pagano and Röell, 1992b).
3 This of course presupposes that there is a dealer who quotes the best price on both sides of the market. Clearly, in equilibrium all dealers will quote the same bid and ask prices (anyone quoting the best price for only one side of the market would, if he were to transact, be strictly worse off because he would not be able

ever to net out a buy and sell order). The tie-breaking rule determining which of the dealers will do the two trades when all quote the same prices is irrelevant. For example, each could transact with probability $1/n$, where n is the number of dealers. It is readily verified that one then obtains the indifference condition (3).

4 We have written the utility functions of customers and speculators as depending only on the liquidation value of the security x, and not also on their initial wealth because initial wealth holdings are irrelevant in the CARA case.

5 Actually, as we have seen, we can show that dealership dominates *for any value of L only when* $b < \beta/2$ (see Proposition 2). In the sub-interval between $\beta/2$ and $\lambda\beta$ we can establish the same result only for extreme values of L (see Proposition 4 in the Appendix).

References

Grossman, S. and M. Miller (1987) 'The Determinants of Market Liquidity', Graduate School of Business, University of Chicago (mimeo).

Ho, T. and H. R. Stoll (1980) 'On Dealer Markets Under Competition', *Journal of Finance*, **35**: 259–68.

Ho, T. and H. R. Stoll (1981) 'Optimal Dealer Pricing Under Transactions and Return Uncertainty', *Journal of Financial Economics*, **9**: 47–73.

Mendelson, H. (1987) 'Consolidation, Fragmentation, and Market Performance', *Journal of Financial and Quantitative Analysis*, **22**: 198–207.

Pagano, M. and A. Röell (1990) 'Trading Systems in European Stock Exchanges: Current Performance and Policy Options', *Economic Policy*, **10**: 63–115.

Pagano, M. and A. Röell (1992a) 'Shifting Gears: an Economic Evaluation of the Reform of the Paris Bourse', Chapter 6 in this volume.

Pagano, M. and A. Röell (1992b) 'Auction and Dealership Markets. What is the Difference?', *European Economic Review*, **36**: 213–23.

Pythiachariyakul, P. (1986) 'Exchange Markets: A Welfare Comparison of Market Maker and Walrasian Systems', *Quarterly Journal of Economics*, **101**: 69–84.

Discussion

ROBERT J. SHILLER

What I like about these chapters is that they are instructive about market phenomena that are of particular concern in this time of rapid change of financial institutions. The studies provide theories of phenomena that have not been given a theoretical treatment before, and theories that can be put to immediate use in understanding the recent market innovations and their consequences. Moreover, there is some valuable empirical work that exploits the 'controlled experiment' offered by a recent institutional reform.

Front-running and stock market liquidity

The front-running study (Chapter 7) shows how the broker–dealer (i.e., dual-capacity dealer) will decide on the optimal amount of front-running to do, how the quantities are determined in a general equilibrium, and establishes a way to measure the consequences of front-running.

Pagano and Röell present two models of front-running, that show two fundamentally different reasons for the price response to demand that is essential to front-running. In the first model, price increases in response to demand increases because the demand increases are a noisy signal of fundamental value. In the second, price decreases in response to demand decreases because of the risk aversion of market makers, their unwillingness to hold more of the asset (to allow customers to hold less) unless its expected yield rises to compensate them for the greater risk in their portfolios. It would seem that their first model is preferable. Risk aversion would not appear to be an important factor in understanding front-running because the risk described here can be averaged over many transactions and many broker–dealers; the N in their expression (3.3) is arbitrarily large. Their risk aversion model presents the broker–dealer as having utility that is a function of this trade only, and where the amount at stake in this trade is substantial relative to the concavity of the utility function. But the typical transaction has only an incremental effect on the broker–dealer's wealth.[1]

The conclusion of all models except for the third model in Section 2 is that the front-running activity does not lose money for the customer of the broker–dealer who betrays the customer's confidence, but makes money for the broker–dealers at the expense of others. This conclusion seems very plausible. After hearing of a buy order from the customer, the front-running broker–dealer takes some of the profits away from the original holder of the stock, by depriving him of the capital gain caused by the customer's purchase. And yet there is no reason to expect that he should cause a price to increase for his customer.

But I think that this conclusion is suspect. If it is possible that the front-running broker–dealer is creating profits for himself without hurting his customer, then the two of them are creating value for themselves. But what did the broker–dealer do to create value? He merely spread out the purchase over two periods, so that the demand increase did not reveal as much information at the time of the first purchase. By spreading out the purchase over two periods, he caused the market to confuse the information traders in period 1 with two groups of noise traders, the period 1 noise traders and the period 2 noise traders, rather than just one group of noise traders. But, surely, the customer did not need the broker–dealer's front-running to do that. Purchasers of large quantities of stocks know well that there is usually an advantage to buying slowly, spreading out the purchase over a number of periods. As described by Laffont and Maskin (1990), the customer will conceal his private information by ensuring that the equilibrium price is not very sensitive to his information variable.

I think that if Pagano and Röell had assumed from the outset that the customers of the front-running firm had already spread out the purchase optimally, over the two periods, so as to minimise the cost of making the whole purchase for themselves, then the front-running broker–dealer would necessarily hurt the customer. The broker–dealer would be competing with the customer in period 0, the first period, and therefore driving up the price that the customer had to pay in that period. This situation may well be approximated by that of the third model in Section 2, where customers traded on the same information in period 1 and period 2.

In their conclusion, Pagano and Röell say that 'front-runners can outbid "honest" broker–dealers by offering lower brokerage fees to offset the implicit transaction cost arising from the price pressure effect of front-running', and that therefore 'public intervention may be in order'.

But I do not see that a case has been made here for public intervention. As they note, in equilibrium all broker–dealers will front-run and charge lower commissions to return their front-running profits to the customers who own the inside information. Carrying this to its logical extreme, I suppose that the consequence of this is that the customer would hand over to the broker–dealer the business of optimally spreading his purchases out over a multiple time period, and pay only a 'market rate' for this services. In this situation, there is no reason for the front-runner to be dishonest about what he is doing. Our front-runner has become nothing more than a block trader, who does business by getting shares for his customer at the lowest possible total cost. What reason is there for the government to intervene?

Auction markets, dealership markets, and execution risk

Chapter 8 was instructive in revealing the consequences of the fundamental similarity and of the fundamental difference between auction markets and dealer markets. The fundamental similarity is that both markets have individuals, call them either speculators or dealers, that will find it advantageous to quote, in effect, a bid–ask spread. The dealers call it such, the speculators instead call it limit orders. The fundamental difference is that when buy and sell orders cross within the bid–ask spread, the dealer earns the bid–ask spread, the speculator earns nothing. As a result, the bid–ask spread will tend to be narrower than the range between the lowest sell limit order and the highest buy limit order.

Pagano and Röell have drawn out some of the consequences of this situation in the context of optimising dealers and their customers. Their principal conclusion is that if dealer markets are to be preferable to auction markets, then a necessary condition is that dealers must be less risk averse than their customers.

I think, though, that the same criticism applies to this model as applies to the risk aversion model of front-running that I described above: pure risk aversion is not the dominant factor determining bid–ask spreads.

A better theory for bid–ask spreads might be one in which the spread arises because the dealer has sometimes to deal with buyers or sellers with superior information. This theory was developed originally by Demsetz (1968), and developed further by Copeland and Galai (1983) and others. Superior information traders buy only when they have reason to believe that price will continue to go up, and sell when they have reason to believe that price will continue to go down. Clearly, the dealer loses by trading with such people, but cannot distinguish them from ordinary noise traders. Hence, the dealer must charge a substantial spread to compensate for the losses he expects to make to such informed traders. The more superior information dealers there are, the wider the spread.

I find such a superior information story of bid–ask spreads attractive because it explains certain phenomena. Gammill and Perold (1989) have pointed out that this theory can explain why liquidity is so much better on stock index futures than on the underlying stocks themselves. They argue that there is more likely to be inside information on individual stocks than on the market as a whole. Traders who do not have information on individual stocks can signal their lack of information by their willingness to trade an index. But surely the Pagano–Röell theory does not explain the better liquidity on the stock index futures market, since the price variability is not much different on the stock index futures market.

I think that if they modified their model by replacing the assumption of risk aversion with risk neutrality and also adding that the four cases illustrated on p. 203 occur only with probability $r < 1$, so that all the probabilities in that table are multiplied by r, and granting a probability of $1 - r$ that the dealer will trade with a single informed trader. Then they could have derived a possibly more attractive model of spreads with much the same features that they produced here. The dealer's bid–ask spread would be narrower than the spread between the lowest ask and highest bid limit orders. But this alternative version of their model has rather different policy conclusions. Investor preference for auction markets versus dealer markets would not depend on their risk aversion relative to that of dealers. For example, the informed traders would always prefer the dealer market.

Shifting gears: An economic evaluation of the Paris Bourse

In Chapter 6 the authors have exploited the recent institutional change in the Paris Bourse to tell us something of the effects of continuous versus batch trading. They find that continuous trading appears to produce lower price volatility than does batch trading. I am prepared to believe that they are probably right on this point, but there are still some ambiguities in interpreting their results.

They claim that their method, comparing volatility before and after the introduction of continuous trading, is better than the existing method of comparing open-to-close prices. But their method suffers a distinct disadvantage: the Paris Bourse switched trading methods only once, over a short period of time. There is thus not much more than one observation here. Other factors beside the transition to continuous trading occurred at about the same time, and so with only one observation we cannot tell whether these other factors were the cause of observed changes in market behaviour over the transition period. The most notable such change is marked by the Stock Market crash of 1987, which occurred right in the middle of the transition period for the stocks listed in Table 6.2. The Stock Market crash produced a tremendous increase in volatility on the Paris Bourse, just as in other stock exchanges. This transient increase in volatility can be seen very clearly in their Figure 6.2. Now, it is good to see that they have included the market volatility as an additional regressor in their regressions. This might control for the effects of the Stock Market crash. On the other hand, it might not. The stocks for which the transition was made may be systematically different from the market as a whole. The other side of this is that the market volatility variable may capture some of the effects of the transition to continuous trading. This would clearly be the case if all stocks made the transition at the same time; then the decline in volatility of individual stocks at the time of their transition would correspond perfectly to a decline in market volatility.

Pagano and Röell also mention several other factors that changed around the same time: the introduction of broker–dealers, i.e., dual-capacity dealers, the liberalisation of commission charges, and the advent of block trading off the floor. It is unclear to me from their discussion to what extent any of these other changes might be held responsible for the changes observed before and after the transition to continuous trading. The date Pagano and Röell give for the law permitting broker–dealers is January 1988. One-third of their firms made the transition to continuous trading in January 1988 or later, and more than half made the transition not substantially earlier than the January 1988 date, so it would appear that any change in these firms' return volatility might be attributed to the advent of broker–dealers. But Pagano and Röell say that the law specified that the phase-in of broker–dealers came gradually, and it is not clear here when the change took effect. Pagano and Röell do not give a clear change date for the liberalisation of commission charges.

Any of the potential for such spurious effect is reduced when one considers that not all stocks switched to the new trading regime at the same time. In their Table 6.2, the earliest transition reported is August 1986, the last February 1988, thus the dates of the transitions range over two and a half years. Two and a half years helps, but is not a long enough time out of a sample of four and a half years.

Another consideration is that the transition dates were not random, but were related to firm size, bigger firms making the transition first. Suppose the Paris Bourse picked high volatility stocks to make the transition. If volatility is a stationary, mean-reverting process, then the stocks chosen for transition will tend to have a subsequent decline in volatility. This might also explain their other result that trading volume declined after the transition, since for individual stocks there is an association between trading volume and volatility.

All of these considerations are especially important since the size of the change that they observed in volatility at the time of the transition was only 5 per cent to 8 per cent of total volatility; at a time when market volatility has changed by a factor of as much as 500 per cent, there is plenty of room for spurious effects to be responsible for their results. The results on trading volume are vulnerable to the same spurious regression effects.

Notes

Robert J. Shiller is Stanley B. Resor Professor of Economics, Cowles Foundation, Yale University.
1 The authoritative paper of Ho and Stoll (1981) which developed a risk aversion theory of bid–ask spreads assumed that the dealer deals in only one stock. They said (p. 53) that 'We leave to future research the development of a more complete multiperiod portfolio analysis of the dealer and the integration of dealer behaviour into the theory of equilibrium asset pricing'.

References

Copeland, Thomas E. and Dan Galai (1983) 'Informational Effects of Bid Ask Spreads', *Journal of Finance*, **38(5)** (December): 1457–69.

Demsetz, Harold (1968) 'The Cost of Transacting', *Quarterly Journal of Economics*, **82**: 33–53.

Gammill, James F. Jr and André F. Perold (1989) 'The Changing Character of Stock Market Liquidity', *Journal of Portfolio Management* (Spring): 13–18.

Ho, Thomas and Hans Stoll (1981) 'Optimal Dealer Pricing Under Transactions and Return Uncertainty', *Journal of Financial Economics*, **9**: (March) 47–74.

Laffont, Jean-Jacques and Eric S. Maskin (1990) 'The Efficient Markets Hypothesis and Insider Trading on the Stock Market', *Journal of Political Economy*, **98** (February): 70–93.

2.3 The bond market

9 The impact of a new futures contract on risk premia in the term structure: an APT analysis for French government bonds

ALESSANDRO CITANNA and
RICCARDO ROVELLI

1   Introduction and summary[1]

What is the effect of the introduction of a futures contract on the spot price of the underlying asset? Empirical research has attempted to measure the effects of futures transactions on the volatility of spot prices.[2] However, we believe that there are situations, related to some kind of market imperfections and investors' risk aversion and heterogeneity, where one should also be able to detect an effect on the price, i.e. on the required return of the underlying asset.

In Section 2 of the chapter we motivate our theoretical *a priori*. We show that, with risk averse investors in the spot market, and if opportunities to hedge interest rate risk were not easily available before the introduction of the futures contract, then in some instances the introduction of such a contract will reduce the required excess return on the underlying asset.

In Section 3 of the chapter we develop an appropriate methodology for testing our conjecture. The excess return on a risky asset may be modelled in terms of premia attached to some specific risk factors, in the tradition of the APT model (Ross, 1976, 1977). Following the introduction of a futures contract, and if it can be argued that this provides new opportunities to hedge interest rate risk, then the premium related to this specific risk factor should decrease significantly.

Section 4 describes the data used to test our model. The French Treasury bond market provides an adequate laboratory for our experiment. In February 1986, a futures contract on Treasury Bonds, the 'Notionnel 10', began trading on the Paris MATIF, and was received with considerable success. Before that date, hedging opportunities were limited and costly. In this section, we also describe the construction and risk–return characteristics of five bond portfolios with constant maturity, which will provide the empirical basis for our APT model.

Section 5 analyses the macroeconomic risk factors and describes the method of estimation. We pre-specify two risk factors – term structure risk and inflation, but find that only the former is significant. In the estimation procedure, we follow Gultekin and Rogalski (1985) in applying the APT model to bond returns. We also use the method of pre-specifying the macro risk factors, suggested by Chen, Roll and Ross (1986). Estimates are obtained with the ITNLSURE estimator used by Burmeister and McElroy (1988).

Finally, Section 6 discusses the empirical results relative to the whole sample 1985–9, and Section 7 the results after splitting the sample in two sub-periods, before and after the MATIF. In the latter section we analyse the estimated change of the risk premium after the introduction of the futures contract. Our results confirm our expectations. Section 8 briefly sums up the main results and draws some normative implications.

2   The theory

Why should the introduction of a futures contract on bonds lower the interest rate required by bondholders?

To develop our argument, we proceed by the following steps. First we characterise a term structure of prices (yields) determined according to the pure expectations theory. In this case, we would expect that the introduction of a futures market should have no consequences on spot prices. In order to get a different result, in the second step of our reasoning we characterise a term structure which embodies risk premia. In a third step, we find that the supply of hedging services will reduce risk premia. We distinguish two cases: if intermediaries are risk neutral, then risk premia will be reduced to zero; if intermediaries are risk averse, then risk premia will only be reduced but remain positive. In a fourth step, we distinguish between hedging on the futures versus the forward markets. We argue that in the first case the reduction of the risk premia should be larger.

2.1   A riskless term structure of security prices

Assume there exist two kinds of securities, discount bonds maturing in N periods, and bills maturing in one period. The latter are reissued each period. Value at maturity is 1 unit of money for bills and bonds.

Each investor is certain that, if she decides to sell part of her portfolio, she will at all times receive the equilibrium price for the securities sold. That is, there is no credit or liquidity risk.

Although we do not model the stochastic behaviour of interest rates, we assume that interest rate risk is one (and for the moment the only) source of risk.

If investors are risk neutral, however, they will be indifferent to risk, and will price securities at the expected price. Thus, for any n, $n = 2, \ldots,$ $N - 1$, it will be true that the price quoted today (t) of a hypothetical bond paying 1 unit maturing at period $t + n$ and with unitary face value, may be indifferently expressed[3] as either

$$P_{n,t} = P_{1,t} E_t\left(\prod_{i=1}^{n-1} P_{1,t+i}\right) \tag{1.1}$$

or equivalently

$$P_{n,t} = P_{N,t} / E_t\left(\prod_{i=n}^{N-1} P_{1,t+i}\right) \tag{1.2}$$

These expressions state that two different strategies, of rolling along the term structure versus rolling out, have the same expected value. Without losing generality, let us simplify the notation by setting $N = 3$ so that $n = 2$. We may thus rewrite the two strategies above as

$$P_{2,t} = P_{1,t} E_t(P_{1,t+1}) \tag{1.3}$$

and

$$P_{2,t} = P_{3,t} E_t(P_{1,t+2}) \tag{1.4}$$

2.2   Risk averse investors

What happens if investors are risk averse? In general, risk aversion causes risk premia in asset markets. However, in the term structure case this is not so obvious. To see this, recall our assumption that the only relevant risk, so far, is interest rate risk. This is defined as the risk that, at time $t = 0$, when an investment is started, the liquidation value at time $t = T$ is not certain. Note that in general each investor will have their own vector of desired liquidation dates, presumably based on the time pattern of desired consumption. However, if zero coupons (or equivalent portfolios) are available maturing at each possible liquidation date in the future, and if their supply matches demand, then each investor will be able to set up an investment immune to risk over the desired horizon. Will this be the case? Will a risk averse investor always choose a horizon-matching investment, if available? The answer in general is negative. For a given horizon and a finite level of risk aversion, there is an optimal amount of risk which investors like to put in their portfolios.

To be more precise, we shall state three propositions. In all cases we assume risk averse investors. We first assume no hedging opportunities, we then introduce risk neutral intermediaries (speculators) who supply hedging services at no cost. Finally intermediaries are assumed to be risk averse.

The model is based on the following assumptions.

Markets
Two markets exist: a one-period bill market and a two-period bond market. The supply of both assets is exogenously given.

Agents
Only investors participate in the market. They are von Neumann–Morgenstern expected utility-maximisers, with negative exponential utility function. a_h is the coefficient of ARA. They are endowed with initial wealth W_0, which can be invested in bills or bonds. They decide in period 0 the composition of their wealth.

Trades
All trades take place in period 0 and all portfolios are liquidated in period 1. Since bills mature in period 1, they are safe assets relative to the holding period which goes from time 0 to time 1. The total return on this riskless asset is fixed to $R = 1 + r$. Bonds are bought in period 0 at the price p_0 and sold in period 1 at the price $\tilde{p}_1$, which is a Gaussian random variable, with variance σ_p^2.

We may now state

Proposition 1

If no hedging is allowed, investors will hold a diversified portfolio of bills and bonds. Bonds will be priced at a discount relative to bills. It is easy to show that, computing the first order condition for the risk averse investor maximisation problem, subject to the wealth constraint

$$W_1 = RW_0 + [E(\tilde{p}_1) - Rp_0]x_h \tag{2}$$

the individual demand of risky bonds is

$$x_h = \frac{E(\tilde{p}_1) - Rp_0}{a_h \sigma_p^2} \tag{3}$$

From the market-clearing condition on the bond market, we get

$$E(\tilde{p}_1) - Rp_0 = \frac{a_h \sigma_p^2 \bar{X}}{N} \tag{4}$$

where N is the number of bond investors, and $\bar{X}$ is the total real supply of bonds. Note that, with ARA, the size of the risky investment does not depend on the amount of initial wealth to be invested. Hence it is possible that $x_h > W_0$ for some individuals. Also notice that, since the utility function exhibits constant ARA, the risk premium is defined in absolute, rather than in percentage terms.

2.3   The supply of hedging services

To state and prove the second proposition we modify the set-up of the model with the following additional assumptions.[4]

Markets
A market for bond futures contracts also exists. The net supply of futures contracts is zero. There is no basis risk in futures contracts. We indicate a long futures position with $f > 0$.

Agents
Investors can trade in the futures market. There is a second class of agents (speculators). They have zero initial net worth, and are restricted to trading only in futures contracts. Speculators are risk neutral. With free entry this ensures zero expected profits.

We may now state the following.

Proposition 2

With risk neutral intermediaries (speculators), investors (hedgers) will want to go short on the futures market. Futures contracts will be priced at the same price as is expected for bonds in period 1. The risk premium in the spot market for bonds is zero.

Hedgers now maximise

$$RW_0 + [E(\tilde{p}_1) - Rp_0]x_h + [E(\tilde{p}_1) - p_f]f_h - \frac{a_h}{2}\sigma_p^2(x_h + f_h)^2 \qquad (5)$$

with respect to x_h and f_h. The two first order conditions are

$$E(\tilde{p}_1) - Rp_0 - a_h\sigma_p^2(x_h + f_h) = 0 \qquad (6)$$

$$E(\tilde{p}_1) - p_f - a_h\sigma_p^2(x_h + f_h) = 0 \qquad (7)$$

Speculators maximise

$$[E(\tilde{p}_1) - p_f]f_s \qquad (8)$$

with respect to f_s. The first order condition for speculators gives a perfectly elastic supply of hedging services. Zero expected profits require that

$$p_f = E(\tilde{p}_1) \tag{9}$$

Substituting this in equation (7) gives:

$$x_h = -f_h \tag{10}$$

which states that the bond portfolio is entirely hedged. Substituting (9) again in equation (6) gives

$$E(\tilde{p}_1) = Rp_0 \tag{11}$$

that is, bonds are priced at the riskless rate and there is no risk premium.

We now modify the model, allowing for risk averse intermediaries (speculators). Our initial assumptions are modified as follows.

Agents

Intermediaries are also von Neumann–Morgenstern expected utility-maximisers, with negative exponential utility function. a_s is their ARA coefficient. They have zero initial net worth, and are restricted to trade only in futures contracts.

In this case we obtain the following proposition.

Proposition 3

With risk averse intermediaries (speculators), the supply of futures contracts is finite. There is 'backwardation' in the futures market. The expected return on bonds include a positive risk premium, but this is lower than in the case where no hedging is possible.

First order conditions for hedgers are again given by equations (6) and (7). Now speculators maximise

$$[E(\tilde{p}_1) - p_f]f_s - \frac{a_s}{2}\sigma_p^2 f_s^2 \tag{12}$$

with respect to f_s. The first order condition is

$$E(\tilde{p}_1) - p_f - a_s\sigma_p^2 f_s = 0 \tag{13}$$

From this equation we solve for the optimal individual supply of hedging services

$$f_s = \frac{E(\tilde{p}_1) - p_f}{a_s\sigma_p^2} \tag{14}$$

Note that speculators will go long (and thus allow hedgers to go short) only if there is 'backwardation', that is if $E(\tilde{p}_1) > p_f$.

In fact, equilibrium in the futures and bond markets requires that

$$Nf_h + Mf_s = 0 \tag{15}$$

and

$$Nx_h = \bar{X} \tag{16}$$

where M is the number of identical speculators. Substituting equations (14), (15) and (16) in (7), we can solve for the equilibrium futures price as a function of total bond supply

$$p_f = E(\tilde{p}_1) - \frac{a_h a_s}{Ma_h + Na_s} \sigma_p^2 \bar{X} \tag{17}$$

Equation (17) shows that there will indeed be 'backwardation' in the futures market, hence hedges will be supplied to investors. Using equation (6) we can now solve for expected return on holding a long position in bonds. Substituting equations (14), (15) and (16) in (6) and rearranging, we obtain

$$E(\tilde{p}_1) - Rp_0 = \frac{a_h a_s}{Ma_h + Na_s} \sigma_p^2 \bar{X} \tag{18}$$

It is immediately apparent that the expected period return to bond-holdings in equation (18) is lower than in equation (4), since it is scaled down by a factor

$$0 < \frac{a_s}{\dfrac{M}{N} a_h + a_s} < 1$$

for any given $\bar{X}$ and σ_p^2 and any positive, finite N, M.

We may finally notice that in equilibrium the risk premium when hedging services are not supplied is higher than the same premium in the case where the supply of hedging services has a finite elasticity, that is

$$E(\tilde{p}_1) - Rp_0|_{f=0} > E(\tilde{p}_1) - Rp_0$$

Note also that the link between the spot and the futures market for bonds is given by

$$p_f = Rp_0 \tag{19}$$

under both Proposition 2 and 3.

This allows us to interpret Rp_0 also as the 'cost of carry' of the futures contract.

We now move on to the fourth step of our analysis, introducing the distinction between futures and forward contracts.

2.4   Forward versus futures hedging

Propositions 2 and 3 stated above suggest that expected rates of return on the spot market are negatively related to the supply of hedging services. This result motivates us to believe that the introduction of a hedging opportunity would lower interest rates on the spot market – more precisely, we would expect that risk premia in the term structure would be reduced: hence the term structure would behave more in line with the pure expectations theory.

Should this theoretical result lead us to investigate whether the opening of an organised futures market does indeed cause lower risk premia in the term structure of spot rates? One possibly relevant objection is that the results proved above depend critically on new agents (the intermediaries–speculators) wanting to trade only after the futures contract has become available. In fact, in our model the futures market simply allows a given amount of risk to be shared by a greater number of agents. A natural question to ask is: where do the intermediaries come from? Why did they not participate in risk-sharing before the futures market was opened? For instance, even in the absence of an organised futures market, investors could always hedge their risk in the forward market. While this objection is correct in principle, we shall argue below that several forms of inefficiency might prevent the smooth – i.e. costless – working of the forward market, and hence decrease the number of participants in risk-sharing. To examine this objection assume that, instead of hedging interest rate risk by selling futures contracts, an investor chooses to sell forward the securities in her portfolio. In this case, she would obviously not face any basis risk – as we assumed in the model above, even if in practice this is a relevant, though diversifiable, source of risk (see Anderson and Danthine, 1981).

However, hedging on the forward market brings two main added sources of risk: the risk of non-performance and the illiquidity risk in the spot market.

As regards the first point, consider a forward contract, established at time 0, for the delivery at time 1 of a bond maturing after this period at an agreed-upon price $F_0(1,1)$. This contract incorporates two options: an implicit put option for the forward buyer and an implicit call option for the forward seller (Kane, 1980, p. 230). The former might be exercised whenever the price of bonds fell below the forward price, the latter when it rose above it. Although exercising either option constitutes non-performance of the explicit forward contract, the true forward price will include the price of the two options, or the cost of perfect performance guarantees.

It is on this last aspect (the cost of perfect performance guarantees) that futures and forward contracts mostly differ: 'a futures contract is to a forward contract as currency is to a check drawn against a demand deposit in a commercial bank. The validity of a genuine \$10 bill . . . does not depend on who offers it in payment, while the validity of a \$10 check depends on the identity of the person who writes or presents it and on the identity of the bank' (Telser and Higinbotham, 1977, p. 973). Since the futures market operates with a margin system, and this is not too costly to access, all potential market participants can access the futures market (as hedgers or speculators), without being regarded as potential credit risks by other participants. Counterparty risk is thus largely disposed of, and at the same time, given increased participation, the liquidity and depth of the market are greatly increased.

Let us turn to the liquidity risk in forward contracts. So far, we have been concerned with interest rate risk only. However, this is only one component of the more general liquidity risk, as defined in Garbade and Silber (1979). Consider again a strategy of rolling out, as defined in equation (1.4) above. Assume for simplicity that expected and realised prices of bills are equal, so that at time $t + 2$

$$P_{1,t+2} = E_t(P_{1,t+2})$$

where $P_{1,t+2}$ defines the equilibrium price of a bill as of time $t + 2$. However, because of lack of liquidity, the actual price of a bond with one period to maturity in period $t + 2$ may be less than the price of a newly issued bill with the same maturity.[5] Then the cost of the uncovered roll-out strategy increases by the same amount as the illiquidity premium. We denote with $P(t)_{1,t+2}$ the price at time $t + 2$ of a security issued at time t and due to mature after one period, i.e. in $t + 3$. If this security suffers a discount relative to a bill with the same residual maturity, this is defined by

$$P(t)_{1,t+2} = P_{1,t+2}(1 - \mu) \qquad \mu > 0 \tag{20}$$

Some aspects of this liquidity price discount are worth noting. First, notice that this discount is expected. So it will be priced by every participant to the market, whether she is averse or neutral to risk. Moreover, it will also be priced in a forward contract. If I sell an illiquid security forward, the buyer of the security will require the same discount that she expects will prevail in the market at the delivery time. Thus forward contracts do not displace liquidity risk out of the term structure.

However, futures markets may do the trick. In fact, futures contracts have some institutional characteristics that differentiate their role rather sharply from that of generic forward contracts: futures are standardised, they are immune from counterparty risk (as was argued above), they may be liquid even if the market for the underlying asset is not. In general, 'It is true that forward contracts are less fungible than are futures contracts. This is the vital point' (Telser, 1981, p. 5). 'The backing of the clearing house behind the futures contracts traded on the exchanges enhances the fungibility of the contract. . . . Consequently a futures contract acquires the same advantages over a forward contract as trade conducted with the aid of money has over barter' (Telser, 1981, p. 12). In the following we briefly examine the liquidity-enhancing characteristics of a futures market, and then discuss why these characteristics should reduce the cost of hedging interest rate risk.

First, futures are non-specific to any particular bond traded in the spot market: on delivery date, one can deliver any instrument with maturity falling in a specified range. On the one hand, this introduces a basis risk in hedging spot positions with a futures contract, but on the other this helps to overcome the possible illiquidity of the single underlying instrument. In underdeveloped markets, where too many different issues (albeit by the same issuer, i.e. the Treasury) have succeeded in fragmenting the spot market, a futures contract can be a powerful instrument to help reduce market segmentation.

Second, as it has been argued above, the margins system helps to dispose of counterparty risk and, given increased participation, increases the liquidity and depth of the market.

Third, futures contracts are standardised and trading takes place in a centralised market place. This again improves liquidity and transparency.

Fourth, futures allow us to manage interest rate exposure of a portfolio, without the need for reallocating the long positions in that portfolio. In some relatively underdeveloped financial markets, this is a considerable improvement. In such markets, some institutional investors are prevented by internal rules from 'undoing' a position at a price lower than the historic price. Also, in these markets the tax on spot market transactions may often effectively discourage hedging transactions such as repurchase agreements. The opportunity to hedge positions in a futures market overcomes both kind of problems, so that futures may be a powerful instrument to increase the allocative efficiency of relatively underdeveloped markets.[6]

Why should the liquidity-enhancing characteristics of a futures market decrease the required returns (inclusive of the premium for liquidity risk) on the spot instruments? The answer is not immediate because the μ discount factor in equation (20) refers to the spot, and not to the futures market. Our argument is twofold. If an 'illiquid' security becomes deliverable in terms of a standardised futures contract, then μ will be reduced.

Moreover, a futures contract may be closed by buying an opposite position on the futures market, rather than on the spot one. Again, this helps to bypass the illiquidity of the underlying spot market.

In conclusion, a futures market relieves the cost of illiquidity of the underlying spot market – and may also increase liquidity itself, by increasing the total volume of trades – and allows investors to buy hedges at the equilibrium futures prices, increasing the price incentive to enter into hedged positions. The result will be that each risk averse investor is more likely to obtain the desired maturity structure of her holdings, and risk premia will accordingly be reduced.

3   The empirical methodology

In order to test the hypothesis of a reduction of the interest rate risk premium we use an Arbitrage Pricing Theory (APT) specification of bond returns. As is well known, the APT model was introduced first by Ross (1976, 1977), and successively elaborated by various authors (e.g. Connor, 1984, Huberman, 1982 and Ingersoll, 1984, 1987). Following this last approach, we can summarise the APT model as follows. Suppose we have an economy with n assets – with n very large[7] – whose returns r_i follow a linear stochastic process in K exogenous factors f_j)

$$r_i = E(r_i) + \sum_{j=1}^{K} b_{i,j} f_j + e_i \qquad i = 1, 2, \ldots, n \qquad (21)$$

where $b_{i,j}$ = *sensitivity of the* ith asset to the jth factor, r_i, f_i and e_i are time variables, but we drop the time subscripts for ease of notation.

We are also assuming that

$$E(e_i) = E(f_j) = E(e_i f_i) = E(f_j f_k) = 0$$

and that both the factor loadings (the sensitivity coefficients) and the factor variances are bounded above. The residuals e_i, called 'idiosyncratic risk', are serially uncorrelated, but not necessarily mutually independent. If we assume absence of (asymptotic) arbitrage profits, then each $E(r_i)$, the expected return, must satisfy the following restriction at each period t:

$$\lim_{n \to \infty} \frac{1}{n} \sum_{i=1}^{n} \left[E(r_i) - \left(\lambda_0 + \sum_{j=1}^{K} \lambda_j b_{i,j} \right) \right]^2 = 0 \qquad (22)$$

λ_0 and λ_j represent respectively the risk-free rate and the risk premia, one for each factor f_j, and are common to all assets.

Some further hypotheses (see Dybvig and Ross, 1985) allow us to rewrite equation (22) as an exact equality

$$E(r_i) - \lambda_0 + \sum_{j=1}^{K} \lambda_j b_{i,j} \qquad i = 1, 2, \ldots, n. \qquad (23)$$

Dybvig (1983) and Dybvig and Ross (1985) – also in reply to Shanken (1982) – have, among others, assessed that the APT is an empirically testable specification even for a finite sub-set of assets, and that the approximation error in equation (23) is extremely small, so that this equation can be considered a testable proposition. However, our purpose in this chapter is not to test the APT model on bond returns. What we do is to use the APT framework as a benchmark to compare bond returns before and after the opening of an interest rate futures market.

There are various ways to model an arbitrage approach to bond prices. In this chapter we refer to Gultekin and Rogalski (1985), who in turn develop the methodology of Fama and MacBeth (1973) and Roll and Ross (1980), extending it to the analysis of the US government bond market.

Before proceeding with the analysis, we should tackle one preliminary question: is the APT model an appropriate framework for testing our hypothesis? Remember that we want to see if the opening of a futures market reduces the risk premia in the term structure of interest rates. For this hypothesis to be testable within an APT framework, we must assume that the risk factors which affect bond returns are indeed of a macro-economic (i.e. not idiosyncratic) nature. Since the two sources of risk we have discussed so far are interest rate variability and market illiquidity, the consequences of their presence should in principle be captured by an APT model.

4   The French government bond market: literature and data

The French government bond market provides an appropriate laboratory to observe the effects of the introduction of an interest rate futures market on the risk premium. Before the opening of the MATIF, hedging opportunities on French government bonds were very costly. Repurchase agreements were rarely used and the market for such instruments was rather thin and illiquid.

Throughout the 1980s, the presence of financial intermediaries on the bond market was increasing, reaching about 65 per cent of total bond holdings by 1987. Non-bank intermediaries (OPCVM) had raised their share of total bond holdings from 6.5 per cent in 1980 to 27 per cent in 1987, while households had decreased theirs from about 40 per cent in 1980 to 25 per cent in 1987.[8] Since it is more likely for financial institutions rather than for individuals to use futures markets to hedge bond portfolios, this evolution of bond holdings created a more favourable environment for the development of a futures market.

Some of the effects of futures trading on spot prices of government bonds have been discussed in Artus and Voisin (1987), while the more general issue of financial market integration is discussed in Bordes (1987). Previous studies of the French term structure (before the MATIF) are Dumas and Jacquillat (1986) and Artus (1987).

Government bonds traded in the French market fall in one of the two main groups[9]:

– *Emprunts d'Etat* (EEs), issued until 1985 through an underwriting syndicate, in a variety of forms (straight bonds, convertible into variable note bonds, zeros, with options to extend, FRNs).
– *Obligations Assimilable du Trésor* (OATs), issued since 1985 as tranches of existing bonds, in a series of Dutch auctions. Primary dealers (SVTs) have made a continuous OTC market in OATs since 1987. OATs have either a fixed rate (with maturities between 7 and 30 years) or a variable rate (with maturities between 5 and 12 years). Some OATs are convertible, and some are issued with warrants.

We used monthly data on 41 bonds, EEs and OATs, all with fixed rate. Some issues had an option for early retirement (through a lottery system) which has been neglected in the analysis.

Prices are end-of-month closing quoations at the Paris Bourse, without interest accrued.[10] The sample starts from January 1985 and ends in April 1989. Monthly returns have been computed by the usual formula:

$$r_{t,i} = \frac{p_{t,i} + w_t C_i - p_{t-1,i}}{p_{t-1,i}} \qquad (24)$$

where $p_{t,i}$ = end-of-month t price of ith bond
C_i = coupon of the ith bond
w_t = interest accrued at the end of month t.

We compute gross returns, assuming that the market is dominated by taxed investors (see also Dumas and Jacquillat, 1986).

As it has been argued by Boquist *et al.* (1975) and Gultekin and Rogalski (1985), when asset pricing models are applied to the bond market, the issue of non-stationarity of betas becomes even more acute than with common stocks.[11]

To alleviate the non-stationarity of betas we choose to follow the approach suggested by Gultekin and Rogalski (1985), clustering government securities into portfolios with constant ranges of maturity. Every portfolio is composed of bonds with life to maturity within the predetermined range, each with the same weight. The portfolio return is the arithmetic mean of individual bond returns. We constructed five portfolios: with less than 2 years to maturity, between 2 and 4 years, between 4 and 6, between 6 and 8, and more than 8 years.

In Table 9.1 we report the characteristics of the five portfolios. We note that mean returns and variances are an increasing function of the life to maturity of the portfolios.

Table 9.1. *Portfolio statistics*

Portfolio	Mean	Variance	Skewness	Kurtosis	K–S test	m1	m2	var1	var2
p1	0.0106231	0.000400	0.081401	0.038278	0.096990	0.019380	0.0071	0.000281	0.000402
p2	0.0098211	0.000180	0.001313	– 0.01039	0.061483	0.015413	0.0076	0.000140	0.000177
p3	0.0095500	0.000104	0.225306	0.930112	0.086559	0.014986	0.0074	0.000092	0.000089
p4	0.0082519	0.000075	0.166997	0.456458	0.073302	0.013806	0.0060	0.000063	0.000061
p5	0.0076269	0.000019	– 0.29174	0.330453	0.098790	0.009940	0.0067	0.000011	0.000019

Notes: *p*1 = life to maturity greater than 8 years.
      *p*2 = life to maturity between 6 and 8 years.
      *p*3 = life to maturity between 4 and 6 years.
      *p*4 = life to maturity between 2 and 4 years.
      *p*5 = life to maturity less than 2 years.
      m1, m2, var1, var2 are respectively the mean returns and variances computed for the periods 01/85–03/86 and 04/86–04/89.
      Returns are expressed as total monthly nominal returns on a monthly basis.

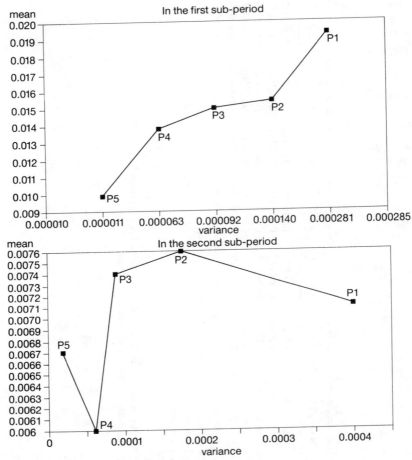

Figure 9.1   Portfolio mean–variance relation

Are observed portfolio returns distributed normally?

A first test of normality of portfolio returns is given by skewness and kurtosis, which in a Gaussian distribution are respectively 0 and 3. It can be observed from Table 9.1 that only the first two portfolios have a very low skewness, while kurtosis is far from the Gaussian value. A non-parametric Kolmogorov–Smirnov test (see Mood, Graybill and Boes, 1982) for all the portfolios tends not to reject the null hypothesis of normality of returns at usual levels of significance. A qualitative analysis of the plot of frequencies for the returns also gives an image of the distribution not so far from a Gaussian. Although the evidence is not strong, the Gaussian model does not seem an implausible description of the data. In any case the estimator and tests we use in the following are asymptotically robust with respect to the normality hypothesis.

We chose to compute means and variances for the two sub-periods January 85–March 86 and April 86–April 89. The breaking point has been chosen with a one-month delay, following the start of trading of the futures contract on French government bonds named 'Notionnel 10'. The delay has been chosen to allow for market adjustment. A strong decrease in mean returns is highlighted by the division. Note that only in the first sub-period are mean and variance of returns distributed along an increasing line, as shown by Figure 9.1.

A reduction of total mean returns is not by itself a proof of a risk premia reduction. Artus and Voisin (1987) notice that *emprunts du gisement*, i.e. deliverable bonds, showed a lower yield to maturity soon after the start of trading on the MATIF. However, this fact may be attributed to a number of different causes. In general, a relative flattening of the term structure is a necessary, but not sufficient, evidence of a reduced risk premium following the introduction of the futures contract.

Since we use the APT as a benchmark for bond returns, we implicitly assume the existence of a term structure based on the expectation theory, augmented by the inclusion of one or more risk premia, depending on which risk components are relevant to the market. In this case, given a sufficiently long sample, a test for the equality of mean returns for the five portfolios is equivalent to test against a risk–return interpretation of the bond market. In the case of equality we can say that no risk premium can be attached to bond returns, and the pure expectation theory would be validated, at least over all the period. However, such a test would have little meaning with a relatively short sample. Nevertheless, casual inspection of Table 9.1 suggests that in the first sub-period (before the MATIF) the five portfolios had very different returns.[12]

The last preliminary step we have accomplished is a principal component analysis. This has the purpose of identifying the maximum number of risk factors to use in the subsequent estimation of risk premia.[13]

The proportion of the total variance explained by the first component is very high: the first two factors account for 95 per cent of the variance of the portfolios. Hence they are sufficient to describe almost all the variability in returns. The grouping of bonds into portfolios was aimed at eliminating the various risk components specific to the single security, and thereby to capture the common ones, assumed to be macroeconomic variables.[14]

5   Macroeconomic factors and estimation method

The findings of the preceding section suggest that we should estimate either a one- or a two-factor model. We use the method of estimating the

APT with pre-specified macroconomic factors. Macrofactors are selected following the Chen *et al.* (1986) criterion. The price of a fixed interest government bond maturing in n periods may be expressed as

$$P(t) = C \sum_{i=1}^{n} \left(\frac{1}{g(TS_{t,i})} \right) + \frac{F}{g(TS_{t,n})} \tag{25}$$

where C is the (fixed) coupon and $g(TS_{t,i})$ is the discount factor between t and $t + i$, a function of the term structure TS at time t, and F is the face value. Changes in interest rates and inflation affect the bond price. The theory allows us to model the function $g(TS_{t,i})$ as a more general function $g(TS_{t,i,}f_k)$, where f_k may be any other (possibly unobservable) factor influencing returns. McElroy and Burmeister (1988) use this argument to include the market portfolio into the vector of exogenous risk factors.[15]

Each macro factor substitutes the exogenous factors of the APT in equation (21).

We define the interest rate risk (the unexpected movement in the term structure) as the difference between the monthly return on a government bond index and the three-month interbank rate (*pensions contre effets*). The resulting variable is sufficiently serially uncorrelated; hence we may interpret it as an innovation factor in the term structure.[16]

Inflation risk has been measured through the monthly difference between actual and expected inflation, measured on a 12-month horizon. Expected inflation has been estimated through a univariate ARIMA(1,1,1) model.[17] The residuals from the ARIMA model are not serially correlated, with some residual seasonality.

Every risk factor has been used in difference from the mean, for consistency with the hypotheses of equation (21).

Given the system described by equations (21) we estimate the risk premia and the factor loadings for each equation, subject to the linear restrictions imposed by the APT on the intercept term $E(r_i)$ (see equation (23)). The exogenous factors are substituted by the following macro factors: interest rate risk, inflation risk and residual market factor, computed as in n. 14.

The risk free rate is λ_0, which is assumed to be observed at the end of the corresponding month, and it is proxied by the interbank 3-month rate *pensions contre effets*, since a series of rates on short-term Treasury bills (BTFs) was not available for the whole sample. We write the system given by equations (21) and (23) as follows

$$\rho_i \equiv r_i - \lambda_0 = [\lambda' \otimes 1_T + F]b_i + e_i \qquad i = 1, 2, \ldots, 5 \tag{26}$$

where ρ_i is a column vector $T \times 1$; λ is the $K \times 1$ vector of the risk premia, including the 'residual market factor'; $\otimes$ is the Kronecker product, 1_T is a $T \times 1$ vector of ones; F is a $T \times K$ matrix, where every column represents the T observations for the jth factor; b_i is the $K \times 1$ vector of sensitivity coefficients for the ith portfolio. e_i has a diagonal covariance matrix. Stacking the five equations (26) we have

$$p = [I_N \otimes X(\lambda)]b + e \tag{27}$$

where p is the $NT \times 1$ (with $N = 5$) vector of returns in excess to the risk-free rate, I is the identity matrix, $X(\lambda)$ is the $NT \times NK$ matrix of the observations (on the factors) and of the parameters (the risk premia), b the $NK \times 1$ vector of factor loadings, equation by equation. $E(e) = 0$ and $E(ee') = \Sigma \otimes I_T$, where Σ is the matrix of covariances among equations, not necessarily diagonal. We apply ITerated Non Linear SURE to the system of equations (14), following Burmeister and McElroy (1988) and Gallant (1975).[18]

6   Estimation results

We started the analysis on the whole sample and adopted the following strategy.

First, we estimated a model with interest rate risk (term structure) and inflation risk factors, plus the residual market factor. In this case, we considered only the orthogonal components of the first two factors. The estimated model was unsatisfactory. No factor turned out to be priced in the sense of the APT, and only the factor loadings related to the interest rate risk were significant (results not reported).

Second, we estimated a model with interest rate risk and the residual market factor. As reported in Table 9.2, $L1$, the interest rate risk premium, is positive and significantly different from zero.

The intercept C, which is a measure of the adequacy of the risk-free rate variable, is not significantly different from zero. All the parameters linked to the residual market factor, i.e. $L2$ and $Bi2$, are not statistically different from zero. Since the t-Student is in this case only asymptotically valid, it could be questioned whether the test t is robust with respect to our sample size. Therefore we have computed a chi-square test, due to Gallant and Jorgenson (1979).[19] The resulting value, compared to the critical one at 10 per cent significance level of a chi-square with 6 df, i.e. 10.6, cannot reject the zero restrictions on the parameters $L2$ and $Bi2$.

As a third step, we estimated a model with only the interest rate risk factor, i.e. without intercept and residual market factor. The estimated coefficients are significant and of the expected magnitude (Table 9.3).

As expected, the sensitivity coefficients increase as the terms to maturity of the portfolios increase.

Note that inflation is not completely excluded as a source of priced risk,

Table 9.2. *ITNLSURE of the model with the interest rate risk and the residual market factor*
(no. obs. 52   no. equations 5   df 49.4)

Parameter	Estimate	Std error	t-ratio	Prob $> |t|$
C	− 2.41E-04	0.00054618	− 0.44	0.66
$L1$	0.00320247	0.0017028	1.88	0.06
$L2$	0.03039	0.03310	0.92	0.36
$B11^*$	1.12654	0.16676	6.76	0.0001
$B21^*$	0.76994	0.11096	6.94	0.0001
$B31^*$	0.61913	0.07817	7.92	0.0001
$B41^*$	0.53452	0.06170	8.66	0.001
$B51^*$	0.21199	0.03947	5.37	0.0001
$B12^{**}$	− 0.03932	0.03536	− 1.11	0.27
$B22^{**}$	− 0.01759	0.02329	− 0.76	0.45
$B32^{**}$	0.00140	0.01655	0.08	0.93
$B42^{**}$	− 0.00703	0.01329	− 0.53	0.59
$B52^{**}$	− 0.00235	0.00843	− 0.28	0.78

$L1$ = interest rate risk premium.
$L2$ = residual market factor risk premium.
  * = interest rate risk sensitivity coefficients.
** = residual market factor sensitivity coefficients.

Table 9.3. *ITNLSURE of the interest rate risk model*
(no. obs. 52   no. equations 5   df 50.8)

Parameter	Estimate	Std error	t-ratio	Prob $> |t|$
$L1$	0.0028237	0.00133349	2.12	0.03
$B1$	1.10525	0.16580	6.67	0.0001
$B2$	0.75885	0.10986	6.91	0.0001
$B3$	0.61826	0.07704	8.02	0.0001
$B4$	0.53105	0.06093	8.70	0.0001
$B5$	0.20740	0.03842	5.40	0.0001

since unexpected changes in the slope of the term structure may also reflect (unexpected) changes in inflation expectations.

7   The effects of the opening of the MATIF

In this section, we report the results of our empirical investigation on the effects of the MATIF on the pricing of interest rate risk. We use the model of Table 9.4 as a starting point. First, we re-estimate the same model for

Table 9.4. *ITNLSURE of the interest rate risk model in the first sub-period, January 1985–March 1986 (no. obs. 15   no. equations 5   df 13.8)*

Parameter	Estimate	Std error	*t*-ratio	Prob > |*t*|
*L*1	0.0042152	0.00134238	3.14	0.007
*B*1	1.47251	0.21878	6.73	0.0001
*B*2	0.99134	0.16244	6.10	0.0001
*B*3	0.90996	0.10547	8.63	0.0001
*B*4	0.74698	0.09384	7.96	0.0001
*B*5	0.26914	0.05278	5.10	0.0002

two separated sub-periods, before and after the opening of the MATIF in February 1986. We report the results in Tables 9.4 and 9.5. In the second period we find that the risk premium is not significantly different from zero, while in the first it is higher than on the entire sample. No significant change has affected the sensitivity coefficients, and this is a proof of a sufficient stability obtained through the bundling of the government bonds into portfolios. The non-stationarity of 'betas' has thereby been effectively avoided.

Because of the asymmetry of the sample size in the two sub-periods, and because the small number of observations could weaken the results of the first sub-sample, we have tried to estimate this change in the risk premium using all the observations and a dummy variable, with the model rewritten as

$$\rho_i = (\lambda_{11} b_{i,1})D_t + (\lambda_{12} b_{i,1})(1 - D_t) + b_{i,1}f_t + e_{i,t} \tag{28}$$

where $D_t = 1$ for $t \leq 15$
$ 0$ for $t > 15$

Table 9.5. *ITNLSURE of the interest rate risk model in the second sub-period, April 1986–April 1989 (no. obs. 37   no. equations 5   df 35.8)*

Parameter	Estimate	Std error	*t*-ratio	Prob > |*t*|
*L*1	− 5.11E-04	0.0016997	− 0.30	0.76
*B*1	0.93574	0.20684	4.52	0.0001
*B*2	0.63642	0.13618	4.67	0.0001
*B*3	0.48386	0.09248	5.23	0.0001
*B*4	0.45169	0.06784	6.66	0.001
*B*5	0.17871	0.04804	3.72	0.0007

Table 9.6. *ITNLSURE of the model with dummy*
(no. obs. 52   no. equations 5   df 50.6)

Parameter	Estimate	Std error	t-ratio	Prob $> |t|$
$L11$	0.00909142	0.00269633	3.37	0.0014
$L12$	0.0001734	0.001505	0.12	0.90
$B1$	1.01584	0.15651	6.49	0.0001
$B2$	0.68763	0.10511	6.54	0.0001
$B3$	0.56945	0.07371	7.73	0.0001
$B4$	0.49859	0.05725	8.71	0.0001
$B5$	0.18884	0.03598	5.25	0.0001

$L11$ = risk premium in the first period.
$L12$ = risk premium in the second period.

and where f_t is the interest rate risk. Results are reported in Table 9.6.

Notice that the risk premium in the second period has a t-ratio of 0.12. To strengthen the validity of this result (which suggests that in the second period the risk premium is not different from zero) we compute the chi-square of Gallant and Jorgenson (1979, see above). The value of the test is 1, lower than the 10 per cent critical value for a chi-square with one degree of freedom, equal to 2.71. Consequently we cannot reject the zero restriction on the second period coefficient for the dummy variable. The risk premium is not significantly different from zero in the second sub-period, indicating that a reduction in the premium has taken place after the opening of the MATIF.

At this point we can interpret the results as follows:

(a) The risk structure of the market, as captured by the portfolios, has not changed ('betas' are always significant and approximately stable in the two sub-periods); nonetheless, since bondholders can now – after the MATIF – diversify away the risk of unexpected movements in interest rates at a lower cost than before, they ask a reduced risk premium (which turns out to be statistically not different from zero).

(b) The 'term structure' of government bond yields behaves now more in accordance with the pure expectations theory: expected holding period rates of returns are equal between the five portfolios and to the risk-free rate.[20]

A possible objection to our conclusion is the following: can we really be sure that these results should be imputed to the introduction of the futures contract in the MATIF?

A change in the estimated risk premium could be attributed, in principle, to two other sets of causes. The first relates to other changes in the structure of financial markets. The second refers to macroeconomic explanations of a flattening of the term structure.

As for the first explanation, it is true that a number of measures have been set up by the French authorities to turn financial markets into a more liquid and efficient system (the new quotation system for the government bonds at the Paris Bourse; the opening at the end of 1986 of a primary dealers' circuit; the reform of the interbank market and the issue of new negotiable short-term Treasuries, the BTF and BTAN). Some of these measures have been effective only far after March 1986; for others, it is not clear how they will affect risk premia on the spot market.

As for the macroeconomic explanation, first note that the variability of returns has not been lower in the second sub-sample, relative to the first (see Table 9.1): hence presumably the amount of perceived interest rate risk, to be taken or hedged, has not decreased. Second, within our sample the level and the slope of the term structure have changed at dates other than March 1986. (Also, an EMS adjustment took place in April 1986.) Our thesis, however, is that risk premia were affected only in March 1986, and not by changes in the slope of the term structure which occurred at other dates (such as, for example, at the end of 1987).

In general, our interpretation that futures markets have caused the change in the risk premium would be strengthened if we could be sure that in our sample there was only one breaking point in March 1986.

To ascertain this point, we have estimated the model recursively,

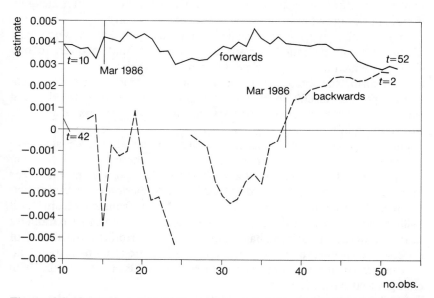

Figure 9.2 Interest rate risk premium, forward and backwards recursive regressions

starting with ten observations and adding a new observation each time. We have repeated this procedure running the regression both forward (from January 1985 onwards) and backward (from April 1989 to January 1985). Figure 9.2 plots the risk premium estimated recursively.

On the forward recursive regression, the risk premium is positive starting with the first observation, and thereafter remains positive for the whole sample. On the backward regression, the risk premium floats around zero or below for the first 37 observations, and becomes significantly positive and stable after the 38th observation is added (i.e. March 86). The premium converges to the same value at the end of both regressions.[21]

Again it seems that only the first 15 observations (in the forward scale) contribute to the occurrence of a positive risk premium. This result strengthens our interpretation of a structural change due to the opening of the MATIF.

8   Conclusions

The motivation for this chapter has been to study whether the introduction of a futures contract in a relatively underdeveloped financial market can significantly change the pricing of securities in that market. Even if the futures contract cannot be thought of as completing the market structure in a strict sense, it might nevertheless offer hedging opportunities previously unavailable because too costly.

In particular, we have constructed a plausible scenario where risk averse investors demand price discounts (risk premia) in order to buy securities which mature at a time different from their chosen horizon. In this scenario, the introduction of a futures contract supplied by risk averse speculators effectively lowers required risk premia, by allowing each investor to construct portfolios with a known, riskless return over their chosen horizon.

Our empirical results seem to conform to the above scenario. We analysed the French government bond market, where a futures contract was introduced in February 1986. We estimated a positive premium for interest rate risk for the period before the introduction of that contract, whereas the premium is not significantly different from zero from April 1986 onwards. This result seems noteworthy because no other parameter in the estimated equations changes around that period (the sensitivity of different portfolios to changes in the term structure remains stable), and no other twist in the term structure (apart from the one of March 1986) changes that parameter.

If our hypothesis is correct, as the evidence we present would suggest, then its normative implications seem of some importance. Financial futures are not only a sophisticated tool for sophisticated investors (often, speculators) in well-developed financial markets. They are also a powerful tool for overcoming some of the shortcomings of relatively under-developed financial systems.

In a poorly developed financial system, the spot market for government securities often lacks liquidity, possibly because there are few institutional investors and because the market is segmented around individual secur-ities, which are poor substitutes for each other. In this market, repurchase agreements are a costly and/or a risky hedging instrument. A futures contract, on the contrary, is by definition (and abstracting from basis risk) a riskless and liquid hedging instrument.

When hedging becomes more easily and cheaply available, then this might help to price interest rate risk away from the term structure. The issuer, that is the Treasury, will benefit from this situation in terms of reduced interest rate premia paid on issues of longer maturity. This would lower the average cost of debt for a given structure of maturities. Also, this might act as an incentive to lengthen the average maturity of the debt; in turn, this would effectively immunise the cost of government debt from monetary policy induced changes in short-term interest rates.

These comments do not imply that a futures contract should be intro-duced as a general remedy for all sorts of market shortcomings. A futures contract can hedge interest rate risk. This is useful in a sufficiently integrated market, where interest rate risk is the main, or maybe even the only, source of priced risk. In a segmented market, each group of secur-ities may be priced also according to some idiosyncratic source of risk. A futures contract would be of no help in hedging against such risks, and should not be recommended as an appropriate remedy against this type of market imperfection.

Before concluding, two further observations may be helpful.

First, it has been claimed in general and also with reference to the French case (see Artus and Voisin, 1987) that futures contracts have increased the volatility of the underlying spot market. Even if it is true, this claim does not imply that futures trading has had a negative impact on the efficiency of the spot market. We have found that futures markets have lowered the slope of the term structure. This is a different, and we believe a more important, point than an increase in the volatility. An increase in volatility *per se* is not necessarily a bad outcome. Illiquid markets might show very low volatility because changes in the infor-mation set did not translate into security prices. As liquidity improves, new information is embedded in security prices and increased volatility is a sign of a more efficient market structure, along with an increased volume of transactions.[22]

Finally, we think that two related areas of further research emerge, relative to the French case. It would be interesting to explore empirically the role of futures prices as collectors of information (Hedge and McDonald, 1986). Also, it could be inquired whether the reduction in risk premia has taken place in the market for corporate bonds, too, despite the presence of a basis risk with the futures contract.

Appendix: data sources

Data on bond prices have been collected at the Chambre de Commerce et d'Industrie in Paris. They are drawn from several issues of the *Les Echos* newspaper. Technical features of the bonds are taken from the *Comptes de la Dette Publique*, a yearly issue of the Direction du Trésor.

As regards the risk factors, the CAC index has been taken as a proxy for the market portfolio. The Government bond index is the Index of the *Emprunts d'Etat* (IEE), which is composed of all the fixed income government long-term securities, and has been taken from the *Bulletin Trimestriel de la Banque de France*, together with the 3-month interbank rate series. Inflation is computed from the CPI index, source INSEE. German interest rates, both long-term yield to maturity and the short-term rate, are drawn from the IMF *International Financial Statistics*.

Notes

1 We are thankful for their criticism and discussions to Ron Anderson, Patrick Artus, Francesco Corielli and Heinz Zimmermann. They all helped considerably in the shaping up of the paper, but any remaining errors are of course our own. We also thank the Chambre de Commerce et d'Industrie in Paris for kindly supplying us with the data on bond prices.
2 The pioneering work on this topic is Froewiss (1978). More recently see Simpson and Ireland (1985).
3 See Kane (1980).
4 For a similar modelling of agents in the market, see also Grossman (1977) and Danthine (1978).
5 See Amihud and Mendelson (1990).
6 Two other market-improving characteristics of futures versus forward contracts are worth noting, even if they do not relate directly to the issue of market liquidity: (i) futures allow investors in the spot market to continue to earn the 'convenience yield', defined as the value derived from simply holding a stock; (ii) futures have a powerful informative role, because they aggregate information from a larger number of market participants, and they then distribute this information to all potential users via prices set in an open market.
7 This statement can be interpreted in two ways: in a 'static' world the number of assets n tends to infinity; in a 'dynamic' world there is a sequence of economies, each one with an increasing number of assets n. See Ingersoll (1987) for more details.
8 See Banque de France (1989).

9 The following information has been obtained courtesy of Morgan Guaranty Trust Co.

10 For a more detailed description of the data, see the Appendix.

11 In fact Boquist *et al.* (1975) show that in a Sharpe–Lintner–Mossin model the 'beta' of a default-free bond is given as follows

$$\beta = -D_{i,t} \frac{\text{cov}(dr_i, R_m)}{\sigma^2(R_m)}$$

where $D_{i,t}$ is the duration *à la* Hicks–McAulay of bond i at time t, dr_i is the bond yield variation and R_m is the market portfolio return. Since the duration varies as time goes by, the 'beta' is also affected and cannot be assumed to be stationary. This argument is valid even in a multifactor model, especially if an interest rate risk factor is included. We found that in our case the dependence of the duration on changes in interest rates was of negligible order.

12 Computing Hotelling's T-square statistics for the second sub-period, for which we have a sufficient number of observations, gives acceptance of the null hypothesis of equality of mean returns. For a description of the T-square statistic, its distribution and properties (UMP among tests invariant to linear transformation), see Anderson (1984). The distribution under the null hypothesis is F with p and $n - p$ degrees of freedom.

13 The eigenvalues of the portfolio returns correlation matrix represent the variance of the extracted components. The right eigenvector indicates the weight each portfolio has in the component. There is a close correspondence between principal components and APT factors, both being orthogonal to each other. The variability of portfolio returns is summed up by the number of distinct components having a large positive eigenvalue.

14 In general, the less segmented the market, the lower is the number of risk factors affecting the behaviour of portfolios. These findings are quite similar to those of Garbade (1986) on the US bond market: the first component, the market 'level', in his analysis accounted for about 70 per cent of the total variability. Gultekin and Rogalski (1985) pick out only five common factors for 12 US Government securities portfolios.

15 The market index has been introduced rewriting equation (21) as

$$r_i = E(r_i) + \sum_{j=1}^{K-1} b_{i,j} f_j + u_i \qquad i = 1, 2, \ldots, 5$$

where $u_i = b_{i,k} f_k + e_i$, with e_i and f_k uncorrelated with each other and with the other factors.

Suppose we wish to construct a well-diversified portfolio, such that its idiosyncratic risk is zero. Let this be the market index. Then its return r_m will be

$$r_m = \lambda_0 + \sum_j \lambda_j b_{m,j} + \lambda_k b_{m,k} + \delta + \sum_j b_{m,j} f_j + b_{m,k} f_k$$

where δ measures the degree of representativity of the securities selected in the portfolio.

Since $b_{m,k}$ is not identified, it is set equal to 1, without loss of generality. Therefore we write the equation as

$$r_m = \lambda_0 + \sum_j \lambda_j b_{m,j} + \lambda_k + \delta + \sum_j b_{m,j} f_j + f_k$$

and the unmeasurable value of f_k in the first equation is substituted by the residuals from the OLS regression of the market index on the observable factors. f_k is said to be the 'residual market factor' (see McElroy and Burmeister, 1988).

16 We also used another measure, suggested by Sweeney and Warga (1986), where the bond index is substituted by the long-term government bond yield to maturity. However, we found it less satisfactory. Using the same kind of measure, we also rejected the significance of the foreign term structure, namely the German one, as a priced factor in the market.

17 The estimation has been conducted with a Kalman algorithm, for the following state–space model:

$$\pi_t^e = a\pi_{t-1}^e + e_t \qquad \text{transition equation}$$

$$\pi_t = b\pi_t^e + w_t \qquad \text{observation equation}$$

where w_t are assumed to have zero mean and to be independently distributed, with variance σ^2; $e(t)$ are assumed zero mean independently distributed with variance V. The order (i.e. the lag) of the univariate model has been chosen such that it gives the highest canonical correlation coefficient between past and future observations derived by the model, once various orders have been compared. To approximate the use of information by individual agents, we compute forecasts of inflation at time t conditioned to the information available at time t. When new information comes up at time $t + 1$, we revise our estimate of inflation in a Bayesian way, keeping in mind the dependence of inflation forecast at time $t + 1$ from expected inflation at time t. Since we use only a sub-space of the entire set of information that individuals have, we smooth the filtered estimate to gain efficiency.

18 The ITerated Non Linear SURE (ITNLSURE) is a three-state procedure: in step 1 we estimate the parameters via OLS equation by equation; in step 2 we compute the sample variance–covariances from the residuals of step 1, to obtain an estimate of Σ; in step 3 we minimise the quadratic form

$$e'(\Sigma \otimes I_T)e$$

with respect to the parameters λ, b. Then we proceed, iterating between the parameters and the matrix Σ: once an estimate of the parameters has been obtained, the covariances are computed again and the quadratic form minimised. This procedure allows, under regularity conditions given by Gallant (1975) to have ML equivalent estimates, given the normality of residuals. Gallant and Jorgenson (1979) showed the robustness of the ITNLSURE even in the absence of normality. ITNLSURE estimates of parameters are in any case consistent, just as a consistent estimate of the covariance of parameters is given by

$$\Omega^{-1} = T[F'(\hat{\Sigma} \otimes I_T)F]^{-1}$$

where F is the Jacobian of the above-mentioned quadratic form. All estimates have been obtained using SAS release 5.18. For another application of the Burmeister and McElroy method, see also Brown and Otsuki (1989).

We preferred this method of estimation, instead of a two-step factor analysis approach for two main reasons. First, we are interested in identifying the interest rate risk factor, while factor analysis does not allow for a straightforward economic interpretation of factor scores. Second, we are constrained to a one-step approach by the relatively small sample of observations.

19 We set $L2$ and the related loadings equal to zero, and constrain the variance–covariance matrix to be the same as in the unrestricted model. We then

estimate the restricted model by ITNLSURE and compute the statistic given by the difference between the quadratic forms, as report in n. 17, in the two cases, that is $253 - 247 = 6$.

20 The argument sub (b) could account for the result of the Hotelling's test reported in n. 11.

21 We refer to significance considerations drawn from the t-Student for each estimate. However we do not report graphically the confidence intervals, because they have only an asymptotic value. In any case, these intervals show that the risk premium is never significantly positive in the second sub-period. CUSUM tests are not viable in this case, because we should standardise a matrix of residuals, and also because standard errors in our model are only valid asymptotically.

22 In 1986, transactions in French bonds increased by 133 per cent relatively up to 1985, up to FF 1673 billions. In 1987 and 1988 the increase was respectively 45 per cent and 41 per cent, while the volume of transactions seemed to have flattened out in 1989 (OECD data).

References

Amihud, Y. and H. Mendelson (1990) 'Liquidity, Maturity, and the Yields on US Treasury Securities' (unpublished).

Anderson, R. W. and J.-P. Danthine (1981) 'Cross-Hedging', *Journal of Political Economy*, **89**: 1182–96 (1984).

Anderson, T. W. (1984) *An Introduction to Multivariate Statistical Analysis*, New York: Wiley.

Artus, P. (1987) 'La structure par terme des taux d'intérêts: théorie et estimations dans le cas français', *Cahiers Economiques et Monétaires*, Banque de France, **27**: 5–47.

Artus, P. and P. Voisin (1987) 'Le MATIF est-il efficace?', *Banque*, **470**: 269–82.

Banque de France (1989) 'Taux d'intérêt à long terme, courbe des rendements et politique monétaire', *Bulletin Trimestriel* (June–July): 51–68.

Boquist, J. A., G. A. Racette and G.G. Schlarbaum (1975) 'Duration and Risk Assessment for Bonds and Common Stocks', *Journal of Finance*, **30** (December): 1360–6.

Bordes, C. (1987) 'Interprétation théorique du mouvement d'intégration des marchés des capitaux', *Cahiers Economiques et Monétaires*, Banque de France, **31**: 5–47.

Brown, S. and T. Otsuki (1989) 'Macroeconomic Factors and the Japanese Equity Markets: The CAPMD project', preliminary draft, New York University (February).

Burmeister, E. and M. B. McElroy (1988) 'Joint Estimation of Factor Sensitivities and Risk Premia for the Arbitrage Pricing Theory', *Journal of Finance*, **43** (July): 721–33.

Burmeister, E., K. D. Wall and J. D. Hamilton, 'Estimation of Unobserved Expected Monthly Inflation Using Kalman Filtering', *Journal of Business and Economic Statistics*, **4** (April): 147–60.

Chen, N., R. Roll and S. A. Ross (1986) 'Economic Forces and the Stock Market', *Journal of Business*, **59** (July): 386–403.

Connor, G. (1984) 'A Unified Beta Pricing Theory', *Journal of Economic Theory*, **34**: 13–31.

Danthine, J.-P. (1978) 'Information, Futures Prices, and Stabilizing Speculation', *Journal of Economic Theory*, **17**: 79–98.

Dumas, B. and B. Jacquillat (1986) 'Le lien entre le marché monétaire et le marché obligataire français', Centre HEC-ISA, *Les Cahiers de Recherche* (September).

Dybvig, P. H. (1983) 'An Explicit Bound on Deviations from APT Pricing in a Finite Economy', *Journal of Financial Economics*, **12**: 483–96.

Dybvig, P. H. and R. A. Ross (1985) 'Yes, The APT Is Testable', *Journal of Finance*, **40** (September): 1173–88.

Fama, E. and J. MacBeth (1973) 'Risk, Return, and Equilibrium: Empirical Tests', *Journal of Political Economy*, **81**: 607–36.

Froewiss, K. (1978) 'GNMA Futures: Stabilizing or Destabilizing?', *Federal Reserve Bank of San Francisco Economic Review*: 20–9.

Gallant, R. A. (1975) 'Seemingly Unrelated Nonlinear Regressions', *Journal of Econometrics*, **3**: 35–50.

Gallant, R. A. and D. W. Jorgenson (1979) 'Statistical Interference for a System of Simultaneous, Non-Linear, Implicit Equations in the Context of Instrumental Variable Estimation', *Journal of Econometrics*, **11**: 275–302.

Garbade, K. (1986) 'Modes of Fluctuations in Bond Yields: An Analysis of Principal Components', in *Topics in Money and Securities' Markets*, Bankers' Trust Co. (June).

Garbade, K. and W. Silber (1979) 'Structural Organization of Secondary Markets: Clearing Frequency, Dealer Activity and Liquidity Risk', *Journal of Finance*, **34**.

Grossman, S. (1977) 'The Existence of Futures Markets, Noisy Rational Expectations and Informational Externalities', *Review of Economic Studies*, **138**: 431–49.

Gultekin, B. N. and R. J. Rogalski (1985) 'Government Bond Returns, Measurement of Interest Rate Risk and the Arbitrage Pricing Theory', *Journal of Finance*, **40** (March): 43–61.

Hedge, S. P. and B. McDonald (1986) 'On the Informational Role of Treasury Bill Futures', *Journal of Futures Markets*, **6**: 629–43.

Huberman, G. (1982) 'A Simple Approach to Arbitrage Pricing Theory', *Journal of Economic Theory*, **28**: 183–91.

Ingersoll, J. E., Jr (1984) 'Some Results in the Theory of Arbitrage Pricing', *Journal of Finance*, **39**: 1021–39.

Ingersoll, J. E., Jr (1987) *Theory of Financial Decision Making*, ch. 7, Totowa, NJ: Rowman and Littlefield.

Kane, E. (1980) 'Market Incompleteness and Divergences Between Forward and Futures Interest Rates', *Journal of Finance*, **35**: 221–34.

McElroy, M. B. and E. Burmeister (1988) 'Arbitrage Pricing Theory as a Restricted Nonlinear Multivariate Regression Model', *Journal of Business and Economic Statistics*, **6**: 29–42.

Mood, A., F. Graybill and D. Boes (1982) 'Introduction to the Theory of Statistics', New York: McGraw-Hill International.

Roll, R. and S. A. Ross (1980) 'An Empirical Investigation of the APT', *Journal of Finance*, **35**: 1073–103.

Ross, S. A. (1976) 'The Arbitrage Theory of Capital Asset Pricing', *Journal of Economic Theory*, **13**: 341–60.

Ross, S. A. (1977) 'Return, Risk, and Arbitrage', in I. Friend and J.L. Bicksler, *Risk and Return in Finance*, vol. 1: 189–218, Cambridge, Mass.: Ballinger.

Shanken, J. (1982) 'The Arbitrage Pricing Theory: Is It Testable?', *Journal of Finance*, **37** (December): 1129–40.

Simpson, W. G. and T. C. Ireland (1985) 'The Impact of Financial Futures on the Cash Market for Treasury Bills', *Journal of Financial and Quantitative Analysis*, **20**: 371–9.

Sweeney, R. J. and A. D. Warga (1986) 'The Pricing of Interest-Rate Risk: Evidence from the Stock Market', *Journal of Finance*, **41**: 393–401.

Telser, L. G. (1981) 'Margins and Futures Contracts', *Journal of Futures Markets*, **1**: 225–54.

Telser, L. G. and H. N. Higinbotham (1977) 'Organized Futures Markets: Costs and Benefits', *Journal of Political Economy*, **85**: 969–1000.

Part III

Banks

3.1 Issues in asset management

10 The role of banks as investors in securities: theoretical and empirical features in an international perspective

UMBERTO CHERUBINI, MASSIMO
CIAMPOLINI and GREGORIO DE FELICE

1 Introduction[1]

In this chapter we analyse a particular aspect of the position of banks in the securities market – that is, their role as investors on their own account. Such a role must be viewed from the perspective of the recent expansion of securities markets and of the progressive blurring of the old demarcation line between commercial and investment banking. However, the increasing interest shown by banks towards securities-related activities has not necessarily implied an increase in their securities holdings. In many cases, the closer relationship between banks and the market has resulted in a more important role for banks in areas such as new-issuing business, brokerage activity, market making activity and portfolio management, which do not require larger investments in securities on banks' own account.

The purpose of this work is to consider how the share of securities holdings in total bank assets has recently developed in some industrialised countries, why a bank decides to invest in securities, what the relations among such investment and other variables are, and whether there are relevant discrepancies in the behaviour of banks across different countries.

In Section 2, we consider the evolution of banks' securities holdings from a comparative point of view. In Section 3, the attention is focussed on a taxonomy of securities markets according to their structures. In Section 4, we study the time-series behaviour of bank deposits, loans and securities' investment in four countries, focussing on the cointegration and causality relationships among these variables. In Section 5 the main issues and conclusions of the chapter are summed up.

2   Banks' securities holdings and asset composition

An international comparison of the role of banks as investors in securities is shown in Figure 10.1 and Table 10.1, where banks' securities holdings

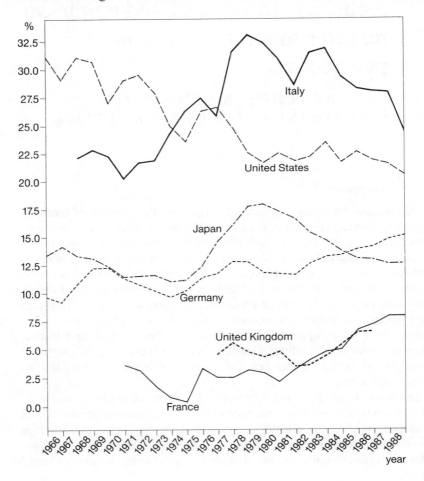

Figure 10.1   Banks' investments in securities* as percentage of total assets
* The figures may present some discrepancies in comparison with those of Table 10.1 for different definitions of banks and for differences in the reference to book or market value data.

Table 10.1. *Investment in securities by commercial banks, as percentage of banks' total assets; end of year figures*

	Total securities		Short-term		Medium–long-term	
	1980	1988	1980	1988	1980	1988
Italy	31.9	23.8	8.7	2.4	23.2	21.4
Germany	12.2	16.3	0.3[a]	0.3[a]	11.9[a]	16.0[a]
France	2.2	7.9	1.5	2.6	0.7	5.3
United Kingdom	7.9	9.7[b]	4.9	4.8[b]	3.0	4.8[b]
Spain	9.1	18.7[b]	1.0	11.4[b]	8.1	7.3[b]
Netherlands	5.7	12.4[b]	3.8	2.7[b]	2.0	9.7[b]
Belgium	20.0	25.2[c]	3.7	8.4[c]	16.4	16.8[c]
United States	25.0	23.0[b]	2.4	—	22.5	—
Japan	16.5[d]	13.1	—	0.1	16.5[d]	13.0

[a] Partially estimated data by referring to OECD, *Financial Accounts*, figures.
[b] The figure given is for 1987.
[c] The figure given is for 1986.
[d] The figure given is for 1981.
Sources: Italy: Banca d'Italia, *Appendice alla Relazione Annuale*; Germany: *Monthly Report of the Deutsche Bundesbank* and *Statistische Beihefte* (Reihe 2); France: Banque de France, *Statistique financières annuelles (series retrospectives)* and *Bulletin Trimestriel*; the United Kingdom, Spain, the Netherlands, Belgium, the United States: OECD, *Financial Accounts*; Japan: Bank of Japan, *Economic Statistics Monthly*.

are presented as a percentage of their total assets. Many differences can be found concerning both the levels of shares of total assets and their more recent evolution.

In Italy, the United States and Belgium, the share of total bank assets invested in securities is higher than 20 per cent, while for other systems (France and the United Kingdom) the same share is below 10 per cent. The levels observed for the Italian banking system between the end of the 1970s and the early 1980s were particularly anomalous (above 30 per cent) and were determined mainly by the holding of public sector securities, which amounted to more than 50 per cent total government securities outstanding.

Diverging trends were also observed considering more recent evolution. In many countries, the wide expansion of securities markets and the progressive blurring of old demarcation lines between banking activities and other forms of intermediation implied a major integration of banks with securities-related services, and the role of banks as investors in securities gathered momentum.[2] On the contrary, the evolution of some other countries where the share was already very high (as for the Italian and the US banking systems) or where previous regulatory constraints were dismantled (Italy[3] and Japan[4]) shows significant reductions in the percentage of total assets invested in securities.

3   Securities markets and the role of banks as investors

3.1   Securities markets' models

In order to understand the role played by banks as investors in securities markets, it seems worthwhile to analyse some features of financial systems as well as some characteristics of the securities markets which may turn out to be relevant. We can consider the share of total assets invested in securities by banks (S^B/A) as the product of three factors:

$$\frac{S^B}{A} = \frac{S^F}{S} \left(1 - \frac{S^{NB}}{S^F} \right) \frac{S}{A}$$

where S represents total outstanding securities, S^F, S^B and S^{NB} are the securities held by the financial system as a whole, by banks and by non-bank financial institutions respectively. S^F/S can be thought of as an indicator of the 'degree of intermediation in securities markets', because it considers to what extent the relation among final investors and final debtors is direct or intermediated by financial institutions. The second factor, $1 - S^{NB}/S^F$, can be viewed as a measure of the 'degree of differentiation among financial investors', where we refer to the differentiation existing in the financial system between intermediaries, the main activity of which is to invest in securities markets, and other financial institutions. The third term, S/A, is an indicator of the size of the securities market compared with that of the banking system. Because of problems relating to availability of statistical information, in this section we will refer exclusively to medium-long term securities.

As we will see, the levels of the former two ratios allow us to identify four models of securities markets (see Table 10.2) which might be

Table 10.2. *Securities markets and financial intermediaries*

	Securities markets	
Financial systems	Direct placing	Highly intermediated
Differentiated (with respect to investors in securities)	Model A1	Model B1
Bank-oriented	Model A2	Model B2

quite important in order to understand the discrepancies previously observed.

3.1.1   The main features of securities markets' models
The first indicator (the 'degree of intermediation in securities' markets') allows us to distinguish between two stylised models. In the first, securities are placed directly with final users. In such an extreme model, savers have to bear the whole risk of debt issues directly. So, it seems reasonable to assume that in this model securities are issued keeping in mind savers' preferences and their placement is probably eased by the activity of rating agencies and disclosure regulations. In the second model, securities are bought mainly by financial institutions that in turn issue their own liabilities in favour of savers. In this model, risk is not borne directly by savers and economies of scale from assets diversification are exploited by the intermediaries, enabling them to earn a spread between funds collected and invested.

We expect different economic systems to be oriented towards one of the models just described, depending on structural features of the market. For example, we expect a securities market to be more intermediated, the greater the share of high-risk issues. So, probably, the market will head for one of the models relying on different 'default-risk' characteristics of issuers and different degrees of liquidity risk. Furthermore, as far as technical features are concerned, we expected intermediated markets to have more 'wholesale' characteristics than the less intermediated ones. Finally, the quality of the financial instruments used by the intermediaries in order to collect funds in competition with final debtors may play an important role.

Let us come to the second structural feature, that we called the 'degree of differentiation among financial investors'. Even in this case, we can consider two extreme models. In the first, the banking system has a dominant role in the various kinds of intermediation activities. In the alternative model, by contrast, the investment in securities is left to non-bank specialised institutions, typically institutional investors (insurance companies, pension funds and mutual funds).

Even in this case, securities markets of countries oriented towards one of these models will present distinct structural features. So, it is more likely to find 'intermediary differentiation' in systems where final debt issuers and the risk features of financial instruments are well differentiated as well: in such a case specialised intermediaries can exploit scale economies from securities markets' monitoring and take advantage of particular technical expertise concerning portfolio selection and hedging techniques. We also expect technical characteristics of notes to make a substantial part of the difference: for example, we are likely to find a strong market for long-term, fixed rate notes in a system in which institutional investors have particular weight and short–medium-term, or floating rate securities, in a system in which banks represent the major investor in securities among financial institutions, so as to ease their typical maturity mismatching and interest risk problems.

3.1.2   The evolution of securities markets

As far as the degree of securities' intermediation is concerned, Table 10.3 shows the share of outstanding bonds held by each category of financial institution in several countries in 1980 and 1988. The final two columns of Table 10.3 enable us to assess the degree of 'securities' intermediation'. It is interesting to notice that there is a trend towards an increasing degree of intermediation (from models (A) to models (B)) in all the countries under consideration, except Italy and Spain.

In Italy the opposite phenomenon took place in a remarkable way: while in 1980 it was the country with one of the highest shares of securities held by financial institutions (62.9 per cent), in 1988 only 42.9 per cent of securities was held by financial institutions and it scored second among the countries with the lowest intermediation ratios (after Belgium).

The Italian figures can be explained by the process of financial deregulation and innovation that took place in the Italian system in the 1980s and by distinctive technical features of the securities market. First of all, at the beginning of the 1980s a series of regulatory provisions heading towards a high degree of financial intermediation were dismantled.[5] After such policy changes had taken place, the Italian market seems to have moved towards a structure that was probably more congenial to the characteristics of the outstanding securities, that is a 'low securities intermediation' model. As a matter of fact, the Italian securities market has features that seem to justify such a transformation.[6]

Another argument that can be given to explain the Italian case refers to the particular character of financial innovation. In Italy we could speak of a 'final debtor-driven' financial innovation, because it involved mainly public debt instruments aimed at attracting ever-new categories of savers. Furthermore, such instruments were typically priced very aggressively with respect to other investment alternatives available to savers. The result has been a progressive reallocation of savers' portfolios in favour of public sector securities. Such a trend has not been contrasted, as happened in other countries, by what we can call 'intermediary-driven' financial innovation; for example, in the United States, innovation deeply involved the financial intermediation system, giving rise to both new kinds of intermediaries (as the Money Market Mutual Funds) and new kinds of financial products on the liability side of the intermediaries' balance sheets (CDs, NOWs, MMDAs, etc.).

Table 10.3. *Bonds held by financial institutions, as % of total bonds outstanding*

| | Commercial banks | | Non-bank financial institutions | | | | | | | | Total financial institutions | |
| | | | Total | | Other financial institutions | | Insurance companies and pension funds | | Unit trusts | | | |
	1980	1988	1980	1988	1980	1988	1980	1988	1980	1988	1980	1988
Italy	57.5	29.8	5.4	13.1	2.5	3.1	2.9	6.4	—	3.6	62.9	42.9
Germany	20.8	22.1	27.1	34.9	15.5	16.3	8.7	13.4	2.9	5.2	47.9	57.0
France	2.9	14.3	39.5	53.5	18.0	15.0	15.6	14.3	5.9	24.2	42.4	67.8
United Kingdom	8.8[b]	17.7[a,b]	56.8[g]	49.6[a,g]	14.1	8.1[a]	42.7[g]	41.5[a,g]	—	—	64.7	67.3[a]
Spain	67.2	52.7[a]	0.0	11.7[a]	0.0	0.8[a]	—	10.9[a]	—	—	67.2	64.4[a]
Netherlands[e]	9.6	11.0[a]	6.4	11.7[a]	—	0.1[a]	6.4	11.6[a]	—	—	16.0	22.7[a]
Belgium	18.0	17.0[c]	22.3	26.5[c]	14.7	20.1[c]	7.6	6.4[c]	—	—	40.3	43.5[c]
United States	20.6	13.9[a,d]	44.6	52.4[a,d]	7.1	14.1[a,d]	36.5	32.2[a,d]	1.0	6.1[a,d]	65.2	66.3[a,d]
Japan	19.4[f]	16.7	44.3[f]	58.1	32.9[f]	38.4	4.1	6.0	7.3[f]	13.7	63.7[f]	74.8

Short term securities are not included.

[a] The figure given is for 1987.
[b] Monetary sector.
[c] The figure given is for 1986.
[d] Government short term securities included.
[e] The data refer only to government securities.
[f] The figure given is for 1981.
[g] The figures include bonds held by unit trusts.

Sources: Italy: Banca d'Italia, *Appendice alla Relazione Annuale*; Germany: *Monthly Report of the Deutsche Bundesbank* and *Statistische Beihefte* (Reihe 2); France: Banque de France, *Statistique financières annuelles (series retrospectives)* and *Bulletin Trimestriel*; the United Kingdom, Spain, the Netherlands, Belgium, the United States: OECD, *Financial Accounts*; Japan: Bank of Japan, *Economic Statistics Monthly*.

In those countries where we observe an increase of the degree of securities' intermediation, securities' characteristics are instead more favourable to a larger presence of financial investors. There is lower significance of public sector securities; bonds have longer maturity; financial intermediaries collect funds by offering to savers more sophisticated financial instruments.

Another particular aspect which has to be taken into consideration is that many of these markets, unlike the Italian one, embody characteristics of 'wholesale securities markets'. In some countries (like Japan[7] and Germany[8]) a market for short-term securities has not reached a sufficient degree of development to compete with banks' deposits. Also in France the short-term market, even though more developed, is typically 'wholesale'.[9] Another aspect regards liquidity of securities available to individuals: in Germany, for example, there are government bonds issued for personal investors having a very low minimum denomination, but also a low degree of liquidity because they are not tradable before maturity.[10]

Let us consider the second relevant institutional aspect of securities markets: the degree of differentiation among financial investors. As Table 10.3 shows, in almost all the countries non-bank institutions hold more securities than commercial banks, highlighting a relative specialisation of these intermediaries as investors in bonds.

Once more the only exception to the general trend are represented by Italy and Spain, where commercial banks hold more securities than other financial intermediaries. In 1980, in Italy more than 90 per cent of total securities held by financial institutions (net of central bank holdings) were placed with banks. Notwithstanding the reduction observed during the 1980s, at the end of 1988 such a share was still around 70 per cent, against values ranging from 20 per cent to 30 per cent in more developed financial markets, like the United States, Japan, France and the United Kingdom. Also in Germany,[11] Belgium and the Netherlands the role of financial investors is mainly carried out by non-bank intermediaries, rather than by commercial banks.

If we compare the 1980 figures with those of 1988, we observe a generalised trend towards an increase in the ratio between securities held by non-bank intermediaries and total securities held by financial institutions, with the exception only of the United Kingdom and France. However, in the United Kingdom, institutional investors traditionally hold huge amounts of securities (more than 40 per cent of total outstanding bonds); in France, in addition, during the 1980s, there was a sharp increase of the role of SICAV,[12] whose investment rose from 5.9 per cent to 24.2 per cent of total securities outstanding in the French market.

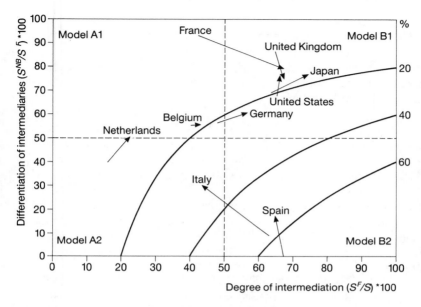

Figure 10.2   Securities market structures: a comparative view, 1980 → 1988, or other benchmark years, as from Table 10.3
Isocurves refer to some levels of the share of securities held by banks.

3.2   Securities market models and the role of banks

The empirical evidence, based on our two indicators, enables us to divide our sample of countries into four groups. In Figure 10.2, the share of outstanding bonds held by banks is represented on a plane where the horizontal axis corresponds to the degree of securities' intermediation and the vertical one to the degree of financial differentiation. Isocurves referring to the same levels of S^B/S are drawn, and the space is divided into four quadrants corresponding to our four models of securities markets.

Considering the evolution during the 1980s, a quite generalised trend may, however, be identified. The previously examined tendency towards an increase both of the degree of intermediation and of the degree of financial differentiation is leading to a predominance of model B1, i.e. of markets where a large share of bonds is held by financial intermediaries and, among these, the role of investors in securities is mainly played by insurance companies, pension funds and unit trusts rather than by commercial banks.

Such a general trend shows countries like the United States, the United Kingdom and Japan in a consolidated position, because in these countries

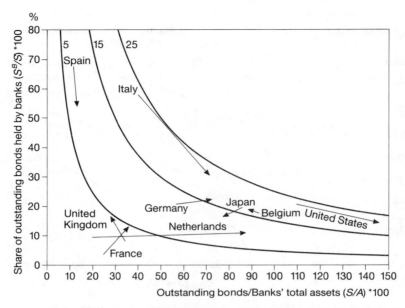

Figure 10.3 Securities market dimensions and the role of banks as investors: a comparative view, 1980→1988, or other benchmark years, as from Table 10.3
Isocurves refer to the investment in securities by commercial banks, as a percentage of banks' total assets.

a model B1 has been predominant for some time. Moreover, as the financial markets of these countries are usually considered more developed, this evidence may also suggest that financial markets development is to some extent correlated with the active presence of professional investors in the market. Many other countries are carrying out important progress towards the realisation of securities markets like those of model B1. Among these systems, France appears to be the country where the process is faster.

Spain and Italy instead appear clear exceptions. Italy left a model B2 (intermediated and bank-oriented securities market) and is moving towards model A2 (direct placing and bank-oriented securities market). In Spain, too, non-bank intermediaries are beginning to play a role, but the system still appears far from the more developed ones. In these countries the weak role of non-bank investors has often required commercial banks to contribute to absorbing a large share of outstanding securities, also by means of compulsory portfolio requirements.

In conclusion, the evolution from one model to another may provide useful information in order to explain the dynamics of the role of banks as securities' investors. Sometimes, however, the countries' evolution is on the same isocurve drawn in Figure 10.2 and in this case the changing of the market structure does not have a significant impact on the role of banks, from our point of view. Moreover, Figure 10.2 relates our four models only by the share of outstanding securities held by banks and not by the dynamics of the securities' portfolio as a share of total assets. In order to do so, it is necessary to take into account the S/A ratio described in paragraph 3.1 above.

In Figure 10.3, the share of bank total assets invested in securities is represented on a plane, where the X axis is the ratio between outstanding bonds and banks' total assets (S/A) and the Y axis corresponds to the S^B/S ratio. The last ratio is the same identified by the isocurves of Figure 10.2. The isocurves of Figure 10.3 instead refer to the same levels of S^B/A. As we can see, very different underlying trends may correspond to similar levels of S^B/A. The comparison between Italian and US figures, for example, is particularly meaningful. Both countries display a level of S^B/A around 20 per cent, but while in the United States the S/A ratio is almost equal to 150 per cent, in Italy the same ratio amounts to about 72 per cent; correspondingly S^B/S is about 14 per cent in the United States and 30 per cent in Italy.

Table 10.4. *Institutional determinants of banks' securities holdings[a], differences between 1988 and 1980; figures in logarithms*

Country	Banks' securities holdings (as % of total assets)	Degree of intermediation of securities markets[b]	Degree of differentiation in the financial structures[c]	Dimensions of securities markets[d]
Italy	− 0.08	− 0.38	− 0.27	0.57
Germany	0.30	0.17	− 0.11	0.23
France	2.02	0.47	1.13	0.42
United Kingdom	0.47	0.04	0.66	− 0.23
Spain	− 0.10	− 0.04	− 0.19	0.13
Netherlands	1.58	0.35	− 0.21	1.44
Belgium	0.02	0.07	− 0.01	− 0.04
United States	− 0.09	0.02	− 0.41	0.30
Japan	− 0.23	0.16	− 0.31	− 0.08

[a] The figures refer only to medium–long-term bonds.
[b] The indicator is equal to the share of outstanding bonds held by all financial institutions.
[c] It is equal to $(1 - S^{NB}/S^F)$, where S^{NB} and S^F correspond to bonds held by non-bank financial institutions and by the financial system as a whole, respectively.
[d] The securities market size is considered in relation to the banks' total assets.

As to the dynamics of the S/A ratio, during the 1980s we observe an increase in most of the countries. This trend is in line with the well-known development of bond markets that was very fast in the 1980s. *Ceteris paribus*, this increase in the size of bond markets calls for an increase of S^B/A. The actual evolution of S^B/A also depends on the qualitative aspects of the securities markets that were considered previously.

In order to summarise how the change in securities markets affected banks' bond holdings, Table 10.4 disaggregates the variations of the shares in banks' total assets invested in bonds into the three factors already mentioned.

In all the countries, at least one of the two indicators relating to the securities market models moved in the same direction of the variation of the share invested in securities. Changes in the degree of financial differentiation were particularly important in France, the United Kingdom, Spain, the United States and Japan. Modifications of the degree of securities' intermediation were instead more relevant in Italy and Belgium.

Finally, in some countries, like Germany and the Netherlands, the increase in securities market dimensions seems to have contributed in a very important way to determining the increasing role of banks in the securities markets. In these two countries, these modifications were more relevant than those of the securities market structure.

4   Deposits, loans and securities of banks: an econometric analysis of causality

4.1   Time-series behaviour of bank aggregates: suggestions from the theory of the banking firm

In order to analyse the role of securities' holdings in bank management, in this section we focus on the cointegration and causality relationships[13] among bank deposits, loans and securities investment in the United States, Italy, Japan and Germany during the 1980s.[14]

The theoretical literature on the banking firm provides essentially three classes of models which can explain a bank's interest in securities investment.[15] A first group of models stems from the application of the traditional portfolio choice theory to the bank:[16] the bank chooses its securities holdings simultaneously with the quantities of other assets (typically, loans) and possibly of (some of) its liabilities, according to risk and return criteria. The Klein–Monti (1971)[17] model, by contrast, assigns a residual role to securities in bank management. Finally, according to a third approach,[18] securities may be bought by banks as a secondary source of liquidity.

The application of the portfolio theory to the banking firm has been criticised on both theoretical and empirical grounds. First, bank interest rates are not explained, but taken as exogenous.[19] Second, the wide differences existing among the various assets (and liabilities) of a bank, and particularly between loans and securities, are completely over-looked.[20] Third, econometric studies generally do not support the port-folio approach to the bank, even when sophisticated dynamic specifi-cations of the model are tested.[21] In sum, it is widely agreed that the application of portfolio theory to the banking firm does not provide a correct representation of the asset (and liability) choices by the bank. Accordingly, we rule out this approach, and will not make any effort to see whether the results of our cointegration and causality analysis conflict or are consistent with this theory.

As to the Klein–Monti model, from our point of view it displays two relevant features. The first is the residual nature of the securities' invest-ment by the bank. First, the profit-maximising bank – which acts as a price (interest rate) taker in the market for securities, but has a monopoly power in the markets for both deposits and loans – determines its optimal levels of deposits and loans. Then, the difference between deposits (and, possibly, other optimally fixed or exogenously given liabilities) and loans (and other assets) defines the room for securities' holdings. Securities essentially play a buffer role: when faced with a shift in the demand curve for loans (deposits), in order to preserve the marginal conditions for profit-maximisation, the bank will increase or reduce loans (deposits) correspondingly squeezing or inflating (inflating or squeezing) securities holdings.

The second interesting feature of the Klein–Monti model is the com-plete separation of deposits decisions and loans decisions. The optimal quantity of deposits (loans) is in no way influenced by the decision making process for loans (deposits). As a consequence, variations in deposits (loans) due to a shift in the demand curve for deposits (loans) will determine changes in securities' holdings, but will have no effect on the amount of loans (deposits).

The Klein–Monti model refers to a static equilibrium framework. If we consider the slow adjustments from one equilibrium to another that occur in reality, however, we can easily translate the predictions of the model into time-series patterns that should be followed by the three variables (bank deposits, loans and securities) of our cointegration and causality analysis (which is intrinsically dynamic). If the model were a correct representation of reality, we would probably find a causal link running from deposits and loans to securities' holdings; on the contrary, we should not find a causal relationship between deposits and loans (in either direction).

As to the models of the banking firm which embody a secondary liquidity rationale for holding securities, similarly to the Klein–Monti model, they imply that the bank will finance loan increases and deposit decreases (giving rise to negative cash flows larger than existing cash reserves) by selling securities. The only difference between the two approaches is that in the secondary liquidity models the 'buffer' securities are held by the bank just for secondary liquidity purposes, while in the Klein–Monti model they are in the bank portfolio only as a residual item.

Consequently, as the econometric analysis that follows deals with all securities held by banks (no matter if for secondary liquidity purposes or residually), from our point of view the secondary liquidity model displays important similarities with the Klein–Monti model: in fact it also implies a causal link running from deposits and loans to securities.

Both the Klein–Monti and the secondary liquidity models raise the following problems. First whereas it is fine to liquidate securities when faced with a stochastic deposit withdrawal, it is a myopic behaviour to do so to finance an expansion of the loan portfolio. In fact, if loan demand is booming, then interest rates will become higher and bond prices lower. If banks choose to liquidate securities in such a situation they will incur a capital loss. A better way to manage a bank's portfolio, in this case, would be through liability management, i.e. by issuing CDs or borrowing on the interbank market.

Second, it is likely that a loan expansion or a deposit contraction will lead to securities sales only when they come to be perceived as permanent. Both these arguments enforce the appropriateness of our causality analysis. In fact, they both imply that a loan expansion or a deposit contraction will eventually determine a securities' sale only with a time lag and our causality analysis is just able to catch only lagged influences of one variable on another.

4.2   Cointegration and causality analysis: methodological aspects and results

Our econometric analysis consists of three steps. First, we perform unit root tests on each variable in each country in order to ascertain whether the series under study are difference stationary. Second, we perform cointegration tests for the three variables in each country. Third a causality analysis is carried out: an error correction model (ECM) specification is used for the countries where the variables are found to be cointegrated, while a simple vector autoregressive (VAR) model in the first differences is estimated in absence of cointegration.[22]

As to the first step, two unit root tests proposed by Dickey and Fuller (1979, 1981) were applied to each variable. Both tests are based on the

Table 10.5. *Unit root tests*

	USA		Italy		Japan		Germany	
	τ_τ	Φ_3	τ_τ	Φ_3	τ_τ	Φ_3	τ_τ	Φ_3
Deposits	− 1.75	1.60	− 3.54	6.27	− 0.80	3.08	− 2.45	3.00
Loans	− 3.17	5.63	− 0.54	1.20	− 1.91	4.89	− 3.24	5.56
Securities	− 2.31	2.97	0.31	1.20	− 0.74	2.37	− 3.42	5.84

The relevant probability distributions of τ_τ and Φ_3 can be found, respectively, in Fuller (1976, p. 373) and Dickey and Fuller (1981).

assumption that the variable under consideration, say x_t, is correctly represented by the model:

$$\Delta x_t = a + \beta t + \rho x_{t-1} + \sum_{i=1}^{p} \theta_i \Delta x_{t-1} + u_t$$

where $\Delta x_{t-i} = x_{t-i} - x_{t-i-1}$, u_t is an independently identically distributed random variable with zero mean and (still by assumption) the constants θ_i are such that a hypothetical AR(p) process with autoregressive parameters $(\theta_1 \ldots \theta_p)$ would be stationary. The tests concern the values of ρ and β: if $\rho = 0$ and $\beta = 0$, the variable x_t is difference stationary, i.e. it is integrated of order 1; if $\rho = 0$ and $\beta \neq 0$, x_t is difference stationary around a linear deterministic trend, i.e. it is integrated of order 1 only when the trend has been removed. When performing the tests, the value selected for the parameter p must be large enough to ensure that the residual u_t is not autocorrelated: this criterion led us to set $p = 12$ for all our variables (this is not surprising, given the strong seasonal component that all of them display).

Table 10.5 shows our results. The τ_τ-statistic (Dickey and Fuller, 1979) tests the unit root hypothesis $\rho = 0$. If $\beta = 0$, this statistic is distributed as in Fuller (1976, p. 373), so that the hypothesis is not rejected at the 5 per cent level if the value of τ_τ falls between − 3.73 and − 0.62. Therefore, should a deterministic trend be absent ($\beta = 0$), for almost all of the variables we would find a unit root. The Φ_3-statistic (Dickey and Fuller, 1981) jointly tests the absence of deterministic trend and the presence of a unit root ($\beta = 0$ and $\rho = 0$). The 5 per cent critical value is 6.49, so that the null hypothesis is accepted for every variable.

The combination of the two tests gives clear-cut evidence in favour of the hypothesis that almost all of the variables under consideration are integrated of order 1, with no evidence of deterministic trend. The joint test based on Φ_3 would suggest that we should accept the same conclusion for all of the variables, and we do so.

Table 10.6. *Engle–Granger cointegration tests*

	USA	Italy	Japan	Germany	5% critical values
CRDW	0.47	0.96	1.77	0.06	0.367
DF	− 3.44	− 5.34	− 8.89	− 3.01	− 3.37
ADF	− 2.29	− 4.80	− 5.83	− 2.69	− 3.13

Critical values are taken from Hall and Henry (1988). While the CRDW and ADF critical values correctly refer to the three-variables case for a sample of 100 observations, the DF value refers to the two-variable case, but the error should be small.

The cointegration relationship among bank deposits, loans and securities' investment in each country was investigated using both some well-known tests proposed by Engle and Granger (1978) and the more recent maximum likelihood approach proposed by Johansen (1988, 1989).

Results from Engle–Granger's approach are shown in Table 10.6. Among the test statistics proposed by the two authors, the most common ones were chosen: the cointegrating regression Durbin–Watson (CRDW), the Dickey–Fuller (DF) and the augmented Dickey–Fuller (ADF).[23] All of these statistics lead us to accept the null hypothesis of no cointegration for Germany at the 5 per cent level. As to the other countries, the evidence clearly favours the existence of cointegration (although the ADF statistic points in the opposite direction for the United States).

The main limitation of Engle–Granger's tests is that they assume that, if a cointegrating vector exists, it is unique. On the contrary, when N variables are involved (in our case $N = 3$), up to $N − 1$ cointegrating vectors may exist. Therefore, Johansen's test seems to be particularly recommended here, as it enables us to assess the number of cointegrating vectors.[24]

Johansen's approach basically confirms the results found in performing Engle–Granger tests. Results are shown in Table 10.7. The statistics reported in the first line of Table 10.7 test the null that there are at most 2 cointegrating vectors ($r \leq 2$). Comparison with the critical values at the 5 per cent level leads us to accept the null for all countries: this means, trivially, that in each country we might have 2, 1 or 0 cointegrating vectors. Statistics in the second row test the null of at most 1 cointegrating vector ($r \leq 1$). Again, the null is accepted for all countries: in each country we might have 1 or 0 cointegrating vectors, so that the possibility of 2 cointegrating vectors is ruled out. Finally, the last row helps to test the null of no cointegration ($r = 0$). Here the null is accepted only for

Table 10.7. *Johansen cointegration tests*

	USA	Italy	Japan	Germany	5% critical values
$r \leq 2$	0.02	1.46	0.24	0.40	3.96
$r \leq 1$	13.30	13.12	13.23	4.52	15.20
$r = 0$	30.79	36.01	65.10	14.57	29.51

r = number of cointegrating vectors.
The critical values are taken from Table T1 in Johansen (1989).

Germany. Therefore, 1 (but not 2) cointegrating vector is found in the United States, Italy and Japan, none in Germany.

Johansen's test is based on a VAR model in the levels of variables: the order k of the VAR model is to be chosen before the test is performed. Results reported in Table 10.7 are obtained setting $k = 5$ for all countries except Japan, where 4 lags were fitted. The test was also repeated using many other parametrisations for each country. In no case was cointegration found in Germany. In no case were we able to find more than 1 cointegrating vector either.[25] The existence of 1 cointegrating vector for Italy, Japan and the United States was confirmed in most (albeit not all) cases.

Summing up, from a joint view of Engle–Granger's and Johansen's tests the empirical evidence in favour of cointegration for all countries except Germany seems to be quite robust, while Johansen's test rules out the existence of more than 1 cointegrating vector.

As anticipated previously, cointegration analysis results provide crucial information in order to set up the dynamic model for the causality tests. For each of the countries where a cointegrating vector was found, the following ECM was adopted for the causality analysis:

$$\Delta y_t = \mu + a z_{t-1} + \sum_{i=1}^{k-1} \Gamma_j \Delta y_{t-j} + \phi D_t + \epsilon_t$$

where y_t is a (3×1) vector including bank deposits, loans and securities investment at time t, Δ is the difference operator, $z_t = \beta' y_t$ is the cointegration residual (β being the cointegrating vector), D_t is a (11×1) vector of seasonal dummies, μ and a are vectors of coefficients and the Γ_js and ϕ are matrices of coefficients. Instead, the causality tests for Germany (where no cointegration was found) were carried out using a traditional VAR model in the first differences (as is obtained setting $a z_{t-1} = 0$ in the ECM above).

Table 10.8 shows the results obtained setting $k = 5$ for the United

States, Italy and Germany and $k = 4$ for Japan, in accordance with the lag structures underlying Johansen's cointegration tests of Table 10.7. The cointegration residuals for causality analysis, when needed, were reckoned using Johansen's estimates of the cointegrating vector obtained assuming the appropriate ks.

The numbers reported under the heading 'Short run' are values of F-statistics: for example, the figure 0.93 in Table 10.8(b) is the value of the F-statistic testing the significance of all of the lagged loans coefficients in the deposits equation appearing in the ECM for the United States and then refers to the causality relation from loans to deposits. Under the heading 'Long run', we report the values of t-statistics relative to the coefficients of z_{t-1} in the ECMs. One asterisk refers to the significance of the F- or t-values at the 5 per cent level, while two asterisks refer to significance at the 10 per cent level.

The significance of the F-value relative to the coefficients of a variable in the ECM equation of another variable indicates short-run causality running from the former to the latter, in Granger's sense. The significance of the coefficient of z_{t-1} in the ECM equation relative to a certain variable – say, securities' holdings – demonstrates that securities' holdings tend to adjust in response to deviations from the long-run equilibrium (the cointegration relationship) in order to restore it: in this sense, it may be referred to as long-run causality, because securities' holdings could be thought as a 'caused' variable in the long run, deposits and/or loans being the 'causing' variable.[26]

4.3   Economic interpretation of the results

Although bank deposits, loans and securities' investments make up a substantial part of the balance sheet of banks, other balance sheet items might be quite important. As a consequence, we should not expect that a cointegrating relationship (i.e. a long-run interrelation) among our three variables *necessarily* holds. In fact, cointegration was found in the United States, Japan and Italy, but not in Germany. This means that in the former countries deposits, loans and securities' investments move in such a way that they do not drift too far apart, while in Germany other variables, such as interbank position or borrowing from Central Bank and issues of bonds (peculiar to the German banking system), may move in order to offset the long-run movements of our three balance sheet items.

In order to assess the contribution of causality analysis to our problem, we might think of the decision making process of a bank as articulated in three levels: a day-by-day cash management, a short-term planning horizon and a long-run strategic horizon. As our causality tests are not

Table 10.8. *Short- and long-run causality*

(a) Italy

	Short run			Long run	
	Deposits	Loans	Securities		
Deposits	—	0.40	1.91	Deposits	1.82
Loans	1.27	—	0.99	Loans	0.25
Securities	0.68	2.71*	—	Securities	− 3.27*

(b) United States

	Short run			Long run	
	Deposits	Loans	Securities		
Deposits	—	0.93	2.12	Deposits	1.70
Loans	2.12	—	1.29	Loans	1.64
Securities	4.93*	3.43*	—	Securities	3.30*

(c) Japan

	Short run			Long run	
	Deposits	Loans	Securities		
Deposits	—	0.78	1.88	Deposits	− 3.61*
Loans	0.41	—	2.22**	Loans	− 5.13*
Securities	0.60	2.90*	—	Securities	− 1.07

(d) Germany

	Short run			Long run	
	Deposits	Loans	Securities		
Deposits	—	0.50	1.30	Deposits	—
Loans	2.22**	—	1.45	Loans	—
Securities	1.43	0.89	—	Securities	—

Note: In the 'Short run' section, row variables represent the (possibly) caused variables, while column variables are the (possibly) causing ones. The figures are F-values and are accompanied by one (two) asterisk(s) in the case of significance at the 5 per cent (10 per cent) level. In the 'Long run' section, the t-values referring to the long-run causality are reported.

able to deal with instantaneous causality, they cannot provide information concerning the very short-run behaviour of banks. It seems, however, that they may represent a useful tool to investigate the decision making process of banks at the short- and long-run levels.

An interesting result of our tests is that we find little evidence of a short-run causal relationship running from deposits to loans: no trace of such a relationship is present in the United States, Japan and Italy, while only at the 10 per cent level is this link assessed in Germany. This finding seems to give an indirect support to that large part of economic literature on the banking firm which considers deposits and loans as two separate outputs of banking activity, in the sense of two different services supplied to customers.[27] The result appears indeed in contrast with the conclusions of other authors who consider the availability of 'funds to be loaned' as an important input of banking activity.[28]

As far as the role of securities' investment is concerned, our causality tests demonstrate that in the short run securities' holdings are caused by, but hardly ever cause,[29] the other bank variables. In particular, securities' holdings turn out to be caused by deposits and loans in the United States and only by loans in Italy and Japan. This outcome is confirmed by the long-run causality analysis. In the long run, securities' holdings are the only variable that carries out the adjustment towards the cointegration relationship both in Italy and in the United States.

This joint evidence seems to demonstrate the 'residual item' role played by securities in the balance sheet of banks, at least in Italy and the United States. This is consistent with the Monti–Klein models of the banking firm, in which securities' investment works as a 'buffer' in face of fluctuations in the demand both for loans and for deposits. As it was noted in paragraph 4.1 above, however, the same evidence could be interpreted as support in favour of a secondary liquidity approach. In any case, securities' holdings seem to display a countercyclical behaviour with respect to the evolution of the demand for loans.

The residual role of securities' holdings is not confirmed for Japan, where in the long-run causality analysis deposits and loans – instead of securities – turn out to adjust towards the cointegrating relationship. This result may appear surprising if compared with those of the other two countries (Italy and the United States), where a cointegrating relationship exists. It must be taken into account, however, that, for a large part of the period considered, Japanese banks could not freely buy and sell securities but were forced to hold previously bought government securities up to their maturity. This constraint clearly prevented a residual role for securities holdings.

5   Summary and concluding remarks

This chapter has tried to examine and explain why banks enter the securities markets as investors and whether cross-country differences exist in banks' securities' holdings, by developing two different lines of analysis. First, the institutional frameworks were considered. Second, in four countries the relation of banks' securities' holdings with deposits and loans during the 1980s was examined by means of a cointegration and causality analysis.

As far as the institutional features of financial markets are concerned, two aspects appear especially relevant. The first concerns the relationship between debtor sectors and final investors, whether it is direct or inter-mediated by financial institutions. From this point of view, two extreme models may be considered and the corresponding underlying features of securities markets identified. In markets in which securities are directly placed with savers, they offer a low degree of risk, have 'retail' character-istics and are household-oriented. On the contrary, in markets in which the role of intermediaries is more developed, outstanding securities may have a higher degree of risk and may also have 'wholesale' characteristics with regard, for example, to the minimum denomination of issues; moreover, intermediaries compete for savings by supplying more sophisti-cated services and developing financial innovations on the liability side.

The second important structural feature of financial markets refers to the degree of specialisation of the intermediaries and, in particular, to what extent institutional investors are present in the various financial systems. We expect more specialisation among intermediaries in countries where securities markets require particular technical expertise, due to their sophistication and differentiation.

Evidence indicates that most of the countries show, or are heading towards, a structure of highly intermediated securities markets and highly differentiated intermediaries. Changes in the securities market models contributed to a large extent in modifying the role of banks as investors in securities. In particular, changes in the degree of differenti-ation among financial investors seem to have played the most significant role in this process. Besides the changes in the securities market struc-tures, in some countries the increase in size of securities markets was also a relevant factor.

The study of the cointegration and causality relationship among bank deposits, loans and securities' investment in four countries during the 1980s revealed interesting aspects of the behaviour of banks. The lack of evidence for a strong causal relation running from deposits to loans seems indirectly to support the bank theories which consider deposits as an output (and not an input) of banking activity. With regard to the role of securities, in the short run securities' holdings do not cause the other two bank variables in any country, while they are caused by deposits and loans in the United States and by loans in Japan and Italy. This result is confirmed by the long-run causality analysis: securities' holdings are the only variable which carries out the adjustment towards the cointegration relationship in both Italy and the United States. This evidence also seems to corroborate those theories of the banking firm which underline the residual role of securities in the balance sheet of banks. It also confirms that the investment in securities displays a countercyclical behaviour with respect to the evolution of the demand for loans.

Notes

1 We would like to thank Rony Hamaui and Riccardo Rovelli for useful comments and suggestions, as well as Mario Noera and other participants of an internal seminar held at BCI, Economic Research Department. We are also grateful to Valentina Corradi, Carlo Favero and Rodolfo Helg for precious suggestions on the cointegration and causality analysis. Any remaining errors are of course our own responsibility. Finally, we wish to thank Simonetta Melotto, who helped us to collect the data, and Giuliana Brenna, for her patience with the editing.

2 This general trend may be explained by the diversification strategies carried out by banks and also by the subsequent changes in authority behaviour. From the first point of view, the broadening and the strengthening of markets for new instruments has increased the need for the banks to diversify their activities, raising investment in marketable assets. See Bröker (1989) and, with regard to the United States, Saunders (1989) and Kaufman (1988). This trend was in many cases accompanied by the behaviour of supervisory authorities, that in recent years made many efforts to improve the efficiency and the working of financial markets.

3 In Italy securities' portfolio constraints were gradually abolished during the 1980s.

4 In various stages, Japanese banks were allowed to sell government bonds in their portfolio if held for more than one year; secondly, banks were allowed to place newly-issued government bonds, and finally they were authorised to act as dealers in the 'over the counter' market. These measures increased the turnover of the securities' portfolio and the role of Japanese banks in the secondary markets, but reduced the bond holdings. See Suzuki (1989).

5 Among these, let us just remember the so-called 'divorce' between the central bank and the Ministry of the Treasury: the Bank of Italy was no longer compelled to subscribe Treasury notes that had not been placed with the market, so that the share of outstanding securities held by the central bank halved from 1980 to 1988. Besides, policy tools, aiming at controlling bank credit directly (such as the ceiling on loans and the securities' portfolio requirement) that had been extensively used in the 1970s and that had boosted the share of banks' portfolios invested in securities, were abandoned in 1983. In January 1986 and September 1987, the ceiling on bank loans was, however, temporarily reintroduced for a six-month period.

6 The share of bonds issued by the public sector is relatively high with respect to

other countries, so that the Italian market does not seem to be excessively concerned with 'default risk'. Furthermore, even though it is not endowed with a high degree of liquidity, it is mainly a market for short-term maturities, so reducing the impact of eventual liquidity costs on the investment decision. Finally, even the technical features of bonds issued in Italy seem to be oriented towards savers' preferences, rather than to those of the intermediaries: for example, the minimum amount of Treasury bonds is quite low, so as to be affordable to small savers.

7 In the Japanese market, short-term government securities amounted at the end of 1988 only to 5.4 per cent of total outstanding securities and only recently the Japanese Ministry of Finance began to increase the issues of Treasury bills.

8 In Germany, less than 1-year government securities do not exist. There are securities with maturity varying between 12 and 24 months, but only with a very high denomination (100,000 DM).

9 In the French government securities market, Treasury bills until 1985 were reserved to interbank participants. Despite the opening to corporations and individuals in January 1986, the market has not become a 'retail' market, because the denomination of these securities requires investment of FF 1 million. This high minimum level regards both BTNs (13, 26, 52 weeks) and BTANs (2 or 5 years) that amount to about 30 per cent of public debt. See Ministère de l'Economie, des Finances et du Budget (1989).

10 These securities have the purpose of increasing savings of individuals with low incomes. They are F-Schätze (with short maturity) or Bundesschätzebriefe (with longer maturity).

11 In Table 10.3 there is an underestimation of the share of securities held by the German banking system, as the item 'commercial banks' does not include Giro institutions.

12 The SICAV are 'Sociétés d'investissement à capital variable', the development of which began in 1983; afterwards there was some legislative intervention.

13 For an application of cointegration and causality analysis to the behaviour of banks, see Corradi, Galeotti and Rovelli (1989).

14 Monthly data are used. Sample periods: Germany, January 1980–May 1989; the United States, August 1981–July 1989; Japan, January 1981–March 1989; Italy, January 1982–September 1989.

15 See Baltensperger (1980) or Santomero (1984) for a survey.

16 See, for example, Parkin (1970); Parkin, Gray and Barrett (1970); Pyle (1971); and Hart and Jaffee (1974).

17 See Klein (1971) and Monti (1971).

18 See, for example, Gray and Parkin (1973).

19 For this criticism see, for example, Baltensperger (1980). Actually, some authors adopting the portfolio approach have taken into account that in some markets banks fix the interest rate and are quantity takers (see Rovelli, 1988, for a survey). This approach, however, did not gain much of a following.

20 Securities are more liquid, more standardised and more easily transferable than loans. Moreover, a loan is part of a peculiar relationship between the bank and the borrower, which involves the production of information on the part of the bank: this aspect has given rise to a substantial body of literature in the 1980s. These differences between securities and loans are so important that risk and return considerations probably represent only one (and, maybe, even a minor) factor affecting the decision of banks about their asset composition.

21 This result has been confirmed for Italy by Ferri and Monticelli (1989).
22 It is by now well known that a simple VAR specification in the first differences is not appropriate for causality analysis when cointegration is found (see, for example, Granger, 1988). On the other hand, VAR models in the levels run into the problem of non-standard asymptotic distribution of the coefficients when the corresponding regressors are integrated: see, for example, Sims, Stock and Watson (1986).
23 We chose bank loans as the left-hand side variable of the cointegrating regression in each country. The outcome of the tests is of course conditional on this (arbitrary) normalisation. By contrast, Johansen's cointegration tests that follow do not depend on any normalisation rule. The ADF cointegration test was performed introducing one lag of the first difference of the cointegrating residuals in the ADF regression.
24 If Johansen's test revealed the presence of 2 cointegrating vectors in some country, the ECM for the causality analysis in that country should include 2 cointegration residuals. In this case, performing only the Engle and Granger tests one would obtain only 1 cointegration residual and would be led to misspecify the ECM. Another advantage of Johansen's test is that its outcome is not conditional on any normalisation rule (see n. 23).
25 The only exception is represented by Japan when $k = 6$.
26 As already pointed out, results reported in Table 10.8 were obtained setting $k = 4$ for Japan and $k = 5$ for the other countries. Actually, for each country we performed the causality tests for many other values of k (each time using the appropriate Johansen estimate of the cointegrating vector to reckon the cointegration residuals, when needed). In each country, the causal links that turned out to be more robust are those shown in Table 10.8. The results obtained for $k = 4$ in Japan and $k = 5$ in the other countries, therefore, can be viewed as representative of a much wider set of results, and this is why they are presented here.
27 See, among the numerous studies following this approach, Goldschmidt (1981).
28 On this approach, see Sealey and Lindley (1977).
29 A causal link from securities to loans is present only in Japan, but only at a 10 per cent level.

References

Assofondi (1988) 'Investitori istituzionali e mercato dei capitali. Un'analisi comparata', *Quademi di documentazione e ricerca*, **3**.

Baltensperger, E. (1980) 'Alternative Approaches to the Theory of the Banking Firm', *Journal of Monetary Economics*, **6**.

Banca d'Italia, *Modello mensile del mercato monetario* (October).

Bank of Japan, *Economic Statistics Monthly* (various issues).

Banque de France, *Bulletin Trimestriel* (various issues).

Banque de France, *Statistique Financières Annuelles* (*series retrospectives*).

Bröker, G. (1989) 'Competition in Banking, Trends in Banking Structure and Regulation in OECD Countries', Paris: OECD.

Corradi, V., M. Galeotti and R. Rovelli (1989) 'A Cointegration Analysis of the Relationship between Bank Reserves, Deposits and Loans: The Case of Italy, 1965–1987', *Journal of Banking and Finance*, **5**.

Courakis, A. (1974) 'Testing Theories of Discount House Portfolio Selection', *Review of Economic Studies*, **42**.

Cumming, C. (1987) 'The Economics of Securitization', *Federal Reserve Bank of New York Quarterly Review* (Autumn).

Deutsche Bundesbank, *Monthly Report* (various issues).

Dickey, D.A. and W.A. Fuller (1979) 'Distribution of the Estimators for Autoregressive Time Series with a Unit Root', *Journal of the American Statistical Association*, **74**.

Dickey, D. A. and W. A. Fuller (1981) 'Likelihood Ratio Statistics for Autoregressive Time Series with a Unit Root', *Econometrica*, **49**.

Engle, R. F. and C. W. J. Granger (1987) 'Cointegration and Error Correction: Representation Estimation and Testing', *Econometrica*, **55**.

Fama, E. F. (1985) 'What's Different about Banks?', *Journal of Monetary Economics*, **15(1)**: 29–39.

Ferri, G. and C. Monticelli (1989) 'L'attività in titoli delle aziende di credito: un'analisi di portafoglio', Banca d'Italia, *Temi di discussione*, **130**.

Fuller, W. A. (1976) *Introduction to Statistical Time Series*, New York: Wiley.

Goldschmidt, A. (1981) 'On the Definition and Measurement of Bank Output', *Journal of Banking and Finance*, **6**.

Granger, C. W. J. (1988) 'Some Recent Developments in a Concept of Causality', *Journal of Econometrics*, **39**.

Gray, W. and A. Parkin (1973) 'Portfolio Diversification as Optimal Precautionary Behavior', in M. Moroshima, *Theory of Demand: Real and Monetary*, Oxford: Oxford University Press.

Hall, S. B. and S. G. B. Henry (1988) 'Macroeconomic Modelling', Amsterdam: North Holland.

Hart, O. D. and D. M. Jaffee (1974) 'On the Application of Portfolio Theory to Depository Financial Intermediaries', *Review of Economic Studies*, **41** (January).

Johansen, S. (1988) 'Statistical Analysis of Cointegration Vectors', *Journal of Economic Dynamics and Control*, **12**.

Johansen, S. (1989) 'Likelihood based Inference on Cointegration. Theory and Applications', *Lecture notes*, Bagni di Lucca (mimeo).

Kaufman, G. G. (1988) 'Securities' Activities of Commercial Banks: Recent Changes in the Economic and Legal Environments', *Midland Corporate Finance Journal* (Winter).

Klein, M. A. (1971) 'A Theory of the Banking Firm', *Journal of Money, Credit and Banking*, **3** (May).

Ministère de l'Economie, des Finances et du Budget (1989) *French Government Securities*, Paris.

Monti, M. (1971) 'A Theoretical Model of Bank Behavior and its Implications for Monetary Policy', *L'Industria*, **2**.

OECD, *Financial Accounts* (various issues).

Parkin, J. M., P. H. Gray and R. J. Barrett (1970) 'The Portfolio Behavior of Commercial Banks', in R. Hilton and D. Heathfield, *The Econometric Study of the United Kingdom*, London: Macmillan.

Parkin, M. (1970) 'Discount House Portfolio and Debt Selection', *Review of Economic Studies* (October).

Pyle, D. H. (1971) 'On the Theory of Financial Intermediation', *Journal of Finance* (June).

Rovelli, R. (1988) 'Le banche e la teoria dell'intermediazione finanziaria', Università L. Bocconi (unpublished).

Santomero, A. M. (1984) 'Modelling the Banking Firm: A Survey', *Journal of Money, Credit and Banking*, **4**.

Saunders, A. (1989) 'Banks and Securities Markets', *Salomon Brothers Center for the Study of Financial Institutions*, Working Paper Series, **509**.

Sealey, C. W. and J. T. Lindley (1977) 'Inputs, Outputs and a Theory of Production and Costs at Depository Financial Institutions', *Journal of Finance*, **4**.

Sims, C. A., J. H. Stock and M.W. Watson (1986) 'Inference in Linear Time Series Models with Some Unit Roots' (unpublished).

Sims, C. A., J. H. Stock and M.W. Watson (1990) 'Inference in Linear Time Series with Some Unit Roots', *Econometrica*, **58**.

Suzuki, Y. (ed) (1989) *The Japanese Financial System*, London: IFR Publishing.

11 Loan sales and balance sheet assets

PAOLO FULGHIERI

1 Introduction

The process of financial innovation that has characterised the international banking system in recent years has led to a rapid transformation of the domain of banks' activity. The creation of new financial instruments has brought the development of new markets and the expansion of the potential operations available to the banking system. The introduction of these new securities has changed the way in which traditional lending is performed, and it has induced banks to engage in extensive off-balance sheet activities. An important component of this process is the so called 'securitisation'.

Securitisation can be broadly defined as the process of originating and selling loans to outside investors.[1] This definition includes two leading forms of securitising loans. The first is more traditional, and it involves the sale of an existing loan to outside investors, either in its entirety or in smaller fractions. This form of securitisation has involved substantially two types of loans. It has first concerned the sale of large commercial and industrial loans, a process that has increased especially in recent years.[2] A second category of loans which have been subject to extensive secondary trade is formed by LDC loans, especially in connection to the process of restructuring the liabilities of some heavily indebted countries. Loans may be sold to outside investors in many different forms. They can be sold as a unique lot to a single acquirer, or can be fragmented in loan participations. Other banks or institutional investors, such as pension funds, are typical targets of the sale. Loans can be sold without recourse or with different degrees of insurance. In the first case, the acquiring investor assumes the default risk connected with the loan, for its share of participation in the loan. In the second case, the selling bank offers various forms of protection against default or pre-payment risk. The type and amount of protection given by the originating bank to the acquirer will determine whether the selling bank is allowed to write the loan off the balance sheet, avoiding in this way reserve and capital requirements.[3]

The second form of securitisation is relatively more recent and involves the pooling of a large number of small, homogeneous loans and their sale to outside investors through the creation of a new marketable security. Although this form of securitisation started as a way to create a secondary market for mortgage loans (especially those granted by Federal Agencies of the US government), it quickly spread to other consumer loans such as credit card receivables, auto loans, and others. There are fundamentally three types of securities which can be issued by the originating institutions to securitise a pool of loans.[4] These securities differ again by the degree of protection that originating banks give to purchasers. In 'pass-through' securities a portfolio of loans (usually mortgages) are pooled in a trust fund and certificates of ownership are sold to investors. Payments from the pool of loans, either in the interest or principal account, are collected by the originating bank and passed through to the investors. In this case, purchasers of the certificates have ownership of the loans and bear all the risk. The originating bank services the fund for a fee and is allowed to write the original loans off its balance sheet. In 'mortgage-backed bonds' the originating bank issues bonds that are collateralised by a pool of mortgages. This form of securitisation is equivalent to secured debt: the bonds are a direct liability of the issuing bank and have their own maturity and interest rate. The original loans are still owned by the bank and remain on its balance sheet. Finally, 'pay-through' securities are an intermediate form of securitisation, sharing characteristics with both of the previous types. In particular, they are bonds collateralised by mortgages, they are direct liabilities of the issuing bank, but now payments from the pool of securitised loans are paid through to the purchasers of the bonds.

The rapid growth of the market share of these new financial instruments has motivated several studies aimed at explaining their development. Kareken (1987) examines several factors thay may help to account for the recent diffusion of these securities, such as the deregulation of the banking system and the lowering of the cost of processing and transmitting information. Other studies have focussed on the properties characterising the securities, and have tried to explain these contractual forms as part of an explicit optimising behaviour by banks. In particular, Benveniste and Berger (1987), note that securitisation with recourse allows banks to create a liability having a claim over part of its assets (the securitised loans) that is senior to, and with lower risk than, the general deposits. This possibility may be valuable if the bank has large, risk averse depositors holding uninsured deposits. In this case the substitution of the uninsured deposits with this new claim would reduce the risk borne by the large investors, allowing a better risk-sharing and producing a lower overall cost of funds. Greenbaum and Thakor (1987) explain securitisation as a way to fund firms which is alternative to standard deposits. In particular, they examine two polar forms of financing firms: a 'deposit funding mode' in which banks issue deposits to risk averse individuals and then lend to firms, and a 'securitised funding mode' in which investors directly fund firms and with banks providing default insurance. It is then shown that if the creditworthiness of borrowers is private information, the amount of insurance purchased from the bank, given the corresponding fee schedule, can be used as a mechanism available to the borrowers to signal their private information to the uninformed investors. By substituting direct screening with signalling, the greater contractual flexibility of the securitisation contract allows the bank to save on the screening costs, but at the price of achieving sub-optimal risk-sharing. Closely related to our study, Pennacchi (1988) considers a model in which financing firms through deposits may be more expensive than direct funding because of the 'intermediation tax'. This tax is determined by the reserve requirements on deposits and, if equity financing is a more expensive source of funds than deposits, by the presence of minimum capital requirements. In this case, a bank may find it optimal to sell a part of its loan to outside investors. But if the probability that a loan is repaid depends on the level of monitoring effort privately chosen by the bank, the sale of a portion of a loan to outside investors may induce a level of monitoring falling short of the first-best. Since outside investors are rational, the costs of inefficient monitoring are shifted back to the bank at the moment the loan is sold, in the form of a discount in the sale price of the loan. The optimal fraction of a loan sold to outside investors is then determined by trading off the agency costs determined by sub-optimal monitoring against the gains from a reduction of the intermediation tax. Finally, in James (1988) it is shown that partial sale of a loan is equivalent to an issue of secured debt. Following Stultz and Johnson (1985), it is then shown that financing with loan sales may reduce the underinvestment problem determined by the conflict between current depositors and stockholders of the bank.

The model discussed in this chapter re-examines the effects of loan sales on the monitoring efforts of banks. In the model discussed in Pennacchi (1988) it is assumed that the agency insuring the deposits of a bank can perfectly observe its monitoring effort and correctly price the insurance premium. In this case, the potential conflict between the bank and the depositors on the level of monitoring is overcome by interposing the insurance agency, eliminating in this way the incentives to sub-optimal monitoring efforts. By financing loans with deposits, banks internalise the returns from monitoring, ensuring first-best effort. The choice of the optimal amount of a loan to be sold can be made then on a loan-by-loan basis. On the other hand, if the amount of monitoring exerted by a bank is not observable even by the insuring agency, the conflict between the bank and the depositors is replaced by an equivalent conflict with the insurance agency, maintaining distorted monitoring incentives. In this case, without loan sales, the optimal amount of monitoring on any loan must be determined simultaneously to all other loans. The sale of a fraction of a loan will now have an impact not only on the choice of the monitoring effort exerted on the loan sold, but also on the incentives to monitor the loans remaining on the balance sheet of the bank. This chapter focusses on these spillover effects, and it studies the effect of loan sales on the incentives to monitor the loans remaining on the balance sheet of the bank. In particular, it will be shown that by selling a loan without recourse, a bank may shield the return from the assets remaining on its balance sheet from the default of the securitised assets. This protection may be valuable because it may increase the incentive of the bank to monitor the assets remaining on its balance sheet. The optimal amount of loan sales will be shown to depend on two opposing incentives. On one hand, the convexity of the return function of equity induces a bank positively to correlate monitoring efforts and to prefer to pool loans in the same portfolio. On the other hand, the partial sale of a loan allows a bank to modify its liability structure, improving the overall distribution of monitoring efforts between balance sheet assets and partially sold loans. Finally, it is shown that if the fractional loan sale is optimal, the quality of the loans remaining on the balance sheet improves.

The basic model is presented in Section 2. As a point of reference, in Section 3 we study the model with deposit financing only. The effects of loan sales on the monitoring incentives of the bank and the optimal amount of loan sales, under specific assumptions of the stochastic structure of the returns, are examined in Section 4. Section 5 concludes the chapter.

2   The model

A bank has the opportunity to initiate two loans with two different customers.[5] These loans require an initial investment at the beginning of a period, say $t = 0$, of X and Y dollars and have a total return $(1 + r_X)X$ and $(1 + r_Y)Y$ at the end of the period, $t = 1$. It will be assumed that the returns r_h, $h = X, Y$, are random variables endowed with a probability distribution $F(r_h, e_h)$ with support $[r_h^0, r_h^1]$. The return on the loans depends on the level of monitoring effort, represented by the parameter $e_h \in [e_h^0, e_h^1] \subset \Re$, exerted by the bank on each loan at the beginning of the period. The level of effort $e = (e_Y, e_Y)$ is privately chosen by the bank, and it originates monitoring costs paid at the beginning of the period according to the cost function $C(e_X, e_Y)$.

The bank starts with some initial cash holding F.[6] Funding for the two loans can be obtained by issuing additional shares for a total value E or by accepting deposits for a total amount D. Let L be the fraction of the total loans financed with deposits: $D = L(X + Y)$. Deposits are insured and yield the risk-free rate r_f. It is assumed that at this rate banks face an infinitely elastic supply of funds. Let ϕ be the insurance premium. Individuals have no personal taxes and the corporate tax rate is τ. Banks are allowed to deduct from taxable income interest payments on deposits, generating a tax-induced preference for financing loans with deposits. At $t = 1$, total taxes will be

$$T_1 = \tau[r_X X + r_Y Y - r_f L(X + Y)]^7 \tag{1}$$

Given (1) and the discount factor for risk-free income $\gamma = 1/(1 + r_f)$, the expected end-of-period profits π_1 are given by

$$\pi_1(L, e_X, e_Y) = E[\max\{(1 + (1 - \tau)r_X)X + (1 + (1 - \tau)r_Y)Y \\ - (1 + (1 - \tau)r_f)L(X + Y); 0\}] \tag{2}$$

where the expectation is taken over the joint probability distribution function $F(r_X, r_Y, e_X, e_Y) = F(r_X, e_X) \cdot F(r_Y, e_Y)$. Expected end-of-period profits π_1 depend on the amount of deposits accepted $L(X + Y)$ and on the levels of monitoring $e = (e_X, e_Y)$ exerted on the two loans.

Consider now the value of the insurance services. If the after-tax value of the assets on the balance sheet of the bank is lower than the after-tax value of the liability to the depositors, the bank defaults and the insurance agency is required to absorb the loss. The expected value of the insurance services on the deposits, I_D, is then given by

$$I_D(L, e_X, e_Y) = \gamma E[\max\{(1 + (1 - \tau)r_f)L(X + Y) \\ - (1 + (1 - \tau)r_X)X - (1 + (1 - \tau)r_Y)Y; 0\}] \tag{3}$$

Since the expectation is taken again over the joint distribution function $F(r_X, e_X)F(r_Y, e_Y)$, the value of these services depends again on the level of monitoring efforts $e = (e_X, e_Y)$ chosen by the bank. Note that the deposit insurance contract can be interpreted as giving the bank the right to sell its assets to the insurance agency at a price equal to the total value of the outstanding deposits. As in Merton (1977), but in a more simplified framework, the value of this service is equal to the value of a put option, given by the option to sell the assets of the bank, with value $(1 + (1 - \tau)r_X)X + (1 + (1 - \tau)r_Y)Y$, at the strike price $(1 + (1 - \tau)r_f)L(X + Y)$.

At the beginning of the period, the bank must decide how much new equity E to issue, how many deposits D to accept, the current dividend δ_0, and the level of monitoring effort $e = (e_X, e_Y)$ in the two loans. To avoid a potential conflict between old and new stockholders, it is assumed that the bank will issue cum-dividend shares. Letting $(1 - a)$ be the fraction of ownership of the bank that must be granted to the new stockholders to raise E, the bank will maximise the fraction of the (cum-dividend) market value of the equity belonging to its original stockholders, and it will choose the vector $(E, \delta_0, a, L, e_X, e_Y)$ to solve

$$\max \ a[\delta_0 + \gamma\pi_1(L, e_X, e_Y)] \tag{4}$$

$$\text{s.t.} \quad \delta_0 + (1 - \tau)C(e_X, e_Y) + \phi + X + Y \leq F + L(X + Y) + E$$
$$E \leq (1 - a)[\delta_0 + \gamma\pi_1(L, e_X, e_Y)]$$
$$\phi \geq I_D(L, e_X, e_Y)$$
$$L \geq 0, \ E \geq 0, \ e_h \in [e_h^0, e_h^1] \ h = X, Y \tag{5}$$

Expression (5) is the cash flow constraint at the beginning of the period, limiting the total outflow for dividends δ_0, the after-tax monitoring costs C, the insurance premium ϕ and the expenditure for the acquisition of the loans $X + Y$ to be not greater than the initial cash F plus the value of the equity issue E plus the amount of deposits accepted. Note that, for simplicity, it is assumed that the bank is allowed to deduct from current taxes the monitoring costs C, but no deduction is allowed for the insurance premium ϕ. The remaining constraints make sure that the bank will indeed be able to issue new equity and to find insurance for its deposits.

Consider now the case in which the bank sells a part of one of the two loans, say loan X. It is assumed that the bank considers the sale without recourse of a fraction S of the face value X raising an amount SX. The remaining part $(1 - S)X$ must be financed with either equity capital or by accepting deposits. Even if, from a general point of view, the bank has great flexibility in determining the contractual form in which the sale of the loan occurs (that is, in designing the payoff of the security issued against the sold loan), in this chapter it will be assumed that the contract of loan sale takes the form of straight debt. This debt is secured by the sold loan, it has a face value $D_X = SX$, interest rate r_s, and a total promised payment of $(1 + r_s)SX$. To simplify the analysis, it is also assumed that this additional debt is itself insured, implying that $r_s = r_f$. Let ψ be the premium paid by the bank at $t = 0$ for insuring the additional debt D_X generated by the sale of the loan.

The sale of loan X will also change the tax liabilities of the bank. To avoid the introduction of inessential asymmetries in the tax status of the different earnings of the bank, it is assumed that banks are taxed at $t = 1$ on the net return from the residual position they hold on the sold loan, but they can deduct from taxable income the fraction $(1 - S)X$ – that is, their share in the purchase of the loan X. In this case the tax function (1) becomes

$$T_1 = \tau[r_Y Y - r_f L(Y + (1 - S)X)$$
$$- \max\{(1 + r_X)X - (1 + r_f)SX; 0\} - (1 - S)X] \qquad (6)$$

Note that for $S = 0$ expression (6) collapses into (1). The expected end-of-period profits of the bank are now given by the expected return on the loan Y remaining on the balance sheet of the bank, plus the proceeds from loan X, after the additional debt D_X has been paid off, that is

$$\pi_1(S, L, e_X, e_Y) = E[\max\{(1 + (1 - \tau)r_Y)Y$$
$$- (1 + (1 - \tau)r_f)LY + \tau(1 - S)X$$
$$+ (1 - \tau)\max\{(1 + r_X)X$$
$$- (1 + r_f)SX; 0\}; 0\}] \qquad (7)$$

In a similar way, the present value of the insurance services on the deposits of the bank, I_D, and on the additional debt issued in correspondence to the sale of the loan, I_S, are given by the value of the respective put options, that is

$$I_D(L, S, e_X, e_Y) = \gamma E[\max\{(1 + (1 - \tau)r_f)LY$$
$$- (1 + (1 - \tau)r_Y)Y - \tau(1 - S)X$$
$$- (1 - \tau)\max\{(1 + r_X)X$$
$$- (1 + r_f)SX; 0\}; 0\}] \qquad (8)$$

$$I_S(S, e_X) = \gamma E[\max\{(1 + r_f)SX - (1 + r_X)X; 0\}] \qquad (9)$$

Note that now the value of the insurance on the debt D_X originating from the securitisation of loan X depends only on the level of monitoring efforts exerted on that loan and on the fraction S of the loan that is securitised. On the other hand, the value of the insurance on the general deposits of the bank depends on the monitoring efforts on both loans, on the fraction S of loan X that is sold and on the total deposits D.

At the beginning of the period, the bank must decide on the optimal equity financing E, the current dividend payment δ_0, the fraction S of the loan X sold, the amount of deposits $L(Y + (1 - S)X)$ accepted, the amount of monitoring efforts e_X and e_Y, and the insurance premia ψ and ϕ to solve

$$\max a[\delta_0 + \gamma\pi_1(S, L, e_X, e_Y)]$$

s.t. $\quad \delta_0 + (1 - \tau)C(e_X, e_Y)$
$$+ \phi + \psi + X + Y \le F + L(Y + (1 - S)X) + SX + E$$
$$\phi \ge I_D(L, S, e_X, e_Y),$$
$$\psi \ge I_S(S, e_X),$$
$$E \le [\delta_0 + \gamma\pi_1(L, S, e_X, e_Y)]$$
$$\delta_0 \ge 0, L \ge 0, 0 \le S \le 1, e_h \in [e_h^0, e_h^1] \, h = X, Y \qquad (10)$$

Problem (10) is the general problem that will be discussed in this chapter under special assumptions on the stochastic structure of the returns.

3   Optimal financing with deposits

As a point of reference, in this section we consider the problem of choosing the optimal level of monitoring when the bank is financed with deposits only. The presence of bankruptcy risk generates a conflict between the stockholders of the bank and its depositors on the optimal level of monitoring. This conflict derives from the fact that, while stockholders bear the full cost of monitoring the two loans (in terms of dividend foregone at the beginning of the period), they capture only a fraction of its benefits. If the bank has some chances of defaulting, its stockholders benefit from monitoring only in those states in which the bank is solvent, creating a distortion in the incentives to monitor the two loans. If deposits are insured, an insurance agency is interposed between the bank and the depositors, and the conflict of interest is shifted from the depositors to the agency. If the level of monitoring is privately chosen by the bank and is not observable by outsiders, it cannot be contracted upon at the moment the insurance contract is designed. In these circumstances the conflict of interest between the bank and the insurance agency cannot be resolved, and the bank may be led to choose sub-optimal levels of monitoring.

From (3), the value of the insurance services depends on the choice of the monitoring efforts e_X and e_Y. At the moment of setting a fair premium ϕ, the agency must then speculate on the level of effort that will be privately chosen by the bank. In particular, the agency will rationally expect that the bank will choose the level of monitoring that is optimal, given its incentive structure. Given that at an optimum the cash flow constraint (5) must be binding and that the bank will post the highest possible ask price E, from problem (4) the level of monitoring privately chosen by the bank will solve

$$\max_{e} F + \gamma E[\max\{(1 + (1 - \tau)r_X)X \\ + (1 + (1 - \tau)r_Y)Y - (1 + (1 - \tau)r_f)K; 0\}] \\ - \phi - (1 - \tau)C(e_X, e_Y) - (1 - L)(X + Y) \qquad (11)$$

where $K = L(X + Y)$ is the value of the outstanding deposits. Since the stockholders will benefit from monitoring only in the states of solvency, the optimal levels of monitoring of the two loans will in general depend on the total liabilities K of the bank. Let $e^*(K) = (e_X^*(K), e_Y^*(K))$ be the solution corresponding to (11). By using the decision rule $e^*(K)$, the insurance agency is able to predict correctly the optimal level of effort privately chosen by the bank for any given total amount K of deposits accepted and to compute a fair premium ϕ accordingly. In this way, the agency costs deriving from the choice of sub-optimal monitoring are shifted back to the bank in the form of higher insurance premia. The maximisation problem of the bank, problem (4), can then be reformulated as

$$\max_{L,e} F + \gamma E[(1 + (1 - \tau)r_X)X + (1 + (1 - \tau)r_Y)Y]$$
$$- (1 - \tau)C(e_X, e_Y) + \gamma\tau r_f L(X + Y) - (X + Y) \quad (12)$$

$$\text{s.t.} \quad e = (e_X, e_Y) \in e^*(K)$$
$$L \geq 0 \quad (13)$$

Expression $\gamma\tau r_f L(X + Y)$ represents the present value of tax savings generated by financing the loan acquisition by accepting deposits. Problem (12) is the maximisation of the *ex ante* net present value from initiating the two loans, net of the monitoring costs C, subject to the constraint that the monitoring effort chosen by the bank is *ex post* optimal, given the amounts of deposits accepted.

To study the solution to this problem, we must re-write the incentive constraint $(e_X, e_Y) \in e^*(K)$ in a more tractable form. Following the traditional principal–agent literature, to characterise (13) with the first order conditions to problem (11) we must ensure that the second order conditions are satisfied as well.[8] Note however that, in constrast to the standard case, we now have a two-dimensional action space and a 'double moral hazard' problem. To simplify the discussion, it will be assumed that loans can either be entirely performing or have a zero net return. In this case, the return on the two loans is given by the two-point distribution

$$r_h = \begin{cases} r_h^1 & p_h(e_h) \\ -1/(1 - \tau) & 1 - p_h(e_h) \end{cases} \quad (14)$$

for $h = X, Y$. It is assumed that increasing monitoring effort will increase the probability of the good state, $p' > 0$, but at a decreasing rate, $p'' < 0$, and that if monitoring is set at its lower limit, the loan will default with probability one, that is $p_h(e_h^0) = 0$. Furthermore, noting that for $r_h < r_h^1$ we have that $F(r_h, e_h) = 1 - p_h(e_h)$, the parameter e_h orders the distributions F by First Order Stochastic Dominance. It will also be assumed that the cost function $C(e_X, e_Y)$ is additively separable and linear, that is $C = c_Y e_Y + c_X e_X$. Furthermore, to ensure that problem (11) is a concave programming problem, the following is assumed:

Assumption A.1
The probability that both loans are repaid

$$\Pr\{r_X, r_Y/e_X, e_Y\} = p_X(e_X)p_Y(e_Y)$$

is a concave function of effort (e_X, e_Y).

Let $R_h = (1 + (1 - \tau)r_h')X$ be the total after-tax return on loan h, $h = X, Y$, with $R_X < R_Y$, and $B = (1 + (1 - \tau)r_f)L(X + Y)$ be the total after-tax liabilities of the bank at the end of the period. The expected end-of-period profits π_1 depend on the total liabilities of the bank, and it is given by

$$\pi_1 = \begin{cases} p_X R_X + p_Y R_Y - B + (1 - p_Y)(1 - p_X)B & \text{for } B \leq R_X \\ p_Y(R_Y - B + p_X R_X) & \text{for } R_X \leq B \leq R_Y \quad (15) \\ p_X p_Y(R_X + R_Y - B) & \text{for } R_Y \leq B \leq R_X + R_Y \end{cases}$$

From (15) it can immediately be seen that an increase in the total liabilities B decreases the end-of-period expected profits, lowering the expected returns from monitoring. This induces the bank to choose a level of monitoring which falls short of the first-best optimum. Since the insurance agency acts rationally, the premium ϕ will reflect this sub-optimal behaviour, compelling the bank to internalise this inefficiency.

Consider now the problem of choosing the total amount of deposit to accept, that is problem (12). In this problem the bank faces two opposing incentives. On one hand, increasing the fraction L of loans financed through deposits allows one to exploit to a larger extent the tax advantages of debt financing. On the other hand, increasing deposits will also induce sub-optimal monitoring, which will result in increasing insurance costs. The overall second-best optimum is then determined by trading off these two opposing incentives, and at the optimum the bank will have a finite deposit–capital ratio. These properties are summarised in the following:

Proposition 1

At the second-best optimum the bank has an inefficient level of monitoring and a finite deposit–capital ratio.

Proof: See Appendix.

Finally, from the incentive constraint (13), note that the allocation of monitoring efforts across loans depends on the total liabilities K of the bank. In the following section it will be shown that loan sales will allow us to influence the distribution of the monitoring efforts across loans by changing the liability structure of the bank.

4   Optimal financing with loan sales

We can examine the incentives of the bank for the fractional sale of a loan. With a procedure similar to the one discussed in the previous section, the problem of choosing the optimal amount of loan X to be sold can be reformulated as follows. If the bank sells a fraction S of loan X, the level of monitoring effort (e_X, e_Y) privately chosen will solve

$$\max_{e} F + \gamma \pi_1(L, S, e_X, e_Y) - \phi - \psi - (1 - \tau)C(e_X, e_Y) \\ - (X + Y) + SX + L(Y + (1 - S)X) \tag{16}$$

s.t. $e_h \in [e_h^0, e_h^1)$ $h = X, Y$

From this problem, the optimal level of monitoring will in general depend on both the total face value of the liabilities of the bank, given now by $K = L(Y + (1 - S)X) + SX$, and on the fraction S of loan X sold on the market. Let $e^*(K, S) = (e_X^*(K, S), e_Y^*(K, S))$ be the corresponding solution. Problem (10) can then be formulated as

$$\max_{e, L, S} F + \gamma E[(1 + (1 - \tau)r_X)X + (1 + (1 - \tau)r_Y)Y] \\ - (1 - \tau)C(e_X, e_Y) - (X + Y) + \gamma r_f \tau K \tag{17}$$

s.t. $(e_X, e_Y) \in e^*(K, S)$
$L \geq 0, 0 \leq S \leq 1$

The term $\gamma \tau r_f \tau K$ again represents the present value of the tax savings generated by financing the bank with deposits and selling loans. It should be noted that the tax function (6) has been designed in a way that the tax benefits depend only on the value of the total debt K of the bank, and not on its composition between deposits and D_X. Therefore, in this model the bank has no tax-induced preference for financing itself with loan sales over deposits. In contrast to Pennacchi (1988), in this model the optimal amount of loan sales will depend entirely on the effects of the liabilities structure on the monitoring incentives of the bank, allowing us to separate the impact of tax and monitoring incentives.

An intuition of the effect of loan sales on the incentive to monitoring both loans can be obtained by examining how the returns from monitoring are affected by the partial sale of loan X. In particular, consider first the case in which the bank finances the purchase of the two loans with deposits only. With unobservable effort, the optimal monitoring levels are determined in problem (11). From examination of the objective function in that problem it is clear that the incentives to monitor will depend on the set of states in which the bank is solvent. For a given level of after-tax liabilities $(1 + (1 + \tau)r_f)K$, the bank will be solvent only in those states of nature for which

$$A(K) = \{(r_X, r_Y): (1 + (1 - \tau)r_Y)Y \\ + (1 + (1 - \tau)r_X)X \geq (1 + (1 - \tau)r_f)K\} \tag{18}$$

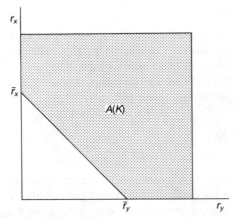

Figure 11.1   In the absence of loan sales, the solvency region A, marked by the shaded area, depends only on the total amount $K = L(X + Y)$ of deposits accepted

These states are represented as the shaded area in Figure 11.1. If the returns from the two loans belong to this region, the bank is solvent and it benefits from the returns to monitoring. In the remaining region, the bank is bankrupt and the returns from monitoring accrue to the insurance agency.

Consider now the case in which the bank sells a fraction of loan X. Since the loan is sold without recourse, the bank can now default on debt D_X but still pay a dividend out of the return from loan Y. This allows the bank to shelter its balance sheet assets from bad returns on the securitised loan. In particular, expected profits $\pi_1(L, S, e_X, e_Y)$ can now be expressed as

$$
\begin{aligned}
\pi_1(L, S, e_X, e_Y) &= E[\max\{(1 + (1 - \tau)r_Y)Y \\
&\quad - (1 + (1 - \tau)r_f)L(Y + SX) + (1 - \tau)\max\{(1 + r_X)X \\
&\quad - (1 + r_f)SX; 0\} + \tau(1 - S)X; 0\}] \\
&= E[\max\{(1 + (1 - \tau)r_Y)Y + (1 + (1 - \tau)r_X)X \\
&\quad + (1 + (1 - \tau)r_f)K + \max\{(1 + r_f)SX \\
&\quad - (1 + r_X)X; 0\}; 0\}]
\end{aligned}
\tag{19}
$$

Comparing (19) with the expression for the expected profits with deposit financing only (2), it can immediately be seen that the sale of a fraction of loan X increases expected profits of the bank by the payoff of the put option generated by the option to default on D_X, given by the last term in (19). This put option has positive payoffs when the proceeds from loan X are not sufficient to repay the debt D_X, that is when $(1 + r_f)SX < (1 + r_X)X$. Allowing for the fractional sale of loan X, the set of states of nature in which the bank is solvent can be described by

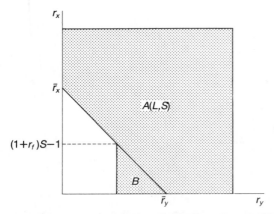

Figure 11.2a In the presence of loan sales the solvency region A, marked by the shaded area, depends on the total liabilities K of the bank and on their composition between deposits and securitised loans

$$A(L, S) = \{(r_X, r_Y): \pi_1(L, S, e_X, e_Y) \geq 0\} \qquad (20)$$

which is represented as the shaded area in Figure 11.2a. By comparing Figure 11.1 and Figure 11.2a it is clear that by selling a fraction of loan X, the region in which the bank has positive profits is enlarged by the area marked B, in which the bank defaults on D_X, but the return on loan Y is still sufficient to repay the deposits.

On the other hand, the sale of a loan X changes the states in which the bank will earn positive return from that asset. In particular, loan X will pay to the bank if $(1 + r_X)X > (1 + r_f)SX$ and if the bank itself is solvent, that is if (r_X, r_Y) belongs to the set

$$A_X(L, S) = \{(r_X, r_Y) \in A(L, S): (1 + r_X) > (1 + r_f)S\} \qquad (21)$$

This region is represented by the shaded area in Figure 2.11b. By comparing Figures 11.2a and 11.2b we can examine the effects of loan sales on the monitoring incentive of the bank. In the absence of loan sales, deposits are backed by loan X and Y simultaneously, and a good return on one loan can be used to compensate for a low return on the other. By selling a fraction of loan X, the bank acquires the option to default selectively on a part of its liabilities, but can still pay a dividend out of the return from the loan remaining on its balance sheet. By selling loan X, however, the states of nature in which this loan originates positive profits to the bank are decreased. *Ceteris paribus*, this increases the incentive to monitor the loan remaining on the balance sheet of the bank and decreases the incentive to monitor the securitised asset. Therefore, by

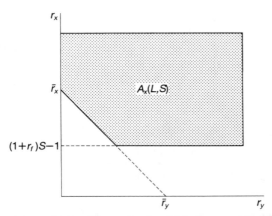

Figure 11.2b   The region in which the securitised loan pays positive returns to the bank

selling a fraction of a loan the bank can adjust the structure of its liabilities, modify the incentives to monitor the two loans and achieve a better distribution of its monitoring efforts across loans.

However, it may not be always in the best interest of the bank to exploit the additional flexibility offered by the sale of a loan, and (partial) loan sales may not always be optimal. In particular, it will be shown that the bank also has an opposing incentive with the effect of discouraging the fractional sale of loans. Limited liability generates a convexity in the return function of banks' equity, inducing a preference for positively correlated returns. This property creates an incentive positively to correlate monitoring efforts as well. By increasing monitoring in one loan, the probability that this loan will be repaid is increased. This reduces the bankruptcy probability of the bank, it decreases the extent of the bank–depositors conflict and creates an incentive to increase monitoring efforts in the remaining loan also.

Therefore, the choice of the optimal amount of loan sale is subject to two opposing incentives. On one hand, the bank has an incentive to sell a fraction of the loan portfolio to achieve a more flexible liability structure and adjust the monitoring efforts across loans. On the other hand, to exploit the spillover effects across loans, it has an opposing incentive to pool loans in the same portfolio. Hence, the optimal amount of loan X to be sold, if at all, is determined by trading off these two opposing incentives and this is discussed in the remainder of this section.

We can now consider the problem of choosing the fraction of loan S to be optimally sold. Since the aim of this chapter is the analysis of the effects of loan sales on the choice of the monitoring efforts of the bank, we will examine only the problem of choosing the fraction S of loan X to be sold, for a given value of the total liabilities $K = L(Y + (1 - S)X) + SX$ of the bank.

The end-of-period expected profits depend on the absolute amount of the after-tax liabilities of the bank. Consider the case in which the earnings of the bank are sufficient to cover the total liabilities even if loan X is performing and loan Y fails – that is, $B = (1 + (1 - \tau)r_f)K < R_X < R_Y$. In this case, expected profits are equal to:

$$\pi_1 = p_X p_Y(R_X + R_Y - B) + (1 - p_X)p_Y(R_Y - \Delta) + (1 - p_Y)p_X(R_Y - B)$$
$$= p_X R_X + p_Y R_Y - B + (1 - p_X)(1 - p_Y)B + (1 - p_X)p_Y(B - \Delta) \qquad (22)$$

where

$$\Delta = (1 + (1 - \tau)r_f)L(Y + (1 - S)X) - \tau(1 - S)X$$
$$= (1 + (1 - \tau)r_f)B - (1 - \tau)(1 + r_f)SX - \tau X \qquad (23)$$

is equal to the after-tax liability of the bank if loan X fails, loan Y performs, and the bank defaults on D_X. Comparing (15) and (22) note that the expected profits with the sale of a fraction S of loan X are equal to the expected profits without the sale of the loan plus the value of the option to default of D_X, given by the last term in (22).

The impact of selling a fraction S of loan X on the monitoring incentive of the bank can be emphasised by considering the effects on the net marginal returns from monitoring the two loans. Differentiating the expected profits (22) with respect to the monitoring efforts, we obtain

$$\frac{\partial \pi_1}{\partial e_X} = p_X'[R_X - B + p_Y\Delta]$$

$$\frac{\partial \pi_1}{\partial e_Y} = p_Y'[R_Y - (1 - p_X)\Delta] \qquad (24)$$

An increase of the fraction S of the loan X sold has two opposing effects on the marginal returns from monitoring. Consider first the impact on the incentives to monitor loan Y. An increase of the fraction of loan X that is securitised has first a direct effect acting through the redistribution of the liabilities of the bank. By increasing S, the bank reduces the amount of deposits accepted (which decreases Δ) and raises the value of the debt secured by loan X only. From Figure 11.2, this process enlarges the set of states in which loan Y generates a positive payoff to the bank and this boosts the incentives to monitor Y, holding p_X constant. At the same time, by a similar argument, an increase of the fraction S reduces the set of states in which loan X has a positive payoff, with the effect of reducing the incentive to monitor loan X, holding p_X constant. Since the return from monitoring loan Y depends also on the probability that loan X performs, the total impact of an increase in S on the incentive to monitor loan Y can then be decomposed into a positive direct effect through the decrease in Δ, and a negative indirect effect induced by a simultaneous decrease in p_X. By a similar argument, it can immediately be seen that the reverse applies to the incentive to monitor loan X. The interaction between the incentives to monitor the two loans derives from the convexity of the payoff structure introduced by limited liability, which induces banks to prefer more correlated returns. In particular, if loan X is performing, the total liabilities of the bank K are risk-free and the bank will have the same incentive to monitoring loan Y as it would have in the first-best case. Hence, limited liability on the deposit contract generates a preference for the bank to increase (or decrease) the monitoring levels of the two loans simultaneously. The total impact of selling a part of loan X on the monitoring incentive of the bank will then depend on the interaction between these two factors, leading to the following propositions. Define $A_X = - p''_X/p'_X$ the coefficient of absolute risk aversion for the function p_X. We have:

Proposition 2

For the given total liabilities K, if $A_X > p'_X/(1 - p_X)$ an increase of the fraction S of loan X sold will increase the optimal monitoring of the loan Y remaining on the balance sheet of the bank, that is $\partial e_Y^*(K, S)/\partial S > 0$.

Proof: See Appendix.

This proposition implies that the sale of a part of loan X may in principle lead to a decrease of the incentive to monitor the loans remaining on the balance sheet of the bank. To ensure that securitisation of loan X does not lead to a decrease in the optimal monitoring of loan Y it is necessary that the probability that loan X performs $p_X(e_X)$ is not too sensitive to its own monitoring level. However, if these conditions are not met and $\partial e_Y^*(K, S)/\partial S < 0$, it is easy to show that the sale of any fraction of loan X will always induce an overall decrease in the level of monitoring in both loans, and it will never be optimal. Hence, in the remaining part of this chapter it will be assumed that the condition in Proposition 2 is met and that is there is a potential gain from securitisation. As an implication of this discussion we obtain the following

Proposition 3

If the probability distribution of the returns from loan X is independent from monitoring, then this loan should be completely securitised.

Note that Proposition 3 implies that banks bear a 'cost' for holding assets that do not require any monitoring. Theories of the demand for liquid assets by banks must then recognise the spillover effect of their liquid position on the loan portfolio.

The effects of an increase of the fraction S on the optimal monitoring of loan X are more complex. In particular, due to the cross-effects just discussed, it may be the case that the positive indirect effect, acting through the increase of the probability that loan Y performs, more than offsets the negative direct effect, at least for low levels of S. Then it may happen that an increase in S may at first improve the monitoring efforts on loan X as well. We have then

Proposition 4

If $A_Y = -p''_Y/p'_Y$ is increasing in e_Y, there is a critical proportion S^c such that

$$\partial e^*_X(K,S)/\partial S \gtrless 0 \quad \text{for} \quad S \lessgtr S^c.$$

Proof: See Appendix.

From Proposition 4 it is clear that if $S^c > 0$, it will always be optimal to sell at least a part of loan X. On the other hand, if $S^c = 0$, a partial sale of loan X will have a positive impact on the incentive to monitor loan Y but a negative impact on the incentive to monitor X. In this case, the overall profitability of a partial securitisation of X will depend on the valuation of the relative gains from an improved monitoring of Y against a decreased monitoring of X. The optimal amount of securitisation is obtained solving the second-best problem

$$\max_{S,e} F + \gamma(p_X R_X + p_Y R_Y) - (1 - \tau)(c_X e_X + c_Y e_Y) + \tau r_f \gamma K \quad (25)$$

$$\text{s.t.} \quad e = (e_X, e_Y) \in (e^*_X(K,S), e^*_Y(K,S))$$

Unfortunately, even in this simplified framework, simple conditions guaranteeing that some securitisation will occur do not seem to arise. However, from Proposition 2 it is possible to state that, if some securitisation occurs, it will increase the monitoring effort exerted in the loan remaining in the balance sheet of the bank, decreasing its riskiness and improving the 'quality' of the asset. This is formally stated in the following

Proposition 5

If a proportion S^* of loan X is optimally sold, then

$$e_Y^*(K, S^*) > e_Y^*(K, 0)$$

and securitisation of X improves the monitoring of the asset remaining in the balance sheet of the bank.

Proof: See Appendix.

From Proposition 5 it can be concluded that, if some securitisation occurs, this will increase the amount of effort exerted on the loan remaining on the balance sheet of the bank. By redistributing its debt between securitised loan and balance sheet assets, the bank is able to achieve a better structure of its liabilities. This allows an overall improvement of the distribution of the monitoring efforts between balance sheet and securitised assets, reducing the agency costs of debt financing for any given level of the total bank liabilities K. As a consequence, by reducing the agency cost of debt, securitisation may induce the bank to achieve a more levered position.

5   Summary and concluding remarks

In this chapter we have developed a model examining the incentives of banks to sell a part of the loans appearing in their portfolios. If the returns from loans depend on the level of monitoring effort exerted by a bank, bankruptcy risk introduces a conflict between the bank and its depositors (or an insuring agency) on the optimal amount of monitoring. If the level of effort is privately chosen by the bank and it cannot be contracted upon, this conflict may lead to the choice of sub-optimal monitoring levels. In a second-best optimum, banks determine the optimal amount of deposits accepted by trading off these agency cost against the tax advantages of financing loan acquisitions with deposits.

This chapter builds on the observation that unobservability of monitoring effort and the limited liability property of the equity contract require banks to choose the level of effort simultaneously for all loans, generating spillover effects across loans. With traditional financing of loans with deposits, the choice of monitoring efforts depends on the total liabilities of the bank – that is, its deposits. On the other hand, by securitising (without recourse) some loans, a bank is allowed to issue liabilities pledged on a sub-set of their assets. This permits the bank to default selectively on a part of its liabilities, but still maintain ownership of the assets remaining on its balance sheet. Asset securitisation allows the bank to change the structure of its liabilities, allowing greater flexibility and inducing a better distribution of the monitoring efforts between balance sheet and securitised assets. It is then shown that loan securitisation may not always be optimal, since it may induce a decrease in the level of monitoring of both balance sheet and securitised assets. However, it is also shown that if some securitisation is optimal from the point of view of the bank, it will lead to improved monitoring of the loans remaining in its balance sheet. For a given total amount of liabilities, securitisation may then improve the 'quality' of the bank's balance sheet. This result is in contrast to the effects discussed in Greenbaum and Thakor (1987) and Lucas and McDonald (1987), where it is shown that, under different circumstances, banks securitise their best loans, worsening the average 'quality' of their balance sheets. The consideration of the positive effects of loan sales on the choice of monitoring efforts by banks may then reduce the concern over the potential destabilising effects of securitisation on the banking system.

Appendix

Proof of Proposition 1

From the *ex post* problem (11) and the profit function (15), the optimal level of monitoring effort in the two loans is determined by solving

$$\max_{e_X, e_Y} \gamma[p_X(R_X - B) + p_Y(R_Y - B) + p_X p_Y B] - (1 - \tau)(c_X e_X + c_Y c_Y) \quad \text{(A.1)}$$

for $B \le R_X$. From assumption A.1, it is immediately seen that (A.1) is a concave programming problem, and that the first order conditions

$$\gamma p'_X(R_X - B) + \gamma p'_X p_Y B = (1 - \tau)c_X$$
$$\text{(A.2)}$$
$$\gamma p'_Y(R_Y - B) + \gamma p'_Y p_X B = (1 - \tau)c_Y$$

are sufficient for a global maximum. Next, note that first-best effort is characterised by the conditions $\gamma p'_h R_h = (1 - \tau)c_h, h = X, Y$. The first order conditions above imply that at a second-best optimum $\gamma p'_X R_X > \gamma p'_X(R_X - B) + \gamma p'_X p_Y B = (1 - \tau)c_X$, that is $e^*_X(B) < e^*_X(0)$, and the second-best level of effort is strictly less than the first-best level. The same argument applies to loan Y, and to different levels of B. The second part of the proposition follows immediately from the fact that for $B \ge R_Y + R_X$ we have that $\pi_1 \equiv 0$, $e^*_X = e^0_X$ and $e^*_Y = e^0_Y$, $p_X = p_Y = 0$ and, from problem (4), the bank will never find it optimal to accept this many deposits. $\square$

Proof of Proposition 2

Consider again the case $B \leq R_X$. The level of monitoring effort (e_X, e_Y) is determined by solving

$$\max_e \; \gamma p_X (R_X - B) + \gamma p_Y (R_Y - \varDelta) + \gamma p_X p_Y \varDelta - (1 - \tau)(c_X e_X + c_Y e_Y) \quad \text{(A.3)}$$

Assumption A.1 implies that the above problem is a concave programming problem: note that the minors H_1 and H_2 of the hessian matrix are

$$H_1 = \gamma p_X''(R_X - K + p_Y \varDelta) < 0$$

$$\begin{aligned} H_2 &= \gamma^2 p_X'' p_Y''(R_X - B + p_Y \varDelta)(R_Y - (1 - p_X)\varDelta) - (\gamma p_X' p_Y')^2 \varDelta^2 \\ &> \gamma^2 \varDelta^2 (p_X'' p_Y'' p_X p_Y - (p_X' p_Y')^2) > 0 \end{aligned} \quad \text{(A.4)}$$

In this case, the first order conditions of problem (A.3)

$$\gamma p_X'(R_X - B + p_Y \varDelta) - (1 - \tau)c_X = 0$$
$$\gamma p_Y'(R_Y - (1 - p_X)\varDelta) - (1 - \tau)c_Y = 0 \quad \text{(A.5)}$$

are again sufficient for a maximum. By implicit differentiation, we obtain that $\partial e_Y^* / \partial S = - D_{YS}/H_2$, where D_{YS} is the determinant

$$D_{YS} = \gamma^2 \begin{vmatrix} -(1 - p_X)p_Y' \varDelta_S & p_X' p_Y' \varDelta \\ p_X' p_Y \varDelta_S & p_X''(R_X - B + p_Y \varDelta) \end{vmatrix}$$

$$\begin{aligned} &< \gamma^2 \varDelta_S \varDelta p_Y' p_Y (1 - (1 - p_X)p_X'' - (p_X')^2) \\ &= \gamma^2 \varDelta_S \varDelta p_Y' p_Y (1 - p_X)p_X'(A_X - p_X'/(1 - p_X)) \end{aligned} \quad \text{(A.6)}$$

Since $\varDelta_S = -(1 - \tau)(1 + r_f)SX < 0$, we have that $\partial e_Y^* / \partial S > 0$ for $A_X > p_X'/(1 - p_X)$. A similar, more simplified argument applies to the case $B \geq R_X$. $\square$

Proof of Proposition 4

For $B \leq R_X$ again, we know from the proof of Proposition 2 that the first order conditions

$$\gamma p_X'(R_X - B + p_Y \varDelta) - (1 - \tau)c_X = 0$$
$$\gamma p_Y'(R_Y - (1 - p_X)\varDelta) - (1 - \tau)c_Y = 0 \quad \text{(A.5)}$$

are sufficient for a maximum. From implicit differentiation, we obtain now that $\partial e_X^* / \partial S = - \varDelta_{XS}/H_2$, where $H_2 > 0$, and

$$\Delta_{XS} = \gamma^2 \begin{vmatrix} p'_X p_Y \Delta_S & p'_X p'_Y \Delta \\ -(1-p_X)p'_Y \Delta_S & p''_Y(R_Y - (1-p_X)\Delta) \end{vmatrix}$$

$$= \gamma \begin{vmatrix} p'_X p_Y \Delta_S & p'_X p'_Y \Delta \\ -(\gamma p'_Y R_Y - (1-\tau)c_Y)\Delta_S/\Delta & \gamma p''_Y(1-\tau)c_Y/p'_Y \end{vmatrix}$$

$$= \gamma p'_X \Delta_S(-p_Y(1-\tau)c_Y A_Y \gamma + p'_Y(\gamma p'_Y R_Y - (1-\tau)c_Y))\text{(A.7)}$$

Hence, since $\Delta_S < 0$,

$$\partial e^*_X(S)/\partial S > 0 \text{ iff } \lambda(S) = p'_Y(\gamma p'_Y R_Y - (1-\tau)c_Y)$$
$$> \gamma p_Y(1-\tau)c_Y A_Y = \mu(S).$$

The proposition follows immediately from the fact that, if $\partial e^*_X(S)/\partial S > 0$ and A_Y is increasing, then $\lambda(S)$ is decreasing in S and $\mu(S)$ is increasing in S. ☐

Proof of Proposition 5

From problem (25) we obtain the first-order condition

$$(\gamma p'_X R_X - (1-\tau)c_X)\partial e^*_X/\partial S + (\gamma p'_Y R_Y - (1-\tau)c_Y)\partial e^*_Y/\partial S = 0 \quad \text{(A.8)}$$

Since $\partial e^*_Y/\partial S < 0 \Rightarrow \partial e^*_X/\partial S < 0$, an interior solution with $S^* > 0$ can occur only if $\partial e^*_Y/\partial S > 0$, and $e^*_Y(K, S^*) > e^*_Y(K, 0)$. ☐

Notes

The author wishes to thank Riccardo Rovelli and the discussant Mervyn King for very helpful comments, and Rony Hamaui for helpful discussions and continuous advice during all the stages of his work.
1 In an even broader definition, securitisation also includes the process of substitution of bank credit with negotiable securities directly sold by firms (see, for example, Cummings, 1987). Although this process is an important aspect of the changing pattern of financing corporate investment, it will not be addressed in this chapter. The problem of choosing between bank credit and direct lending is examined in Berlin and Loeys (1988).
2 The ratio of loans sold to total assets grew from 1.2 per cent in the second quarter of 1983 to 4 per cent in the first quarter of 1987. For the largest 20 US banks, this ratio rose from 1.5 per cent to 9 per cent in the same period, characterising loan sales as a phenomenon stemming from 'money center' banks; see Becketti and Morris (1987).
3 This aspect of the securitisation process raises substantial regulatory issues since the possibility of escaping the intermediation tax provides one of the incentives to the sale of loans.
4 For an extensive discussion, see Pavel (1986).
5 An important problem is to explain why the banking system can provide competitive intermediation, even in the presence of the burden of the intermediation tax. A possible explanation, consistent with the model discussed in this chapter, is in Fama (1985).

6 We can always interpret the initial cash holding F as the proceeds from a previous equity issue.
7 Note that the tax function (1) is symmetric, allowing a transfer from the government to the bank in the bad states of nature.
8 In the agency theoretic framework, this problem is known as the first order approach problem, and it is extensively discussed in Grossman and Hart (1983), Rogerson (1985), and Jewitt (1988).

References

Becketti, S. and C. Morris (1987) 'Loan Sales: Another Step in the Evolution of the Short-Term Credit Market', *Economic Review*, Federal Reserve Bank of Kansas City (November): 22–31.
Benveniste, L. and A. Berger (1987) 'Securitization with Recourse', *Journal of Banking and Finance*, **11**: 403–24.
Berlin, M. and J. Loeys (1988) 'Bond Covenants and Delegated Monitoring', *Journal of Finance*, **43**: 397–412.
Cumming, C. (1987) 'The Economics of Securitization', *Federal Reserve Bank of New York Quarterly Review* (Autumn): 11–23.
Fama, E. (1985) 'What's Different about Banks?', *Journal of Monetary Economics*, **15(1)**: 29–39.
Greenbaum, S. and A. Thakor (1987) 'Bank Funding Modes: Securitization versus Deposits', *Journal of Banking and Finance*, **11**: 379–401.
Grossman, S. and O. Hart (1983) 'An Analysis of the Principal–Agent Problem', *Econometrica*, **51**: 7–45.
James, C. (1988) 'The Use of Loan Sales and Standby Letters of Credit by Commercial Banks' (mimeo).
Jewitt, I. (1988) 'Justifying the First-Order Approach to Principal–Agent Problems', *Econometrica*, **56**: 1177–90.
Kareken, J. (1987) 'The Emergence and Regulation of Contingent Commitment Banking', *Journal of Banking and Finance*, **11**: 359–77.
Lucas, D. and R. McDonald (1987) 'Bank Portfolio Choice with Private Information about Loan Quality: Theory and Implications for Regulation', *Journal of Banking and Finance*, **11**: 473–98.
Merton, R. (1977) 'An Analytical Derivation of the Cost of Deposit Insurance and Loan Guarantees: An Application of Modern Option Pricing Theory', *Journal of Banking and Finance*, **1**: 3–11.
Pavel, C. (1986) 'Securitization', *Economic Perspectives*, Federal Reserve Bank of Chicago (July–August): 16–31.
Pennacchi, G. (1988) 'Loan Sales and the Cost of Bank Capital', *Journal of Finance*, **43**: 375–96.
Rogerson, W. (1985) 'The First-Order Approach to Principal–Agent Problems', *Econometrica*, **53**: 1357–68.
Stultz, R. and H. Johnson (1985) 'An Analysis of Secured Debt', *Journal of Financial Economics*, **14**: 501–22.

Discussion

MERVYN KING

Innovation was the key word in financial markets during the 1980s. Liberalisation of financial markets – often accompanied by a restructuring of the regulatory system – led to a wave of financial innovation. This covered both new instruments and new markets for both financial intermediaries and ultimate borrowers and savers.

Fulghieri's Chapter 11 is a theoretical study of the motives for securitisation of part of the assets of a financial intermediary. It is clear that one of the major developments in the 1980s has been the growth of off-balance sheet activities of which 'securitisation' has been perhaps the main example. This has affected both firms themselves and the regulators of financial institutions. Securitisation can mean the substitution of finance from bank intermediaries by the issue of marketable securities directly to investors, as well as the packaging and selling of parts of the total loan book to outside investors. This chapter is concerned with the latter aspect of securitisation. Fulghieri sets up a sophisticated optimisation model to examine the impact of changes in the ratio of securitised loans to the size of the total loan book on the optimal degree of monitoring by banks of agents to whom they have lent funds. The basic idea is that by securitising one part of the loan book they have more incentive to monitor carefully the remaining part of the loan book that has not been sold. It is assumed that the return to the bank on the loans made depends on the level of monitoring. Moreover, the level of monitoring by the bank intermediary is not only chosen by the bank but is unobservable to the rest of the market. Some of the analysis assumes that deposits are insured by a regulator although the chapter does not follow this up by analysing the requirements on capital adequacy that such a regulator is almost certain to wish to impose.

Fulghieri analyses a one-period model. At the beginning of the period, the bank decides on its debt–equity ratio and the level of monitoring that it will make. A crucial feature of the chapter is that there is bankruptcy risk for the bank which generates a conflict between the stockholders and the depositors about the optimal level of monitoring. Because stockholders bear the full costs of monitoring but do not capture all of the benefits if the bank defaults in some states of the world, there is a conflict between the interests of the two groups. The bank may choose a suboptimal level of monitoring. Fulghieri argues that the same result would occur if deposits were insured by a regulator because the conflict would simply be one between stockholders and the regulatory agency. But the regulator has an additional policy tool that is normally not part of the contract between a bank and its depositors. This is the level and composition of capital that the bank should hold. Capital requirements are normally imposed precisely to prevent the existence of such conflict. If we leave this possibility to one side, then it is clear that selling some of the loans alters the incentive of the bank to monitor. Fulghieri considers the special case of two loans. By selling a certain fraction of one loan, the returns on the other asset are less likely to be infected by bad returns on the first, thus increasing the potential benefit from monitoring the second loan. But of course the opposite applies to the first loan, on which monitoring is likely to decrease. The choice as to whether or not to sell the first loan will then depend on the interaction of these two opposing effects.

The trade-off between the two is analysed by Fulghieri in the special case when the returns on loans have a two-point distribution. This is a reasonable assumption in order to simplify the exposition, but it may give a false impression of the importance of the effect. Fulghieri shows that if the return is sufficiently sensitive to monitoring the securitisation will be optimal. A natural question is, therefore, what limits the extent of the securitisation? Fulghieri argues that in the second-best outcome, banks trade off the benefits of securitisation in terms of increased monitoring against the tax advantage of financing the loan book by deposits. I find this less plausible. In most European countries, the tax advantage of debt over equity is not large because of the introduction of imputation systems of corporation tax. Moreover, the existence of deposit finance long pre-dates the corporate tax system. Surely, the benefits of being able to collect and pool savings from a national system of retail branches has given banking an historical advantage in the provision of loan finance? Technical change both in the retailing of saving schemes and the operation of the payments mechanism may lead to substantial changes in the structure of banking, of which securitisation is only one example. Hence the chapter is good in analysing the advantages of securitisation but weaker in its analysis of the advantages of direct deposit finance. In essence, the question that I would like to pose to the author is: why do banks appear to have a comparative advantage in the provision of certain kinds of finance? Is there something special about banks that enables them to transform highly liquid deposits into illiquid long-term loans, or is this an outdated structure of the balance sheet that will disappear with changes in the payments system and the existence of new financial markets?

Note

Mervyn King is Executive Director, Bank of England. Any statements made are a matter of personal opinion and do not involve the Bank of England.

3.2 The liability side

12   A comparative analysis of the liabilities structure in seven banking systems

MAURO MACCARINELLI, GIUSEPPE
MAROTTA and MASSIMO PROSDOCIMI

1   Introduction[1]

Deregulation and financial innovation in the 1980s have deeply affected the liability side of banks' balance sheets, through the twofold challenge of the spread of institutions and instruments directly competing for the funds traditionally channelled into deposits, often non- or low and regulated interest-bearing, and of the savers' enhanced financial sophistication. The banks have experienced changes on the asset side as well, because of the shift from top customers, able directly to access financial markets, to medium–smaller business debtors and to households; furthermore, lending abroad has widened.

The overall increase in the exposure to asset risk, the reduced chances to rely on the cheap stable inflows from savers and the severe stance of monetary policy, curtailing the room for easy adjustments in case of liquidity needs, have urged changes in the asset and liability management. Concurrent regulatory developments (such as the BIS minimum asset-to-capital ratios) have called for a strengthened equity position.

The end results on the funding side have been an enlarged range of new (marketable) instruments, a move from personal to market relationships with customers, a reduction of the room allowed to cross-subsidisation practices and a structural increase in the average cost of funding.

Our aim in this chapter is to provide a broad overview of the changing patterns in banks' liabilities structure of the four larger continental European countries (France, Germany, Italy and Spain) and of Japan, the

United Kingdom and the United States. The distinctive feature of our examination is that, acknowledging the blurring of the traditional distinctions between banks and other institutions, both in lending and in funding activities, and in accordance with the insight provided by the recent literature on financial intermediation, we take a broad view of the banking industry, rather than considering only the commercial banks, due to their privileged status of suppliers of (narrow) money.[2]

Indeed, the literature on financial intermediation characterises banks as those institutions (a) with a large proportion of assets – i.e. loans – highly illiquid, because incorporating private information, (b) whose liabilities are of a standard debt-contract type, although a sizeable amount of equity is also needed on coinsurance grounds and (c) that distribute and produce liquidity through the issue of demand deposits or else of contingent liabilities, such as binding (for the bank) lines of credit (see Baglioni and Marotta, 1992).

Section 2 provides a cross-country overview of the balance sheet structures of the extended domestic banking systems, both on consolidated and on aggregate (gross) data, during the 1980s. Section 3 concentrates on the extent and on the implications of the increasing share of deposits bearing market interest rates. Section 4 examines the role of the main non-price funding tool, namely the branches network. Section 5 contains concluding remarks. An Appendix details the statistical methodology of the reconstruction of the extended banking systems and provides individual tables for the seven countries.[3]

2   Banking systems' balance sheets: a cross-country overview

In this section we present a cross-country overview of domestic banking systems' balance sheets during the 1980s. In order to control for institutional aspects, such as the presence of within intermediation due to specialised financial circuits, the data are presented both on a consolidated and on an aggregate (gross) basis. This allows us to appreciate the contribution to the 'depth' of the banking intermediation due to the internal transfer of funds via the issue and the subscription of bonds and the funding through the interbank market.

The chosen time span is characterised by some common aspects:

 – The nominal interest rate cycle, with a reduction in the first half of the 1980s and subsequently a stabilisation, has stimulated both the issue (because of the cost) and the subscription (because of the prospective capital gains) of securities; together with the strengthened profitability, the positive effects of declining rates on the liquidity position have slowed down the demand for loans by (large) non-financial firms, thus stimulating the banks to enlarge their range of customers among small firms and consumers.

- The increasing interpenetration of the national banking systems has widened the scope for the money markets, especially the domestic interbank market, in order to provide resources to the usually thin retail base of the foreign banks.
- Many countries experienced key changes in the banks' environment around the mid-decade: Italy (end of the permanent credit ceilings in 1983), Spain (1978–83 banking crisis), France (1984 banking reform), the United States (thrifts' wave of failures).

As a first broad overview let us consider the relative size of the extended banking systems, through a rough indicator such as the total assets to GDP ratio (Table 12.1). Despite the spread of off-balance sheet items, which we are unable to consider in our data, the trends that emerge are quite impressive, as they show rather different paths across countries.

Even in a period of often claimed disintermediation of the banking systems, the indicator has increased everywhere, with a range of values in 1988 more than double relative to 1980, though with a slower growth in the second half of the period; the only striking exception to the trend is Italy, where it has actually declined. At end-1988, the range of values of the indicator had widened, singling out pairs of countries – the United Kingdom and Japan, France and Germany, Italy and Spain – and the United States.[4]

The main implication of this evidence is that no disintermediation is detectable, except for those countries, Italy first of all and Spain to a lesser extent, where the competitive edge of the high interest-bearing public debt

Table 12.1. *Size of the extended banking systems, total balance sheet/GDP*

	1980	1985	1988
France	—	1.54	1.86
Germany	1.59	1.82	1.89
Italy	1.41	1.35	1.25
Japan	1.62	1.93	2.29
Spain	1.14	1.44	1.39
UK	1.55	2.49	2.67
USA	0.81	0.86	0.87[a]

[a] 1987 data.
Source: see Appendix.

instruments has crowded out bank liabilities from savers' (be they individuals or institutional investors) portfolios.[5] In all other countries, except for the United States, the deepening of banking intermediation can instead, as a first approximation, be related to the recycling into (medium–long-term) bank liabilities of funds catered for large institutional investors (such as pension funds, insurance companies and mutual funds).

It is interesting to remark how the likely effects of the liberalisation of capital markets show up dramatically in the United Kingdom and France (the latter between 1985 and 1988 drew level with Germany).

In the following sections we examine the composition of the balance sheets and especially of their liability side.

2.1   Consolidated banking systems

A distinction between the collection of outside resources from non-banks and the intrasectoral provision of funds is useful, because the different degrees of within intermediation affect the gross size of the interbank market and of the banks' bonds issues, both sensitive elements in an international comparison of banks' liabilities.

Accordingly, we provide an overview of the consolidated extended banking systems and reclassify the balance sheets adapting at the aggregate level the basic identity suggested by Tobin (1982) for a commercial bank:

> **Stable sources of funds** (non-banks' deposits and bonds
> + shareolders' equity, including other subordinated debt instruments)
> = **Stable uses of funds** (loans and investments
> + required reserves) + **defensive position** (cash + deposits at the
> Central bank net of borrowed reserves + net interbank loans +
> liquid securities)

We acknowledge, but do not implement in our work, due to data constraints, that only retail (or non-marketable) deposits should be included in the category of a stable source of funds, considering the wholesale market negotiable term instruments (such as CDs) as a component of the defensive position, given their substitutability with the securities. Also, only short-term net interbank loans should be considered as a liquidity adjustment instrument; permanent customer relationships between retail collectors of funds and their central institutes or between large and small banks or else between domestic headquarters and foreign branches should rather be taken as another stable use of funds.

The cross-country comparison of the latest (1988) available consolidated balance sheets (1987 for the United States), besides some well-known stylised facts, such as the special case of the United Kingdom

Table 12.2. *Consolidated credit systems, selected items, per cent end-year figures*

		Assets					Liabilities		
		A	B[a]	C	D	E	F	G	H[a]
France	1985	89.7	15.1[a]	− 5.2	—	48.6	70.3	24.1[a]	5.7
	1988	84.5	17.4[a]	− 3.5	—	47.8	67.7	25.2[a]	7.1
Germany	1980	95.8	5.2	− 2.2	1.0	62.7	78.3	16.4	5.3
	1985	92.8	6.8	− 1.3	4.0	62.8	76.0	18.4	5.6
	1988	90.5	8.0	− 0.7	6.6	60.8	79.4	14.7	5.9
Italy	1980	67.9	23.4	2.3	− 5.2	54.5	88.3	3.8	6.5
	1985	67.7	28.2	1.2	− 7.1	53.5	82.5	5.1	10.4
	1988	72.9	23.0	0.8	− 9.2	57.7	79.2	7.4	11.9
Japan	1980	68.7	18.5	8.5	—	81.9	89.9	6.4	3.7
	1985	71.3	19.1	10.0	—	80.3	90.7	6.8	2.5
	1988	70.4	20.2	10.3	—	80.4	89.8	7.1	3.1
Spain	1980	72.5	19.1	− 1.9	− 3.6	76.2	87.6	1.7	10.7
	1985	57.7	31.1	− 1.9	− 1.1	68.6	83.4	4.6	12.1
	1988	61.9	33.6	− 2.6	− 4.3	70.4	83.3	3.3	13.3
UK	1980	90.5	13.1	11.5	− 21.5	43.7	89.1	—	10.8
	1985	96.1	18.0	6.7	− 24.7	41.2	87.3	—	12.8
	1988	92.7	13.6	4.5	− 14.1	48.0	87.3	—	12.7
USA	1980	76.3	17.9	− 1.8	1.1	82.2	91.7	0.4	7.9
	1985	77.1	18.7	− 2.6	2.0	81.3	92.3	0.1	7.6
	1987	78.8	23.4	− 2.7	1.7	80.3	92.5	0.1	7.4

A: Loans/Non-banks' claims.
B: Non-banks' securities + Participations/Non-banks' claims.
C: Net interbank assets/Non-banks' claims.
D: Net external assets/Non-banks' claims.
E: Non-banks' claims/Total assets.
F: Non-banks' deposits/Non-banks' claims.
G: Net banks' securities/Non-banks' claims.
H: Equity/Non-banks' claims.
[a] Gross of intrasectoral items.

because of London's role in the Euromarket, shows other features, which indicate a clustering of the continental European banking systems relative to the other three on many features (Table 12.2).[6]

 – The degree of intrasectoral intermediation (proxied by the ratio to total assets of non-banks' deposits and banks' equity and net bonds issued) goes from around 1/2 for France and the United Kingdom to 3/5 for Italy and Germany, 7/10 for Spain and 4/5 for Japan and the United States.
 – The net funding through the issue of bonds is sizeable in France (1/3 of

deposits on average, gross), in Germany (1/5), in Italy[7] and in Japan (1/10). By contrast, this funding mode is negligible in the United States and in the United Kingdom.
– On the asset side, Germany, France and the United Kingdom are more than fully loaned-up, with a ratio of loans to non-banks' deposits greater than 1; holdings of securities (net of intrasectoral items) and participations are at the highest in countries with sizeable public debt (Italy, Spain and the United States) and amount from 1/3 to 1/2 of the loans, whereas Germany is at the opposite end, with less than 1/10.

Across time, the main aspects that show up are that:

– The equity component has increased, though with different intensity, in all European countries, slightly declining or staying approximately constant in the United States and in Japan. The contribution of non-banks' deposits to the stable funding has diminished (except for Germany).
– The net external lending (for Germany) or borrowing (for Italy and Spain) has consistently increased, as a result of international financial integration.
– The ratio of loans to stable funding has considerably increased only in Italy; an opposite trend can be detected in Spain[8] and, to a lesser extent, in Germany, although after 1985 with signs of an inversion or, at least, of a slowing down.

Overall, besides the shrinking relative size, the Italian banking system has experienced during the decade the largest changes in the balance sheet structure, both on the asset (more loans, especially after the end of the credit ceiling regime in 1983, decumulating securities and borrowing from abroad) and on the liability side (with a shift from deposits to bonds and, especially, equity resources).

2.2   Aggregate banking systems

Have the extended banking systems reacted in a similar way to the changing environment, first of all to the spread of competitors for the traditional consumer deposits and to the likely shift in the composition of depositors towards the institutional investors? The cross-country evidence on the liabilities maturity structure using some key aggregate (gross) balance sheets ratios provides qualified support to the hypothesis of analogous patterns (Table 12.3).

The time and savings component of the non-banks' deposits has increased, except for Italy and Germany. In these two countries, however, the time component, that includes CDs, has expanded, so that overall (with the exception of Spain) the stabilisation of the funding has implied the decline, or at least a slower growth, of the more traditional savings deposits. The lengthening of the maturity of the deposits has matched the similar pattern for loans in the continental European countries, and especially in Japan.

The size of domestic interbank funding, excluding the component of bank bonds, distinguishes the European countries (from 39 per cent of total balance sheets on average for France to 17 per cent for Germany, 16 per cent for the United Kingdom, 12 per cent for Spain, and 9 per cent for Italy) from the United States (8 per cent, including Repos) and Japan (5 per cent). It is difficult to disentangle the causes, namely whether the size of the market results from the presence of foreign banks with a weak retail funding base and/or from the existence of specialised financial circuits.

Indeed, among the factors that account for the unusual size of the market in *France*, the key ones are the presence of specialised financial circuits (notably, Treasury – *Caisse des dépôts et consignations*) and of two-tier structures for local banks, as well as the structural imbalance between the excess funding of some institutions (large commercial banks, *Caisse des dépôts*, savings and cooperative banks) and the excess lending of others (*établissements spécialisés*, merchant banks, foreign banks)[9] (Table 12A.3).

In *Germany*, the split between major categories of banks into those that typically act as lenders and those that typically act as borrowers intensified during the 1980s.[10] Considering the intrasectoral pattern, three categories of banks (Commercial, Giro institutions and Regional institutions of credit cooperatives) alone accounted in 1988 for two-thirds of the domestic funding (against a 44 per cent of their share over total assets); the distribution is even more skewed in the short-term side of the market. Within the system of the savings banks, the two-tier structure has only partially been recently weakened by the major savings banks, through an increased demand for longer-term interbank funds outside the giro system.

In *Spain*, the interbank market has increased in relative terms during the 1980s, mostly because of the widening structural imbalance between net borrowers and lenders. The former include the large commercial and most foreign banks, limited in their possibilities of collecting retail deposits;[11] the latter include first of all the savings banks, but also the two other categories of commercial banks, small and industrial.

Once more, the evidence shows a peculiar development of the *Italian* system, the only one among the continental European systems with a slight decline in the share of time and saving deposits and with shrinking interbank funding.[12]

The latter phenomenon has partly been caused by a structural change in the two-tier structure of the savings banks. The main factor is, however, the removal of the credit ceiling in 1983, with the ensuing competition process in lending, which has led to a relative decline in the market share of the large commercial banks, structurally net borrowers in the interbank market, despite their further reliance on this source of funds (Ferri and Marullo, 1989; Di Giovanni *et al.*, 1991).

Table 12.3. Selected balance sheet ratios, per cent end-year figures

	M/L term loans/Loans			Time and savings deposits/Deposits			Time deposits/Deposits			Banks' deposits/Total balance sheet			Bonds issued/Total balance sheet		
	1980	1985	1988	1980	1985	1988	1980	1985	1988	1980	1985	1988	1980	1985	1988
France	—	72.8	79.3	—	67.9	70.5	—	23.0	28.1	—	38.2	39.3	—	11.7	12.0
Germany	81.1	82.0	84.1	84.9	85.5	85.2	31.2	33.8	35.3	18.5	16.7	17.3	17.6	19.9	17.7
Italy	49.0	50.0	51.0	49.3	49.9	48.5	2.3	7.2	15.6	10.6	9.4	7.8	11.2	8.6	9.0
Japan	33.2	34.5	41.8	67.2	73.2	75.5	—	—	—	3.4	5.6	5.6	6.7	6.9	7.0
Spain	—	—	—	73.7	78.5	77.7	—	46.0	43.0	9.8	13.7	12.1	2.0	3.3	2.4
UK	—	—	—	—	—	—	19.2	25.3	24.3	16.9	16.7	14.2	—	—	—
USA	—	—	—	48.2	56.0	59.2ᵃ	—	—	—	9.3	8.1	7.5ᵃ	0.3	0.1	0.1ᵃ

ᵃ 1987.

In the following section we examine the extent of, and draw some implications from, the evolution in the deposit maturity structure during the 1980s and of the concurrent phenomenon of the deregulation of interest rates.

3   Interest rates' deregulation and securitisation of funding

The deregulation of interest rates and the spread of securitisation of funding, through consumer and large CDs, bank bonds and time deposits, have been widespread processes, though until now not fully completed (Table 12.4).

By deregulation we mean, besides the lifting of formal limitations in setting nominal interest rates, the dismantling of informal arrangements, such as the supply of free banking services, that imply *de facto* regulated (mostly nil) interest rates on demand deposits in Germany and, until very recently, in Spain, and in the United Kingdom.[13] Only in Italy have market rates been always paid on demand deposits, actually an instrument fit for both transactions and saving purposes.

Table 12.4. *Deposit interest rates' deregulation in the 1980s*

France	1985: introduction of CDs December 1989: interest rates on time deposits with a maturity of at least 1 month freely set, remuneration of demand deposits as yet prohibited
Germany	May 1986: introduction of domestically issued CDs
Italy	December 1982: introduction of CDs Free rates over the period
Japan	1979: introduction of CDs March 1985: interest rates on MMCs freely set up to a limit not exceeding CDs rates October 1985: deregulation of interest rates on large time deposits with a minimum denomination of 1 million yen and maturity of 3 months to 2 years; since then, the coverage of the deposits eligible for deregulated interest rates has been widened in terms of minimum denomination and maturity; remuneration of demand deposits as yet prohibited
Spain	1981: deregulation of interest rates for large time deposits 1987: all interest rates liberalised
UK	1983: Building societies issue CDs Free rates over the period
USA	1982: phase-out of the 25 basis points' differential on passbook rates over commercial banks; remuneration of demand and up to 7-days' time deposits as yet prohibited

It is difficult to disentangle cause and effect relationships between the deregulation of interest rates and the shift from low- or non-interest-bearing deposits to market interest-bearing instruments, and it is anyway a task we do not try to pursue in this chapter. What is important to stress, for our purposes, is the common pattern of securitised funding detectable in most countries, except for Italy.

Besides the well-known case of the *United States'* commercial banks (Table 12A.14), the Savings and Loans Institutions have also had a similar trend away from traditional passbook deposits towards time and interest-bearing checkable accounts: in 1987, just 9.4 per cent of savings deposits were of the first type, against 77 per cent of the latter (Gart, 1989).

In *France*, the share of CDs over total deposits of the commercial and the mutual and cooperative banks grew from 1.2 in 1985 to 10.6 per cent in 1988 (Table 12A.2). In *Japan*, whereas in 1985 the funding through instruments with deregulated interest rates accounted for 75 per cent of the new liabilities, in 1988 it had reached around 120 per cent (Osugi, 1990). In *Spain*, the most important effect on the composition of the bank liabilities has been the increase of cheap deposits, especially with the commercial banks. Deposits of the private sector, which accounted for one-half of total liabilities of this category, had dropped to nearly one-third by the end of 1988 (Table 12A.10).[14] In the *United Kingdom* during the 1980s building societies faced competition on their funding, traditionally realised through ordinary share accounts, earning regulated interest rates by issuing, besides CDs, 'high' (i.e. market) interest accounts. As a result, by 1988 the ordinary share accounts had nearly disappeared, despite the fact that the customer base is drawn from the least financially sophisticated section of the population (Salomon Brothers, 1990).

In *Germany*, the securitisation of funding has mainly happened through the bond type instrument. Within the time deposits, the component over 4 years (including bank borrowers' notes and registered bonds) has grown steadily[15] (Table 12A.5). The declining savings component of deposits would have been even smaller but for the high-yielding special savings schemes (mostly bank savings bonds), which at the end of 1988 accounted for one-quarter of all savings deposits. By issuing bank savings and bearer bonds not only specialised institutions, but also commercial banks have been promoting 'securitised' saving. Indeed, out of the bearer bonds amounting to more than one-third of non-banks' deposits, in 1988 the commercial banks' component reached 12 per cent; on a consolidated basis, bonds reached in 1988 about one-fifth of the deposits. The savings bank sector has further widened the range of the liabilities issuing long-term time deposits, including price–risk-free registered bonds; moreover, 'primary institutions' of the savings bank sector have stepped up their own issues of marketable bearer bonds.

The stability of the demand deposits share only in *Italy*, where this component has always earned market interest rates, is suggestive of one important explanation for the phenomenon on the demand side.[16] Indeed, the enhanced savers' sophistication has exclusively affected the more traditional saving deposits, with a shift towards the CDs[17] (see Di Giovanni *et al.*, 1991).

Patterns similar to customers' deposits can be detected in the evolution of the interbank liabilities in the continental European countries, namely a lengthening of the maturity and an increasing role for negotiable CDs, except for Italy, where the oversized ordinary accounts and (formally) sight deposits result from the as yet predominant bilateral customer relationships (Ferri and Marullo, 1989; Tables 12A.15–12A.18).

What are the implications of the growing securitisation and of the lengthening maturity of bank liabilities, as well as of the concurrent interest rates' deregulation?

First, the shrinking of the cheap (demand and savings) deposit components implies a structural increase in the banks' funding cost. Moreover, the reduction of the spread between the money market rates and the average cost of the deposits reduces the room for cross-subsidising different types of deposits and loans, thus putting pressures on the banks for a careful pricing of the services (among which is liquidity insurance) supplied to customers. The loss of the privileged access to cheap funds stresses the dependence of the viability of banks on their strategic role as private information producers in their lending activity, as the theory on financial intermediation suggests.

Second, the shift in the customer composition, from individuals to institutional investors,[18] further reduces the bargaining power of banks in setting interest rates and reduces the advantages of exploiting the low interest elasticity demand arising from long-term customer relationships. As a consequence, banks can be led to reassess the role of the main non-price instrument to collect funds directly, namely the branches network.

4   The branch network

The diffusion of branches is remarkably different across countries (Table 12.5).

Besides the demand factors (such as number of inhabitants, level of GDP *per capita*, population density), limitations on the opening of branches, due to the regulatory framework aimed at ensuring the stability (see Bröker 1989) have unevenly affected, on the supply side, the various banking systems.

Table 12.5. *Selected indicators of bank branch diffusion, as of 1986*

	Branches per 10,000 inhabitants	GDP per branch (mn. ECU)	Employees per branch	Interest spread
France*	6.5	20.6	17	6.15
Germany	6.5	22.8	14	3.72
Italy	2.4	44.8	23	3.62
Japan†	3.6	45.3	35	—
Spain	8.4	7.1	7	11.65
UK*	4.3	22.6	12	4.57
USA	4.6	38.4	16	—

* 1983 data; † 1985 data.
Source: Own calculation. 4th column: 1980–5 weighted average of the spread between money market and demand and savings deposits rates (Neven, 1989, Table 7).

With the exception of Italy (in 1989), formal limitations were lifted during the 1960s (in Germany in 1962, in France in 1967) and in the early 1970s (in Spain in 1974) or never applied (as in Japan and in the United Kingdom) or were greatly eased during the 1970s and the 1980s, as in the United States.[19] Despite the fact that specific regulations, often aimed at geographical freedom of establishment (as in France, from 1982–6, or in Spain until 1985 for the savings banks) or at the foreign banks (as in Japan and in Spain) have been kept, indirect evidence of the effectiveness of the regulations can be inferred from the 'race' to the opening of branches after their lifting (8.4 per cent annual growth rate in Germany during the 1960s; in Spain, from 1975–7 the number of commercial banks' branches doubled, with an annual growth rate of 8 per cent till 1982, until the process stopped in 1985 (Caminal *et al.*, 1989).

The case of Japan, that immediately follows Italy for the lowest branch density, suggests the need to take into account among the supply side factors also the presence of institutions (the Post Office, mainly) that can act as substitutes in supplying bank-like payment services and savings instruments. In Japan, the branches of the Post Office amounted, as in France, Germany and the United States, to about half of those of the banks (BIS, 1985, data referring to 1983), but the Post Office accounts amounted to about one-third of total deposits by individuals (Osugi, 1990, data as of end-1988).[20] In Italy, by contrast, the branches of the Post Office outnumbered banks (14262 vs 12960 in 1984) and the Post Office accounts amounted in 1988 to one-sixth of total deposits by individuals.

Overall, in the light of past experiences, the abnormally low branch density in Italy – though partially offset by their size in terms of employees – could change dramatically after the liberalisation in the branching policy in 1989. Inferences from past trends should be resisted, however, if the branch network is to be considered as just a tool of quality competition adopted by the banks as a substitute for price competition (Neven, 1989).

According to this view, in those countries as well as in those periods in which the competition through interest rates is low (i.e. spreads of money market rates over deposit ones are thick), banks have stronger incentives to open branches in order to attract cheap funds from the customers (see Steinherr and Gilibert, 1988). The joint examination of the pattern of branch density and of interest spreads for Germany, France, and Spain on the one hand and for Italy on the other, seem to provide support for this hypothesis.

On the grounds of the enhanced price competition in the 1980s through deregulated interest rates, as well as of the increasing availability of low labour-intensity substitutes for the payment services (ATM cash dispensers, POS terminals, etc.), it is thus unsurprising that the growth of branches slowed down during the 1980s; the trend was confirmed also in Japan, considering together banks' and Post Office outlets (Bröker, 1989). In Europe, the downwards trend is likely to intensify, at least in the domestic markets (in Germany the number of branches actually declined after 1985), save for the offsetting influence of the entry of foreign banks into new markets due to the process of financial integration in the EC.

Though the branch density appears to have no relation with the composition of liabilities in the aggregate, it has an impact on the relative position of the biggest banks within each banking industry, as their central role in the payment system and in retail funding is enhanced the larger is the geographical coverage of their branch network. The net lending position in the interbank market of the French and of the largest German banks[21] is coherent with the relative size of the branch network (the largest Japanese and Italian banks have, on average, 300–500 domestic branches, the German ones around 1,000 and the French, Spanish and British ones, on average, 2,000–3,000).

Given the initial branch density – the lowest in our sample – the thin presence of foreign banks,[22] the shortage of an extensive network for its major banks and the competition for the deposits of the households with highest saving propensity in an integrated EC financial market, Italy could be the country most likely to experience an expansion of the domestic branch network.

5   Concluding remarks

The funding of banking systems considerably changed during the 1980s, via the shrinkage of the low interest rate-bearing saving deposits and of the non-interest-bearing (except for Italy) demand deposits offset by the time component, and especially of the marketable CDs.

The differential between average and marginal costs of funding has structurally diminished; the shift from the traditional retail saving deposits towards (wholesale) market instruments carries with it a change in the customers' mix, from individual savers, with low or no market power to more sophisticated investors and to intermediaries. Indeed, the bank liabilities end up being the most likely use of the long-term funds collected from the savers, except in countries, such as Italy and, partially, Spain, where the lack of large institutional investors goes along with sizeable public sector borrowing requirements, or where the capital markets are highly developed, as in the United States. The patterns of the total assets to GDP ratios during the 1980s across countries provide suggestive evidence in this regard.

The lengthened maturity of the deposits (both customers' and banks') has mostly offset the reduction of the buffer role provided by traditional interest-inelastic individuals' deposits, against an increasing risk of mismatch between the assets (among which the maturity of loans has generally lengthened) and the liabilities. The recourse to an alternative long-term funding instrument, such as bonds, has remained viable, but stable in relative terms, in most continental European countries and in Japan, though often (also due to the regulatory framework) in order to fund specialised institutions in the long-term lending activity; bonds issued remain negligible in the United Kingdom and in the United States.

Overall, the features of each national banking system have remained rather stable during the 1980s. The outstanding case is the Italian one, which on the one hand has deeply modified the structure of both asset and liability sides of the balance sheet, with a shrinking of the interbank funding, and on the other, has not experienced a lengthening of the deposit maturity structure. The latter aspect, we have argued in this chapter, could be related to the composite nature of demand deposits in Italy – both a transactions and a savings instrument – as they have, differently from all other countries but for a very recent exception, always earned market interest rates.

Appendix: Synoptic table on assets and liabilities and reclassified balance sheet in seven extended banking systems

	Assets						
Items	France	Germany	Italy	Japan[a]	Spain	UK	USA
CASH + BALANCE WITH CENTRAL BANK	Caisse, Instituts d'Emission, Trésor Public et Comptes Courants Postaux	Cash Balances and Balances with the Bundesbank	Liquidità in lire, riserva obbligatoria, deposito sconfinamento massimale (ICS: cassa e depositi)	Cash – Checks and bills	Efectivo y otros depositos transferibles en pesetas y moneda extranjera – exterior – Banco de España	Notes and Coin + Balances with Bank of England	Currency and Coin (Savings and Loans: Cash)
LENDING TO BANKS	Etablissements de Crédit et Institutions Financières (c/ordinaire prêts et compte à terms) + Valeurs Reçues en Pension ou Achetées Fermé	Lending to Banks – Bank securities	Conti interbancari + conti con ICS (ICS: depositi da aziende di credito)	Deposits with others + Call loans + Bills bought	Pasivos de Instituciones Financieras – Banco de España – Empresas de Seguro + otros depositos sistema bancario	LGS Market loans – CD – Overseas + Other Currencies Market Loans – Advances – CD – Overseas (Building Societies: Deposits with Monetary Sector)	Loans to Depository Institutions + Acceptances of Other Banks + non-Interest Bearing Balances due from Commercial Banks (Savings and Loans: All Other non-Mortgage Loans)

Appendix (cont.)

Items	France	Germany	Italy	Japan[a]	Spain	UK	USA
	Assets						
LENDING TO NON-BANKS	Credit à la Clientèle + Comptes Ordinaires Débiteurs de la Clientèle	Lending to non-Banks – Treasury Bill Credits – Securities	Impieghi e accettazioni bancarie + crediti in sofferenza (ICS: impieghi sull'interno totali)	Loans and Discounts	Creditos – Instituciones Financieras – exterior + pasivos de Administra-ciones Publicas de empresas no financieras y familias + otros depositos familias	LGS Advances – Overseas + Other Currencies Advances – Overseas (Building Societies: Mortgages)	Loans – Lease Financing Receivables
SECURITIES	Bons du Trésor et Créances Negociables sur les Marches + Operations sur Titres + Titres de Placement	Securities + Treasury Bill Credits + Bank Securities	BOT + titoli a medio-lungo termine (ICS: titoli di proprietà meno partecipazioni)	Securities + Commodity Bonds	Titulos: mercado monedario, de renta fija negociables + de renta fija no necogiables	LGS Investments + Other Currencies Investments + LGS T. Bills + Other Currencies T. Bills + Eligible Local Authorities Bills + Eligible Bank Bills + Other Bills (Building Societies: British Government Securities + Treasury Bills + Local Authority Long-Term Debt)	Securities

EQUITY INVESTMENTS	Titres de Partecipation	Participations	Partecipazioni e azioni	All Banks and City Banks: Stocks and Shares	Titulos de renta variable		
FOREIGN ASSETS		External Assets	Attività sull'estero		Exterior	Overseas	Balances with Banks in Foreign Countries
OTHER ASSETS	Total assets *less* previous items	Total assets *less* previous items	Altre partite – spese e perdite e sopravvenienze passive	Total assets *less* previous items including acceptances and guarantees	Total assets *less* previous items	Total assets *less* previous items	Total assets *less* previous items

[a] In order to reduce biases in the international comparison due to the multi-tier system of the Credit Cooperatives and of the Shinkin Banks, we con-solidated the balance sheets of the Credit Cooperative and of their National Federations, and of the Shinkin Banks and of their central institute, i.e. the Zenshinren Bank, respectively.

Appendix (cont.)

Items	Liabilities						
	France	Germany	Italy	Japan	Spain	UK	USA
BORROWED MONEY FROM CENTRAL BANK	Instituts d'Emission, Trésor Public et Comptes Courants Postaux	Bundesbank Lending to Domestic Banks	Crediti da Banca Italia o UIC (ICS: risconto)	Borrowed Money from the Bank of Japan	Activos de Banco de España + otros depositos Banco de España		Loans + Float + Other Federal Assets of Central Bank
DEPOSITS FROM BANKS	Etablissements du Crédit + Valeurs Données en Pension ou Vendues Fermé	Deposits and Borrowing from Banks	Conti interbancari + depositi di ICS (ICS: conti attivi di aziende di credito con ICS)	Call Money + Bills Sold + Borrowed Money	Efectivo y depositos transferibles en pesetas de istituciones financieras – Banco de España – Empresas de Seguro + otros activos de istituciones financieras	UK Monetary Sector Deposits (Sight and Time in LGS and in other Currencies) (Building Societies Bank Borrowing + Bonds + Monetary Sector Deposits and CD)	Deposits of Commercial Banks and Other Deposits of Financial Institutions
DEPOSITS FROM NON-BANKS	Comptes Créditeurs de la Clientéle + Comptes d'Epargne Régime Spéciale + Bons de Caisse + Certificats de Dépôt	Total Deposits and Borrowing from non-Banks	Depositi di clienti + altra raccolta all'interno (ICS: CD al netto di CD e BF inclusi in attività delle aziende di credito)	Deposits + CD	Efectivo y depositos transferibles en pesetas y moneda extranjera exterior – instituciones financieras	LGS Sight and Time Deposits + Other Currencies Sight and Time Deposits – Overseas	Total Deposits – Deposits from Banks

BONDS	Obligations et Emprunts Participatifs + Operations sur Titres	Bearer Bonds Oustanding	ICS: obbligazioni altre	Bank Debentures Issued	Titulos del mercado monedario	CD and Other Short-Term Money Market Paper Issued	Subordinated debt
FOREIGN LIABILITIES		External Liabilities	Raccolta all'estero (ICS: prestiti in valuta)		Exterior	Overseas	
CAPITAL AND RESERVES	Capital + Reserves	Capital	Patrimonio	Capital	Cuentas de capital + títulos de renta variable	Capital and Other Funds	Equity Capital (Savings and Loans: Regulatory Capital)
OTHER LIABILITIES	Residual	Residual	Altre partite – rendite e profitti e sopravvenienze attive	Residual Including Acceptances and Guarantees	Residual	Residual	Residual
STATISTICAL SOURCES	*Rapport de la Commission Bancaire*; BIS, *Payment System in Eleven Developed Countries* (1985); OECD, *National Accounts*	*Monthly Report of the Deutsche Bundesbank*; OECD, *National Accounts*	*Banca d'Italia, Relazione Anuale e Bollettino Statistico*; ABI, *Annuario delle Aziende di Credito e Finanziarie*	Bank of Japan, *Economic Statistic Annual*; OECD, *Bank Profitability* (1988); Bröker (1989)	Banco de España, *Informe Annual*; OECD, *Bank Profitability* (1988); Gorria, *The Retail Banking Revolution in Spain*, IEF Papers (1989)	Central Statistical Office, *Financial Statistics*; OECD, *Financial Accounts*; BIS, *Payment System in Eleven Developed Countries* (1985)	*Federal Reserve Bulletin*; Federal Home Loan Bank Board, *Combined Financial Statements FSLIC-Insured Institutions*; US Department of Commerce, *Statistical Abstract of the United States*

Appendix (*cont.*)

Items	Liabilities						
	France	Germany	Italy	Japan	Spain	UK	USA
EXTENDED BANKING SYSTEM: LIST AND NUMBER (1988) OF INSTITUTIONS	Banques (408) Banques Mutualistes ou Coopératives (178) Caisses D'Epargne et de Prévoyance (301) Caisses de Crédit Municipal (21) Société Financières (1059) Institutions Financières Spécialisées (32)	Kreditbanken (317) Girozentralen (12) Sparkassen (585) Genossenschaftliche Zentralbanken (6) Kreditgenossenschaften (3361) Realkreditinstitute (38) Kreditinstitute Mit Sonderaufgaben (16)	Banche (284) Casse di Risparmio e Monti di Credito su Pegno (37) Istituti Centrali di Categoria (5) Istituti di Credito Spaciale (83)	All Banks (87) Sogo Banks (68) Shinkin Banks (455) The Zenshiren Bank (1) The Shoko Chukin Bank (1) Credit Cooperatives (419) National Federation of Credit Cooperatives (1) The Norinchukin Bank (1) Agricultural Cooperatives (3979) Credit Federation of Agricultural Cooperatives (47)	Banca Privada (136)* Cajas de Ahorro (79)* Cooperativas de Credito (134)*	Monetary Sector (588)** Building Societies (138)**	Insured Commercial Banks (domestic offices) (14,235)* FSLIC-Insured Institutions (Savings and Loans) (3147)**

* 1986 figures.
** 1987 figures.

Table 12A.1. *France: balance sheet composition, end-year*

Assets	1985	1988
Cash and CB reserves	2.2	1.5
Loans to banks	35.7	37.6
Loans to customers	43.6	40.4
Securities	5.6	6.3
* money market	2.7	2.3
Participations	1.8	2.0
Other assets	11.1	12.1
Total	100.0	100.0

Liabilities	1985	1988
Borrowing from CB	2.5	1.7
Deposits from banks	38.2	39.3
Deposits from customers	34.1	32.3
* current accounts	15.3	12.4
* special savings	14.9	13.0
* CD and *bons de caisse*	3.9	6.9
Bonds	11.7	12.0
Equity	2.8	3.4
Other liabilities	10.7	11.2
Total	100.0	100.0

Note: In all Appendix tables, totals are not the sum of the data, because of rounding.

Table 12A.2. *France: composition of deposits with customers Banques and Banques Populaires ou Mutualistes*

	1985	1988
Current accounts	32.1	29.5
Time deposits	11.6	9.7
Special savings	45.0	42.5
Bons de caisse	10.2	7.8
CD	1.2	10.6
Total	100.0	100.0

Table 12A.3. *France: breakdown of the system by categories of institution, end-1988*

Assets	BC	BMC	CE	CM	SF	IFS	TOT
Cash and CB reserves	74.2	17.1	3.3	0.3	1.3	3.9	100.0
Loans to banks	55.9	11.3	18.5	0.1	11.0	3.2	100.0
Loans to customers	44.3	22.9	4.6	0.3	8.6	19.2	100.0
Securities	60.5	20.0	0.5	0.0	15.5	3.5	100.0
* money market	56.7	24.1	0.0	0.1	15.7	3.4	100.0
Participations	57.0	6.6	0.5	0.0	29.9	6.0	100.0
Other assets	43.9	18.7	2.6	0.1	28.6	6.2	100.0
Total	50.4	17.4	9.2	0.2	12.7	10.1	100.0

Liabilities	BC	BMC	CE	CM	SF	IFS	TOT
Borrowing from CB	87.8	5.6	0.6	0.0	0.1	5.9	100.0
Deposits from banks	58.4	6.4	7.0	0.1	18.4	9.6	100.0
Deposits from customers	43.7	31.2	19.0	0.3	4.4	1.5	100.0
* current accounts	63.4	29.2	3.0	0.2	3.0	1.2	100.0
* special savings	22.2	32.8	44.5	0.0	0.5	0.0	100.0
* CD and *bons de caisse*	48.3	31.8	0.1	0.8	14.2	4.8	100.0
Bonds	39.0	15.0	0.1	0.1	13.1	32.7	100.0
Equity	39.0	15.9	5.8	0.4	33.2	5.7	100.0
Other liabilities	52.0	21.3	1.1	0.1	11.0	14.5	100.0
Total	50.4	17.4	9.2	0.2	12.7	10.1	100.0

BC   = Banques
BMC = Banques mutualistes ou cooperatives
CR   = Caisse d'épargne et de prévoyance
CM   = Crédit municipal
SF   = Sociétés financières
IFS   = Institutions financières spécialisées

Table 12A.4. *Germany: balance sheet composition, end-year*

Assets	1980	1985	1988
Cash and CB reserves	3.0	2.3	2.2
Loans to banks	17.1	15.9	16.9
Loans to customers	60.1	58.3	55.0
Securities	9.8	11.7	12.7
Foreign assets	6.6	8.0	9.7
Participations	0.8	0.9	1.0
Other assets	2.6	2.9	2.5
Total	100.0	100.0	100.0

Liabilities	1980	1985	1988
Borrowing from CB	2.4	3.2	3.6
Deposits from banks	18.5	16.6	17.3
* sight and 1–3 months	3.0	2.4	2.4
* others	15.5	14.2	14.9
Deposits from customers	49.1	47.6	48.3
* sight	7.3	6.9	7.1
* time	41.8	40.7	41.2
Bonds	17.6	19.8	17.7
Foreign liabilities	6.0	5.5	5.7
Equity	3.3	3.5	3.6
Other liabilities	3.1	3.8	3.8
Total	100.0	100.0	100.0

Table 12A.5. *Germany: composition of deposits with customers and securities in portfolio*

	1980	1985	1988
Sight deposits	15.1	14.5	14.8
* demand	14.3	13.6	14.1
* < 1 month	0.8	0.9	0.7
Time deposits	31.2	33.8	35.3
* 1–3 months	11.0	10.7	9.8
* 3–12 months	5.2	5.0	4.0
* 1–4 years	0.4	0.2	0.3
* > 4 years	14.6	17.9	21.2
Bank savings bonds	8.2	10.3	9.7
Savings deposits	41.4	38.0	37.2
Loans on a trust basis	4.1	3.4	3.0
Total	100.0	100.0	100.0
	1980	1985	1988
Treasury bills	1.4	1.4	0.9
Securities	24.4	27.7	30.0
* medium term	6.3	3.3	1.5
* long term	18.1	24.4	28.5
Bank bonds	74.2	70.9	69.1
Total	100.0	100.0	100.0

Table 12A.6. *Germany: breakdown of the system by categories of institutions, end-1988*

Assets	KB	GI	SK	GZ	KG	RKI	KIS	P	TOT
Cash	25.3	1.8	48.2	0.9	23.3	0.1	0.4	—	100.0
Borrowing from CB	33.1	4.9	27.6	3.0	14.5	0.7	0.8	15.4	100.0
Loans to banks	24.0	22.9	8.1	11.2	8.5	12.2	12.4	0.7	100.0
Loans to customers	23.7	14.4	23.0	1.5	12.4	18.3	5.7	1.0	100.0
Securities	19.0	10.2	39.5	6.1	17.8	1.5	2.3	3.6	100.0
* bank securities	10.6	9.5	48.2	4.1	21.7	0.7	1.5	3.7	100.0
Participations	56.3	17.6	7.8	11.3	5.2	0.5	1.3	—	100.0
Other assets	24.9	11.4	28.8	2.1	18.1	9.9	4.8	—	100.0
Total	23.7	15.6	21.7	4.6	12.3	13.9	6.7	1.5	100.0

Liabilities	KB	GI	SK	GZ	KG	RKI	KIS	P	TOT
Deposits from banks	34.0	18.8	11.9	14.2	5.7	6.8	8.4	0.2	100.0
* sight and 1–3 months	41.7	23.3	8.2	16.5	3.6	2.9	3.2	0.6	100.0
* time	29.0	18.2	12.6	14.2	5.8	9.2	11.0	—	100.0
Deposits from customers	21.2	6.9	33.3	0.6	19.9	10.0	5.2	2.9	100.0
* sight	34.0	4.5	32.6	1.1	21.0	0.3	0.9	5.6	100.0
* time	19.3	5.9	34.6	0.5	20.4	11.5	5.3	2.5	100.0
Bonds	12.0	37.6	2.6	2.4	1.0	36.2	8.2	—	100.0
Equity	34.9	10.1	22.4	4.3	13.3	9.2	5.8	—	100.0
Other liabilities	32.1	10.6	22.4	2.8	9.1	13.0	8.4	1.6	100.0
Total	23.7	15.6	21.7	4.6	12.3	13.9	6.7	1.5	100.0

KB = Kreditbanken
GI = Girozentralen
SK = Sparkassen
GZ = Genossenschaftliche Zentralbanken
KG = Kreditgenossenschaften
RKI = Realkreditinstitute
KIS = Kreditinstitute mit Sonderaufgaben
P = Postgiro und Postsparkassenaemter

Table 12A.7. *Italy: balance sheet composition, end-year*

Assets	1980	1985	1988	1988[a]
Cash and CB reserves	7.2	7.5	7.9	100.0
Loans to banks	11.8	10.0	8.3	94.8
Loans to customers	37.0	36.2	41.9	64.8
Securities	21.1	19.8	16.5	92.3
Foreign assets	5.5	6.9	6.0	94.2
Participations	0.7	1.1	1.4	77.7
Other assets	16.5	18.3	18.0	87.4
Total	100.0	100.0	100.0	80.6
Liabilities	1980	1985	1988	1988[a]
Borrowing from CB	0.6	0.9	0.5	83.8
Deposits from banks	10.6	9.4	7.8	91.2
Deposits from customers	48.1	44.2	45.6	93.5
* CDs	1.1	3.2	7.1	58.3
Foreign liabilities	8.4	10.7	11.3	78.6
Bonds	11.2	8.6	9.0	0.0
Borrowing from government	0.8	1.1	0.9	0.0
Equity	3.5	5.6	6.8	72.6
Other liabilities	16.9	19.5	18.1	86.0
* statistical discrepancies	0.4	0.6	0.4	—
Total	100.0	100.0	100.0	80.6

[a] Aziende di credito: share on the extended banking system.

Table 12A.8 *Japan: balance sheet composition, end-year*

Assets	1980	1985	1988	1988[a]
Cash and CB reserves	0.9	0.7	0.6	16.8
Loans to banks	10.4	13.6	13.8	18.6
Loans to customers	56.3	57.2	56.6	38.2
Securities	16.7	16.7	17.5	25.9
* bank bonds	1.5	1.4	1.2	35.8
Other assets	15.8	11.6	11.5	45.9
Total	100.0	100.0	100.0	34.4

Liabilities	1980	1985	1988	1988[a]
Borrowing from CB	0.5	0.6	0.8	85.4
Deposits from banks	3.4	5.6	5.6	58.1
Deposits from customers	72.7	71.2	70.3	31.7
Due to trust accounts	0.9	1.7	1.9	3.1
Securities	6.7	6.9	7.0	9.3
Equity	3.1	2.0	2.5	44.1
Other liabilities	12.7	12.1	12.0	53.8
Total	100.0	100.0	100.0	34.4

[a] City banks' share on the extended banking system.

Table 12A.9. *Spain: balance sheet composition, end-year*

Assets	1980	1985	1988
Cash and CB reserves	6.7	9.1	9.4
Loans to banks	8.3	12.4	10.4
Loans to customers	55.5	38.6	43.6
Securities	12.8	19.9	21.0
* bank securities	0.7	0.1	0.1
Foreign assets	7.9	7.3	4.6
Participations	2.5	1.9	2.8
Other assets	6.4	9.8	8.3
Total	100.0	100.0	100.0

Liabilities	1980	1985	1988
Borrowing from CB	2.4	2.4	1.7
Deposits from banks	9.8	13.7	12.2
Deposits from customers	66.8	57.2	58.7
* sight	17.6	12.3	13.0
* time and savings	49.2	44.9	45.6
Foreign liabilities	10.7	8.0	7.6
Money market paper	2.0	3.3	2.4
Equity	8.1	8.3	9.3
Other liabilities	0.3	7.1	8.0
Total	100.0	100.0	100.0

Table 12A.10. *Spain: structure of deposits of the private sector, per cent of total deposits, end-year*

	Commercial banks		Savings banks		Cooperative banks	
	1985	1988	1985	1988	1985	1988
Sight deposits	27.9	38.0	13.8	15.8	15.7	15.0
Saving deposits	15.1	15.7	48.2	62.5	32.0	33.4
Term deposits	57.0	43.4	49.9	41.7	52.3	51.6
– less than 6 months	0.2	7.1	0.4	3.9	0.6	10.8
– from 6 months to 1 year	11.6	16.5	2.6	4.7	5.0	9.0
– from 1 to 2 years	41.5	19.0	40.5	30.2	46.7	31.8
– more than 2 years	3.7	0.8	6.4	2.9		
Total (ESP bn)	11,183	11,599	7,804	10,850	959	1,229
Share in total deposits with the banking sector	56.1	49.6	39.1	45.2	4.8	5.1

Source: Lygum *et al.* (1989).

Table 12A.11. *Spain: breakdown of the system by categories of institution, end-1988*

Assets	B	CR	COOP	TOT
Cash and CB reserves	53.4	42.5	4.0	100.0
Loans to banks	64.8	28.6	6.6	100.0
Loans to customers	65.0	32.1	2.9	100.0
Securities	50.9	46.9	2.2	100.0
* bank securities	80.3	18.8	1.0	100.0
Foreign assets	95.4	4.5	0.0	100.0
Participations	77.5	22.0	0.5	100.0
Other assets	61.5	36.3	2.7	100.0
Total	62.2	34.8	3.0	100.0

Liabilities	B	CR	COOP	TOT
Borrowing from CB	96.0	4.0	0.0	100.0
Deposits from banks	88.3	10.1	1.6	100.0
Deposits from customers	51.7	44.3	4.0	100.0
* sight	66.5	30.7	2.8	100.0
* time and savings	47.2	48.4	4.3	100.0
Foreign liabilities	90.5	9.4	0.1	100.0
Money market paper	47.9	51.5	0.6	100.0
Equity	67.7	28.7	3.6	100.0
Other liabilities	66.4	31.9	1.7	100.0
Total	62.2	34.8	3.0	100.0

B   = Banca privada
CR   = Cajas de ahorro
COOP = Cooperativas de credito

Table 12A.12. *United Kingdom: balance sheet composition, end-year*

Assets	1980	1985	1988	1988[a]
Cash and CB reserves	0.6	0.4	0.4	93.8
Loans to banks	22.0	19.4	16.3	90.0
* in foreign currency	11.6	10.1	6.5	
Loans to customers	39.6	39.6	44.5	70.8
* in foreign currency	12.8	13.6	10.7	
Securities	5.7	7.4	6.5	88.2
* in foreign currency	1.1	1.3	0.6	
Foreign assets	28.4	30.2	29.3	100.0
Other assets	3.8	3.0	3.0	87.0
Total	100.0	100.0	100.0	84.2

Liabilities	1980	1985	1988	1988[a]
Deposits from banks	16.9	16.7	14.2	91.5
* in foreign currency	11.9	10.5	6.9	
Deposits from customers	31.5	26.9	31.7	60.6
* in foreign currency	1.6	2.2	2.7	
CDs + time deposits	7.5	9.1	10.2	
* in foreign currency	5.9	7.3	6.4	
Foreign liabilities	37.8	40.3	36.0	99.6
Equity	4.7	5.3	6.1	86.9
Other liabilities	1.7	1.8	1.8	71.7
Total	100.0	100.0	100.0	84.2

[a] 'Monetary sector' share on the extended banking system.

Table 12A.13. *United States: balance sheet composition, end-year*

Assets	1980	1985	1987	1987[a]
Cash and CB reserves	2.6	2.0	1.8	76.7
Loans to banks	4.5	2.1	2.0	98.7
Funds sold and repos	3.3	3.9	3.3	100.0
Loans to customers	62.7	62.7	63.3	60.9
Securities	14.7	16.0	18.8	79.1
Foreign assets	0.9	1.6	1.4	100.0
Other assets	11.3	11.7	9.5	70.4
Total	100.0	100.0	100.0	68.1

Liabilities	1980	1985	1987	1987[a]
Borrowing from CB	0.7	0.6	0.5	100.0
Funds purch. and repos	6.2	6.4	6.1	100.0
FHLB Advances	2.2	2.5	3.1	0.0
Deposits from banks	3.1	1.7	1.4	0.0
Deposits from customers	75.4	75.0	74.3	98.2
Other borrowed money	1.3	3.6	5.2	32.8
Subordinated debt	0.3	0.1	0.1	93.1
Equity	6.5	6.2	5.9	79.3
Other liabilities	4.3	3.9	3.5	83.3
Total	100.0	100.0	100.0	68.1

[a] 'Commercial banks' share on the extended banking system.

Table 12A.14. *United States: breakdown of total deposits (banks' and customers') of commercial banks*

	1980	1985	1988
Demand	36.4	25.2	21.7
Time and savings:	63.6	74.8	78.3
– time < 100,000 $	25.2	24.7	25.3
– time CDs > = 100,000 $	19.8	15.3	16.2
– all NOW accounts	1.9	2.6	9.3
– open/acc. > = 100,000 $	1.6	2.0	1.6
– other time/savings	15.0	30.2	25.8
* MMDA	—	18.7	16.6
Total	100.0	100.0	100.0

Table 12A.15. *France: interbank liabilities of 'Banques' (in FF with residents), annual average end-quarter figures, per cent*

Items	1980	1985	1987
Ordinary accounts	9.6	10.6	10.2
Due on demand	17.6	18.0	14.9
Term borrowing	72.8	70.4	71.3
– < 1 year	46.0	40.5	39.2
– > 1 year	26.8	29.9	33.1
Others	—	1.0	3.6
Total (% total balance sheet)	35.2	36.1	35.6
– CDs	—	2.5	11.7

Source: Banque de France (1989).

Table 12A.16. *Germany: interbank domestic liabilities, annual averages, per cent*

Items	1980	1987
Short term	47.7	43.5
– due on demand	14.8	14.0
– < 1 year	29.9	26.6
– bill-based borrowing	3.1	2.9
Medium term (1–4 years)	7.3	9.5
Long term (> 4 years	44.9	47.0
Total (DM bn)	400.9	607.0

Source: Deutsche Bundesbank (1988).

Table 12A.17. *Italy: interbank liabilities, commercial banks, annual averages, per cent*

Items	1979	1985	1988
Ordinary accounts	41.9	40.7	38.1
Loans	5.5	5.7	11.0
Sight deposits	37.6	44.1	34.9
Time deposits	15.0	9.5	16.0

Source: Ferri and Marullo (1989).

Table 12A.18. *Spain: interbank liabilities, end-year figures, per cent*

Items	1980	1985	1988
Overnight	20.8	18.2	22.4
1–30 days	22.7	7.4	9.2
> 30 days	56.5	74.4	68.4
Total (ESP bn)	213.8	961.7	2904.5

Source: Lygum *et al.* (1989).

Notes

1 We thank Rony Hamaui, Mario Monti and Gianni Pittaluga for helpful comments. The usual disclaimer applies.

2 Only the French (since 1984) and the German banking statistics adopt the same comprehensive approach.

3 A fuller set of tables with time series data from 1980 to 1988 for the structure of the balance sheets and the disaggregation in 1988 of each domestic extended banking system into its component categories is available from the authors upon request.

4 The patterns do not change if instead of a total balance sheet, gross of intrasectoral items, we take as a proxy of the size of banking intermediation the non-banks' claims, as defined in Section 2.1.

5 A feature that could have further imposed handicaps on the Italian and Spanish commercial banking systems relative to the others is the burden of the reserve requirements. Indeed, the average coefficients, respectively, of 19.8 and 17.0 as a percentage of deposits in 1989 are to be compared with 5.9 and 3.2 for Germany and France (Banca Commerciale Italiana, 1990).

6 The net domestic interbank assets should by construction be zero; aside from mere statistical discrepancies, the dimension of the item can be taken as an indicator of the degree of coverage of the data, both for the instruments and for the operators. In our data, the net domestic interbank lending is close to nil for only two countries (Germany and Italy) with the broadest coverage for instruments and operators, due to the relative underdevelopment of the money market; the omission of some bank-like institutions in other countries such as Japan's Securities Houses, France's Caisse des Dépôts et Consignations, Spain's Credito Oficial and the United States's and the United Kingdom's institutional investors and large non-financial firms that operate in the money market and the United States's investment banks shows up with much larger figures (especially in Japan and in the United Kingdom).

7 Bonds are issued only by the Special Credit Institutions; commercial and saving banks are as yet prevented from adopting this funding instrument in the current regulatory framework, which limits, with only partial exceptions, to the short term (up to 18 months) both the lending and the funding activities of these institutions.

8 Even in Spain the ratio has increased through time, once the step conversion to state-backed securities of loans to the firms involved in the 1978–83 banking crisis has been taken into account.

9 A further factor behind the inflated interbank market was until quite recently (1985, when interbank operations were included in the computations of prudential ratios) the customary attribution of no risks to the transactions with banking counterparts (Banque de France, 1989, pp. 67–8).

10 The mortgage banks have changed their net position since end-1983 *vis-à-vis* other categories of domestic banks, becoming net lenders (Deutsche Bundesbank, 1988).

11 Foreign banks that operate in Spain under the law of 1978 are subject to restrictions that concern (1) the structure of their funding – they may not fund more than 40 per cent of their loans to Spanish residents with domestic non-bank liabilities – and (2) the maximum (three) number of branches they may have. Since the accession of Spain to the EC some changes have been made with respect to EC banks. The upper bound on the ratio of domestic liabilities to loans to Spanish residents has increased 10 per cent every year, from 50 per cent in 1988 to 90 per cent in 1992. In addition, foreign banks were able to open one additional branch in 1990 and two more in 1992 (Lygum *et al.*, 1989). Foreign banks get their funds mainly from the interbank market (60 per cent versus 16 per cent for national banks in 1987, Caminal *et al.*, 1989).

12 Most of the decline is due to the commercial banks (from 12.9 per cent in 1983 to 8.9 per cent in 1988).

13 In September 1989 Banco Santander started to pay market interest rates on current accounts of at least 500,000 pesetas, followed soon by the other largest banks (*The Wall Street Journal* (Europe) 8–9 June 1990). Large retail banks introduced interest-bearing demand deposits early in 1989 (Bank of England, 1990).

14 The non-financial private sector has replaced these low-yielding deposits with instruments paying interest rates closer to market rates, primarily in the form of repurchase agreements (endorsements of Treasury notes mainly), but also of negotiable liabilities ('*pagarés bancarios*') (Lygum *et al.*, 1989).

15 The trend does not appear to have been altered by the 1986 reform, according to which bank liabilities with a maturity greater than 4 years were free from reserve requirements.

16 An additional supply side explanation could be the lack of differentiation, except for CDs (see n. 17), in the reserve requirement of deposits according to their maturity, as is usual in most other countries.

17 CDs are also the only deposit component with a lower reserve requirement burden, because of a differential of 3 percentage points in the interest rate earned on their reserves. Moreover, CDs enjoy a favourable fiscal treatment relative to sight saving deposits, with a withholding tax rate of 25 instead of 30 per cent.

18 The scanty information available supports this conjecture. In the United States, the proportion of demand deposits held by consumers has declined from one-third in 1980 to just over one-fourth in 1987 (Gart, 1989). In Germany, a large part of the long-term deposits come from insurance companies, recycling some of their inflows of funds from savers (Deutsche Bundesbank, 1989).

19 Legislation relaxing constraints on the geographic expansion of banks and bank holding companies has come principally from the states. After 1970, the number of states reducing branching restrictions grew markedly, rising from 6 during the 1970s to 22 during the 1980s. As a result, 35 states currently allow unlimited state-wide branching or state-wide expansion through acquisition of existing banks. Only four states remain unit banking states. See Federal Reserve Board (1989).

20 In Japan, Postal Savings accounts have various advantages over bank deposits, such as high liquidity, a long maximum maturity of 10 years and half-yearly compounded interest rates.
21 The shares in the interbank liabilities and assets of the three largest commercial banks, that in France at end-1988 accounted for 39.4 per cent of the total assets of the 'Banques', were equal to 27.9 and 32.9 per cent; in Germany, the corresponding figures for the Commercial banks were 37.6, 26.5 and 31.0.
22 The market shares (as a percentage of total balance sheet) of foreign institutions were at end-1987 3 for Italy, 4 for Germany, 11 for Spain, 16 for France and 60 for the United Kingdom (Steinherr and Gilibert, 1988).

References

Baglioni, A. and G. Marotta (1992) 'Deposit Insurance: Implications From Financial Intermediation Theory', Chapter 13 in this volume.
Banca Commerciale Italiana (1990) *Tendenze Monetarie*, **61**.
Bank of England (1990), 'Monetary Aggregates in a Changing Environment: A Statistical Discussion Paper', *Discussion Papers*, **47**.
Banque de France (1989) 'Le marché interbancaire', *Bulletin Trimestriel*, **69**.
BIS (1985) *Payment System in Eleven Developed Countries*, Basle: BIS.
Bröker, G. (1989) *Competition in Banking, Trends in Banking Structure and Regulation in OECD Countries*, Paris: OECD.
Caminal, R., J. Gual and X. Vives (1989) 'Competition in Spanish Banking', *CEPR Discussion Paper*, **314**.
Deutsche Bundesbank (1988) 'Domestic Banks' Interbank Assets and Liabilities Since 1980', *Monthly Report* (March).
Deutsche Bundesbank (1989) 'Longer-term Trends in the Banking Sector and Market Position of the Individual Categories of Banks', *Monthly Report* (April).
Di Giovanni, M., G. B. Pittaluga and A. Tamagnini (1991) 'L'evoluzione nelle politiche di raccolta delle banche: il caso italiano', in V. Conti and R. Hamaui (eds), *Operatori e mercati nel processo di liberalizzazione*, vol. III, *Gli intermediari bancari*, Bologna: Il Mulino.
Federal Reserve Board (1989) 'Trends in Banking Structure Since the Mid-1970s', *Federal Reserve Bulletin* (March).
Ferri, G. and P. Marullo Reedtz (1989) 'Mercato interbancario e gestione degli attivi bancari: tendenze recenti e linee di sviluppo', Banca d'Italia *Temi di discussione*, **117**.
Gart, A. (1989) *An Analysis of the New Financial Institutions*, New York: Quorum Books.
Lygum, B., E. Perée and A. Steinherr (1989) 'The Spanish Financial System', *EIB Papers* (December).
Neven, D. J. (1989) 'Structural Adjustment in European Retail Banking. Some Views From Industrial Organization', *CEPR Discussion Paper*, **311**.
Osugi, K. (1990) 'Japan's Experience of Financial Deregulation Since 1984 in an International Perspective', *BIS Economic Papers*, **26**.
Salomon Brothers (1990) 'Higher Bank Capital = Securitization', London.
Steinherr, A. and P. L. Gilibert (1988) 'The Impact of Freeing Trade in Financial Services and Capital Movements on the European Banking Industry', *EIB Papers* (August).
Tobin, J. (1982) 'The Commercial Banking Firm: A Simple Model', *Scandinavian Journal of Economics*, **84(4)**: 495–530.

13 Deposit insurance: implications from financial intermediation theory

ANGELO BAGLIONI and
GIUSEPPE MAROTTA

1   Introduction[1]

Starting with the seminal paper by Black (1970), a stream of studies based on information asymmetries has been focussing on the nature of financial intermediation, in the attempt to provide a theoretical foundation to the uniqueness of the banks, denied by the 'new view' and, more recently, by the so called 'Legal Restrictions Theory' (LRT).[2]

The features, embedded in a bank, which this literature tries to explain, in order to provide a rationale for a special role among the intermediaries and hence a conceptual framework for a regulatory and supervision policy, are that:[3]

(1)   a large proportion of the assets – i.e. loans – in a diversified portfolio is highly illiquid;
(2)   most of the liabilities are of a standard debt-contract type, with predetermined money value, regardless of the performance of the underlying portfolio;
(3)   a portion of the debt liabilities has the form of perfectly liquid demand deposits.

In the 'new view' proposed by Gurley, Shaw and Tobin in the early 1960s, banks differ from other intermediaries simply because of the regulations imposed on them. Fixed-value liabilities convertible at will into cash, such as demand deposits, are the result of an historical event, namely the central role of the banks in the payment system. Similar reasoning, though with different implications, has been pursued by the proponents of LRT (Kareken, Wallace, Fama), whose claim is that the production of monetary services is not associated with any specific intermediary. According to Fama (1980), for instance, both banks and non-bank intermediaries can provide (a) delegated portfolio management and (b) payments services.

As for the first function, the usual rationale for the existence of financial intermediaries is offered by portfolio theory-cum-transaction costs. Economies of scale in diversification provide a cost advantage to risk neutral intermediaries over risk averse individuals; in particular, whereas search costs seem to justify the existence of brokers (Leland and Pyle, 1977; Chan, 1983), costs related to the acquisition and holding of marketable assets account for mutual fund-type intermediaries (Klein, 1973; Kane and Buser, 1979). Ruling out perfect diversification, due to systematic or undiversifiable risk, opportunities of mutually beneficial exchanges can arise if investors differ with respect to their attitudes toward risk. The intermediary explained by the combination of both diversifiable and systematic risks would be more complex than a mutual fund, but still would not match the other characteristics of deposit taking institutions (Chant, 1987).

As for the second function, the historical – and hence logically contingent – involvement in the payment system, entailing the issue of fixed-value convertible liabilities, explains why banks differ from brokers and mutual funds in holding liquid assets (cash and securities), for precautionary reasons. As subsequently remarked (Fama, 1985), the LRT fails, however, to explain why deposit taking institutions' portfolios include highly illiquid, due to the lack of a secondary market, loans.

Relying on the approach of information asymmetries we utilise a logical framework which incorporates the key features of the banking firm and thus allows us to assess especially the role of deposit insurance schemes – that is, one of the main components of the complex net of regulatory policies aimed at the typical mode of the banks' fund raising.

The origin of banking intermediation can be found in the informational asymmetries between borrowers and lenders and in the economies of scale – through delegation – in screening and monitoring. The (private) information thus gathered is embedded in the loans which are highly illiquid. As a counterpart, the intermediary can issue fixed-value liabilities (deposits); in addition, the liquidity-insurance service provided by banks to their depositors explains why they issue demand (together with time) liabilities. We argue that the issue of demand deposits can also be seen as an effective way to supply the depositors with a cheap checking device over the choices of managers (acting on behalf of the controlling shareholders).

In drawing the implications for banking regulation we make the following points: (a) the need of own-equity resources of the intermediary as a coinsurance device; (b) the liquidity production operated by banks – through the holding of unmarketable assets together with the issue of demand deposits – makes them particularly vulnerable to 'runs', which in turn calls for the existence of a lender of last resort as well as for some kind of deposit insurance; (c) the unmarketability of loans makes socially costly the liquidation of troubled banks, thus lending support to timely reorganisation policies, in order to prevent the liquidation itself.

As far as deposit insurance is concerned, we utilise the logical framework so far outlined to assess the many proposals put forward in the United States for a reform of the existing (1990) scheme.

First of all, we argue that the existence of undiversifiable risk in banking calls for a public insuring agency, a claim justified also by the need for such an agency to have supervisory powers over the banks. We then argue that the proposed 'narrow bank' solution is not satisfactory, as it would simply translate the liquidity risk currently incurred by banks to other types of intermediaries (apart from its feasibility problems). On the contrary, a strong case can be made in favour of a system of risk-related insurance premia, which would restrain the amplitude of the moral hazard and of the cross-subsidisation among banks implied by the present scheme of flat premia. The major drawback of risk-based premia lies in the problems connected with their estimation, making difficult, at present, their implementation.

The social benefits of avoiding the disruption of customer relationships with the borrowers, together with the goal of minimising the costs of the insuring agency, point to the desirability of endowing it with powers of timely intervention, in order to prevent the economic net worth of a troubled bank becoming negative, originating a confidence crisis among depositors, which in turn could lead to liquidation. The microeconomic goal of an efficient handling of problem banks thus turns out to provide the basic rationale for a public deposit insurance agency, endowed with some supervisory powers.

The other two motivations at the base of the US deposit insurance system – namely protection against a collapse of the money supply and of the payment system and protection of small depositors – have on the contrary lost much of their relevance. Indeed, while the macroeconomic goal of stabilising the money supply can be left to the lender of last resort, the protection of small depositors seems less necessary when a large portion of households' wealth is managed by institutional investors and it can anyway be obtained through other (fiscal, for instance) means.

The balance of the chapter is organised as follows. Section 2 selectively surveys the literature dealing with the three key characteristics of a bank. Section 3 draws some implications for the asset and liability management and for the principles of banking supervision, with special emphasis on deposit insurance. Section 4 examines the motivations and drawbacks of the US deposit insurance system, a natural term of reference for any discussion of the topic. Section 5 assesses some proposals of reform for the present US system, which have some bearing on the recent evolution of deposit protection schemes in most other industrialised countries and raises some issues connected with the process of financial integration in Europe. Section 6 concludes the chapter.

2   Banking intermediation theory: some building blocks

Building blocks of the recent financial intermediation theory are information asymmetries between lenders and borrowers in a principal–agent setting. Economies of scale, through delegation, in monitoring outcomes of the financed projects or in screening potential ones and feasibility of portfolio diversification may establish the superiority of indirect to direct transfer of funds.

In Diamond (1984), under the hypotheses of universal risk neutrality and (*ex post*) information asymmetry about the outcomes of the projects, observed only by the would-be borrowers, it can be shown that a standard debt contract (SDC)[4] is incentive-compatible in direct lending, as the problem of revealing truthfully the outcome to be shared can be solved by a fixed payment subject to a deadweight bankruptcy penalty. If the outcome could be observed through (costly) monitoring, this (utility) loss could, however, be avoided. Furthermore, indirect lending would be preferable should the economies of scale allow a per-project reduction of the fixed monitoring cost and the ensuing cost savings more than offset the expected agency (or delegation) cost of providing the incentives to the agent (intermediary) to meet its commitment with the principals (depositors).

Indeed, Diamond shows not only that a SDC between the intermediary and the ultimate lenders (depositors) is incentive-compatible, but also, in order to make indirect lending viable, that the delegation cost, namely the intermediary's deadweight bankruptcy penalty, can be driven to zero, for independently distributed projects, through diversification across borrowers.

Two important implications of the model are (1) well-diversified, across illiquid information-intensive assets, highly leveraged intermediaries; (2) once removed the information asymmetry on the realised outcomes of the projects, more efficient financing contracts than the SDC could be agreed upon (e.g. equity contracts).[5]

Terlizzese (1988) provides a deeper foundation of the intermediary's activity taking into account a more fundamental issue of adverse selection due to (*ex ante*) information asymmetry about the return distribution of the projects and stressing the credibility issue of the commitment with the depositors.

Under (*ex ante*) information asymmetry, entrepreneurs who know the return distribution of the projects better than do potential investors have an incentive to misrepresent the prospects of the projects they want to finance, offering the investors a contract that might be a 'lemon'. In a setting of risk neutral borrowers and risk averse lenders this asymmetry could even preclude the signing of a SDC or at best limit its extension (i.e. credit rationing). Removing this information asymmetry, thus avoiding the chance of being cheated, could imply bearing a (fixed) screening cost; following the same reasoning as Diamond, this task could be delegated to an agent (intermediary), due to economies of scale.

The ensuing standard agency problem arising from the privacy of the information thus gathered could be solved through the offer of a SDC provided the promise of a fixed payment in *all* states could be made credible. Ruling out perfect risk diversification, this problem could be at least partially eased allowing ultimate lenders to monitor the intermediary. Typical solutions would be the (coinsuring) commitment of a significant amount of the agent's own wealth or the holding of (precautionary) lower yield-bearing 'safe' assets, all of them entailing however for the savers, according to Terlizzese, informational requirements somewhat too heavy; hence the preferred solution is based on the incentives provided by reputation, which in a long-term credit relationship could substitute the actual evaluation of the riskiness of the bank's assets. But reputation is costly, for the intermediary is often forced to choose an amount of reserves larger than that resulting from a static optimisation, so that in general there is no guarantee that one of the agents would in fact choose to act as intermediary, unless the cost is decreasing with diversification.

Some features of the model are worth stressing: (1) whereas in Diamond the (costly) monitoring allows one under certain conditions to improve on an already feasible SDC in direct lending, here the screening activity is to some extent a prerequisite for a SDC; (2) even having removed the (*ex ante*) information asymmetry, the SDC between the intermediary and the borrowers is optimal; (3) on both asset and liability sides, together with well diversified information-intensive loans and debt, the model predicts the presence of reserves and of own-equity.

The ratonales that until now provided for the existence of financial intermediaries do not, however, apply uniquely to the deposit taking institutions. Indeed, as Terlizzese acknowledges, all the devices available for an intermediary to establish a reputation of credible commitments – a sufficiently extended time horizon or an initial large wealth – could also be used by ultimate debtors to borrow directly issuing *ex ante* riskless liabilities. A combination of debt and equity, bundled with a portfolio of unmarketable information-intensive assets, could thus characterise, rather than a deposit taking institution, a non-financial holding company with a sufficiently diversified range of businesses.

One further explanation of why banks are the unique issuers of demand instead of (or together with) time liabilities to our mind grounds their role in the payment system as distributors and producers of liquidity. This key step is realised in the contributions by Bryant (1980) and Diamond and Dybvig (1983), in which the issue of demand deposits is rationalised with the 'liquidity insurance' argument. Due to the *ex post* information asymmetry, uncertainty on the time profile of the liquidity requirements of agents cannot be coped with by private arrangements; the banks provide an insurance service against liquidity shocks through the issue of demand deposits, thus enhancing welfare.

The mismatch between illiquid assets (loans) and the perfectly liquid liabilities (demand deposits) is however the potential cause of bank runs. Early realisation of information-intensive assets forced on a solvent but temporarily illiquid bank could in fact cause a bankruptcy. The chance of such an event, with its spillover effects throughout the system, could spark, lacking some sort of savers' claims insurance, a generalised flight from deposits.[6]

To summarise, within the framework of information asymmetries, rationales are provided for a financial intermediary to hold in its diversified portfolio illiquid assets (loans) and 'safe' securities; the liabilities' counterpart bundle, equity and debt, is explained as well. Only the 'liquidity insurance' argument singles out, however, a particular intermediary, namely a bank, motivating among the debt liabilities the issue of demand deposits.

3   The banking firm and regulatory implications

The literature surveyed offers key insights for the existence of the typical features of a bank. What is still missing, though, is a thorough examination of the implications of the logical framework so far outlined for asset and liability management.[7]

Fama (1985) has indicated two avenues through which the information production via different banking functions has an impact both within the bank itself and in the market. First, the periodic assessment of the creditworthiness of borrowers implied by the renewal of short-term credit (be it a part or the totality of the credit granted to the entrepreneur) is not only a feasible internal monitoring device. The continuation of the customer relationship also signals to the market the good reputation of the borrower; thus, rather than being a substitute, the loans are complementary to the raising of funds directly from the market, which could even be unavailable to an entrepreneur without a performance track and/or costly to monitor. Analogously, the provision of a contingent back-up facility, entailing a binding commitment to create liquidity at request (Diamond and Dybvig, 1986), would act as an implicit rating of creditworthiness; the reputation-enhancing effect would however be strengthened by a firmer commitment of the bank's own resources through the extension of a loan.

Second, another link between the credit granting and the liquidity production is to be found in the easing of information collection through the management of the payments of the borrower, thus allowing a reduction in monitoring costs. This link, however, could be weaker the more these functions are performed by other intermediaries, as the evolution of the payment systems in developed countries shows.

In our opinion, a further, often overlooked, implication of the issue of demand deposits is the influence on the optimal choice of the balance sheet structure, as a consequence of the monitoring powers thus conferred on the depositors.

The need for an intermediary to maintain the confidence of both its customers and third parties restrains the choices on the portfolio and/or on the commitment of own resources. If it could be shown that the portfolio is held in stable-valued securities, then the costs of verifying the safety of depositors' claims would be reduced. The monitoring of the bank's portfolio could however necessitate too heavy informational requirements for the savers. Our claim is that the threat of a withdrawal of demand deposits alone is a feasible and informationally cheap device to deter the bank manager from pursuing a risky investment policy. Intuitively, the continuous monitoring, rather than the discrete one allowed by term liabilities, provides on its own a stricter check.

Besides, as a consequence of the random assessments of the quality of the bank's portfolio through deposit withdrawal and of the ensuing need to cope with the liquidity constraint, the managers are liable to a progressively tighter scrutiny over their choices. In fact, in order to offset a deposit drain there are three main alternatives:

(1) Selling marketable securities. The availability of a sufficient (in the market's perception) amount in the first place would signal the soundness of the bank.

(2) Purchasing funds in the wholesale or in the interbank market or via recourse to the central bank. This would amount to the managers being screened and monitored by operators more sophisticated than consumer depositors;

(3) Selling loans. This could imply high liquidation costs due to the private information they embed, with potential disruptive effects on solvency. The discount would in general be related to the market's perception of the shortage of liquidity as well as to the degree of risk accepted by the managers.

Despite the magnified likelihood of a run if ever rumours arose of inability to meet the terms of the sight deposit contract, the increasing costs of the three above alternatives of offsetting a liquidity drain on the one hand as well as, in a principal–agent setting, the signalling effects on the soundness of a bank on the other could motivate a large supply-driven component of sight liabilities, such as demand deposits. The case would be strengthened by considering the implications of the supply of contingent liabilities by the bank in its unique capacity of creator of new liquidity (Diamond and Dybvig, 1986).

The framework so far outlined allows us to examine key aspects of banking regulation. In fact, the coinsurance issue in a principal–agent setting points to the role of the own-equity resources and hence to the capital ratios requirements; the liquidity production, at the origin of runs, calls for the setting up of deposit insurance schemes; the unmarketability, due to the content of privileged information, of loans can provide grounds for conferring on a (public) agency the powers for a timely intervention in a troubled bank, thus preventing liquidation and the consequent fire-sales of the assets.

3.1   Capital requirements

Capital-to-assets ratios requirements have mostly to do with the coinsurance solution to the principal–agent problem, although they can also affect the illiquidity risk.

The asymmetric information–monitoring story, with the distinction between controlling (owners) and portfolio shareholders, gives a different interpretation to the problem of bank capital than do arguments based on risk diversification. In these latter theories the bank capital problem can be viewed as part of the optimal choice made by portfolio shareholders; in contrast, the former theory suggests that equity creates confidence among depositors (as well as non-controlling shareholders and other debt-holders), so that they are willing to provide their funds to the institution.

The difference between the two approaches can be illustrated by the prediction of the consequences of an exogenous shock that increases the riskiness of the investment in the bank equity. The portfolio model suggests a reduction of the risky component; the alternative view would instead recommend the opposite, to assure depositors and other non-controlling claim holders. In this instance, 'the equity rationing' argument of Greenwald *et al.* (1984) could however easily apply. Even with the owners' commitment enhanced by an additional inflow of own wealth, there could be difficulties in the collection of further equity capital, as it could be taken as a signal of the owners' dim view about the prospects of the bank, or else of a perceived loss of confidence by depositors.

The complementarity between the raising of equity and debt-type funds would suggest a role for both time – subordinated (or uninsured) debt – and demand deposits. In the first case, the renewal of the debt would allow a periodic assessment by informed investors of the performance of the bank, which could be signalled to the market through the required return on their investment; in the other, the collection of callable funds in the time intervals within each renewal of the previous type of debt would allow a continuous, though weaker, monitoring of the bank itself.

In this framework, compulsory minimum capital requirements can be assessed in a setting in which the public authorities' (principal) aim is strengthening the stability of the financial system through the reduction of the likelihood of a bank's (agent's) insolvency, because of the risky investment policy of the controlling private shareholders, and the ensuing costs to the taxpayers.[8] The coinsurance aspect of a minimum level of commitment of shareholders' resources should help restrain moral hazard effects or at least provide bounds to the extent of their risk taking (see Section 5.2 below on risk-related premia for some remarks on this topic).

3.2   Deposit insurance and timely restructuring

Normal or diversifiable risk in banking – namely interest rate, asset and liquidity risk – results basically from the production of liquidity, thus justifying a comprehensive approach to the stability problem.

Interest rate risk arises from the mismatch of maturities between assets and liabilities; asset risk derives from banks holding claims with uncertain returns against debt liabilities; in addition, disregarding the degree of marketability of assets, a portion of the liabilities is perfectly liquid, thus implying that amounts and timing of the withdrawals are unknown to the bank. Events such as deposit withdrawals or poor performance of assets are usually sufficiently independent to be coped with by ordinary insurance-type risk pooling and diversification, supplemented by capital ratios and liquid reserves.

Systematic or undiversifiable risk arises instead from a loss of confidence that the bank will meet its commitments and shows up in self-fulfilling runs, where each depositor tries to transfer the possible losses to the others anticipating the withdrawal of deposits. In this case, events are highly correlated, making it impossible to face them with ordinary policies.

This latter argument leads to the issue of the nature of the deposit insurance agency, as it suggests that a private one would not be credible and hence that government intervention could be unavoidable. Besides, a private deposit insurance scheme could not efficiently exploit the high degree of complementarity–substitutability between fair insurance premia and prudential regulation rules, determined prevalently by governmental bodies.

In fact, the setting of a fair deposit insurance premium is not independent of other regulatory constraints to which the banks can be subject. An insurance contract is fair when the present value of the liability faced by the insurer is exactly compensated by the premium paid by the insured agent. Thus, for instance, that liability is clearly inversely correlated with the capital-to-assets ratio, which represents indeed an implicit premium charged on the shareholders. The same reasoning applies to other forms of prudential controls (like limitations to loan concentration and liquid reserve requirements) which can lower both the expected return and the risk of banking activity. The fairness of a deposit insurance contract must therefore be judged on the basis of all these implicit and explicit premia, taking into account the possible trade-offs between them.[9]

In the light of the previous selective survey of the literature, two strong messages from a regulatory viewpoint come out.

The *prima facie* contradiction between the liquidity production through the issue of demand deposits, seen as a monitoring device for the depositors, and the deposit insurance, which would weaken such an instrument, could be coped with providing that any insurance scheme did not rule out, explicitly or implicitly, a bank defaulting; fully insured deposits, though with a low upper threshold, could be justified, if ever, only for equitable purposes.

The switch on of a pure deposit insurance scheme, after the liquidation of the bank, would however imply dissolving the bundle of information-intensive ties with its borrowers; consequently the minimisation of social costs could lead one to prefer an (impure) interventionist insurance system managed by an agency endowed with powers of timely restructuring for the problem bank. In addition, leaving aside the issue of the comparison of the costs caused by a bank failure relative to any other line of businesses,[10] transaction costs' considerations – such as the large number of creditors relative to debtors and the frequent turnover of both debtors and creditors which make costly the apportionment of claims – could motivate the choice of a preventive rather than a remedial (*ex post*) approach to the regulation.

4   The US deposit insurance scheme: motivations and drawbacks

Among the reasons behind the introduction of the federal deposit insurance in the early 1930s in the United States, three are usually singled out as the most important, namely the protection against a collapse of the money supply and of the payment system, the protection of small depositors, and the protection of unit – i.e. small local – banks (Benston and Kaufman, 1988). It seems worthwhile to start by examining whether these sources of concern are today still relevant and justify a public deposit insurance scheme, and what are its costs. The discussion refers to the US system,[11] where a sizeable literature has assessed the topic on both theoretical and empirical grounds; in the other major industrialised countries only recently have deposit insurance or protection schemes been introduced or restyled, though with important differences with respect to the US one.[12]

In principle, the deposit insurance is a preventive device to guarantee unconditionally the liquidity of the (sight component of) deposits, thus avoiding the possibility that the perception of a temporary difficulty of a bank to meet its commitments might spark a run; moreover, the automatic inflow of liquidity through the switch on of the insurance scheme would avoid, even in the case of inability of the monetary authorities fully to compensate, as in the early 1930s, the risk that a flight from deposits to cash might disrupt the money supply. The other channel of provision of liquidity, that is the lending of last resort, involves instead an *ex post*, mostly collateralised (through sterilised discount window lending or open market operations) discretionary intervention with respect to illiquid but solvent banks, aimed at implementing monetary targets at the macro level (Goodfriend and King, 1988).

It has been often remarked, however, that events such as the flight from deposits to (domestic) currency are a rather unlikely event in today's economies, given that the more widespread is the role of banks in the payment system, the less important are the leakages from deposits to currency and hence the lower the likelihood of a contraction in the money supply. A drain in the deposits of a bank could in fact simply imply a re-deposit in the remaining ones, with only second order effects on the money multiplier.

The equitable case of the 'small or uninformed depositors' protection' can be rationalised on the grounds that, because of costs of information gathering and processing, some people need guidance to avoid unsustainable wealth losses. In today's developed financial systems, with a large component of household wealth managed by institutional investors and consumers' increasing financial sophistication, the case for the deposit insurance looks however rather weak, even leaving aside the implied disincentives to acquire information. At any rate, costs and benefits of ways of protecting small depositors' wealth as an alternative to deposit insurance should be preliminarily assessed so to provide it in the most cost effective way. For instance, it has been suggested that the government could allow an income tax credit so that the depositors could deduct their losses, up to a legislated maximum (Chant, 1987). More fundamentally, the small depositor argument clashes with the main aim of the deposit insurance, namely the prevention of runs, which *per se* requires that no upper limit be set. Indeed, any depositor afraid even of a minimum loss would have the incentive of starting the run, exactly the event to be prevented in the first place.

Whereas the first two macroeconomic motivations of deposit insurance seem to us in today's economic environment of a lesser importance (see, however, Section 5.4 below), the third one, which refers to the efficient handling at the micro level of the problem banks, appears the most relevant and justifies the public nature of the insurance agency.

In accordance with the view of banks as inside lenders it has been emphasised that, instead of focussing on the liability side, the effects of a deposit drain should rather be evaluated with reference to its asset counterpart, that is the economic costs of the disruption of customer relationships, most importantly with the ultimate debtors (Bernanke, 1983). Even with an unchanged aggregate money stock, the unmarketability of these information-intensive assets at the micro level would not only further reduce the economic net worth of the bank, conceivably transforming an illiquid though otherwise financially sound institution in an insolvent one, but would cause deadweight losses to the borrowers. They would not be able to recover the bank-specific costs in building up credit relationships; in addition to the transaction costs of changing the bank partner they could face a credibility crisis in the financial market, sparked by the troubles of their creditworthiness signaller. This last effect would have further distributive consequences, as it would be enhanced the smaller–younger or anyway less established the firm.

The US unit banking system, inhibiting a nationwide portfolio diversification, is less effective in absorbing the effects of macroeconomic shocks,[13] thus making the small local banks more liable to insolvency. The increased likelihood of runs then raises the issue of the credibility of the deposit protection through insurance. As an *ex ante* device to avoid the threat that rumours of illiquidity will spark a run only a public insurance scheme appears viable and credible, being immune from paucity of resources. In turn, the role of the public authority in shaping, through the design of the insurance policy and also of the related regulation and supervision policies, the portfolio choices of the bank, can help to restrain moral hazard effects.

The well known drawbacks of the flat rate premia, namely the weakening of the market discipline and the incentive for banks' riskier portfolios, require only a brief treatment. As for the first aspect, insured depositors have no incentives to choose a bank carefully and to monitor its behaviour; unless regulators have a policy of timely intervention in potentially insolvent institutions, it is up to the shareholders, the uninsured depositors and the other subordinate claims' holders to impose market discipline. However, even these agents could be induced to a passive attitude, should the perception arise that, because of the policies applied towards some large banks through bail-out operations and the like, some banks are too big to fail and all deposits are, *de facto*, protected. From the banks' viewpoint, the flat rate insurance provides them with a no-risk source of funding, as the insured depositors need not be compensated (through higher interest rates) when substantial risks are undertaken.

On both grounds, the capital base that would be chosen falls below the minimum required to fend off abnormal withdrawals; *ceteris paribus*, the deposit insurance scheme, combined with the shareholders' limited liability, creates an incentive for riskier bank portfolios.

5   Deposit insurance: current issues

In the following three sub-sections we examine the main proposals aimed at reforming the current deposit insurance system in the United States. We consider first of all the radical proposal of the 'narrow bank', which according to its proponents could help to remove the liquidity risk itself; on the grounds that this suggestion does not conform with the characteristics proper to a deposit taking institution, we examine the issues of the risk-related insurance premia and of the timely reorganisation policies. In the fourth sub-section we explore some implications of the integration of the European financial markets for the working of domestic deposit insurance schemes.

5.1   Narrow bank

A drastic solution to the deposit run, sparked by illiquidity risk, is the proposal to impose a 100 per cent reserve requirement, so that intermediaries offering demand deposits could hold only cash or interest-bearing liquid government claims or securities (Kareken, 1986).

Leaving aside the feasibility issue of the supply of enough short paper in the economy, the net effect of such a policy would be to divide the banking industry into two components: the regulated part supplying liability side services, like a money market mutual fund; the other part offering the maturity transformation services. Even if banks would now be 'almost' fail-proof (see below), the proposal would just pass along to their substitutes in the intermediary business the instability problem, which arises from the financing of illiquid assets with short-term fixed claims (which need not be demand deposits).

Moreover, as Benston and Kaufman (1988) point out, if the 100 per cent reserve requirement were satisfied with interest-bearing government securities instead of with central bank balances, the Treasury would have to guarantee to redeem all the securities at par value; otherwise, interest rate increases could reduce the market value of the securities below the par value of the deposits, and the institution could become insolvent.

Thus the only condition under which the modern fail-safe bank would be equivalent to the Simons–Friedman 100 per cent reserve requirement institution would be if it held monetary base. But, then, the issue of the economic viability of the purely payment intermediary would become crucial. As an aside, even if the narrow banks were prevented from taking asset and interest rate risks, they would still be liable to, admittedly less relevant, operating risks; the spillover effects of the participation in the payment network would still leave ample room for regulatory practices.

The main drawback of the proposal of the narrow bank is however that it considers just *one* of the services offered by a bank, namely the payments service, disregarding the transfer of risk and the production of liquidity associated with the lending activity, each of them exploiting externalities from the joint production of the banking services. As stressed by Diamond and Dybvig (1986), overlooking the distinction between the 'distribution' and the 'production' of liquidity, the proposal would adversely affect the borrowers who currently are not dependent on banks, such as firms raising short-term funds on the market *and* demanding back-up lines of credit, in order to be able to tap an emergency source to circumvent a potential liquidity need. Offering binding lines of credit that are not fully collateralised by the liquidation value of assets is one way of providing the typical bank transformation service, as it is functionally equivalent to issue demand deposits. Providers of this transformation service other than banks would thus still be liable to runs.

To summarise, should the 'no payment' banks be unable to issue short-term liquid claims, the proposal would be dangerous, as it would end up reducing the overall amount of liquidity; otherwise, also these bank-like intermediaries would be liable to the liquidity risk.

5.2   *Risk-related premia*

The advantage of risk-based insurance premia is the ability to restrain the amplitude of the moral hazard and the cross-subsidisation among banks implied by the present scheme of flat premia.

The disregard of the riskiness of the bank's portfolio in fact increases *ceteris paribus* the liability of the insurer, leaving unchanged the risk (and hence the compensation) of the insured depositors. Thus, if the controlling shareholders are less risk averse than depositors, bank managers will have an incentive to undertake riskier strategies. The nature of the moral hazard problem itself indicates the way to solve it, that is: internalise the cost of a riskier strategy to the bank, by making the deposit insurance premium correlated to the risk incurred. The other drawback of a flat premium is that it forces safer banks to subsidise riskier ones, thereby inducing an undesirable distortion in the market mechanism.[14] Indeed, all empirical studies estimating risk-based deposit insurance premia show that the distribution should be quite skewed, with most banks paying below average premia.[15]

The advantages of risk-related premia notwithstanding, the debate is open on two major controversial points.

First, risk-related premia would be simply redundant, in the presence of a set of regulations (such as the 1988 BIS risk-weighted capital ratio requirements) which enable the supervisory authorities to charge implicit premia on the banks. Indeed, an insurance premium can be made fair even if it is flat, by modifying the probability of failure of the bank, which in turn can be achieved by regulatory and examination procedures.

It could however be argued that there cannot be a perfect equivalence between the two devices, since while the implicit premia impose a constraint which may or may not be binding on the probability of bank failure, the risk-related ones are a more flexible instrument, influencing at the margin the risk incentive of bank management over a range of possible choices. Let us take, for example, the risk-weighted minimum capital requirements, which can easily be seen as setting a ceiling to the probability of bank failure. If such a ceiling happens to be binding for all banks, so that all of them are aligned on the same probability of failure, then risk-related insurance premia are redundant; if for some banks ceilings are slack, so that the probability of failure can differ cross-sectionally, then risk-related premia would be useful in order to discriminate between riskier and safer banks.

Second, in a macroeconomic perspective, there could be undesirable effects on some debtors, as the risk bearing would be shifted from the financial to the non-financial sector (Goodman and Santomero, 1986). As banks would tend to modify their assets' composition by making more costly and/or less available the credit to those categories of debtors which increased the riskiness of their portfolio (and, consequently, the burden of the insurance premium), the reduction in the probability of bank failure guaranteed by the risk-based insurance mechanism would tend to be counterbalanced by a greater probability of failure of some debtors. Although this is in principle what correct risk-pricing should indeed achieve, a comprehensive assessment of the social costs incurred because of the failure of a bank or of debtors (such as new–high growth firms) could justify a public agency accepting an underpricing of the insurance coverage.

A related subtler problem is tied in with the undiversifiable component of risk originating from the busienss cycle. Intuitively, the economic prospects of most firms worsen in the downswing; should correspondingly the *average* insurance premium increase, borrowers already affected by the cyclical phase would further bear the higher cost of the loans. On the other hand, it would seem rather cumbersome to devise cycle-adjusted risk-related premia over the maturity span of the loan. Incidentally, it can be noted that the same problem applies to risk-weighted capital ratios, which also tend to alter the asset composition and pricing of banks in an unfavourable way for riskier debtors (Kim and Santomero, 1988).

This type of macroeconomic objection notwithstanding, the implementation of risk-related premia would overall make more transparent and correct the mechanism of deposit insurance. In fact, under the current system of flat premia, riskier banks receive an implicit subsidy not only from other (safer) banks, but also – in the event of an overall underpricing of deposit insurance – from the insuring agency and, in the end, from the lender of last resort, who stays *de facto* ready to cover the uninsured deposits as well as the insurance agency itself. As an end result, the whole economic system implicitly and unknowingly subsidises – through the banking system and the lender of last resort – the riskier economic activities, because of an improper pricing of risk. A system where all deposits are explicitly insured with appropriate risk-related premia would not only force banks to price the credit correctly in relation to the debtors' riskiness, but also would openly let the society assess whether to subsidise riskier lines of business, avoiding improperly charging bank managers with distributive as well as with allocative tasks.

In the end, however, the main obstacle to the implementation of risk-related premia comes from the practical difficulties in their estimation, as they should relate to the marginal increase of risk of each bank rather than to the risk of the class of instruments considered on its own, as in the case of the risk-weighted capital requirements.[16] Many solutions have been proposed in the literature (see FDIC, 1989), falling into two main categories based on (a) market information – some forms of private insurance or coinsurance, interest rates paid on uninsured liabilities, applications of the option pricing – and (b) information directly collected by the supervisory authority.

As for the first set of solutions, it has already been argued that a purely private deposit insurance appears infeasible, due to the impossibility of diversifying the risk causing the runs. Some type of coinsurance could be preferable, where a small portion of deposits would be privately insured, with the remainder left to the public agency, at a price set equal to that of the private one (Baer, 1985). This solution would exploit the market expertise to determine the insurance price, and at the same time the ability of a public agency to cope with the systematic risk. Another way of relying on the market evaluation would be to infer from interest rates the risk premium paid by the banks on their uninsured liabilities.[17] The main objection to this method is that its accuracy would suffer from any market imperfection, such as: a non-competitive deposit market, high transaction costs, and above all the expectation of a *de facto* coverage for all deposits of the large banks.

A third method of estimating premia exploiting market information is the one derived from the option pricing theory.[18] A deposit insurance contract is seen as a put option on bank assets, issued by the agency in favour of the equity holders of the bank: the latter ones may choose to 'sell' the assets to the former at the exercise price equal to the face value of the insured liabilities. Formulae originally developed for option pricing may then be applied to the estimation of the premia, which is equivalent to the value of the option; they are in general a function of five variables: the nominal value of insured deposits (corresponding to the exercise price); the market value of assets; the variability of such value and the risk-free interest rate (both variables rather heroically assumed to be constant); and, finally, the time to maturity or lifetime of the option, measured by the interval between bank examinations, when the market value of the bank can be only conjectured.

A major difficulty in implementing this method is that it requires a market evaluation of the equity, which is not always feasible for all the banks (due to the underdevelopment of the stock market and/or to the public sector's ownership). Moreover, relevant measurement errors may be present in the estimation of bank assets' value and variability from data on stock prices. Such difficulties are reflected in the remarkable differences among the various estimates of deposit insurance premia available in the literature (even with regard to homogeneous samples).

In addition to the 'technical' drawbacks of market-based methods of estimating deposit insurance premia, a major theoretical objection arises from the content of private information of the banking activity itself. Borrowers demand loans – rather than issuing marketable securities – precisely because public information on their economic and financial positions is not available (or too costly to obtain); markets should not then be expected to evaluate accurately the prospects of a bank.

Indeed, market evaluations of banks' risk seem to be primarily based on their past and current performance, thus entailing substantial limitations for their efficacy in estimating risk, because (1) estimates may have only a short time horizon, becoming unstable for longer periods; (2) if risk is detected only when it has resulted in losses and then incorporated in higher premia, the insurance mechanism loses much of its preventive capabilities; (3) premia based on '*ex post*' information can further penalise, being wrongly timed for institutions already in difficulty.

The difficulties of implementing market-based risk-related premia could induce one to exploit the ability of the supervisory authorities to obtain 'inside' information in order to develop '*ex ante*' measures of risk. The use of the CAMEL ratings[19] for such a purpose has been for instance considered in the United States (FDIC, 1989). A major drawback of these proposals is that they do not take into account the confidentiality of such information, with the likely trade-off between the spread of 'reliable private' information and its quality deterioration in order not to enable competitors to exploit it to their advantage.

Summarising, although desirable in principle, the setting-up of a system of risk-related deposit insurance premia still poses substantial conceptual and estimation problems; the methods based on market information need in particular further research before providing applicable results.

5.3   Timely restructuring policies

Rather than intervening only after the manifestation of a bank crisis, covering any (*ex-ante* predetermined) depositors' loss, it could be preferable to increase the preventive capabilities of the public insurance agency (or at any rate one endowed with powers of intervention over private institutions) through the provision of a range of timely implementable devices aimed at avoiding the risk that the economic net worth of the bank might fall below some threshold limit and hence might spark a confidence crisis.

In many respects, such proposals match closely the microfoundations of the bank previously surveyed.

First, the reference to the economic rather than the accounting net worth, despite all the difficulties in implementing suitable indicators,[20] stresses the forward-looking approach of the insurance deposit scheme. The unmarketability of a portion of the assets implies large enough liquidation costs to make it often preferable to an insurer to intervene in advance, through restructuring and merging, to avoid altogether the emergence of the insured event (or effectively to cancel the insurance cover). This type of policy could thus prevent the disruption of the customers' relationships and hence the loss of the ongoing value of the problem bank. As Horvitz (1983) emphasises, it is the time factor – the delay in closing down a bank running into difficulties – that is often responsible for turning an *ex ante* risk position into an *ex post* loss-making state.[21] With a purely insurance scheme, it is in the interest of both short-sighted supervisors and (potentially fired off) bank managers to defer the closure in the hope of some recovery or rescue.

Second, subordinated claims (be they non-controlling shares or debt) holders could be willing to signal to the market their commitment to the bank providing additional resources, so to reestablish an adequate capital-to-assets ratio. Should they not do it voluntarily, a timely request of the agency would lead them to disclose their intentions. A refusal to comply could lead the agency to take over the management of the bank, with the loss of the rights for the not-to-be-protected claim holders.

Third, though the timely interventions alone would not prevent a run, they would still reinforce the dissuasion effects over the actions of managers and of uncommitted shareholders of banks of any size. In particular, should a public agency intervene, the bargaining power of those banks 'too big to fail' would be checked, thus removing the unequitable distinction between small and large ones.

Fourth, the intensive monitoring and the intervention at an early stage of the crisis, possibly started with unusual deposits withdrawals, by reducing the costs for the insurer, would allow a rebate of the premia and thus minimise the cross-subsidisation from safer to riskier banks.

To sum up, if banks were closed before their net worth became negative, depositors would be protected and no losses would be imposed on the insurance agency nor eventually on the tax payers; premia would be needed only to pay for the operational expenses.

The timely reorganisation policies recommended most particularly by Benston and Kaufman (1988) require explicit criteria for a public intervention with respect to banks, exploiting the many options open to a public cost-minimising insurance agency. Despite the normative efficacy, in promoting competition, of letting inefficiently run institutions go bust, once the characteristics of a bank as a bundle of assets and liabilities which cannot be, after the dissolution, market-priced on an item-by-item basis and the welfare costs of disruption of customers' relationships in an economy plagued by imperfect information are taken seriously, the goal of devising a coherent system of timely implementable trouble-resolution policies fits naturally the theoretical framework of the banking firm outlined in the chapter. Indeed, contrary to the usual justifications for a bank being 'too large to fail', the prejudice against failure should rather apply to the small–local ones, less likely to be substitutable by other institutions in providing funds for the young–high growth firms they mostly deal with, and whose ability to raise funds in the market is low or nil.

5.4   Domestic deposit insurance in the transition to integrated financial markets

We have argued that the main rationale of the US deposit insurance is to be found in the intervention powers to handle problem institutions in a banking sytem more easily affected by external shocks as a consequence of the geographical limitations in portfolio diversification (not to mention the further constraint as to the type of assets allowed under the commercial–investment banking divide). On the contrary, the European banking systems are more concentrated, due also to the nation-wide branch banking, and with a sizeable public sector ownership. These factors contribute to lessen the risk that bank troubles, at any rate less probably caused by insufficient portfolio diversification, might affect depositors, so far *de facto* protected through the policy of bailing out insolvent institutions.

Why is it then that since the late 1970s the largest EC countries have implemented or strengthened already existing domestic deposit protection schemes? They are characterised by mutual–voluntaristic arrangements among the member banks, with an informal involvement of the Central Bank and/or of the supervisory authorities, whereas they often lack some key features of the system currently operating in the United States, namely own resources through the *ex ante* funding scheme, the facility of temporary financing by the Treasury and the public status, with the impaired regulatory powers, of the agency.

The main reason seems to have been, on the whole, to relieve the monetary authorities, empowered with the lending of last resort and the general supervisory activity, of the tasks of monitoring and managing potential bank crisis at the micro level. Contrary to the US experience, however, most of the motivations behind that deposit insurance system are not present, lacking two central prerequisites: a previous experience of bank failures implying depositors' losses and the widespread presence of private shareholders and other subordinated debtholders acting so as to impose the market discipline upon the management.

The as yet hybrid nature of the deposit protection schemes implemented in the EC countries could indeed result from the only partial adherence to the market rules of (publicly owned) large components of the banking systems;[22] this is rather worrying because while in the transition to the full markets' integration the efficacy of domestic (i.e. for deposits at local branches of resident banks) insurance schemes is not foolproof.

Let us consider a macroeconomic rationale for the introduction of the deposit insurance in the United States, namely the prevention of shocks to the money supply in case of lack of intervention by the lender of last resort, anyway made less compelling because in a *financially closed economy* the flight from the deposits to cash is unlikely, with no repercussions to the aggregate money supply (except for an increase in precautionary reserves by banks). In a *financially open economy*, a flight from deposits held domestically to deposits held abroad could instead cause a reduction in the domestic money supply, which could not however be offset by the switching on of a domestic deposit insurance scheme.

The uniqueness of loans as well as small depositors' protection arguments lose much of their relevance. Foreign banks entering another country's market are in fact likely to be less dependent on the privileged information content of lending – they will do their business with top customers – and on the retail funds – until well established, they will collect resources wholesale via marketable instruments such as large CDs or, most likely, through the interbank market.

The rather generalised absence of insurance cover for the interbank deposits in the European countries – a remarkable difference with the United States – seems coherent with an implicit reliance on the reciprocal monitoring role which, missing a supranational authority, uninsured peer banks and other informed agents can exercise.

Indeed, in a setting where supervision is hampered by the absence of a unified supervisory framework, the checks by peer banks operating in the uninsured wholesale deposits market appear the most (only) effective ones. On the one hand, in fact, the deficiency as yet of world-wide consolidated accounts weakens (because of lack of information) the case for an effective monitoring role of domestic consumer creditors and of subordinated claims holders; on the other hand, entrusting different monetary authorities with the supervision of aspects of an essentially unique business – such as assigning to the Central Bank of the home country the supervision for the solvency of the parent bank on a consolidated basis, leaving the supervision for the liquidity (i.e. the deposits) to the monetary authorities of the host country, according to the 1983 (revised) Basle Concordat – can create an incentive for the exploitation of the arbitrage opportunities created by different domestic deposits' protection systems.

In this environment, the monitoring role of peer informed operators could be exploited or even motivated, restating a recent proposal by Baltensperger and Dermine (1987) of adding to the *ex ante* funding of the domestic insurance agency an *ex post* penalty funding system. Their point is that in order to enhance the depositors' incentives for bank monitoring, not only shareholders but also current and former depositors of the troubled bank(s) should bear the costs incurred by the insurance agency. 'The major difference between the *ex post* penalty and deposit insurance is that, in the first case, losses are borne by depositors while, in the second case, they are shifted to the deposit insurance agencies and, in the case of deposit insurance failure, to the lender of last resort. The complete privatization of costs in the *ex post* penalty system is a clear advantage' (Baltensperger and Dermine, 1987, p. 82). Unfortunately, the feasibility chances of such a proposal seem rather small, as remarked by Goodhart (1987b), due to the difficulties in determining when, and how, the run begins, or the date after which a former depositor would still be liable, or how to reach non-residents and others whose status has changed in the meantime.

On top of the absence of the insurance cover for the interbank deposits, a charge for the domestic banks to contribute on an *ex post* basis to replenish the own resources of the national agency, should they fall below some threshold (see, for the latter proposal of reform of the US system, FDIC, 1989) would preserve the gist of the Baltensperger and Dermine proposal, namely the at least partial internalisation of the moral hazard effects.

6   Concluding comments

In this chapter, drawing on the logical framework derived from the asymmetric information literature on financial intermediation, we have assessed some proposals of reform of the US deposit insurance system. The main conclusions we draw are that:

(a)   The undiversifiable component of bank risk, connected with the occurrence of runs, calls for a public insuring agency credibly endowed with sufficient own resources to pay off insured deposits.

(b)   In order to motivate depositors to monitor the bank managers (acting on behalf of controlling shareholders), the upper threshold of insured deposits should be low, once the diminished strength of the case for the 'uninformed small depositor' has been taken into account.

(c)   Risk-related premia are desirable, but as yet difficult to implement, for both empirical and logical reasons. The latter derive in particular from the unavailability for the market of the private information produced through the lending activity.

(d)   A cost-minimising insurance agency should prevent the liquidation event of a bank, as the ongoing value of the institution would rapidly shrink because of the disruption of the information-intensive customer relationships. Hence, the set of proposals of reform that better fit the adopted theoretical framework are those advocating an agency endowed with powers of timely restructuring.

The European banking systems are somewhat different from the US one, because they are more concentrated, lessening the instability coming from both high competition and insufficient portfolio diversification of small–local banks, the public sector ownership is widespread and the monetary authorities are traditionally more involved in managing problem banks at the micro level. For these reasons, in recent years, in order to cope with the probable effects of the intensifying competition in deregulated financial markets, many European countries have implemented or strengthened the already existing deposit protection schemes, although with as yet ill-defined goals, resources and powers. This raises some doubts about their efficacy, further weakened by their domestic scope in the wake of the process of integration of the EC financial markets.

In a longer-term perspective, a cost-effective deposit insurance scheme in a unified European financial area will be viable if institutional reforms in the banking system structure shift from peer banks, as it now implicitly has because of the absence of cover for the interbank deposits, to the private shareholders and to the subordinated debtholders as well as to the depositors the task of implementing the market discipline. It is our opinion that the examination of the US experience provides useful insights on how effectively to manage the challenges arising in this new context.

Notes

1 We thank Rony Hamaui, Mario Monti, Gianni Pittaluga, Marco Ratti and Daniele Terlizzese for useful comments.

2 Chant (1987) and Giannini (1986) provide a detailed review of this literature, in connection with the issues of banking regulation and supervision.

3 These features refer to a commercial bank, not entitled to provide equity resources to a firm as in the case of a universal bank.

4 A standard debt contract (SDC) is a sharing contract whereby the borrower agrees to pay a fixed amount in all states of nature, remaining a residual claimant to income, except for the state(s) of bankruptcy, in which the net worth of the project is appropriated by the lenders.

5 This is indeed suggestive of what a universal bank does, when it subscribes shares issued by some of its borrowers. It must be noted, however, that even this mode of resource transfer is generally accompanied by the more traditional one of the loan.

6 Actually, as Kaufman (1988) remarks, Diamond and Dybvig consider only a run on the banking system as a whole. Should a run hit a sub-set of the banking system, however, it would rather represent an indirect redeposit, which would probably not lead to an economy-wide contraction in total deposits. They also consider, in a partial equilibrium setting, only runs into consumption rather than currency. In a general equilibrium perspective, the negative consequences of a bank run could be at least partially offset by the multiplier effects of higher consumption.

7 For an interesting example in this direction see Conti and Noera (1988).

8 This further constraint can however motivate a riskier policy of the banks, thus at least partially offsetting its aimed at effects (Kim and Santomero, 1988).

9 A theoretical appraisal of the interdependence between capital ratios and deposit insurance premia is made by Sharpe (1981). Buser et al. (1981) remark that the recognition of the existence of implicit as well as explicit prices for the FDIC insurance allows us to see that the agency achieves a comparable effect by employing a risk-related structure of implicit premia in the form of regulatory interference. Recent developments in banking supervision are examined in De Felice et al. (1988).

10 For contrasting views see Kaufman (1988), who points out that the uniqueness of the bank–customer relationship is more an exception than the norm, and Goodhart (1987a), who stresses the costs to the borrowers of having to switch the source of loans from the troubled institution to other sound ones.

11 Our analysis focusses on the Federal Deposit Insurance Corporation (FDIC), whose main features are the following: membership is compulsory for all bank members of the Fed system; the funding is based on flat premia, with the

possibility of *ex post* rebates; temporary financing facility with the US Treasury, up to \$3 bn; all deposits (including CDs and interbank) are covered up to \$100,000; the range of possible interventions, given the overall goal of own-cost minimisation, with the explicit proviso of the discretionality in singling out essential banks not allowed to fail, goes from financial assistance to temporarily illiquid banks to the management of an insolvent bank's crisis; the FDIC is also entitled to carry out supervisory activities. As of August 1989, following the approval by Congress of the Financial Institutions Reform, Recovery and Enforcement Act, the FDIC absorbed the Federal Savings and Loan Insurance Corporation (FSLIC). A smaller agency, the National Credit Unions Insurance Fund, was created in 1970 for the Federal Credit Unions.

12 For fuller discussion, see the Appendix in the enlarged Italian version of this study (Baglioni and Marotta, 1991). Very briefly, in contrast to the United States, the European deposit insurance systems are generally the result of voluntary agreements among member banks, with a largely private administration (somewhere jointly with the Central Bank). Accordingly, they do not have supervisory and regulating powers. Their powers to intervene and manage a bank crisis in order to avoid liquidation is also quite limited compared with the US system. The funding is usually set on an *ex post* basis. For a cross-country summary of the main features of the deposit insurance schemes, see Table 13.1.

Table 13.1 *Deposit protection schemes for commercial and savings banks in seven countries*

	USA	Japan	UK	France	Germany	Italy	Spain
Membership[a]	C[d]	C	C	V	V	V	V
Administration[b]	PU	J	PU	PR	PR	J	J
Funding[c]	E.A.[e]	E.A.	E.A.[f]	E.P.	E.A.[f]	E.P.	E.A.
	F.P.	F.P.	F.P.	F.P.[g]	F.P.	F.P.[g]	F.P.
Access to lender of last resort financing	NO	YES	NO	NO	NO	NO	YES
Supervisory powers of insuring agency	YES	NO	NO	NO	NO	NO	YES
Deposit coverage:							
– limited amount	YES	YES	YES	YES	YES	YES	YES
– interbank	YES	NO	NO	NO	NO	NO	NO
– foreign currency	YES	NO	NO	NO	YES	YES	NO
– at local branches of foreign banks	YES	NO	YES	YES	YES	YES	YES
– at branches abroad of domestic banks	NO	NO	NO	NO	YES	YES	NO

[a] V = Voluntary, C = Compulsory.
[b] PU = Public authority, PR = Private arrangements among banks, J = Joint.
[c] E.A. = *Ex ante*, E.P. = *Ex post*, F.P. = Flat premia.
[d] Only for nationally chartered banks and members of Fed system.
[e] With *ex post* rebate.
[f] With *ex post* additional contributions.
[g] With a regressive scale.

13 The nearly 6,000 bank failures that occurred during the 1920s in the United States were of small unit banks in agricultural regions. By contrast in Canada,

with nationwide branch banking, many branches in agricultural regions closed, but no bank failed (Bordo, 1989).

14 As Goodhart (1987a) remarks, in a dynamic perspective a case could be made for this distributive effect, as it could help new (and presumably riskier) banks to enter the market, thus avoiding the occurrence of an increasing concentration.

15 Unfortunately, up to now such studies are available (as far as we know) only for the United States and Canada. See, for example: Ronn and Verma (1986), Marcus and Shaked (1984), McCulloch (1985), Avery *et al.* (1985) and, for Canada, Gianmarino *et al.* (1989).

16 As far as capital requirements are concerned, disregarding the likely degree of arbitrariness behind their determination, their major drawbacks are that: first, they take into account only the asset risk, while they do not consider the interest rate and the liquidity risks coming from the maturity mismatching between bank assets and liabilities; second, they consider only the risk specific to each bank asset, failing to take into account the correlations among the risks of different assets, obviously of great importance in determining the performance of the portfolio; finally, they concentrate only on the asset side of balance sheets, leaving aside the correlation between returns on assets and on liabilities.

17 See Thompson (1987). Hannan and Hanweck (1988) provide evidence of the existence of such a risk premium on American CD's larger than $100,000 (not covered by deposit insurance).

18 As far as we know, studies of this kind are available only for the United States and for Canada. See Avery *et al.* (1985), McCulloch (1985), Crouhy and Galai (1986), Pyle (1986), Ronn and Verma (1986), Pennacchi (1987), Penati and Protopapadakis (1988) and, for Canada, Gianmarino *et al.* (1989).

19 CAMEL ratings (referred to capital adequacy, asset quality, management, earnings and liquidity) are assigned to each US bank after periodical onsite examinations by the supervisory authorities.

20 See however Berger, Kuester and O'Brien (1989) who, starting from the acknowledged unmarketability of a part of bank assets, provide some recommendations for a more realistic accounting system, combining the elements of both market and book value methods.

21 Horvitz (1983) forcibly argues that advocates of risk-related premiums have been imprecise as to the meaning of 'risk of bank failure', often identified with the risk to an insurance system, as if deposit insurance were like life insurance. For a life insurance company, risk of death of the insured and risk of loss to the insurance company are identical. But the analogy is not as valid as the one with the fire insurance. 'Risk to the insurer is not the same as the risk of fire. Other variables, such as how quickly the fire is detected, whether there are sprinklers, and how quickly the fire department responds, affect the extent of the damage and the cost to the insurer. Small fires quickly extinguished that do less damage than the deductible in the policy may be very disturbing and expensive to the insured, but represent no loss to the insurance company' (Horvitz, 1983).

22 Out of the 100 largest banks in the EC countries in 1987, 43 were publicly controlled and 14 of a cooperative and mutual type. Their respective asset shares were 40.9 and 12.5 per cent (Revell, 1988).

References

Avery, R. B., G. A. Hanweck and M. L. Kwast (1985) 'An Analysis of Risk-Based

Deposit Insurance for Commercial Banks', in Federal Reserve Bank of Chicago, *Bank Structure and Competition* (May).

Baer, H. (1985) 'Private Prices, Public Insurance: the Pricing of Federal Deposit Insurance', Federal Reserve Bank of Chicago, *Economic Perspectives* (September-October).

Baglioni, A. and G. Marotta (1991) 'L'assicurazione dei depositi: implicazioni della teoria dell'intermediazione finanziaria', in V. Conti and R. Hamaui, (eds), *Operatori e mercati nel processo di liberalizzazione*, vol. III, Bologna: Il Mulino.

Baltensperger, E. and J. Dermine (1987) 'Banking Deregulation in Europe', *Economic Policy*, **2(1)**: 64–109.

Benston, D. and G. G. Kaufman (1988) 'Risk and Solvency Regulation of Depository Institutions: Past Policies and Current Options', Monograph Series in Finance and Economics, **1988–1**, Salomon Brothers Center for the Study of Financial Institutions and New York University.

Berger, A. N., K. A. Kuester and J. M. O'Brien (1989) 'Some Red Flags Concerning Market Value Accounting', *Finance and Economics Discussion Series*, Federal Reserve Board, **85** (August).

Bernanke, B.S. (1983) 'Nonmonetary Effects of the Financial Crisis in the Propagation of the Great Depression', *American Economic Review*, **73(3)**: 257–76.

Black, F. (1970) 'Banking and Interest Rates in a World Without Money', *Journal of Bank Research*, **1(3)** (Autumn): 8–28.

Bordo, M. D. (1989) 'The Lender of Last Resort: Some Historical Insights', *NBER Working Paper*, **3011** (June).

Bryant, J. (1980) 'A Model of Reserves, Bank Runs, and Deposit Insurance', *Journal of Banking and Finance*, **4**: 335–44.

Buser, S. A., A. H. Chen and E. J. Kane (1981) 'Federal Deposit Insurance, Regulatory Policy, and Optimal Bank Capital', *Journal of Finance*, **35(1)**: 51–60.

Chan, Y. (1983) 'On the Positive Role of Financial Intermediation in Allocation of Venture Capital in a Market With Imperfect Information', *Journal of Finance*, **38**: 1543–68.

Chant, J. (1987) 'Regulation of Financial Institutions – A Functional Analysis', *Bank of Canada Technical Reports*, **45**.

Conti, V. and M. Noera (1988) 'Quale banca per il mercato o quale mercato per la banca: le ragioni di una ricerca ancora aperta', in Banca Commerciale Italiana, *Banca e Mercato*, Bologna: Il Mulino.

Crouhy, M. and D. Galai (1986) 'An Economic Assessment of Capital Requirements in the Banking Industry', *Journal of Banking and Finance*, **10(2)**.

De Felice, G., D. Masciandaro and A. Porta (1988) 'Evoluzione del sistema bancario nella struttura finanziaria e problemi di regolamentazione: un'analisi comparata', in Banca Commerciale Italiana, *Banca e Mercato*, Bologna: Il Mulino.

Diamond, D. W. (1984) 'Financial Intermediation and Delegated Monitoring', *Review of Economic Studies*, **51** (July): 393–414.

Diamond, D. W. and P. H. Dybvig (1983) 'Bank Runs, Deposit Insurance, and Liquidity', *Journal of Political Economy*, **91(3)**: 401–19.

Diamond, D. W. and P. H. Dybvig (1986) 'Banking Theory, Deposit Insurance and Bank Regulation', *Journal of Business*, **59(1)**: 55–68.

Fama, E. F. (1980) 'Banking in the Theory of Finance', *Journal of Monetary Economics*, **6(1)**: 39–57.

Fama, E. F. (1985) 'What's Different About Banks?', *Journal of Monetary Economics*, **15(1)**: 29–39.

Federal Deposit Insurance Corporation (FDIC) (1989) *Deposit Insurance for the Nineties. Meeting the Challenge* (staff study).

Gianmarino, R., E. Schwartz and J. Zechner (1989) 'Market Valuation of Bank Assets and Deposit Insurance in Canada', *Canadian Journal of Economics*, **22(1)**: 109–27.

Giannini, C. (1986) 'Innovazione finanziaria e teoria dell'intermediazione: una rassegna della letteratura', Banca d'Italia, Rome (mimeo).

Goodfriend, M. and R. G. King (1988) 'Financial Deregulation, Monetary Policy and Central Banking', *Federal Reserve Bank of Richmond Working Paper*, **88(1)**.

Goodhart, C. (1987a) 'Why Do We Need a Central Bank?', *Oxford Economic Papers*, **39**: 75–89.

Goodhart, C. (1987b) 'Discusson of Baltensperger [and] Dermine [1987]', *Economic Policy*, **2(1)**: 95–8.

Goodman, L. S. and A. M. Santomero (1986) 'Variable-Rate Deposit Insurance: A Re-examination', *Journal of Banking and Finance*, **10(2)**: 203–18.

Greenwald, B., J. Stiglitz and A. Weiss (1984) 'Informational Imperfections and Macroeconomic Fluctuations', *American Economic Review*, **74(2)**: 194–9.

Hannan, T. H. and G. A. Hanweck (1988) 'Bank Insolvency Risk and the Market for Large Certificates of Deposit', *Journal of Money, Credit and Banking*, **20(2)**: 203–11.

Horvitz, P. M. (1983) 'The Case Against Risk-Related Deposit Insurance Premiums', *Housing Finance Review*, **2(3)**: 253–63.

Kane, E. J. and S. A. Buser (1979) 'Portfolio Diversification at Commercial Banks', *Journal of Finance*, **34**: 19–34.

Kareken, J. H. (1986) 'Federal Bank Regulatory Policy: A Description and Some Observations', *Journal of Business*, **59(1)**: 3–48.

Kaufman, G. G. (1988) 'Bank Runs: Causes, Benefits, and Costs', *Cato Journal*, **7(3)**: 559–88.

Kim, D. and A. M. Santomero (1988) 'Risk in Banking and Capital Regulation', *Journal of Finance*, **43(5)**: 1219–33.

Klein, M. A. (1973) 'The Economics of Security Divisibility and Financial Intermediation', *Journal of Finance*, **28**: 923–31.

Leland, H. E. and D. H. Pyle (1977) 'Information Asymmetries, Financial Structure and Financial Intermediation', *Journal of Finance*, **32(2)**: 371–87.

McCulloch, J. H. (1985) 'Interest-Risk Sensitive Deposit Insurance Premia. Stable ACH Estimates', *Journal of Banking and Finance*, **9**: 137–56.

Marcus, A. J. and I. Shaked (1984) 'The Valuation of FDIC Deposit Insurance Using Option-pricing Estimates', *Journal of Money, Credit and Banking*, **16(4)** Part I (November).

Peltzman, J. (1972) 'The Costs of Competition: an Appraisal of the Hunt Commission Report', *Journal of Money, Credit and Banking*, **4** (November).

Penati, A. and A. Protopapadakis (1988) 'The Effect of Implicit Deposit Insurance on Banks' Portfolio Choices With an Application to International Overexposure', *Journal of Monetary Economics*, **21**: 107–26.

Pennacchi, G. G. (1987) 'A Reexamination of the Over- (or Under-) Pricing of Deposit Insurance', *Journal of Money, Credit and Banking*, **19(3)**: 340–60.

Pyle, D. H. (1986) 'Capital Regulation and Deposit Insurance', *Journal of Banking and Finance*, **10(2)**: 189–202.

Revell, J. R. S. (1988) 'Come le banche si preparano al 1992', *Banca Impresa Società*, **7(3)**: 305–25.

Ronn, E. I. and A. K. Verma (1986) 'Pricing Risk-Adjusted Deposit Insurance: An Option-Based Model', *Journal of Finance*, **41(4)**: 871–95.

Sharpe, W. F. (1981) 'Bank Capital Adequacy, Deposit Insurance, and Security Values', in S. J. Maiser (ed.), *Risk and Capital Adequacy in Commercial Banks*: Chicago and London, University of Chicago Press.

Terlizzese, D. (1988) 'Delegated Screening and Reputation in a Theory of Financial Intermediaries', Banca d'Italia, *Temi di discussione*, **111**.

Thompson, J. B. (1987) 'The Use of Market Information in Pricing Deposit Insurance', *Journal of Money, Credit and Banking*, **19** (November): 528–37.

Discussion

MARIO MONTI

The studies commented upon here are rich on an informative level, and combine well the three elements which characterise all the research of the Banca Commerciale Italiana presented in this volume: the theoretical element, the empirical one, and the institutional one. In doing so, they satisfy the fundamental objective which appears to me to pull together the research: they develop useful reflections at a policy level, both for an individual bank and for the authorities. I have no observations on the philosophy of these two studies; I will, however, briefly comment on each of the works.

The study by M. Maccarinelli, G. Marotta, and M. Prosdocimi in Chapter 12, proposes to gather comparable statistical data for the purpose of making significant comparisons between countries with very different institutional structures. It is an attempt which is to be appreciated since comparative analyses often neglect this problem and reach conclusions which are less than reliable.

There is a very broad range of data and indicators contained in the work. It is to be hoped that the authors will make further use of them in the future so as to get deeper into the implications of the differences between the various structures and how they may affect the competition between systems after 1992.

The 'consolidated banking system' proposed by the authors traces the system of the statistics already being used in Germany and France, and includes savings banks and investment banks in addition to the commercial banks.

The picture which emerges from reconstructed data on the banking system within this broad meaning is interesting from various points of view. I will only touch upon a few points.

A particularly significant aspect concerns the size of the banking system (Table 12.1 of the study) and perhaps merits more attention than the authors have given it.

The data in Table 12.1 show a growth trend in the ratio of total assets – GDP between 1980 and 1988 for all countries studied except Italy. I would like to formulate two questions on the other countries as a whole, and then some considerations on Italy.

In the first place, the process of disintermediation in banking, about which so much has been written in recent years, does not seem to be borne out over the 1980s if we consider, as the authors do, an enlarged version of the banking system. Should it be concluded from this therefore that the process has concerned the more restricted version of the banking system (commercial banks)? Or rather that the disintermediation also involved the consolidated banking system, but in order to make it evident it would be necessary to look at the size of banking assets not as a percentage of GDP but as a measure of total financial assets for the country?

Secondly, with regard to the relationships between these indicators and financial structure 'models' (or 'stereotypes'), it is very surprising that the United States has a very low ratio (0.87 in 1987) which is in especially sharp contrast with the ratio for the United Kingdom (2.67). Both countries are often presented as examples of 'market-oriented' financial structures. The financial structure of the United States, which has the lowest ratio of the countries studied, confirms this connotation. The situation for the United Kingdom is very different; it emerges as the banking system with the largest size (2.67 vs 1.89 for Germany). Perhaps the greater weight of foreign assets and liabilities for the United Kingdom comes into play (at least in part)?

Coming to Italy, two peculiar characteristics are noted: (a) it is the only country in which the ratio goes down over the course of the 1980s; (b) it is the country which has the lowest ratio at the end of the 1980s (with the exception of the United States).

(a)   With regard to the reduction of the ratio, the authors single out its cause in the 'advantage of the yield on public debt instruments [which] has switched investor portfolios . . . away from debt instruments issued by the banks'. This topic would merit being examined more deeply.

In 1980, the ratio in Italy was relatively high even considering the absence of administrative or legislative constraints on the level of interest rates on deposits, constraints which were present in many other countries during the 1960s and 1970s. But it certainly would have been expected to grow further, at least as of 1983 since the elimination of administrative constraints on assets (and in particular the lending ceiling) brought lower 'taxation' on banking intermediation. Instead, the

ratio went down. This was no doubt due to the reason which the authors
supported (the financial crowding out due to high public debt) but it was
also probably due to three other reasons:

* tax policy, both that which is explicit (growing differential during the
  1980s between the tax rate on interest earned on bank deposits and the
  rates on the yield from other financial assets) and that which is implicit
  (a growing burden from mandatory reserves);
* financial regulation, to the extent (mentioned by the authors in n. 6)
  that it prevented banks from collecting funds on the classic segment of
  public debt, that of bonds;
* a debt management policy which has displayed the Treasury's financing – formally bonds – to an extreme represented by monetary
  equivalents (either BOTs, for their short-term maturities; or variable
  rate medium term CCTs, for their reference to short-term interest
  rates), accordingly maximising their substitutability with banking
  deposits.

A qualification is necessary in this regard. The public sector has
maximised the competition facing banks over short-term borrowing. It
has, however, developed very little in competing with them in their other
function, that of placing the public debt. Under this profile, the Treasury
has remained almost totally dependent on the banking system although
other aspects of the financial system – in particular, the widespread
deposit system offered through branches of the Post Office – could
favour the development of alternative distribution channels to the
banking system. (The authors note that in Japan, where the number of
Post Office branches is about 50 per cent of the bank branches – about
what it is in the France, Germany, and the United States – the volume of
postal deposits is about one-third of total private deposits. In Italy, on
the other hand, the number of Post Office branches is greater than the
number of bank branches but monies on deposit with the Post Office
represent only about one-sixth of total private deposits.)

(b)   With regard to the ratio's low value, this topic should be considered with
particular attention at the current time when Italy is completing its
process of deregulation which also includes banking deposits. One could
argue that the ratio is lower because the constraints in force in the Italian
banking system (within the scope of regulation and the policy for public
debt) have reduced the incentive for savers to leave their money on
deposit with banks; and that without removing these constraints, it is
probable that a part of Italian savings will flow into deposits with foreign
banks.

The preceding observations refer to the size of the banking system as
expressed by deposits. The authors also offer interesting indicators
regarding the composition of bank financial statements.

Two issues in particular differentiate the Italian banking system from
foreign systems and are to be carefully considered in the current environment: the lower weight of certificates of deposit (notwithstanding their
growth in recent years as shown by the figures in Tables 12.2 and 12.3,
third indicator) and the significant weight (which has grown over time) of

net liabilities to foreign entities (see Table 12.2). Relative to both of these aspects, we could ask here if the process of integration might not be destined to pose problems for the Italian banking system.

Finally, an observation which ties the method followed by the authors to a possible policy issue. The authors chose to carry out their comparative analysis by looking at enlarged banking systems which include special credit institutions in addition to banks and savings banks. We can conclude from their analytical choice that they would consider with favour a system of mandatory reserves distributed more uniformly over the various areas which make up the enlarged banking systems.

The work of A. Baglioni and G. Marotta in Chapter 13 offers an excellent example of the line adopted in various studies of the present research: in order to face a well defined problem of operating importance – in this case, that of insurance on deposits – the authors find it necessary, and justifiably so, to go deeper into recent theoretical literature on the specifics of banks as financial intermediaries and to draw useful implications from this for credit policy.

On the basis of the theoretical analysis and an examination of the case in the United States they suggest that the insurance should have the following characteristics: an insurance fund of a public nature, endowed with regulatory and supervisory power, applicable to banks as broadly defined; premiums correlated to the risk of banking assets; partial coverage (and not very high coverage) of the deposit; the discretional criterion in valuing risk to be put into the hands of the public entity charged with the supervision and based on confidential information; broad use of procedures to prevent institutions from collapsing into insolvency; discretional selection of the banks for which a bailout would be provided without any possibility of bankruptcy.

Against the background of the authors' conclusions, it would be of particular interest to know their evaluation of the Interbank Deposit Guarantee Fund in force for the Italian banking system. I would encourage them to develop this theme, perhaps on another occasion.

Another observation concerns the introduction, within the framework of deposit insurance, of problems tied to the risk of the individual bank. The advantages of introducing this are clear from a theoretical point of view. Moreover, it can be asked – in addition to what has been pointed out by the authors – if the presence of other forms of prudential control implicit or explicit, could not, by being put on top of the premium, cause a phenomenon of risk reduction by the bank, even below the optimal choice for the portfolio. The possibility should then be evaluated that a distortion in the banking system might occur towards less risky uses of funds, such as government securities, thus favouring banks' demand for public debt with some constraint (or at least induced convenience) on their portfolio. With this prospect, the introduction of a system with premiums tied to risk, in addition to capital ratios (in turn, possibly graded in such a way as to make the employment of funds in government securities weigh less) could in some way constitute a disincentive in asserting a more entrepreneurial management of the banks.

Note

Mario Monti is Rector, Bocconi University.

Index

369

376   **Index**